THE 15 MINUTE PLANT-BASED DIET

The Ultimate Cookbook With 600 Quick & Easy Recipes for Beginners. From Prep to Table in 15 Minutes or Less.

© **Copyright 2021 - All rights reserved.**

This document is geared towards providing exact and reliable information in regard to the topic and issue covered.

- From a Declaration of Principles which was accepted and approved equally by a Committee of the American Bar Association and a Committee of Publishers and Associations.

In no way is it legal to reproduce, duplicate, or transmit any part of this document in either electronic means or in printed format. All rights reserved.

The information provided herein is stated to be truthful and consistent, in that any liability, in terms of inattention or otherwise, by any usage or abuse of any policies, processes, or DIRECTIONS contained within is the solitary and utter responsibility of the recipient reader. Under no circumstances will any legal responsibility or blame be held against the publisher for any reparation, damages, or monetary loss due to the information herein, either directly or indirectly.

Respective authors own all copyrights not held by the publisher.

The information herein is offered for informational purposes solely and is universal as so. The presentation of the information is without contract or any type of guarantee assurance.

The trademarks that are used are without any consent, and the publication of the trademark is without permission or backing by the trademark owner. All trademarks and brands within this book are for clarifying purposes only and are owned by the owners themselves, not affiliated with this document.

Join our Free Facebook Group
"The Happy Cookbook: Healthy Recipes and Diet Plan"

In order to maximize the value that you receive from this book, I highly encourage you to join our tight-knit community on Facebook. Here you will be able to connect and share with other people passionate about cooking.

Taking this journey alone is not recommended, and this can be an excellent network for you. It would be great to connect with you there,

Ann Claire

www.facebook.com/groups/ann.claire.love/

https://bit.ly/AnnClaireLove

Get a peek at our new recipes before they're published and the chance to leave reviews for your favorite recipe!

Buy Now or Download FREE ...

US: https://www.amazon.co.uk/dp/B092C6B5RW
UK: https://www.amazon.co.uk/dp/B092C6B5RW
CA: https://www.amazon.ca/dp/B092C6B5RW

FREE: https://happyhealthyrecipes.net/free-reader-books-club

Table of Contents

- Table of Contents 5
- Introduction 15
- Chapter 1. Benefits of Plant-Based Diet . 17
- Chapter 2. Breakfast Recipes 19
  1. French Fries 19
  2. Crispy Zucchini Wedges 19
  3. Sweet Potato Chips 19
  4. Baked Potatoes With Broccoli and Cheese 19
  5. Crispy Kale 20
  6. Garlic Mushrooms 20
  7. Rosemary Potatoes 20
  8. Roasted Spicy Carrots 20
  9. Baked Artichoke Fries 20
  10. Baked Tofu Strips 21
  11. Avocado Fries 21
  12. Crispy Vegetables 21
  13. Onion Appetizers 21
  14. Crispy Brussels Sprouts 22
  15. Sweet Potato Tots 22
  16. Lemon Tofu 22
  17. Buffalo Cauliflower 22
  18. Chipotle, Pinto, and Green Bean 22
  19. Mixed Vegetable Medley 23
  20. Spicy Lentils 23
  21. Pinto and Green Bean Fry 23
  22. Indonesian-Style Spicy Fried Tempeh Strips .. 24
  23. Fried Rice and Vegetables 24
  24. Spanish-Style Saffron Rice With Black Beans .. 24
  25. Simple Lemon Dal 24
  26. Gingered Black-Eyed Peas With Black Tea 25
  27. Creamy Polenta With Sautéed Mixed Mushrooms 25
  28. Pan-Fried Baby Potatoes 25
  29. Yellow Split Peas and Rice 26
  30. Indian-Style Potatoes and Cauliflower 26
  31. Red Lentil and Cauliflower Tomato Pilaf 26
  32. Chickpea, Cauliflower, and Potato Coconut Curry 27
  33. Pineapple Breeze Smoothie 27
  34. Pumpkin Spice Smoothie 27
  35. Mint Chocolate Smoothie 28
  36. Super Green Smoothie 28
  37. Tempeh and Kale Breakfast Skillet 28
  38. Vanilla Blueberry Overnight Oats 28
  39. Protein Pancakes 28
  40. Apple Cinnamon Quinoa Porridge 29
  41. Savory Steel-Cut Oats 29
  42. Classic Tofu Scramble 29
  43. High-Protein Granola 29
  44. Chickpea Omelet 30
  45. Chocolate Zoats 30
  46. Greens on Toast with Tofu Ricotta ... 30
  47. Staple Smoothie 30
  48. Cashew Cheese Spread 30
  49. Fruit and Nut Oatmeal 31
  50. Almond and Banana Granola 31
  51. Polenta with a Dose of Cranberries and Pears 31
  52. Smoked Tempeh 31
  53. Quiche With Cauliflower 32
  54. Oatmeal and Carrot Cake 32
  55. Coconut Butter Banana Overnight Oats 32
  56. Peach and Chia Seed Breakfast Parfait 32
  57. Guacamole with White Beans Toast .. 33
  58. Oatmeal and Peanut Butter Breakfast Bar 33
  59. Chocolate Chip Banana Pancake 33
  60. Breakfast Sandwich 33
  61. Gingerbread Waffles 34
  62. Easy Hummus Toast 34

63. Flaxseed and Blueberry Porridge 34
64. Avocado and Strawberry Bowl 34
65. Coconut and Strawberry Bars 34
66. Avocado Breakfast Bowl 35
67. Granola 35
68. Flaxseed Pancakes 35
69. Breakfast Cereal 35
70. Eggplant Hash Browns 35
71. Cantaloupe Smoothie Bowl 36
72. Fruity Oatmeal 36
73. Green Mango Smoothie 36
74. Fruit Salad 36
75. Flaxseed Porridge 36
76. Spicy Hash Browns 36
77. Kiwi Slushy 37
78. Chia Seed Smoothie 37
79. Mango Smoothie 37
80. Quinoa and Chocolate Bowl 37
81. Vegetable Hash 37
82. Walnut Porridge 37
83. Spinach With Fried Eggs 38
84. Green Bagel Topped With Poached Eggs 39
85. Egg and Honey Toast 39
86. Baked Rotini 39
87. Vegetarian Meatballs 39
88. Impossibly Easy Spinach and Feta Pie 40
89. Tomato Tart 40
90. Puff Pizza Tart 40
91. Veggie Pizza 40
92. Seeded Flatbreads 41
93. Roasted Veggie Flatbread 41
94. Dilly Veggie Pizza 41
95. 5-Ingredients Vegetable Fried Brown Rice 42
96. Garlic Roasted Carrots 42
97. Baked Parmesan Mushrooms 42
98. Buttery Garlic Green Beans 42
99. Roasted Butternut Squash Puree 43
100. Sweet and Easy Corn on the Cob 43
101. 5-Ingredients Coconut Curry 43
102. Dairy-Free Chocolate Pudding 43

Chapter 3. Lunch Recipes 44
103. Curry Spiced Lentil Burgers 44
104. Maple Dijon Burgers 44
105. Cajun Burgers 44
106. Grilled AHLT 45
107. Black Bean Pizza 45
108. Mediterranean Hummus Pizza 45
109. Curried Mango Chickpea Wrap 45
110. Thai Noodle Bowl 46
111. Sushi Bowl 46
112. Sweet Potato Patties 46
113. Spring Rolls 46
114. Potato Skin Samosas 47
115. Simple Sesame Stir-Fry 47
116. Sun-Dried Tomato and Pesto Quinoa 47
117. Olive and White Bean Pasta 48
118. BBQ Fruit Sliders 48
119. Hawaiian Luau Burgers 48
120. Falafel Burgers 49
121. Easy Vegan Pizza Bread 49
122. Baked Mac and Peas 49
123. Savory Sweet Potato Casserole 49
124. BBQ Tofu and Mashed Potato Bowl 49
125. Sunday Slow Roast 50
126. Rice-and-Vegetable Stir-Fry 50
127. Mango-Ginger Chickpea Curry 50
128. Italian Bean Balls 50
129. Crispy Rice-and-Bean Tostadas 51
130. Stuffed Peppers 51
131. Burrito Bowl With Oil-Free Tortilla Chips .. 51

132. Baked Taquitos With Fat-Free Refried Beans 51
133. Broccoli and Mushroom Stir-Fry 52
134. Slow Cooker Chili 52
135. Quinoa Lentil Burger 52
136. Hummus Quesadillas 53
137. Spaghetti Alla Puttanesca 53
138. Crispy Baked Falafel 53
139. Gluten-Free Mango and Black Bean Tacos ..53
140. Butternut Squash and Cranberry 54
141. Avocado Hummus Bowl 54
142. Slow Cooker Pumpkin Chili 54
143. Broccoli Pesto With Pasta and Cherry Tomatoes 54
144. Southwest Sweet Potato Vegan Meal Prep Bowls 55
145. Asian Quinoa and Edamame 55
146. Mushroom Pecan Burgers 55
147. Avocado Toast With White Beans 55
148. Veggie Spring Rolls 56
149. Smoky Coleslaw 56
150. Baked Ratatouille 56
151. Tasty Tabouli 56
152. Skillet Seitan Stew 56
153. Two-Alarm Chili 57
154. Basic Buddha Burrito Bowl 57
155. Spicy Tostadas 57
156. Red "Risotto" 57
157. Kale Pesto Penne 58
158. Cheesy Zucchini 58
159. Pea Nutty Carrot Noodles 58
160. Sweet Potato Alfredo 58
161. Chana Masala 58
162. Sautéed Red Lentils and Fennel Seed 59
163. Ratatouille 59
164. Peanut Coconut Curry Veggies 59

165. Stuffed Portobello Mushrooms With Walnut and Thyme 60
166. Green Beans With Lemon Toasted Almonds 60
167. Mashed Cauliflower With Garlic 60
168. Spicy Cauliflower Burgers 61
169. Vietnamese Summer Rolls 61
170. Chickpea-Free Falafel With Coriander 62
171. Hearty Italian Bean and Barley Stew 62
172. Pea Soup 62
173. Sweet Potato Chili 62
174. Spicy Sweet Potato Enchiladas 63
175. Raw Nut Cheese 63
176. Italian Tomatoes 63
177. Gluten-Free, Raw Bread With Caraway Onion 64
178. Flaky Honey Biscuits 64
179. Curried Apple Chips 64
180. Baked Sweet Potato Latkes 64
181. Huevos Rancheros Potato Skins 65
182. Cheddar and Broccoli–Stuffed Sweet Potatoes 65
183. Caramelized Mushrooms Over Polenta 65
184. Garlic and Parmesan Spaghetti Squash 66
185. Roasted Broccoli Bowl With an Egg 66
186. Lentil Potato Salad 67
187. Warm Grain Salad With Miso Butter 67
188. Lemony Kale, Avocado, and Chickpea Salad 67
189. Roasted Cauliflower and Rice Bowl With Tomatoes 68
190. Tomato Galettes 68
191. Taco Pizzas With Refried Beans 68
192. Avocado Toasts With Hummus 68
193. Buddha Mix 69
194. Corn Pasta With Brown Butter 69
195. Simple Garlic Bread Snack 69

196. Potato Chips 69
197. Bell Peppers 69
198. Crunchy Roasted Edamame 70
199. Toasted Pumpkin Seeds 70
200. Grilled Cheese Sandwich 70
201. Greek Cheese Sandwich 70
202. Linguine With Mushrooms 70
203. Baked Eggs With Herbs 71
204. Green Chickpea Flour Pancakes 71

Chapter 4. Dinner Recipes 72
205. Pad Thai Bowl 72
206. Green Pea Risotto 72
207. Three-Bean Chili 72
208. Chinese Black Bean Chili 73
209. New World Chili 73
210. Butternut Squash Gnocchi 73
211. No-Cook Quesadilla 74
212. BBQ Sandwich 74
213. Cauliflower Chickpea Sheet Pan Meal 74
214. Mediterranean Quesadilla 74
215. Cauliflower Nachos 75
216. Simple Pasta 75
217. Sweet and Savory Tofu 75
218. One-Pot Pumpkin Curry 76
219. Millet Stuffed Zucchini Boats 76
220. Meat(less) Loaf 76
221. Tropical Protein Bowl 76
222. Rainbow Pinwheels 76
223. Spaghetti Squash With Sundried Tomato Sauce 77
224. Simple Stir Fry 77
225. Quinoa Lentil Burgers 77
226. Sage Zucchini Noodles 77
227. Twice Baked Butternut Squash 78
228. Ultra-Crispy Roasted Potatoes 78
229. Gluten-Free Cauliflower Fried "Rice" 78
230. Mushroom Cauliflower Risotto 78
231. Halloumi Burger 79
232. Creamy Green Cabbage 79
233. Cheesy Broccoli and Cauliflower 79
234. Green Beans With Roasted Onions 79
235. Eggplant Fries 79
236. Garlic Focaccia 80
237. Portobello Mushrooms 80
238. Butter-Fried Green Cabbage 80
239. Asian Garlic Tofu 80
240. Stuffed Mushrooms 81
241. Creamy Leeks 81
242. Parmesan Croutons 81
243. Quesadillas 81
244. Cheesy Cauliflower 82
245. Parmesan Roasted Bamboo Sprouts 82
246. Brussels Sprout With Lemon 82
247. Cauliflower Hash Browns 82
248. Cauliflower Parmesan 82
249. Cauliflower Mash 83
250. Millet Pilaf 83
251. Spiced Quinoa and Cauliflower Rice Bowls .83
252. Black Beans and Rice 84
253. Chickpea Curry 84
254. Vegetable Pea Soup 85
255. Spanish Rice 85
256. Spiced Brown Rice 85
257. Salsa Brown Rice and Kidney Beans 86
258. Walnut Lentil Tacos 86
259. Citrusy Black Beans 86
260. Tofu Curry 87
261. Pumpkin Walnut Chili 87
262. Lentil Curry 88
263. Pasta Puttanesca 88
264. BBQ Meatballs 88

265. Lentil Sloppy Joes 89
266. Green Coconut Curry 89
267. Potato Carrot Medley 89
268. Jackfruit Curry 90
269. Potato Curry 90
270. Squash and Cumin Chili 91
271. Fried-Up Avocados 91
272. Hearty Green Beans 91
273. Parmesan Cabbage Wedges 91
274. Extreme Zucchini Fries 92
275. Easy Fried Tomatoes 92
276. Roasted Up Brussels 92
277. Roasted Brussels and Pine Nuts ... 92
278. Low-Calorie Beets Dish 93
279. Broccoli and Parmesan Dish 93
280. Fried-Up Pumpkin Seeds 93
281. Jalapeno Poppers 93
282. Air Fried Olives 93
283. Breaded Artichoke Hearts 94
284. Bruschetta With Basil Pesto 94
285. Cajun Zucchini Chips 94
286. Cheesy Apple Roll-Ups 95
287. Cheesy Jalapeño Poppers 95
288. Cheesy Steak Fries 95
289. Crispy Cajun Dill Pickle Chips 96
290. Summer Rolls With Peanut Sauce ... 96
291. Cheesy White Bean Cauliflower Soup ... 96
292. Split Pea Soup 97
293. Quinoa and Chickpea Tabbouleh ... 97
294. Cauliflower Caesar Salad With Chickpea Croutons 97
295. Vegetable Rose Potato 98
296. Rice Arugula Salad 98
297. Tomato Salad 98
298. Kale Apple Roasted Root Vegetable Salad ... 98
299. Rice Arugula Salad With Sesame Garlic Dressing 99
300. Roasted Lemon Asparagus Watercress Salad 99
301. Pumpkin and Brussels Sprouts Mix ... 99
302. Almond and Tomato Salad 99
303. Strawberry Spinach Salad 100
304. Apple Spinach Salad 100
305. Kale Power Salad 100
306. Falafel Kale Salad With Tahini Dressing 101

Chapter 5. Salad and Soup Recipes 102
307. Tomato Gazpacho 102
308. Tomato Pumpkin Soup 102
309. Cauliflower Spinach Soup 102
310. Avocado Mint Soup 102
311. Creamy Squash Soup 103
312. Zucchini Soup 103
313. Creamy Celery Soup 103
314. Avocado Cucumber Soup 103
315. Creamy Garlic Onion Soup 103
316. Avocado Broccoli Soup 104
317. Green Spinach Kale Soup 104
318. Cauliflower Asparagus Soup 104
319. African Pineapple Peanut Stew ... 104
320. Cabbage and Beet Stew 104
321. Basil Tomato Soup 105
322. Hearty Chickpea Soup 105
323. Cream of Tomato Soup 105
324. Creamy Mushroom 105
325. Tofu Miso Soup 106
326. Hot and Sour Tofu Soup 106
327. Creamy Cauliflower Soup 106
328. Pumpkin Soup 106
329. Wild Rice Stew 107
330. Black-Eyed Pea and Sweet Potato Soup 107
331. Creamy Garlic-Spinach Rotini Soup 107

332. Tuscan White Bean Soup 107
333. Minestrone 108
334. Italian Wedding Soup 108
335. Corn Chowder 108
336. Coconut Curry Soup 109
337. Ruby Grapefruit and Radicchio Salad 109
338. Apple and Ginger Slaw 109
339. Spinach and Pomegranate Salad 109
340. Pear Veggie Salad 110
341. Apple and Fennel Salad 110
342. German Potato Salad 110
343. Tabbouleh 110
344. Kale and Root Vegetable Salad 111
345. Brown Rice and Pepper Salad 111
346. Three-Bean Salad 111
347. Satsuma, Fruit Salad 111
348. Quinoa Pilaf 111
349. Lemon and Thyme Couscous 112
350. Spicy Picnic Beans 112
351. Chickpeas with Lemon and Spinach 112
352. Spicy Chickpeas 112
353. Coleslaw Salad 113
354. Corn Avocado Salad 113
355. Couscous With Chickpeas Salad 113
356. Black and White Bean Salad 113
357. Caesar Salad 114
358. Red Cabbage Salad 114
359. Spicy Roasted Chickpeas 114
360. Fresh Salsa and Peachy Mango Chutney on the Side 115
361. Spicy Sweet Potato Tofu Scramble 115
362. Avocado Salad Collard Wrap 115
363. Artichoke, Radish, Carrot, and Strawberry Bowls 116
364. Tofu Stir Fry 116
365. Macaroni and Cheese 117

366. Berry Fruit Salad With Chocolate Coconut Whipped Cream 117
367. Aloo Gobi 118
368. Jackfruit Carnitas 118
369. Baked Beans 118
370. Brussels Sprouts Curry 118
371. Jambalaya 118
372. Mushroom-Kale Stroganoff 119
373. Sloppy Joe Filling 119
374. Hoppin' John 119
375. African Sweet Potato Stew 119
376. Sweet-and-Sour Tempeh 120
377. Jackfruit Cochinita Pibil 120
378. Delightful Dal 120
379. Moroccan Chickpea Stew 120
380. Tex-Mex Taco Filling 121
381. Cauliflower Bolognese 121
382. Delectable Dal 121
383. Almond Roasted Veggies Salad 121
384. Apple Almond 122
385. Asian Cabbage 122
386. Avocado Chat 122
387. Avocado Protein Salad 122
388. Beetroot Hummus 122
389. Beans Salad 123
390. Broccoli Roasted Toasts 123
391. Butternut Squash Hummus 123
392. Butternut Squash With Vegan Yogurt ... 123
393. Cauliflower and Squash Mix 123
394. Chickpeas Avocado Salad 124
395. Chickpeas Cucumber Salad 124
396. Crunchy Pomegranate Flower Sprouts ... 124

Chapter 6. Snack Recipes 125
397. Cinnamon Baked Apple Chips 125
398. Acorn Squash with Mango Chutney 125
399. Carrot Chips 125

400. Brussels and Pistachio 125
401. Buffalo Cashews 125
402. Morning Peach 126
403. Mango Rice 126
404. Pecan Fruity Crumble 126
405. Healthy Rice Pudding 126
406. Oatmeal Cookies 126
407. Apple Slices 127
408. The Garbanzo Bean Extravaganza 127
409. Roasted Onions and Green Beans 127
410. Lemony Sprouts 127
411. Hummus Without Oil 127
412. Tempting Quinoa Tabbouleh 128
413. Quick Peanut Butter Bars 128
414. Healthy Cauliflower Popcorn 128
415. Hummus Made With Sweet Potato 128
416. Crisp Balls Made With Peanut Butter 129
417. Healthy Protein Bars 129
418. Tempeh Bacon-Smoked 129
419. Delicious Quiche Made With Cauliflower and Chickpea 129
420. Carrot Cake with Oatmeal 130
421. Tasty Oatmeal Muffins 130
422. Omelet with Chickpea Flour 130
423. A Toast to Remember 130
424. Tasty Panini 131
425. Chickpea and Tomato 131

Chapter 7. Dessert Recipes 132
426. Banana Chocolate Cupcakes 132
427. Minty Fruit Salad 132
428. Mango Coconut Cream Pie 132
429. Cherry-Vanilla Rice Pudding 132
430. Mint Chocolate Chip Sorbet 133
431. Peach-Mango Crumble 133
432. Zesty Orange-Cranberry Energy Bites 133
433. Almond-Date Energy Bites 133
434. Pumpkin Pie Cups 134
435. Coconut and Almond Truffles 134
436. Fudgy Brownies 134
437. Chocolate Macaroons 134
438. Chocolate Pudding 135
439. Lime and Watermelon 135
440. Coconut-Banana Pudding 135
441. Beets Bars with Dry Fruits 135
442. Cocoa, Avocado, and Chia Cream 136
443. Coconut Balls With Lemon Rinds 136
444. Coconut Rice Pudding With Cardamom ... 136
445. Nutty Cake 136
446. Dark Honey Hazelnut Cookies 137
447. Energy Dried Figs Brownies 137
448. Hearty Apple Bran Muffins 137
449. Honey Raisins Crispy Balls 137
450. Protein Banana Cream 138
451. Protein Carrot Macaroons 138
452. Raw Lemon "Cheesecake" 138
453. Semolina Cake With Brown Sugar Syrup ... 138
454. Strawberries, Quinoa and Silk Tofu Dessert 139
455. Strawberry and Banana Ice Cream 139
456. Strawberry Coconut Ice Cream 139
457. Chocolaty Oat Bites 139
458. Peanut Butter Mousse 139
459. Salted Coconut-Almond Fudge 140
460. Peanut Butter Fudge 140
461. Coconut Bars With Chocolate Chips 140
462. Coconut Rice With Mangos 140
463. Spiced Apple Chia Pudding 141
464. Fudge 141
465. Dark Chocolate Raspberry Ice Cream 141
466. Coconut and Chocolate Cake 141
467. Tamari Toasted Almonds 141
468. Express Coconut Flax Pudding 142

469. Mango Coconut Chia Pudding 142
470. Cacao Nut Bites 142
471. Avocado-Based Chocolate Mousse 142
472. Oatmeal and Peanut Butter Bar 143
473. Maple-Pumpkin Cookies 143
474. Coconut Chocolate Truffles 143
475. Avocado Toasts 143
476. Sweet and Spicy Snack Mix 143
477. Melon Dessert 144
478. Mango and Strawberry Ice Cream 144
479. Watermelon Pizza 144
480. Roasted Mango and Coconut 144
481. Fruit Compote 144
482. Creamy Cashew Sauce 144
483. Choco Peanut Butter 145
484. Ginger Cranberry Sauce 145
485. Avocado Pancakes 145
486. Oatmeal with Pears 145
487. Thai Oatmeal 146
488. Tropical Oats 146
489. Sweet Potato Hash Browns 146
490. Apple, Pecans, and Cinnamon Oatmeal 146
491. Pumpkin Oats 146
492. Melon Muesli 146
493. Citrus Vinaigrette 147
494. Lemon Garlic Tahini Sauce 147
495. No-Carb Cereal Bars 147
496. Nutty Chocolate Bombs 147
497. No-Bake Hazelnut Chocolate Bars 148
498. Coconut Chocolate Balls 148
499. Raspberry Cheesecake Fudge 148
500. Blueberry Lemon Choco Cups 148
501. Creamy Coconut Vanilla Cups 149
502. Peanut Butter Power Bars 149
503. Dark Chocolate Mint Cups 149

504. Low-Carb Pistachio Gelato 150
505. Toasted Cashews With Nut Flakes 150
506. Chocolate and Yogurt Ice Cream 150
507. Choco Chip Ice-Cream With Mint 151
508. Crispy Cheese Snacks 151
509. Crème Brule 151
510. Avocado Chocolate Pudding 152
511. Black Olive and Thyme Cheese Spread 152
512. Egg Muffins 152
513. Chia Pudding With Blueberries 153
514. Papaya Smoothie 153

Chapter 8. Appetizer Recipes 154
515. Veggie Salad 154
516. Baked Kale Chips 154
517. White Bean Dip With Olives 154
518. Roasted Eggplant Dip 154
519. Stuffed Dates with Cashew Cream and Roasted Almonds 155
520. Crunchy Vegetable Spring Rolls 155
521. Coconut Bacon 155
522. Portobello Bacon 155
523. Roasted Carrots and Chickpeas 156
524. Cauliflower Buffalo Wings 156
525. Crispy Crunchy Coconut Tofu 156
526. Sweet Potato Latkes 157
527. Italian-Style Spaghetti Squash 157
528. Roasted Brussels Sprouts With Warm Maple Sauce 157
529. Baked Oatmeal and Fruit 157
530. Hemp and Oat Granola 158
531. Warm Farro With Dried Sweet Cherries and Pistachios 158
532. Pineapple, Cucumber, and Mint Salad 158
533. Bright, Beautiful Slaw 158
534. Baked Apples With Dried Fruit 159
535. Chocolate Protein Bites 159

536. Crunchy Granola 159
537. Almond Bars 159
538. Spicy Nut and Seed Snack Mix 160

Chapter 9. Smoothie Recipes 161
539. Healthy Green Smoothie 161
540. Chocolate Mint Smoothie 161
541. Green Pumpkin Spice Smoothie 161
542. Apple Spinach Protein Smoothie 161
543. Banana Berry Tropical Breeze 161
544. Banana Peanut Butter Cranberry Protein Smoothie 162
545. Blueberry Oatmeal Protein Smoothie 162
546. Carrot Orange Smoothie 162
547. Chocolate-Strawberry Heaven 162
548. Cherry Limeade Smoothie 162
549. Layered Smoothie 163
550. Eat Your Kale Smoothie 163
551. Green Apple Orange Banana Spice 163
552. Maple Fig Smoothie 163
553. Mint Protein Smoothie 164
554. Chocolate Smoothie 164
555. Mint Smoothie 164
556. Cinnamon Roll Smoothie 164
557. Coco Milk Smoothie 164
558. Almond Smoothie 164
559. Blueberry Smoothie..................................165
560. Nutty Protein Shake 165
561. Cinna-Pear Smoothie 165
562. The Perfect Milkshake 165
563. Berry Protein Shake..................................165
564. Raspberry Nut Smoothie 165
565. Chocolate Strawberry Almond Protein Smoothie 166
566. Beet Blast Smoothie 166
567. Green Power Smoothie 166
568. Tropical Bliss Smoothie 166

Chapter 10. Juice Recipes 167
569. Switchel: The Original Sports Drink 167
570. Lemon-Lime Electrolyte Drink 167
571. Switchel Sports Drinks With Juice 167
572. Cucumber-Lime Electrolyte Drink 167
573. Cranberry-Citrus Electrolyte Drink 167
574. Miso-Maple Electrolyte "Broth" 168
575. Umeboshi Electrolyte Drink 168
576. Frozen Matcha Latte 168
577. Margarita Recovery Drink 168
578. "Bulked-Up" Drink 168
579. Banana Weight Loss Juice 168
580. Citrus Detox Juice 169
581. Metabolism Water....................................169
582. Stress Relief Detox Drink..........................169
583. Strawberry Pink Drink 169
584. Spiced Buttermilk....................................169
585. Mexican Hot Chocolate Mix 170
586. Health Boosting Juices 170
587. Thai Iced Tea 170
588. Colorful Infused Water 170
589. Hibiscus Tea 171
590. Lemon and Rosemary Iced Tea 171
591. Lavender and Mint Iced Tea 171
592. Pear Lemonade 171
593. Energizing Ginger Detox Tonic 171
594. Warm Spiced Lemon Drink 172
595. Soothing Ginger Tea Drink 172
596. Nice Spiced Cherry Cider 172
597. Classic Switchel 172
598. Lime and Cucumber Electrolyte Drink 172
599. Trope-Kale Breeze 173
600. Mango Madness 173

Conclusion 174

Introduction

A plant-based diet is a strict vegetarian diet that eliminates all meat, eggs, and dairy products. It's rare to find someone who follows this way of eating 100% of the time, but it may be worth bearing in mind if you're watching to improve your health or lose weight.

A plant-based diet is high in several vitamins and minerals, including carotenoids, fiber, calcium, folate, iron, magnesium, potassium, and zinc. It's also a good source of antioxidants namely flavonoids (found in fruits and vegetables) and polyphenols (found in wine).

This diet has been linked to lower rates of obesity and weight gain. A plant-based diet has the potential to reduce the risk of some types of cancer, heart disease, and diabetes.

A plant-based diet may also be more accessible or more sustainable for people with allergies or intolerances to certain foods. It is a good option for people who want to be more environmentally friendly. However, it is essential to eat various foods in this way of eating because there are approximately nutrients that only originate in animal products, and the amounts of certain nutrients may be too low without consuming them.

How to Transition to a Plant-Based Diet?

The first step would be trying out some meatless dishes to see what you like most. For example, your first test dinner may be something like this:

"A dead cow, a chicken thigh, and some vegetables could be your baseline for testing the limits of plant-based food."— Michael Pollan.

You can then start to incorporate more vegan foods into your diet by researching recipes online or deciding on a plan that best fits your current lifestyle.

Plant-Based Diet Nutrition

Since most plant-based foods are naturally organic, many people who eat this way usually have a more nutritious diet than those who don't. It's also recommended for people with certain health conditions because it can help lower cholesterol and blood sugar levels, provide you more energy and help you feel satiated.

Many plant foods contain phytochemicals, which are chemicals found in plants that offer additional health benefits to humans. Studies have shown that these phytochemicals can help to protect the heart, reduce inflammation, prevent cancer, and slow down the aging process.

Plant-Based Diets and Diseases

A plant-based diet can complicate some diseases. For example, if you're unsure how to include legumes in your meal plan or if you have an intolerance to certain plants, it would make sense to consult a doctor before starting this way of eating.

Plant-Based Diet for Weight Loss

The reason why most people, especially women, decide to go plant-based is for health reasons. If you are overweight and want to start losing weight, we recommend making changes that will be sustainable in the long run and can be incorporated into your everyday life. For example, you can choose to eat primarily whole foods and only occasionally have the animal-based foods you like.

Plant-Based Diet and Protein

Getting enough protein in your diet is necessary, and the most common misconception about a plant-based diet is that it's protein deficient. While it's true that animal products are high in protein, it's also possible to get enough from plant sources. These include beans and nuts, which contain complete proteins.

Plant-Based Diet and Veganism

Vegetarians who choose not to eat animal-based foods are called vegans. While a vegan diet is an excellent choice for people who want to improve their health and live an ethical lifestyle, it's essential to know that people trying to lose weight through plant-based eating will tell you otherwise. It's highly improbable that you will lose weight if you eat high-fat vegan food like cookies and cream ice cream.

Plant-Based Diet for Children

Kids can also benefit from a plant-based diet. It's essential to introduce them to rich nutrients and whole foods at an early age. It can help them grow up healthy and avoid the adverse effects of junk food on their health. If your children ask for junk food, try substituting a vegetable or fruit they like. Have them taste it first before offering it to them so that they know what's been added.

Chapter 1. Benefits of Plant-Based Diet

Slight Chances of Type 2 Diabetes and Heart Disease

A plant-based diet is characterized by a significant increase in vegetables, fruits, grains, and legumes. They are likewise high in fiber then lower in the glycemic index.

These diets are very beneficial for individuals with diabetes and cardiovascular diseases since they are high in soluble fiber, which helps to reduce blood glucose levels after eating. Numerous studies have created that there are benefits associated with the consumption of plant-based diets. In addition, most individuals who have a plant-based diet base their lifestyle on an ethical and environmental standpoint. For these reasons, it is not astonishing to see the rising popularity of these diets.

Supports Your Immune System

Plant-based diets are high in antioxidants. Antioxidants help to lower inflammation and this, in turn, helps to support your immune system. Reducing inflammation is beneficial for your immune system and the health of your gut microbiome. The gut microbiome has been related to numerous chronic health issues and diseases, including cancer, cardiovascular disease, heartburn, and irritable bowel disease.

Weight Management

Plant-based diets are low in calories which allows for easy weight control. As you begin to eat a plant-based diet, you will notice that carbohydrates are reduced. For example, rice and pasta are high in the glycemic index. While these foods provide sustenance, they cause insulin surges and spikes in blood sugar. Plant-based diets do not have this problem, and in turn, weight loss can be achieved easier on these diets.

Better Digestion

Dietary fiber is critical as it helps to break down food particles so that they can be properly digested. When carbohydrates are consumed, they spike blood sugar levels. Fiber is vital as it absorbs water in the digestive tract, which helps to keep the stool soft and easier to pass.

Better Brain Function

Plant-based diets reduce inflammation which is an essential factor for maintaining cognitive function. Many chronic

diseases of the brain are linked to inflammation due to their role as a signaling molecule in our bodies. Plant-based diets have been shown to enhance cardiovascular health and, therefore, brain health as well.

Reduces Inflammation

Plant-based diets are rich in antioxidants such as carotenoids and flavonoids. Antioxidants reduce inflammation, and therefore, there is less oxidative damage to our cells. Our cells carry out a process called apoptosis, where they signal to the body that it is time for them to die. When there is too much oxidative damage, then this process is not carried out properly, resulting in chronic diseases.

Prevents Obesity

There is evidence that plant-based diets can reduce obesity when compared to traditional Western diets. Plant-based diets are high in carbohydrates and can cause insulin spikes and spikes in blood sugar. There is a solid link between obesity and diabetes. Many individuals that develop diabetes have never been exposed to a plant-based diet, so it is possible that they are not aware of the consequences of eating a Western-type diet.

Reduces Your Risk for Other Diseases Too

There is a strong link between diet and disease. Plant-based diets can lessen the risk of many diseases, including cardiovascular disease, cancer, and Alzheimer's.

Reduces Blood Pressure

Plant-based diets are rich in fiber, especially soluble fiber. Soluble fiber binds to cholesterol, causing it to be extruded from the body. Reducing cholesterol helps to lower blood pressure as well as providing additional benefits for the heart.

It Protects Your Brain and Keeps You Young

Plant-based diets have been shown to improve cognitive function and reduce the risk of developing Alzheimer's disease. A study printed in the Journal of Alzheimer's Disease found that following a plant-based diet was highly effective for reducing your risk of developing this disease.

Chapter 2. Breakfast Recipes

1. FRENCH FRIES
(PREP. TIME: 10 MIN | COOKING: 5 MIN | SERVING 3)

INGREDIENTS
- 2 potatoes, sliced into thick strips
- 1 bowl water
- 2 tbsp. light olive oil
- 1/4 tsp. paprika
- 1 tbsp. cornstarch
- Salt and pepper to taste

DIRECTIONS:
1. Soak potato strips in water for 30 minutes
2. Drain and pat try.
3. Toss in light olive oil.
4. Season with salt, pepper, and paprika.
5. Cover with cornstarch.
6. Spray air fryer basket with oil.
7. Cook at 360°F for 30 minutes shaking every 5 minutes
8. Garnish with green onion.

Nutrition: Calories: 185 | Fat: 9 g | Protein: 2 g

2. CRISPY ZUCCHINI WEDGES
(PREP. TIME: 10 MIN | COOKING: 4 MIN | SERVING 6)

INGREDIENTS
- 1/2 cup all-purpose flour
- 2 vegan eggs
- 1 zucchini, sliced into wedges
- 1/2 tbsp. red-wine vinegar
- 2 tbsp. tomato paste
- 2 tbsp. water
- Breadcrumbs as needed

DIRECTIONS:
1. Spray air fryer basket with oil.
2. Put the flour in a dish.
3. In another dish, combine vegan eggs and 2 tbsp. water.
4. In a third dish, put the breadcrumbs.
5. Dip each zucchini strip into the three dishes, first the flour, then the eggs and water, and lastly the 1 1/2 breadcrumbs.
6. Cook in the air fryer at 360°F for 12 minutes, shaking once.
7. Incorporate the rest of the **INGREDIENTS** in a bowl.
8. Serve zucchini fries with dipping sauce.

Nutrition: Calories: 235 | Fat: 12 g | Protein: 6 g

3. SWEET POTATO CHIPS
(PREP. TIME: 10 MIN | COOKING: 5 MIN | SERVING 4)

INGREDIENTS
- 1 sweet potato, sliced into thin rounds
- 1 bowl water
- 1 tbsp. light olive oil
- Salt and pepper to taste
- Cooking spray

DIRECTIONS:
1. Immerse sweet potato slices in a bowl of water for 30 minutes
2. Drain and then dry with paper towels.
3. Toss in oil and season with salt and pepper.
4. Spray air fryer basket with oil.
5. Cook sweet potato at 350°F for 15 minutes, shaking every 5 minutes

Nutrition: Calories: 62 | Fat: 4 g | Protein: 0.1 g

4. BAKED POTATOES WITH BROCCOLI AND CHEESE
(PREP. TIME: 4 MIN | COOKING: 10 MIN | SERVING 8)

INGREDIENTS
- 4 potatoes
- 1 cup almond milk, divided
- 2 tbsp. all-purpose flour
- 1/2 cup vegan cheese, divided
- 1 cup broccoli, florets, chopped
- Salt and cayenne to taste

DIRECTIONS:
1. Poke all sides of potatoes with a fork.
2. Microwave on a high level for 5 minutes
3. Flip and microwave for another 5 minutes
4. In a saucepan over medium heat, heat 3/4 cup of milk for 2 minutes, stirring frequently.
5. Add the remaining milk to a bowl and stir in the flour.
6. Mix in the mixture the pan and bring to a boil.
7. Reduce heat
8. Reserve 2 tbsp. vegan cheese.
9. Stir in the rest of the cheese to the pan and stir until smooth.
10. Add the broccoli, salt, and cayenne.
11. Cook for a minute then pull away from heat.

12. Slice the potatoes and arrange them on a single layer inside the air fryer.
13. Top with the broccoli mixture.
14. Add another layer of potatoes and broccoli mixture.
15. Sprinkle reserved cheese on top.
16. Cook at 350°F for 5 minutes
17. Garnish with chopped chives.

Nutrition: Calories: 137 | Fat: 3 g | Protein: 5 g

5. CRISPY KALE
(PREP. TIME: 5 MIN | COOKING: 10 MIN | SERVING 2)

INGREDIENTS
- 6 cups kale leaves, torn
- 1 tbsp. light olive oil
- 1 1/2 tsp. low-sodium soy sauce
- 1/4 tsp. ground cumin
- 1/2 tsp. white sesame seeds
- Salt to taste

DIRECTIONS:
1. Spray air fryer basket with oil.
2. Toss kale in oil, salt, and soy sauce.
3. Cook at 375°F for 10 minutes Shake every 3 minutes
4. Sprinkle with cumin and sesame seeds before serving.

Nutrition: Calories: 140 | Fat: 9 g | Protein: 4 g

6. GARLIC MUSHROOMS
(PREP. TIME: 10 MIN | COOKING: 5 MIN | SERVING 2)

INGREDIENTS
- 8 oz. mushrooms, rinsed, dried, and sliced in half
- 1 tbsp. light olive oil
- 1/2 tsp. garlic powder
- 1 tsp. Worcestershire sauce
- 1 tbsp. parsley, chopped
- Salt and pepper to taste

DIRECTIONS:
1. Toss mushrooms in oil.
2. Season with garlic powder, salt, pepper and Worcestershire sauce.
3. Cook at 380°F for 11 minutes, shaking halfway through.
4. Top with parsley before serving.

Nutrition: Calories: 90 | Fat: 7.4 g | Protein: 3.8 g

7. ROSEMARY POTATOES
(PREP. TIME: 5 MIN | COOKING: 10 MIN | SERVING 4)

INGREDIENTS
- 4 potatoes, cubed
- 1 tbsp. garlic, minced
- 2 tsp. dried rosemary, minced
- 1 tbsp. lime juice
- 1/4 cup parsley, chopped
- 2 tbsps. oil
- Salt and pepper to taste

DIRECTIONS:
1. Toss potato cubes in oil and season with garlic, rosemary, salt, and pepper.
2. Put in the air fryer.
3. Cook at 400°F for 15 minutes
4. Stir in lime juice and top with parsley before serving.

Nutrition: Calories: 244 | Fat: 10.5 g | Protein: 3.9 g

8. ROASTED SPICY CARROTS
(PREP. TIME: 5 MIN | COOKING: 10 MIN | SERVING 4)

INGREDIENTS
- 1/2 lb. carrots, sliced
- 1/2 tbsp. light olive oil
- 1/8 tsp. garlic powder
- 1/4 tsp. chili powder
- 1 tsp. ground cumin
- Salt to taste

DIRECTIONS:
1. Prep your air fryer at 390°F for 5 minutes
2. Cook the carrots at 390°F for 10 minutes
3. Transfer to a bowl.
4. Mix the oil, salt, garlic powder, chili powder, and ground cumin.
5. Coat the carrots with the oil mixture.
6. Put the carrots back into the air fryer and cook for another 5 minutes
7. Garnish with sesame seeds and cilantro.

Nutrition: Calories: 82 | Fat: 3.8 g | Protein: 1.2 g

9. BAKED ARTICHOKE FRIES
(PREP. TIME: 10 MIN | COOKING: 4 MIN | SERVING 4)

INGREDIENTS

- 14 oz. canned artichoke hearts, drained, rinsed, and sliced into wedges
- 1 cup all-purpose flour
- 1/2 cup almond milk
- 1/2 tsp. garlic powder; paprika
- 1 1/2 cup breadcrumbs
- Salt and pepper to taste

DIRECTIONS:
1. Dry the artichoke hearts by pressing a paper towel on top.
2. In a bowl, mix the flour, milk, garlic powder, salt, and pepper.
3. In a shallow dish, add the paprika and breadcrumbs.
4. Dip each artichoke wedge in the first bowl and then coat with the breadcrumb mixture.
5. Cook at 450°F for 10 minutes
6. Serve fries with your choice of dipping sauce.

Nutrition: Calories: 391 | Fat: 9.8 g | Protein: 12.7 g

10. Baked Tofu Strips
(Prep. Time: 7 Min | Cooking: 8 Min | Serving 4)

INGREDIENTS
- 2 tbsp. light olive oil
- 1/2 tsp. basil; oregano
- 1/4 tsp. cayenne pepper; paprika
- 1/4 tsp. garlic powder; onion powder
- 15 oz. tofu, drained

DIRECTIONS:
1. Combine all the **INGREDIENTS** except the tofu.
2. Mix well.
3. Slice tofu into strips and dry with a paper towel.
4. Marinate in the mixture for 10 minutes
5. Situate in the air fryer at 375°F for 15 minutes, shaking halfway through.

Nutrition: Calories: 132 | Fat: 10 g | Protein: 7 g

11. Avocado Fries
(Prep. Time: 10 Min | Cooking: 5 Min | Serving 4)

INGREDIENTS
- Salt to taste
- 1/2 cup panko breadcrumbs
- 1 cup aquafaba liquid
- 1 avocado, sliced into strips

DIRECTIONS:
1. Mix the salt and breadcrumbs in a bowl.
2. In another bowl, pour the aquafaba liquid.
3. Dip each avocado strip into the liquid and then dredge with breadcrumbs.
4. Cook in the Air fryer at 390°F for 10 minutes, shaking halfway through.

Nutrition: Calories: 111 | Fat: 9.9 g | Protein: 1.2 g

12. Crispy Vegetables
(Prep. Time: 7 Min | Cooking: 8 Min | Serving 4)

INGREDIENTS
- 1 cup rice flour
- 2 tbsp. vegan egg powder
- 1 cup breadcrumbs
- 1 cup squash; zucchini
- 1/2 cup green beans; cauliflower
- 1 tbsp. nutritional yeast
- 2/3 cup of water

DIRECTIONS:
1. Set up three bowls.
2. One is for the rice flour, another for the egg powder, 1 tbsp. nutritional yeast and 2/3 cup of water, another for the breadcrumbs.
3. Dip each of the vegetable slices in the first, second, and third bowls.
4. Spray the air fryer basket with oil.
5. Cook at 380°F for 8 minutes or until crispy.

Nutrition: Calories: 272 | Fat: 2.2 g | Protein: 7.9 g

13. Onion Appetizers
(Prep. Time: 10 Min | Cooking: 4 Min | Serving 4)

INGREDIENTS
- 2 lb. onions, sliced into rings
- 2 vegan eggs
- 1 tsp. garlic powder; cayenne pepper
- 1 tbsp. ketchup; paprika
- 1 cup almond milk
- 2 cups flour
- Salt and pepper to taste
- ½ cup vegan sour cream
- ½ cup mayo
- ½ tbsp. paprika

DIRECTIONS:
1. Combine the eggs and 1 cup almond milk on one plate.
2. On another plate, mix the 2 cups flour, paprika, salt, pepper, garlic powder, and cayenne pepper.
3. Dip each onion into the egg mixture before coating it with the flour mixture.
4. Spray with oil.

5. Air fryer at 350°F for 4 minutes
6. Serve with the dipping sauces such as vegan sour cream or mayo.

Nutrition: Calories: 364 | Fat: 14.5 g | Protein: 8.1 g

14. CRISPY BRUSSELS SPROUTS
(PREP. TIME: 5 MIN | COOKING: 1 MIN | SERVING 2)

INGREDIENTS
- 2 cups Brussels sprouts, sliced
- 1 tbsp. light olive oil
- 1 tbsp. balsamic vinegar
- Salt to taste

DIRECTIONS:
1. Toss all the **INGREDIENTS** in a bowl.
2. Air fry for 10 minutes at 400°F; shake once or twice during the cooking process.
3. Check to see if crispy enough.
4. If not, cook for another 5 minutes

Nutrition: Calories: 100 | Fat: 7.3 g | Protein: 3 g

15. SWEET POTATO TOTS
(PREP. TIME: 10 MIN | COOKING: 5 MIN | SERVING 10)

INGREDIENTS
- 2 cups sweet potato puree
- 1/2 tsp. salt
- 1/2 tsp. cumin
- 1/2 tsp. coriander
- 1/2 cup breadcrumbs

DIRECTIONS:
1. Prep your air fryer to 390°F.
2. Combine all **INGREDIENTS** in a bowl.
3. Form into balls.
4. Arrange on the air fryer pan.
5. Spray with oil.
6. Cook for 6 minutes or until golden.
7. Serve with vegan mayo.

Nutrition: Calories: 77 | Fat: 0.8 g | Protein: 1.8 g

16. LEMON TOFU
(PREP. TIME: 5 MIN | COOKING: 9 MIN | SERVING 4)

INGREDIENTS
- 1 lb. tofu, sliced into cubes
- 1 tbsp. arrowroot powder; tamari
- 1/4 cup lemon juice
- 1 tsp. lemon zest
- 2 tbsp. coconut sugar

DIRECTIONS:
1. Coat the tofu cubes in tamari.
2. Dredge with arrowroot powder.
3. Let sit for 15 minutes
4. Add the rest of the **INGREDIENTS** to a bowl, mix and set aside.
5. Cook the tofu in the air fryer at 390°F for 10 minutes, shaking halfway through.
6. Put the tofu in a skillet over medium-high heat.
7. Stir in the sauce.
8. Simmer until the sauce has thickened.
9. Serve with rice or vegetables.

Nutrition: Calories: 112 | Fat: 3 g | Protein: 8 g

17. BUFFALO CAULIFLOWER
(PREP. TIME: 10 MIN | COOKING: 5 MIN | SERVING 4)

INGREDIENTS
- 1 cauliflower, sliced into florets
- 2 tbsp. hot sauce; nutritional yeast
- 1 1/2 tsp. maple syrup
- 2 tsp. avocado oil
- 1 tbsp. arrowroot starch

DIRECTIONS:
1. Preheat your fryer to 360°F.
2. Incorporate all the **INGREDIENTS** except the cauliflower.
3. Mix well.
4. Toss cauliflower into the mixture to coat evenly.
5. Cook in the air fryer for 14 minutes, shaking halfway during the cooking.

Nutrition: Calories: 52 | Fat: 0.7 g | Protein: 3.7 g

18. CHIPOTLE, PINTO, AND GREEN BEAN
(PREP. TIME: 5 MIN | COOKING: 10 MIN | SERVING 2)

INGREDIENTS
- 2 tbsp. extra-virgin light olive oil
- 1 1/2 cups fresh or frozen corn
- 1 cup green beans, chopped
- 2 green onions
- 1/2 tbsp. garlic
- 1 medium tomato
- 1 tsp. chili powder
- 1/2 tsp. chipotle powder
- 1/2 tsp. ground cumin
- 1 (14 oz.) can pinto beans
- 1 tsp. sea salt

DIRECTIONS:
1. Cook light olive oil in a huge skillet over medium heat. Add the corn, green beans, green onions, and garlic and stir for 5 minutes
2. Add the tomato, chili powder, chipotle powder, and cumin and stir for 3 minutes, until the tomato starts to soften. In a bowl, mash some of the pinto beans with a fork. Add all of the beans to the skillet and stir for 2 minutes
3. Pull away from the heat and stir in the salt. Serve hot or warm.

Nutrition: Calories: 391 | Fiber: 15 g | Protein: 15 g

19. MIXED VEGETABLE MEDLEY
(PREP. TIME: 5 MIN | COOKING: 9 MIN | SERVING 2)

INGREDIENTS
- 1 cup coconut oil
- 1 large potato
- 1 onion
- 1/2 tbsp. garlic
- 1 cup green beans
- 2 ears fresh sweet corn
- 1 red bell pepper
- 2 cups white mushrooms

DIRECTIONS:
1. Warm-up half of coconut oil in a large nonstick skillet over medium-high heat. Stir in the potato and cook, stirring frequently, for 15 minutes
2. Mix in the rest of the coconut, turn down the heat to medium, and add the onion, garlic, green beans, and corn. Cook, stirring frequently, for 5 minutes
3. Add the red bell pepper and mushrooms. Stir for another 5 minutes Add more coconut oil, if necessary.
4. Pull out from heat and season. Serve hot.

Nutrition: Calories: 688 | Fiber: 11 g | Protein: 11 g

20. SPICY LENTILS
(PREP. TIME: 8 MIN | COOKING: 7 MIN | SERVING 3)

INGREDIENTS
- 1 cup dried red lentils
- 2 1/2 cups water
- 1 tbsp. extra-virgin light olive oil
- 1 tbsp. garlic
- 1 tsp. cumin
- 1/2 tsp. coriander
- 1/2 tsp. turmeric
- 1/4 tsp. cayenne pepper
- 1 medium tomato
- 1 (16 oz.) package spinach
- 1 tsp. salt

DIRECTIONS:
1. In a saucepan, boil lentils and water.
2. Partially cover the pot, reduce the heat to medium, and simmer, stirring occasionally, for 15 minutes
3. Drain the lentils and set them aside.
4. In a big nonstick skillet, heat the light olive oil over medium heat. Once hot, add the garlic, cumin, coriander, turmeric, salt, and cayenne. Sauté for 2 minutes
5. Cook tomato for 4 minutes
6. Add handfuls of the spinach at a time, stirring until wilted.
7. Stir in the strained lentils and cook for another few minutes
8. Season well and serve hot.

Nutrition: Calories: 237 | Fiber: 18 g | Protein: 16 g

21. PINTO AND GREEN BEAN FRY
(PREP. TIME: 5 MIN | COOKING: 9 MIN | SERVING 4)

INGREDIENTS
- 1/2 cup water
- 1/3 cup couscous
- 2 tbsp. extra-virgin light olive oil
- 1 small onion
- 1/2 tbsp. garlic
- 1 cup green beans
- 1 cup fresh corn
- 1 1/2 tsp. chili powder
- 1/2 tsp. ground cumin
- 1 large tomato
- 1 (14 oz.) can pinto beans
- 1 tsp. salt

DIRECTIONS:
1. Boil water. Pull out from the heat and stir in the couscous. Cover and put aside for 10 minutes
2. Gently fluff the couscous with a fork.
3. While cooking, preheat light olive oil in a large skillet over medium heat. Cook onion and garlic. Then, cook green beans for 4 minutes Stir in corn for another 2 minutes, then add the chili powder and cumin to coat the vegetables.
4. Simmer tomato for 4 minutes Stir in the pinto beans and couscous and cook for 3 to 4 minutes Stir often.
5. Sprinkle salt and serve.

Nutrition: Calories: 267 | Fiber: 10 g | Protein: 10 g

22. Indonesian-Style Spicy Fried Tempeh Strips

(Prep. Time: 5 Min | Cooking: 9 Min | Serving 4)

INGREDIENTS

- 1 cup sesame oil
- 1 (12 oz.) package tempeh
- 2 medium onions
- 1 1/2 tbsp. tomato paste
- 3 tsp. tamari
- 1 tsp. dried red chili flakes
- 1/2 tsp. brown sugar
- 2 tbsp. lime juice

DIRECTIONS:

1. Preheat sesame oil in a large wok over medium-high heat. Add more sesame oil as needed to raise the level to at least 1 inch.
2. Once hot, put the tempeh slices and cook, stirring frequently, for 10 minutes
3. Add the onions and stir for another 10 minutes Situate in a large bowl lined with several sheets of paper towel.
4. While the tempeh and onions are cooking, whisk together the tomato paste, tamari or soy sauce, red chili flakes, brown sugar, and lime juice in a small bowl.
5. Remove the paper towel from the large bowl and pour the sauce over the tempeh strips. Mix well to coat.

Nutrition: Calories: 317 | Fiber: 1 g | Protein: 17 g

23. Fried Rice and Vegetables

(Prep. Time: 5 Min | Cooking: 5 Min | Serving 4)

INGREDIENTS

- 3/4 cup long-grain white rice
- 1 1/2 cups water
- 2 tbsp. sesame oil
- 2 large eggs
- 2 carrots
- 1 1/4 cups white mushrooms
- 1 tbsp. garlic
- 6 green onions
- 2 tbsp. tamari
- 1/2 cup frozen green peas

DIRECTIONS:

1. Rinse the rice and add to a small saucepan. Boil water and decrease the heat to low, then simmer for 15 minutes Fluff with a fork and set aside.
2. While cooking, heat 1/2 tbsp. sesame oil in a wok over medium heat. Mix in eggs and cook without stirring for 5 minutes Slice into small strips. Set aside.
3. Return the saucepan or wok to the heat. Cook remaining 2 1/2 tbsp. sesame oil. Cook the carrots for 2 minutes
4. Stir in mushrooms, garlic, and the white parts of the green onions for 3 more minutes
5. Mix cooked rice and tamari. Cook, stirring frequently, for 10 minutes
6. Throw in the green parts of the green onions, peas, and egg. Pull away from the heat and serve.

Nutrition: Calories: 271 | Fiber: 3 g | Protein: 9 g

24. Spanish-Style Saffron Rice With Black Beans

(Prep. Time: 3 Min | Cooking: 11 Min | Serving 6)

INGREDIENTS

- 2 cups vegetable stock
- 1/4 tsp. saffron threads
- 1 1/2 tbsp. light olive oil
- 1 small red onion
- 1 tbsp. garlic
- 1 tsp. turmeric
- 2 tsp. paprika
- 1 cup long-grain white rice
- 1 (14 oz.) can black beans
- 1/2 cup green beans
- 1 small red bell pepper
- 1 tsp. salt

DIRECTIONS:

1. In a small pot, boil vegetable stock. Add the saffron, if using, and remove from the heat.
2. Preheat light olive oil in a huge nonstick skillet over medium heat. Add the onion, garlic, turmeric, paprika, and rice and stir to coat.
3. Pour in the stock, and mix in the black beans, green beans, and red bell pepper. Boil, set the heat to medium-low, cover, and simmer for 20 minutes
4. Sprinkle salt and serve.

Nutrition: Calories: 332 | Fiber: 9 g | Protein: 11 g

25. Simple Lemon Dal

(Prep. Time: 5 Min | Cooking: 8 Min | Serving 4)

INGREDIENTS

For lentils:

- 1 cup dried red lentils
- 2 1/2 cups water

- 1/2 tsp. turmeric
- 1/2 tsp. ground cumin
- 2 tbsp. lemon juice
- 1/3 cup fresh parsley
- 1 tsp. salt
- For finishing:
- 1 tbsp. extra-virgin light olive oil
- 2 tsp. garlic
- 1/2 tsp. dried red chili flakes

DIRECTIONS:

1. Boil lentils to a medium saucepan and mix in turmeric and cumin.
2. Select heat to medium-low, cover, and simmer, stirring occasionally, for 20 minutes
3. Drizzle lemon juice, parsley, and salt, and pull away from the pan from the heat.
4. Using the saucepan, heat the oil over medium-high heat. Once hot, stir in the garlic and red chili flakes or cayenne and stir for a minute.
5. Swiftly pour the oil into the cooked lentils, cover, and let sit for 5 minutes
6. Stir the lentils and serve immediately.

Nutrition: Calories: 207 | Fiber: 15 g | Protein: 13 g

26. GINGERED BLACK-EYED PEAS WITH BLACK TEA

(PREP. TIME: 5 MIN | COOKING: 10 MIN | SERVING 4)

INGREDIENTS

- 2 tbsp. light olive oil
- 1 tbsp. garlic
- 1 1/2 tbsp. fresh ginger
- 1 or 2 fresh green chilies
- 1 tsp. ground cumin
- 1/2 tsp. turmeric
- 2 (14 oz.) cans of black-eyed peas
- 1/4–1/3 cup fresh cilantro
- 1 1/2 tsp. salt
- 2 cups brewed black tea
- 2 tbsp. lime juice

DIRECTIONS:

1. In a big saucepan, cook light olive oil over medium heat. Stir in the garlic, ginger, and fresh chilies and sauté for a few minutes
2. Stir in the cumin, turmeric, black-eyed peas, cilantro, and salt. Boil brewed tea. Select the heat to medium and simmer for 11 minutes
3. Put off heat, stir in the lime or lemon juice, cover, and set aside for 5 minutes

Nutrition: Calories: 245 | Fiber: 12 g | Protein: 12 g

27. CREAMY POLENTA WITH SAUTÉED MIXED MUSHROOMS

(PREP. TIME: 4 MIN | COOKING: 9 MIN | SERVING 4)

INGREDIENTS

For polenta:
- 4 cups vegetable stock
- 1 tsp. salt
- 1 cup yellow cornmeal
- For mushrooms:
- 1 tbsp. light olive oil
- 1 large shallot
- 2 garlic cloves
- 1 (16 oz.) package mixed mushrooms
- 1/2 cup dry red wine
- 1 tsp. dried rosemary
- 1/2 tsp. dried thyme
- 3/4 cup vegetable stock
- 1 tsp. cornstarch
- 2 1/2 tbsp. coconut oil
- Salt and pepper to taste

DIRECTIONS:

For polenta:
1. In a medium saucepan, boil the vegetable stock and salt to a boil. Gradually pour in the cornmeal, whisking as you go to avoid lumps.
2. Put heat to low, cover, then simmer for 12 minutes, stirring every few minutes

For mushrooms:
1. While cooking, preheat light olive oil in a huge nonstick skillet over medium heat. Sauté shallot or onion and garlic for a few minutes to soften.
2. Increase the heat to medium-high and stir in the mushrooms. Cook for 5 minutes
3. Pour in the red wine, add the rosemary and thyme, and simmer for another 5 minutes, until most of the liquid has evaporated.
4. Whisk together the vegetable stock and cornstarch and pour into the pan. Simmer for another few minutes to thicken. Season with salt and pepper.
5. Stir the coconut into cooked polenta. Top with sautéed mushrooms and sauce.

Nutrition: Calories: 265 | Fiber: 4 g | Protein: 7 g

28. PAN-FRIED BABY POTATOES

(PREP. TIME: 4 MIN | COOKING: 9 MIN | SERVING 4)

INGREDIENTS
- 3 tbsp. light olive oil
- 1 medium onion
- 1 lb. baby potatoes
- 2 tbsp. water
- 1 tsp. ground cumin
- 1/2 tsp. ground coriander
- 1/2 tsp. turmeric
- 1 cup green or red cabbage
- 1 cup green or red kale
- 1/2 tsp. chili powder
- 1 tsp. salt

DIRECTIONS:
1. In a nonstick pan, prep light olive oil over medium heat. When hot, mix in onion and sauté for 5 minutes
2. Stir in the potatoes and fry, stirring occasionally, for 10 minutes
3. Sprinkle in 1 tbsp. of water, cumin, coriander, and turmeric, and cover the pan. Cook for another 5 minutes
4. Stir in the cabbage, kale, and remaining 1 tbsp. of water. Cook, stir often.
5. Add the chili powder to the pan, reduce the heat to medium-low, and cook for another 5 minutes, until the cabbage is tender.
6. Stir in the salt and serve immediately.

Nutrition: Calories: 183 | Fiber: 4 g | Protein: 4 g

29. YELLOW SPLIT PEAS AND RICE
(PREP. TIME: 5 MIN | COOKING: 8 MIN | SERVING 5)

INGREDIENTS
- 3/4 cup dried yellow split peas
- 4 cups boiling water
- 3 tbsp. light olive oil
- 1 medium onion
- 1/2 tbsp. ginger
- 2 cups cauliflower
- 1 large tomato
- 1/2 tsp. ground cumin
- 1/2 tsp. chili powder
- 3/4 cup long-grain white rice
- 2/3 cup green peas
- 3 tbsp. lemon juice
- 1 tsp. salt

DIRECTIONS:
1. Clean split peas. Pour the boiling water over the split peas and set them aside.
2. While the split peas are soaking, heat the light olive oil in a huge saucepan over medium heat. Put the onion and ginger and cook, stirring often, for 3 minutes
3. Add the cauliflower and stir for 2 minutes Add the tomato, cumin, and chili powder and cook for 5 minutes
4. Pour in the split peas and water and add the rice and green peas. Boil, select heat to low, and cover. Simmer for 18 minutes
5. Pull out from the heat and stir in the lemon juice and salt. Serve.

Nutrition: Calories: 401 | Fiber: 14 g | Protein: 15 g

30. INDIAN-STYLE POTATOES AND CAULIFLOWER
(PREP. TIME: 4 MIN | COOKING: 9 MIN | SERVING 5)

INGREDIENTS
- 3 tbsp. extra-virgin light olive oil
- 2 tbsp. minced fresh ginger
- 1 tsp. turmeric
- 1 1/2 tsp. ground coriander
- 1 tsp. ground cumin
- 1/4 tsp. cayenne pepper
- 2 large potatoes
- 2 cups cauliflower
- 3 medium tomatoes
- 1 (14 oz.) can chickpeas
- 1/4 cup cilantro
- 2 tbsp. lime juice
- Salt and pepper to taste

DIRECTIONS:
1. In a big nonstick saucepan, heat the light olive oil over medium heat. Stir in the ginger, sauté for 1 minute, and then stir in the turmeric, coriander, cumin, and cayenne and cook for another minute.
2. Mix potatoes and cauliflower to the pan to coat, and fry, stirring often, for 5 minutes
3. Stir in the tomatoes. Boil, decrease heat and then cover and simmer over medium-low heat for 11 minutes
4. Add the chickpeas and cilantro and cook for extra 5 minutes
5. Stir in the lime juice, season with salt and freshly ground black pepper, and serve hot.

Nutrition: Calories: 358 | Fiber: 12 g | Protein: 11 g

31. RED LENTIL AND CAULIFLOWER TOMATO PILAF
(PREP. TIME: 5 MIN | COOKING: 8 MIN | SERVING 5)

INGREDIENTS

- 1/2 tbsp. extra-virgin light olive oil
- 1 small red onion
- 1/2 tbsp. garlic
- 1/2–1 tbsp. fresh ginger
- 2 fresh green chilies
- 1 1/2 tsp. ground coriander
- 1 tsp. ground cumin
- 1/2 tsp. turmeric
- 2 medium tomatoes
- 2 cups cauliflower
- 1/2 cup red lentils
- 1/2 cup long-grain white rice
- 2 cups water
- 3 tbsp. lemon juice
- 1 tsp. salt

DIRECTIONS:

1. Prep light olive oil in a saucepan over medium heat. Place the onion and sauté for 5 minutes Stir in the garlic, ginger, and chilies and sauté for 1 minute.
2. Add coriander, cumin, and turmeric. Mix in tomatoes and simmer for extra5 minutes, stirring occasionally.
3. Stir in the cauliflower, lentils, and rice and stir for 1 minute.
4. Boil water over medium-high heat.
5. Press heat to medium-low, and simmer for 12 minutes
6. Turn off the heat, and drizzle the lemon juice and salt.
7. Toss with a fork and serve hot.

Nutrition: Calories: 227 | Fiber: 11 g | Protein: 10 g

32. CHICKPEA, CAULIFLOWER, AND POTATO COCONUT CURRY

(PREP. TIME: 5 MIN | COOKING: 8 MIN | SERVING 6)

INGREDIENTS

- 1 tbsp. extra-virgin light olive oil
- 1 tbsp. fresh ginger
- 1 tsp. ground cumin
- 1/2 tsp. turmeric
- 1/4–1/2 tsp. cayenne pepper
- 2 cups cauliflower
- 1 medium potato
- 1 medium carrot
- 1 large tomato
- 2/3 cup coconut milk
- 1 cup water
- 1 (19 oz.) can chickpeas
- 1 red bell pepper
- 1 tsp. garam masala
- Salt to taste

DIRECTIONS:

1. In a nonstick saucepan, warm up light olive oil over medium heat. Mix ginger and sauté for a few minutes Stir in the cumin, turmeric, and cayenne and stir for another minute.
2. Cook cauliflower, potato, and carrot for few minutes adding a few tsp. of water as necessary to prevent sticking.
3. Cook in tomato for extra minutes Pour in the coconut milk and water and stir in the chickpeas. Bring to a gentle boil. Select heat to medium-low, cover, and simmer for 10 minutes, stirring occasionally.
4. Add the red pepper, garam masala, and few tbsp. of water if the mixture seems too dry. Cover and continue to simmer for extra 10 minutes
5. Season with salt and serve hot.

Nutrition: Calories: 230 | Fiber: 7 g | Protein: 8 g

33. PINEAPPLE BREEZE SMOOTHIE

(PREP. TIME: 5 MIN | COOKING: 0 MIN | SERVING 1)

INGREDIENTS

- 1 (1 oz.) scoop vanilla protein powder
- 1 tsp. sized piece of fresh ginger
- 1 cup frozen spinach
- 1/2 cup pineapple chunks
- 1 1/4 cups unsweetened plant-based milk

DIRECTIONS:

1. Blend all **INGREDIENTS** and process at high speed until smooth.

Nutrition: Calories: 148 | Fat: 2 g | Protein: 22 g

34. PUMPKIN SPICE SMOOTHIE

(PREP. TIME: 5 MIN | COOKING: 0 MIN | SERVING 1)

INGREDIENTS

- 1 (1 oz.) scoop vanilla protein powder
- 1/2 cup canned pumpkin purée
- 1 small frozen banana
- 1 tsp. fresh ginger
- 1 tsp. fresh turmeric
- 1/2 tsp. cinnamon
- 1/4 tsp. nutmeg
- 2 tbsp. hemp hearts
- 1 tsp. ground flaxseed

- 1 1/4 cups unsweetened plant-based milk

DIRECTIONS:
1. Blend all **INGREDIENTS** and process at high speed until smooth.

Nutrition: Calories: 463 | Fat: 19 g | Protein: 31 g

35. Mint Chocolate Smoothie
(Prep. Time: 5 Min | Cooking: 0 Min | Serving 1)

INGREDIENTS
- 1 (1 oz.) scoop chocolate protein powder
- 1/4 cup fresh mint leaves
- 1 cup frozen spinach
- 1 small frozen banana
- 1 tsp. spirulina
- 1 1/4 cups water

DIRECTIONS:
1. Blend all **INGREDIENTS** and process at high speed until smooth.

Nutrition: Calories: 253 | Fat: 5 g | Protein: 24 g

36. Super Green Smoothie
(Prep. Time: 5 Min | Cooking: 0 Min | Serving 1)

INGREDIENTS
- 1 (1 oz.) scoop vanilla protein powder
- 1 cup frozen spinach
- 1/2 cucumber
- 2 celery stalks
- 1 tsp. spirulina
- 1/2 small banana
- 1 1/4 cups water

DIRECTIONS:
1. Blend all **INGREDIENTS** and process at high speed until smooth

Nutrition: Calories: 214 | Fat: 2 g | Protein: 27 g

37. Tempeh and Kale Breakfast Skillet
(Prep. Time: 5 Min | Cooking: 10 Min | Serving 3)

INGREDIENTS
- 1 tbsp. light olive oil
- 1 white onion
- 2 garlic cloves
- 1 (9 oz.) package tempeh
- 3 tbsp. tamari
- 2 tbsp. apple cider vinegar
- 4 cups kale
- Salt to taste
- 1 cup water
- 1 tbsp. chili flakes

DIRECTIONS:
1. In a medium skillet, warm the oil over medium-high heat. Sauté onion and a big pinch of salt for 5 minutes Cook in the garlic and chili flakes.
2. Stir tempeh, amino, and vinegar. Steam tempeh for 10 minutes Put water to deglaze the skillet.
3. Stir in kale and cook uncovered for 3 minutes Season well.

Nutrition: Calories: 279 | Fat: 14 g | Protein: 19 g

38. Vanilla Blueberry Overnight Oats
(Prep. Time: 5 Min | Cooking: 0 Min | Serving 1)

INGREDIENTS
- 1/2 cup rolled oats
- 1 1/2 tbsp. chia seeds
- 1 (1 oz.) scoop vanilla protein powder
- 1 cup unsweetened plant-based milk
- 1/4 cup blueberries
- Salt to taste

DIRECTIONS:
1. Combine the oats, chia, and salt in a 2 cups food storage container. Mix together the protein powder and the plant-based milk. Stir liquid over the oat mixture.
2. Top your oats with blueberries, put the lid on, and chill overnight.

Nutrition: Calories: 466 | Fat: 17 g | Protein: 30 g

39. Protein Pancakes
(Prep. Time: 5 Min | Cooking: 10 Min | Serving 2)

INGREDIENTS
- 1 ripe banana
- 1 cup unsweetened plant-based milk
- 1 cup rolled oats
- 1 (1 oz.) scoop vanilla protein powder
- 1 tbsp. ground flaxseed
- 1 tsp. cinnamon
- 1 tsp. baking powder
- Salt to taste

- 2 tbsp. coconut oil

DIRECTIONS:
1. Mix the bananas and milk in a blender on high. Blend oats, protein powder, flaxseed, cinnamon, baking powder, and salt and process on high.
2. Lightly grease the surface of a nonstick pan with coconut oil over medium-high heat. Once hot, pour in the batter in about 1/3 cup portions.
3. Cook for about 4 minutes repeat this process.

Nutrition: Calories: 392 | Fat: 16 g | Protein: 18 g

40. Apple Cinnamon Quinoa Porridge
(Prep. Time: 2 Min | Cooking: 13 Min | Serving 3)

INGREDIENTS
- 1 cup quinoa
- 1 1/2 cups water
- 1 tsp. vanilla extract
- 3/4 tsp. cinnamon
- 3/4 cup unsweetened plant-based milk
- 2 tsp. chia seeds
- 2 tsp. maple syrup
- 1 tbsp. coconut oil
- 1 large apple
- 1 ginger
- Salt to taste
- Hemp hearts

DIRECTIONS:
1. Boil quinoa, water, vanilla, 1/2 tsp. cinnamon, and salt. Then simmer for 12 minutes
2. Once cooked, stir in the milk, chia seeds, and 1 tsp. of maple syrup. Transfer into 3 containers. Set aside.
3. Warm the coconut oil over medium heat. Cook apple, ginger, remaining 1 tsp. maple syrup, and remaining 1/4 tsp. cinnamon for 15 minutes, covered.
4. Top each with apple mixture and hemp hearts.

Nutrition: Calories: 332 | Fat: 10 g | Protein: 9 g

41. Savory Steel-Cut Oats
(Prep. Time: 11 Min | Cooking: 3 Min | Serving 3)

INGREDIENTS
- 1 cup steel-cut oats
- 2 cups vegetable broth
- 1 tbsp. coconut oil
- 1 yellow onion
- 2 garlic cloves
- 1/2 tsp. dried thyme
- 1/2 tsp. dried rosemary
- A pinch of salt

DIRECTIONS:
1. Boil steel-cut oats and vegetable broth. Then simmer, for 20 minutes
2. Warm the oil over medium heat. Sauté onion, garlic, and a big pinch of salt, set heat to low, for 20 minutes Stir in the thyme and rosemary.
3. Mix the onion mixture with the steel-cut oats. Season well.

Nutrition: Calories: 184 | Fat: 7 g | Protein: 7 g

42. Classic Tofu Scramble
(Prep. Time: 10 Min | Cooking: 5 Min | Serving 6)

INGREDIENTS
- 1 tbsp. light olive oil
- 1 white onion
- 2 garlic cloves
- 1 tsp. turmeric
- 1 (16 oz.) package organic firm tofu
- 1/4 cup nutritional yeast
- 1 tsp. black salt
- 4 cups spinach
- Salt to taste
- 1 cup water

DIRECTIONS:
1. Warm the oil over medium heat. Sauté the onions with salt and water for 5 minutes add the garlic then stir in the turmeric.
2. Mix in the crumbled tofu, nutritional yeast, and black salt. Cook to warm the tofu. Add in the spinach. Serve.

Nutrition: Calories: 191 | Fat: 10 g | Protein: 19 g

43. High-Protein Granola
(Prep. Time: 8 Min | Cooking: 7 Min | Serving 5)

INGREDIENTS
- 2 cups rolled oats
- 1/2 cup sunflower seeds
- 1/2 cup walnuts
- 1/4 cup ground flaxseed
- 1/2 cup vanilla protein powder
- 1/4 tsp. salt
- 1/3 cup coconut oil, melted
- 1/4 cup maple syrup

DIRECTIONS:
1. Prepare oven to 325°F and line a baking sheet with parchment paper or a silicone liner.

2. Mix oats, sunflower seeds, walnuts, flaxseed, protein powder, and salt. Mix melted coconut oil and maple syrup.
3. Evenly arrange the granola on a baking sheet, bake for 15 minutes and then stir the granola. Bake for 10 minutes more and remove from the oven. Allow the granola to cool before transferring it to an airtight container.

Nutrition: Calories: 431 | Fat: 26 g | Protein: 19 g

44. Chickpea Omelet
(Prep. Time: 4 Min | Cooking: 10 Min | Serving 2)

INGREDIENTS
- 1 cup chickpea flour
- 1 cup water
- 1 tbsp. nutritional yeast
- 1/4 tsp. turmeric
- 1/4 tsp. salt
- Black pepper to taste
- 1 tbsp. oil

DIRECTIONS:
1. Scourge the chickpea flour, water, nutritional yeast, turmeric, salt, and as much black pepper as you'd like. Set aside for a few minutes
2. Warm a large nonstick sauté pan over medium-high heat. Lightly grease the surface with oil. Pour half of the batter into the sauté pan. Cook both sides for 10 minutes
3. Repeat this process one more time. Enjoy immediately on your own or with a side of your choice. Hot sauce, salsa, guacamole, sliced tomatoes, or a lightly dressed salad pair nicely with this dish.

Nutrition: Calories: 269 | Fat: 11 g | Protein: 14 g

45. Chocolate Zoats
(Prep. Time: 3 Min | Cooking: 12 Min | Serving 1)

INGREDIENTS
- 1/2 cup rolled oats
- 3/4 cup water
- 1/2 small zucchini, grated (about 1/2 cup)
- 2 tbsp. powdered chocolate peanut butter

DIRECTIONS:
1. In a small saucepan, bring oats, water, and zucchini to a boil. Cook for 14 minutes Stirs in the powdered peanut butter until it's evenly mixed.

Nutrition: Calories: 249 | Fat: 6 g | Protein: 16 g

46. Greens on Toast with Tofu Ricotta
(Prep. Time: 5 Min | Cooking: 9 Min | Serving 1)

INGREDIENTS
- 2 slices Ezekiel bread
- 1 tbsp. light olive oil
- 2 garlic cloves
- 4 cups greens, your choice
- Juice of 1/2 lemon
- Tofu Ricotta, to taste
- Salt and pepper to taste

DIRECTIONS:
1. Toast the Ezekiel bread or English muffin. Meanwhile, warm the oil in a small sauté pan over medium heat. Cook garlic. Mix greens and lemon juice and cook for 3 minutes or until the greens are nicely wilted. Season with salt and pepper.
2. Spread about 2 tbsp. of tofu ricotta on each slice of toast, and then top with even amounts of greens. Crack a bit of pepper over them if desired and enjoy right away.

Nutrition: Calories: 491 | Fat: 20 g | Protein: 23 g

47. Staple Smoothie
(Prep. Time: 5 Min | Cooking: 0 Min | Serving 1)

INGREDIENTS
- 1 (1-ounce) scoop protein powder
- 1 tsp. sized piece of fresh ginger
- 1 tsp. sized piece of fresh turmeric
- 1 cup frozen spinach
- 1/2 cup frozen blueberries
- 1 tsp. spirulina
- 1 1/4 cups water

DIRECTIONS:
1. Blend all **INGREDIENTS** and process at high speed until smooth.

Nutrition: Calories: 187 | Fat: 3 g | Protein: 28 g

48. Cashew Cheese Spread
(Prep. Time: 5 Min | Cooking: 0 Min | Serving 5)

INGREDIENTS
- 1 cup of water
- 1 cup raw cashews
- 1 tsp. nutritional yeast
- 1/2 tsp. salt
- Optional: 1 tsp. garlic powder

DIRECTIONS:
1. Immerge the cashews for 6 hours in water.
2. Drain and transfer the soaked cashews to a food processor.
3. Add 1 cup of water and all the other INGREDIENTS and blend.

Nutrition: Calories: 151 | Fat: 10.9 g | Protein: 4.6 g

49. Fruit and Nut Oatmeal
(Prep. Time: 4 Min | Cooking: 11 Min | Serving 2)

INGREDIENTS
- 1 1/2 cups of water
- 3/4 cup rolled oats
- 1/4 cup berries, fresh
- 1/2 ripe banana
- 2 tbsp. nuts
- 1/2 tsp. cinnamon
- A pinch of salt

DIRECTIONS:
1. Position oats in a medium saucepan and add 1 1/2 cups of water. Stir and over high heat, boil. Decrease heat and cook for 5 minutes
2. Stir in the cinnamon and add the pinch of salt. Serve in 2 bowls and top each with the chopped fruit and nuts.

Nutrition: Calories: 420 | Fat: 21.5 g | Protein: 14 g

50. Almond and Banana Granola
(Prep. Time: 5 Min | Cooking: 7 Min | Serving 8)

INGREDIENTS
- 2 peeled and chopped ripe bananas
- 4 cups of rolled oats
- 1 tsp. salt
- 2 cups of freshly chopped and pitted dates
- 1 cup of slivered and toasted almonds
- 1 tsp. almond extract

DIRECTIONS:
1. Heat the oven to 275°F.
2. With parchment paper, line two 13 x 18-inch baking sheets.
3. In an average saucepan, boil water, 2 cup of dates. On medium heat, cook them for 10 minutes keep on adding water to the saucepan so that the dates do not stick to the pot.
4. After removing the dates from the high temperature, allow them to cool before you blend them with salt, bananas, almond extract.
5. To the oats, add this mixture and mix.
6. Split the mixture into equal halves and lay over the baking sheets.
7. Bake for 32 minutes and stir every 10 minutes
8. After removing the baking sheets, allow them to cool. Add the almonds.

Nutrition: Calories: 248 | Fat: 9.4 g | Protein: 8 g

51. Polenta with a Dose of Cranberries and Pears
(Prep. Time: 45 Min | Cooking: 10 Min | Serving 4)

INGREDIENTS
- 2 pears
- 1 batch warm basic polenta
- 1/4 cup brown rice syrup
- 1 tsp. ground cinnamon
- 1 cup cranberries

DIRECTIONS:
1. Heat up the polenta in a medium-sized saucepan. Stir in the cranberries, pears, rice, and cinnamon powder.
2. Cook everything, stirring occasionally.
3. Split the polenta equally among the 4 bowls. Stir some pear compote as the last finishing touch.

Nutrition: Calories: 185 | Fat: 4.6 g | Protein: 5 g

52. Smoked Tempeh
(Prep. Time: 5 Min | Cooking: 10 Min | Serving 4)

INGREDIENTS
- 3 tbsp. maple syrup
- 8 oz. packages tempeh
- 1/4 cup of soy sauce
- 2 tsp. liquid smoke

DIRECTIONS:
1. Using a steamer basket, steam the block of tempeh.
2. Incorporate the maple syrup, liquid smoke, and tamari in a bowl.
3. Once the tempeh cools, cut into strips and add to the prepared marinade.
4. Using a sauté pan, cook the tempeh on medium-high heat with a bit of the marinade.
5. When the strips get crispy on one side, flip them over so that both sides are equally cooked.
6. You can stir some more marinade to cook the tempeh, but they should be correctly caramelized.

Nutrition: Calories: 130 | Fat: 1 g | Protein: 12 g

53. Quiche With Cauliflower
(Prep. Time: 8 Min | Cooking: 7 Min | Serving 4)

INGREDIENTS
- 1/2 tsp. salt
- 1 cup of grated cauliflower
- 1 cup of chickpea flour
- 1/2 tsp. baking powder
- 1/2 zucchini
- 1 tbsp. flax meal
- 1 cup of water
- 1 sprig of fresh rosemary
- 1/2 tsp. Italian seasoning
- 1/2 freshly sliced red onion
- 1/4 tsp. baking powder

DIRECTIONS:
1. Mix all the dry ingredients.
2. Cut the onion and zucchini.
3. Shred the cauliflower so that it has a rice-like consistency and add it to the dry ingredients. Now, pour in the water and mix well.
4. Stir in the zucchini, onion, and rosemary last.
5. Use a metal cake tin with a removable bottom. Now place the mixture in the tin and press it down mildly.
6. The top should be left muddled to resemble a rough texture.
7. Bake at 350°F for 30 minutes. You will know your quiche is ready once the top is golden.

Nutrition: Calories: 420 | Fat: 8.5 g | Protein: 7.5 g

54. Oatmeal and Carrot Cake
(Prep. Time: 5 Min | Cooking: 10 Min | Serving 2)

INGREDIENTS
- 1 cup of water
- 1/2 tsp. cinnamon
- 1 cup of rolled oats
- Salt to taste
- 1/4 cup of raisins
- 1/2 cup of shredded carrots
- 1 cup of non-dairy milk
- 1/4 tsp. allspice
- 1/2 tsp. vanilla extract

Toppings:
- 1/4 cup of chopped walnuts
- 2 tbsp. maple syrup
- 2 tbsp. shredded coconut

DIRECTIONS:
- Position pot on low heat and simmer non-dairy milk, oats, and water.
- Combine carrots, vanilla extract, raisins, salt, cinnamon, and allspice. Simmer all the ingredients, stir for 10minutes
- Transfer the thickened dish to bowls. You can top them with coconut, maple syrup, or walnuts.

Nutrition: Calories: 210 | Fat: 11.2 g | Protein: 3.8 g

55. Coconut Butter Banana Overnight Oats
(Prep. Time: 5 Min | Cooking: 10 Min | Serving 2)

INGREDIENTS
- 1/2 cup rolled oats
- 1 cup almond milk
- 1 tbsp. chia seeds
- 1/4 tsp. vanilla extract
- 1/2 tsp. ground cinnamon
- 1 tbsp. honey or maple syrup
- 1 banana, sliced
- 2 tbsp. natural coconut butter

DIRECTIONS:
1. Mix oats, milk, chia seeds, vanilla, cinnamon, and honey.
2. Stir to incorporate then split half of the mixture between two bowls.
3. Put banana and peanut butter on top then add the remaining mixture.
4. Cover then pop into the fridge overnight.

Nutrition: Calories: 227 | Fat: 11 g | Protein: 7 g

56. Peach and Chia Seed Breakfast Parfait
(Prep. Time: 5 Min | Cooking: 10 Min | Serving 4)

INGREDIENTS
- 1/4 cup chia seeds
- 1 tbsp. pure maple syrup
- 1 cup coconut milk
- 1 tsp. ground cinnamon
- 3 medium peaches
- 2/3 cup granola

DIRECTIONS:
1. Mix chia seeds, maple syrup, and coconut milk.
2. Stir well then cover and chill for 1 hour.
3. Mix the peaches and sprinkle with the cinnamon in a separate bowl. Put aside.
4. When it's time to serve, take two glasses and pour the chia mixture between the two.

5. Sprinkle the granola over the top, keeping a tiny amount to one side to use to decorate later.
6. Top with the peaches and top with the reserved granola and serve.

Nutrition: Calories: 260 | Fat: 13 g | Protein: 6 g

57. GUACAMOLE WITH WHITE BEANS TOAST
(PREP. TIME: 5 MIN | COOKING: 6 MIN | SERVING 4)

INGREDIENTS
- 1/2 cup canned white beans
- 2 tsp. tahini paste
- 2 tsp. lemon juice
- 1/2 tsp. salt
- 1/2 avocado, peeled and pit removed
- 4 slices whole-grain bread, toasted
- 1/2 cup grape tomatoes, cut in half

DIRECTIONS:
1. Mix beans, tahini, 1/2 the lemon juice, and 1/2 the salt. Crush with a fork.
2. Mash avocado and the remaining lemon juice and salt together.
3. Situate your toast onto a flat surface and stir in the mashed beans, spreading well.
4. Garnish with the avocado and the sliced tomatoes then serve and enjoy.

Nutrition: Calories: 140 | Fat: 5 g | Protein: 6 g

58. OATMEAL AND PEANUT BUTTER BREAKFAST BAR
(PREP. TIME: 10 MIN | COOKING: 0 MIN | SERVING 8)

INGREDIENTS
- 1 1/2 cups date, pit removed
- 1/2 cup peanut butter
- 1/2 cup old-fashioned rolled oats

DIRECTIONS:
1. Grease a baking tin and pop to one side.
2. Grab your food processor, add the dates, and whizz until chopped.
3. Add the peanut butter and the oats and pulse.
4. Scoop into the baking tin then pop into the fridge or freezer until set.
5. Serve and enjoy.

Nutrition: Calories: 232 | Fat: 9 g | Protein: 5 g

59. CHOCOLATE CHIP BANANA PANCAKE
(PREP. TIME: 15 MIN | COOKING: 3 MIN | SERVING 6)

INGREDIENTS
- 1 large ripe banana, mashed
- 2 tbsp. coconut sugar
- 3 tbsp. coconut oil, melted
- 1 cup of coconut milk
- 1 1/2 cups whole wheat flour
- 1 tsp. baking soda
- 1/2 cup vegan chocolate chips
- Light olive oil, for frying

DIRECTIONS:
1. Grab a large bowl and add the banana, sugar, oil, and milk. Stir well.
2. Add the flour and baking soda and stir again until combined.
3. Add the chocolate chips and fold through then pop to one side.
4. Put a skillet over medium heat and add a drop of oil.
5. Pour 1/4 of the batter into the pan and move the pan to cover.
6. Cook for 3 minutes then flip and cook on the other side.
7. Repeat with the remaining pancakes then serve and enjoy.

Nutrition: Calories: 271 | Fat: 16 g | Protein: 5 g

60. BREAKFAST SANDWICH
(PREP. TIME: 13 MIN | COOKING: 2 MIN | SERVING 1)

INGREDIENTS
- 1 vegan sausage patty
- 1 cup kale, chopped
- 2 tsp. extra virgin light olive oil
- 1 tbsp. pepitas
- Salt and pepper, to taste
- 1 tbsp. vegan mayo
- 1/8 tsp. chipotle powder
- 1 tsp. jalapeno chopped
- 1 English muffin, toasted
- 1/4 avocado, sliced

DIRECTIONS:
1. Situate a sauté pan over high heat and add a drop of oil.
2. Add the vegan patty and cook for 2 minutes
3. Flip the patty then add the kale and pepitas.
4. Season well then cook for another few minutes until the patty is cooked.
5. Find a small bowl and add the mayo, chipotle powder, and jalapeno. Stir well to combine.

6. Place the muffin onto a flat surface, spread with the spicy may then top with the patty.
7. Add the sliced avocado then serve and enjoy.

Nutrition: Calories: 573 | Fat: 35 g | Protein: 21 g

61. Gingerbread Waffles
(Prep. Time: 5 Min | Cooking: 6 Min | Serving 6)

INGREDIENTS
- 1 cup spelled flour
- 2 tsp. baking powder
- 1/4 tsp. salt
- 1 tbsp. ground flax seeds
- 1 1/2 tsp. ground cinnamon
- 2 tsp. ground ginger
- 4 tbsp. coconut sugar
- 1/4 tsp. baking soda
- 1 1/2 tbsp. light olive oil
- 1 cup non-dairy milk
- 1 tbsp. apple cider vinegar
- 2 tbsp. blackstrap molasses

DIRECTIONS:
1. Find your waffle iron, oil generously, and preheat.
2. Find a large bowl and add the dry ingredients. Stir well together.
3. Put the wet INGREDIENTS into another bowl and stir until combined.
4. Stir the dry and wet together until combined.
5. Pour the mixture into the waffle iron and cook at a medium temperature for 20 minutes
6. Open carefully and remove.
7. Serve and enjoy.

Nutrition: Calories: 137 | Fat: 5 g | Protein: 3 g

62. Easy Hummus Toast
(Prep. Time: 10 Min | Cooking: 0 Min | Serving 1)

INGREDIENTS
- 2 slices sprouted wheat bread
- 1/4 cup hummus
- 1 tbsp. hemp seeds
- 1 tbsp. roasted unsalted sunflower seeds

DIRECTIONS:
1. Start by toasting your bread.
2. Top with the hummus and seeds then eat!

Nutrition: Calories: 316 | Fat: 16 g | Protein: 19 g

63. Flaxseed and Blueberry Porridge
(Prep. Time: 9 Min | Cooking: 6 Min | Serving 2)

INGREDIENTS
- 1/4 cup coconut flour
- 1/4 cup flaxseed, ground
- 1 cup almond milk
- Salt to taste
- 1 tsp. cinnamon
- 1 tsp. vanilla
- 10 drops of stevia

Garnish:
- 1 oz. coconut, shaved
- 2 tbsp. pumpkin seeds
- 2 Ounces Blueberries

DIRECTIONS:
1. Heat 1 cup almond milk in a saucepan over low heat, whisking in your coconut flour, salt, 1 tsp. cinnamon and flaxseed
2. Once it bubbles, adds in your 1 tsp. vanilla and 10 drops of stevia
3. Remove from heat, garnishing as desired.

Nutrition: Calories: 405 | Fat: 34 g | Protein: 10 g

64. Avocado and Strawberry Bowl
(Prep. Time: 13 Min | Cooking: 0 Min | Serving 1)

INGREDIENTS
- 1 cup strawberries
- 1 cup avocado, peeled, and pitted
- 1 tsp. lime
- Stevia to taste
- A pinch sea salt

DIRECTIONS:
1. Blend all INGREDIENTS until smooth.

Nutrition:: Calories: 140 | Fat: 10 g | Protein: 2 g

65. Coconut and Strawberry Bars
(Prep. Time: 11 Min | Cooking: 4 Min | Serving 2)

INGREDIENTS
- 1 tbsp. coconut oil
- 1 cup strawberries, chopped
- 16 oz. coconut butter, melted
- 1 tsp. stevia
- 1/4 cup coconut flakes, unsweetened

DIRECTIONS:

1. Mix your stevia, oil, and butter together, transferring it to a prepared baking dish.
2. Add your strawberries and coconut, and then refrigerate for four hours. Chop into bars.

Nutrition: Calories: 294 | Fat: 28 g | Protein: 3 g

66. Avocado Breakfast Bowl
(Prep. Time: 6 Min | Cooking: 0 Min | Serving 1)

INGREDIENTS
- 2 tbsp. tahini
- 1 carrot, shredded
- 1 avocado, halved and pit removed

Sauce:
- 1 tbsp. poppy seeds
- 1/4 cup lemon juice

DIRECTIONS:
- Blend all of your sauce INGREDIENTS together, and then mix all other INGREDIENTS together.
- Drizzle your sauce over your bowl before serving.

Nutrition: Calories: 562 | Fat: 52 g | Protein: 8 g

67. Granola
(Prep. Time: 8 Min | Cooking: 7 Min | Serving 7)

INGREDIENTS
- 1/2 cup maple syrup, pure
- 1/4 cup coconut oil
- 3/4 cup coconut, unsweetened, and shredded
- 1 cup almonds, slivered
- 5 cups rolled oats

DIRECTIONS:
1. Start by heating your oven to 250°F and then mix all of your ingredients together in a bowl.
2. Spread your granola out over two baking sheets, making sure it's spread out evenly.
3. Bake for an hour and fifteen minutes, but you'll need to stir every twenty minutes
4. Allow it to cool before serving.

Nutrition: Calories: 239 | Fat: 11 g | Protein: 6 g

68. Flaxseed Pancakes
(Prep. Time: 7 Min | Cooking: 8 Min | Serving 1)

INGREDIENTS
- 3 tbsp. water
- 2 tbsp. flaxseeds
- 1 1/2 tbsp. coconut oil
- 1/2 scoop vanilla vegan powder
- 1/4 teaspoon baking powder
- Salt to taste

DIRECTIONS:
1. Mix 1 tbsp. flaxseeds with water, and then mix in your oil.
2. Mix your baking powder, vegan powder, flaxseed, and salt together in a bowl.
3. Stir in wet and dry ingredients together then preheat a nonstick pan over medium heat.
4. Scoop batter into your pan, cooking for five minutes flip cooking for two minutes on the other side. Repeat until you've finished all your batter.

Nutrition: Calories: 309 | Fat: 27.1 g | Protein: 13.4 g

69. Breakfast Cereal
(Prep. Time: 6 Min | Cooking: 9 Min | Serving 6)

INGREDIENTS
- 1/4 tbsp. coconut butter
- 2 1/4 cups water
- 1 tsp. cinnamon
- 1 cup brown rice, uncooked
- 1/2 cup raisins, seedless

DIRECTIONS:
1. Start by combining your cinnamon, raisins, rice, and coconut butter in a saucepan before adding in your water. Boil, and allow it to simmer while covered for forty minutes Fluff with a fork.
2. Serve with honey.

Nutrition: Calories: 160 | Fat: 1.5 g | Protein: 3 g

70. Eggplant Hash Browns
(Prep. Time: 6 Min | Cooking: 9 Min | Serving 8)

INGREDIENTS
- 1 eggplant; red onion
- 2 red bell peppers, seeded, and diced
- 1/4 cup almonds; mint leaves
- 1/2 tsp. coriander seeds; cinnamon
- 1/4 tsp. cayenne pepper
- 1 tbsp. oil
- 4 garlic cloves
- 1/2 cup sundried tomatoes

DIRECTIONS:
1. Start by heating oil in a skillet, searing your bell pepper and eggplant, cooking for three minutes make sure to stir occasionally.

2. Add in your onion and 4 garlic cloves, cooking for two minutes
3. Toss in your mint leaves, almonds, and 1/2 cup sundried tomatoes. Make sure to heat all the way through, and then add in the rest of your ingredients.

Nutrition: Calories: 100 | Fat: 6.4 g | Protein: 2.42 g

71. Cantaloupe Smoothie Bowl
(Prep. Time: 9 Min | Cooking: 0 Min | Serving 2)

INGREDIENTS
- 3/4 cup carrot juice
- 4 cups cantaloupe, frozen, and cubed
- Mellon balls or berries to serve
- A pinch sea salt

DIRECTIONS:
1. Blend everything together until smooth.

Nutrition: Calories: 135 | Fat: 1 g | Protein: 3 g

72. Fruity Oatmeal
(Prep. Time: 7 Min | Cooking: 8 Min | Serving 2)

INGREDIENTS
- 1/2 cup apple juice, fresh, and frozen
- 1/2 cup oatmeal; water
- 3 prunes; apricots
- 1 apple, small, and diced
- 4 pecans, diced
- 1/4 tsp. cinnamon

DIRECTIONS:
1. Start by getting out a small saucepan and mix together your apple juice and water, bringing the mixture to a boil.
2. Add half a cup of oatmeal, cooking for a minute. Add in your pecans, 1/4 tsp. cinnamon and fruit pieces. Make sure to stir.

Nutrition: Calories: 230 | Fat: 5.6 g | Protein: 4.6 g

73. Green Mango Smoothie
(Prep. Time: 6 Min | Cooking: 0 Min | Serving 1)

INGREDIENTS
- 2 cups spinach
- 1–2 cups coconut water
- 2 mangos, ripe, peeled, and diced

DIRECTIONS:

1. Blend everything together until smooth.

Nutrition: Calories: 417 | Fat: 2.8 g | Protein: 7.2 g

74. Fruit Salad
(Prep. Time: 15 Min | Cooking: 0 Min | Serving 4)

INGREDIENTS
- 1/8 tsp. cinnamon; cardamom; ginger
- 2 cups pineapple, fresh, and cubed
- 1 cup banana; orange
- 1 cup mango, ripe, diced, and peeled
- 1 tbsp. lime, zest, and juiced

DIRECTIONS:
1. Throw everything together, and allow it to sit chilling for an hour before serving.

Nutrition: Calories: 276 | Fat: 12.3 g | Protein: 3.1 g

75. Flaxseed Porridge
(Prep. Time: 6 Min | Cooking: 9 Min | Serving 2)

INGREDIENTS
- 1 cup almond milk
- 1 tsp. cinnamon; vanilla extract
- 1/4 cup coconut flour
- 1/4 cup ground flaxseed
- 10 drops of stevia
- Salt to taste

DIRECTIONS:
1. Heat your almond milk in a saucepan using low heat, and whisk your coconut flour, salt, cinnamon, and flaxseed together.
2. Add in your stevia and vanilla once it's bubbling
3. Remove it from heat, mixing all of your ingredients together.
4. Garnish with blueberries, coconut, pumpkin seeds, and almonds before serving.

Nutrition: Calories: 405 | Fat: 34 g | Protein: 10 g

76. Spicy Hash Browns
(Prep. Time: 23 Min | Cooking: 22 Min | Serving 5)

INGREDIENTS
- 1 tsp. paprika
- 1/4 tsp. red pepper
- 3/4 tsp. chili powder
- 2 tbsp. light olive oil
- 6 1/2 cups potatoes, diced
- Salt and black pepper to taste

DIRECTIONS:
1. Set oven to 400°F, and then get out a large bowl.
2. Mix together your light olive oil, chili powder, red peppers, salt, black pepper, and paprika. Stir well.
3. Coat your potatoes in the mixture, and then arrange your potatoes on a baking sheet in a single layer Bake for about thirty minutes

Nutrition: Calories: 227 | Fat: 5.7 g | Protein: 3.9 g

77. Kiwi Slushy
(Prep. Time: 6 Min | Cooking: 0 Min | Serving 2)

INGREDIENTS
- chocolate tea ice cubes
- 1 cup vanilla rice milk
- 2 ripe kiwi fruits, sliced, and frozen

DIRECTIONS:
1. Blend everything together until smooth.

Nutrition: Calories: 42.1 | Fat: 0.4 g | Protein: 0.8 g

78. Chia Seed Smoothie
(Prep. Time: 7 Min | Cooking: 0 Min | Serving 3)

INGREDIENTS
- 1 tbsp. chia seeds; ginger
- 2 Medjool dates, pitted
- 1 cup alfalfa sprouts; water
- 1 banana
- 1/2 cup coconut milk, unsweetened

DIRECTIONS:
1. Blend everything together until smooth.

Nutrition: Calories: 477 | Fat: 29 g | Protein: 8 g

79. Mango Smoothie
(Prep. Time: 6 Min | Cooking: 0 Min | Serving 3)

INGREDIENTS
- 1 carrot, peeled, and chopped
- 1 cup strawberries
- 1 cup peaches, chopped
- 1 banana, frozen, and sliced
- 1 cup mango, chopped

DIRECTIONS:
1. Blend everything together until smooth.

Nutrition: Calories: 376 | Fat: 2 g | Protein: 5 g

80. Quinoa and Chocolate Bowl
(Prep. Time: 24 Min | Cooking: 11 Min | Serving 2)

INGREDIENTS
- 1 cup almond milk; quinoa; water
- 1 banana
- 2 tbsp. coconut butter; cocoa powder
- 1 tbsp. chia seeds, ground
- 1/4 cup raspberries, fresh
- 1 tbsp. cinnamon
- 1 tbsp. flaxseed
- 1 cup water

DIRECTIONS:
1. Place your cinnamon, milk, water, and quinoa in a pot, bringing it to a boil before turning it down to low heat to simmer. Cover, simmer for twenty-five to thirty minutes
2. Puree your banana, mixing in your coconut butter, flaxseed, and cocoa powder.
3. Scoop a cup of quinoa into a bowl, and then top with pudding, raspberries, chia seeds, and walnuts if you're using them before serving.

Nutrition: Calories: 392 | Fat: 19 g | Protein: 12 g

81. Vegetable Hash
(Prep. Time: 2 Min | Cooking: 13 Min | Serving 4)

INGREDIENTS
- 1 tbsp. sage leaves; parsley
- 1 bell pepper; onion
- 3 red potatoes, diced
- 15 oz. black beans, canned
- 2 cups Swiss chard, chopped
- 3 garlic cloves
- Salt and pepper to taste
- 2 tbsp. oil

DIRECTIONS:
1. Start by cooking the bell pepper, potatoes, 3 garlic cloves, and onion in a skillet with oil. This will take 20 minutes
2. Add in your Swiss chard and beans, cooking for 3 more minutes
3. Sprinkle it with salt and pepper, then serve with parsley and sage leaves.

Nutrition: Calories: 273 | Fat: 11 g | Protein: 9 g

82. Walnut Porridge
(Prep. Time: 9 Min | Cooking: 6 Min | Serving 2)

INGREDIENTS

- 1/2 cup coconut milk, unsweetened
- 1 cup water
- 1 cup teff, whole grain
- 1/2 tsp. cardamom, ground
- 1/4 cup walnuts, chopped
- 1 tbsp. maple syrup, pure

DIRECTIONS:
1. Start by combining your coconut milk and water, bringing it to a boil before stirring in your teff.
2. Add the cardamom, and then allow it to simmer for 20 minutes
3. Mix in your walnuts and maple syrup before serving.

Nutrition: Calories: 312 | Fat: 18 g | Protein: 7 g

83. SPINACH WITH FRIED EGGS
(PREP. TIME: 11 MIN | COOKING: 4 MIN | SERVING 4)

INGREDIENTS
- 1 onion chopped
- 1 lb. spinach, cleaned and chopped roughly
- Salt to taste
- Ground black pepper to taste
- 4 eggs
- 2 tbsp. Light olive oil

DIRECTIONS:
1. Using a big frying pan, add light olive oil and heat over medium heat. Add in diced onion and cook for about five minutes
2. Add spinach then spice with salt and ground black pepper. Cook till the spinach sags and becomes tender.
3. Sink some 4 small reservoirs in the spinach mixture and break an egg on each reservoir. Cook for 4 minutes
4. Spay black pepper and salt on each egg.
5. Serve while hot.

Nutrition: Calories: 161 | Fat: 11.9 g | Protein: 9.1 g

84. Green Bagel Topped With Poached Eggs
(Prep. Time: 5 Min | Cooking: 6 Min | Serving 2)

INGREDIENTS
- 1 seeded wholemeal bagel, halved
- 1/2 avocados, ripe
- 1/4 lemon slice
- 1 egg
- 5 ml of water
- Salt and black pepper to taste

DIRECTIONS:
1. Boil 5ml of water in a skillet and toast the bagel while the water boils.
2. Mix black pepper, salt, and avocado in a mixing bowl. Mash until smooth. Squeeze in the lemon slice.
3. Crash the egg on a small plate and put it into the boiling water. Cook for three minutes then lower the heat to simmer.
4. Meanwhile, spread the avocado mixture onto the two bagel halves. Place them on warm saucers.
5. Using a chopstick, remove the egg from the boiling water and drain it. Put on top of the bagels and then serve.

Nutrition: Calories: 274 | Fat: 13.2 g | Protein: 9.8 g

85. Egg and Honey Toast
(Prep. Time: 6 Min | Cooking: 5 Min | Serving 4)

INGREDIENTS
- 2 eggs
- 2 tbsp. honey, clear
- 2 bread slices, wholemeal
- 3 oz. berries
- Cooking spray
- ¼ cup yogurt
- ¼ cup Cheese

DIRECTIONS:
1. Crash the eggs in a small dish and mix with honey. Soak one of the bread slices till it absorbs the egg.
2. Add cooking spray oil in a non-stick pan and heat. Place the egg-soaked bread slice on the hot pan and cook for two minutes Flip the other side using a spatula, cook further for 2 minutes Remove from the pan, and place on a plate. Do the process again with the other bread slice
3. Cut the bread into two halves, top with honey, yogurt cheese, and mixed berries, and serve.

Nutrition: Calories: 244 | Fat: 7.5 g | Protein: 18.5 g

86. Baked Rotini
(Prep. Time: 9 Min | Cooking: 6 Min | Serving 8)

INGREDIENTS
- 16 oz. whole wheat rotini noodles
- 1/2 cup pasta (reserved liquid)
- 17 oz. jarred spaghetti sauce
- 2 cups soft white cheese
- 2 cups mozzarella cheese, shredded
- Salt to taste
- Water
- 1 egg

DIRECTIONS:
1. Preheat roaster to 350°F
2. Cook pasta 2 minutes less than according to the package instructions in salty boiling water. Drain it reserving 1/2 of cooking liquid.
3. Mix reserved sauce together with cooked pasta, soft white cheese, egg, sauce, and 1 cup cheese shreds.
4. Pour the mixture into a large cooking vessel 9x13 or casserole dish and top with the remaining white cheese.
5. Bake until cheese is fizzy, or for 30 minutes
6. You can prepare earlier up to baking, and if coming from the fridge add 20 minutes to the baking time.

Nutrition: Calories: 685 | Fat: 13.2 g | Protein: 26.4 g

87. Vegetarian Meatballs
(Prep. Time: 4 Min | Cooking: 11 Min | Serving 10)

INGREDIENTS
- 3 cups cauliflower
- 3 cups brown rice and/or cooked quinoa
- 3/4 cups oat flour, breadcrumbs, or almond meal
- 4 eggs
- 1 tbsp. spices (paprika, chili powder, and/or cumin)
- Water
- 1 layer of light olive oil

DIRECTIONS:
1. Put cauliflower florets in a bowl of boiling water for about 5 minutes, until fork-tender. And drain.
2. Blend cauliflower and quinoa until semi-smooth transfer the mixture into a large bowl and mix with all other ingredients, blend until everything is

incorporated. Measure about 1 piled up tbsp. and roll into balls.
3. Pour a thin layer of light olive oil into a cooking pot and heat over medium heat.
4. Add the balls and cook gently for a few minutes turning every side often to get browned all around.
5. Serve with sauces, salad, or freeze for later.

Nutrition: Calories:: 134 | Fat: 7.6 g | Protein: 5 g

88. IMPOSSIBLY EASY SPINACH AND FETA PIE
(PREP. TIME: 9 MIN | COOKING: 6 MIN | SERVING 6)

INGREDIENTS
- 10 oz. chopped spinach (frozen) defrosted and squeezed to drain
- 1/2 cup feta cheese, crushed
- 4 sliced green onions
- 1/2 cup reduced-fat baking mix or original Bisquick.
- 2 eggs

DIRECTIONS:
1. Heat skillet up to 400°F grease pie pan 9x1 1/4 inches. Mix spinach, onions, and cheese in a pan.
2. Mix remaining ingredients in a bowl until blended and pour into the pie pan.
3. Cook 30 to 35 minutes or test by inserting a knife in the center and comes out clean.
4. Let rest for 5 minutes before serving.

Nutrition: Calories: 123 | Fat: 6.3 g | Protein: 6.8 g

89. TOMATO TART
(PREP. TIME: 3 MIN | COOKING: 12 MIN | SERVING 4)

INGREDIENTS
- 4 tbsp. cheese, soft
- 1 tbsp. Dijon mustard
- 1 lb. puff pastry
- Olives for decorate
- Chunk parmesan
- 1 tomato, sliced

DIRECTIONS:
1. Preheat your oven to 395°F.
2. Mix the cheese with Dijon mustard in a mixing bowl.
3. Roll the pastry on a dusted surface into a rectangle.
4. Place the rectangle pastry on a baking sheet. Trim wiggly edges.
5. Mark an even border around the pastry edges then spread cheese inside the border.
6. Arrange tomato on the cheese then garnish with olives.
7. Spread-grated parmesan all over.
8. Place the tart in your preheated oven to bake until the pastry is golden brown.
9. Remove from oven, let cool, and serve. Enjoy.

Nutrition: Calories: 508 | Fat: 38 g | Protein: 10 g

90. PUFF PIZZA TART
(PREP. TIME: 6 MIN | COOKING: 9 MIN | SERVING 4)

INGREDIENTS
- 1 lb. sheet puff pastry, ready rolled
- 5 tbsp. red pesto
- 2 oz. salami, sliced
- 4 oz. ball mozzarella, pieces
- Handful rocket
- Light olive oil to taste

DIRECTIONS:
1. Preheat oven to 400°F.
2. Unfold the puff pastry on a baking sheet and use a fork to prick its surface.
3. Mark a border around the edges of the pastry then spread the red pesto inside the border.
4. Layer the sliced salami and mozzarella on the pesto.
5. Season to taste then bake until the pastry is golden brown.
6. Drizzle light olive oil and scatter a handful of rockets. Serve and enjoy.

Nutrition: Calories: 597 | Fat: 47 g | Protein: 18 g

91. VEGGIE PIZZA
(PREP. TIME: 4 MIN | COOKING: 11 MIN | SERVING 4)

INGREDIENTS
- 1 lb. carton passata
- 5 large flatbreads
- 1 garlic clove
- 3 balls mozzarella, pat dry, and tore into pieces
- ½ cup Nutmeg, freshly grated
- ½ cup Spinach
- 1 egg
- Basil for garnish

DIRECTIONS:
1. Preheat your oven to the highest level of hotness.
2. Meanwhile, spread passata on each flatbread.

3. Squeeze water from spinach then scatters them on top of the passata leaving a space at the center.
4. Divide garlic and mozzarella among the flatbreads. Put two pizzas on a baking tray and crack an egg into space at the center of each pizza.
5. Season with nutmeg and basil as you desire.
6. Cook until the egg is cooked and the cheese has melted.
7. Repeat the process with all the pizzas.
8. Cut into pieces and serve. Enjoy.

Nutrition: Calories: 444 | Fat: 22 g | Protein: 28 g

92. SEEDED FLATBREADS
(PREP. TIME: 4 MIN | COOKING: 11 MIN | SERVING 4)

INGREDIENTS
- 1/2 oz. sachet yeast, dried
- 14 oz. white bread flour
- 7 oz. wholemeal bread flour
- 1 tbsp. black onion seeds
- 2 tbsp. sesame seeds
- 2 tbsp. water
- Caster sugar to taste
- 1 tbsp. salt

DIRECTIONS:
1. Mix the dried yeast with 2 tbsp. water and caster sugar. Let rest for a few minutes
2. Tip both flours in a mixing bowl and add 1 tbsp. salt. Mix well.
3. Add the yeast mixture with a half-liter of warm water into the mixing bowl.
4. Mix well with a wooden spoon.
5. Tip the dough on a work surface and knead until elastic and smooth.
6. Oil a bowl and place the dough in it. Wrap with a towel and leave it in a warm place.
7. Let it rise until the dough doubles its size.
8. Knock out all the air in the dough then knead in the seeds. Make sure they are evenly distributed.
9. Portion the dough into twelve equal pieces and roll out each piece as thinly as you can.
10. Cook the flatbreads in a nonstick skillet until both sides are well cooked, and bubbles appear.
11. Wrap the flatbreads in foil and store.

Nutrition: Calories: 189 | Fat: 3 g | Protein: 7 g

93. ROASTED VEGGIE FLATBREAD
(PREP. TIME: 3 MIN | COOKING: 12 MIN | SERVING 2)

INGREDIENTS
- 16 oz. pizza dough
- 6 oz. goat cheese, divided
- 3/4 cup parmesan cheese, divided
- 3 tbsp. fresh dill, divided
- 1 red pepper, sliced
- Salt and pepper to taste
- Oil to taste

DIRECTIONS:
1. Preheat oven to 400°F
2. Roll the pizza dough into a rectangle.
3. Spray a parchment paper with nonstick spray and place the dough on it.
4. Spread half the goat cheese on half the pizza dough.
5. Sprinkle half parmesan cheese and red pepper and half the dill.
6. Fold the other half of the dough carefully over the cheese. Sprinkle the remaining goat cheese and parmesan cheese.
7. Layer the vegetables on the cheese creating your desired pretty pattern.
8. Brush oil and season with salt, pepper, and dill to taste.
9. Bake until the edges are golden brown. Cut into two-inch slices and serve when warm.

Nutrition: Calories: 170 | Fat: 6 g | Protein: 8 g

94. DILLY VEGGIE PIZZA
(PREP. TIME: 4 MIN | COOKING: 10 MIN | SERVING 15)

INGREDIENTS
- 8 oz. refrigerated crescent rolls
- 1 cup vegetable dill dip
- 1 cup fresh broccoli
- 1 cup chopped tomatoes, seeded
- 1 can ripe olives, drained and sliced
- 1 cup carrots
- 1 cup onions

DIRECTIONS:
1. Preheat your oven to 375°F
2. Unroll the crescent rolls into a rectangle.
3. Grease a baking pan then press the dough on it. Make sure you seal the seams.
4. Bake until golden brown then cool completely.
5. Spread the dill dip on the crust then sprinkle broccoli, tomatoes, olives, carrots, and onions.
6. Cut into squares. Serve and enjoy.
7. Leftovers can be refrigerated.

Nutrition: Calories: 225 | Fat: 20 g | Protein: 2 g

95. 5-Ingredients Vegetable Fried Brown Rice
(Prep. Time: 6 Min | Cooking: 9 Min | Serving 4)

INGREDIENTS
- 1 cup mixed vegetables (frozen)
- 2 cups brown rice (cooked)
- 2 lightly whisked eggs
- 1/4 cup of soy sauce (low-sodium)
- 2 tbsp. oil
- Salt and pepper to taste

DIRECTIONS:
1. Heat oil in a frying pan (large) over medium-high heat.
2. Add mixed vegetables then cook for about 2 minutes while stirring.
3. Add rice and soy sauce. Cook for 5 minutes
4. Make a well in the mixture center then add eggs to the frying pan.
5. Let the eggs cook and set for about 1 minute then use a spoon to break them up into small pieces.
6. Season with additional soy sauce, pepper, and salt to taste.
7. Serve with Sriracha and enjoy.

Nutrition: Calories: 279 | Fat: 8 g | Protein: 10.5 g

96. Garlic Roasted Carrots
(Prep. Time: 4 Min | Cooking: 11 Min | Serving 6)

INGREDIENTS
- 24 baby carrots (tops 2-inches trimmed)
- 2 tbsp. balsamic vinegar
- 5 minced garlic cloves
- 1 tbsp. thyme (dried)
- 2 tbsp. parsley leaves (chopped)
- 2 tbsp. light olive oil
- Salt and pepper to taste

DIRECTIONS:
1. Preheat your oven to 350°F.
2. Coat a baking sheet with nonstick spray.
3. Situate carrots on the baking sheet in a single layer.
4. Add vinegar, light olive oil, garlic, and thyme then season with pepper and salt.
5. Toss gently to combine then place in the oven.
6. Bake for about 40 minutes until tender.
7. Garnish with parsley and serve immediately.

Nutrition: Calories: 59.5 | Fat: 4.6 g | Protein: 0.4 g

97. Baked Parmesan Mushrooms
(Prep. Time: 9 Min | Cooking: 6 Min | Serving 4)

INGREDIENTS
- 1 1/2 lb. cremini mushrooms, thinly sliced
- 1/4 cup lemon juice + zest
- 3 minced garlic cloves
- 1/4 cup parmesan (grated)
- 2 tbsp. thyme (dried)
- 3 tbsp. light olive oil
- Salt and pepper to taste

DIRECTIONS:
1. Preheat your oven to 350°F.
2. Coat a baking sheet with nonstick spray.
3. Place mushrooms on the baking sheet in a single layer.
4. Add light olive oil, lemon zest, lemon juice, garlic, parmesan, and thyme then season with pepper and salt.
5. Throw gently to combine and place in the oven.
6. Bake for about 15 minutes until tender and browned. Toss occasionally.
7. Serve immediately and enjoy.

Nutrition: Calories: 163.5 | Fat: 12.2 g | Protein: 6.9 g

98. Buttery Garlic Green Beans
(Prep. Time: 9 Min | Cooking: 6 Min | Serving 4)

INGREDIENTS
- 1 lb. trimmed and halved fresh green beans
- 3 minced garlic cloves
- 2 pinches lemon pepper
- 1 tbsp. coconut butter
- Water
- Salt to taste

DIRECTIONS:
1. Place fresh green beans in a skillet (large) then cover with water. Boil over medium-high heat.
2. Reduce to medium-low heat and simmer the beans for about 5 minutes until beans soften lightly.
3. Drain excess water then add coconut butter and cook for about 3 minutes while stirring until butter melts.
4. Add garlic, stir and cook for about 4 minutes until garlic is fragrant and tender.
5. Season with salt and lemon pepper.

Nutrition: Calories: 116 | Fat: 8.8 g | Protein: 2.3 g

99. ROASTED BUTTERNUT SQUASH PUREE

(PREP. TIME: 9 MIN | COOKING: 6 MIN | SERVING 4)

INGREDIENTS
- 1 large seeded and halved butternut squash
- 2 cups chicken stock
- Salt and pepper to taste

DIRECTIONS:
1. Preheat your oven to 400°F.
2. Situate squash on a baking sheet with the flesh side up.
3. Roast in the oven for about 45 to 60 minutes until slightly brown and tender. Cool until it can be easily handled.
4. Scoop the squash flesh into a blender and blend until smooth.
5. Add 1/4 cup chicken stock at a time while blending until smooth.
6. Season with pepper and salt.
7. Serve and enjoy.

Nutrition: Calories: 159 | Fat: 0.6 g | Protein: 3.7 g

100. SWEET AND EASY CORN ON THE COB

(PREP. TIME: 4 MIN | COOKING: 10 MIN | SERVING 6)

INGREDIENTS
- 2 tbsp. coconut sugar
- 1 tbsp. lemon juice
- 6 ears corn on the cob (silk and husks removed)
- Water

DIRECTIONS:
1. Pour water into a large pot to about 3/4 full and boil.
2. Stir in sugar and lemon juice and stir until sugar dissolves.
3. Place the ears of corn gently into the boiling water.
4. Put off heat, close, and let the ears of corn cook for about 10 minutes until tender in hot water.
5. Serve and enjoy.

Nutrition: Calories: 94 | Fat: 1.1 g | Protein: 2.9 g

101. 5-INGREDIENTS COCONUT CURRY

(PREP. TIME: 9 MIN | COOKING: 9 MIN | SERVING 4)

INGREDIENTS
- 2 broccoli heads (small)
- 1 can coconut milk
- 2 tbsp. red curry paste
- 1 can rinse and drained chickpeas
- 12 tbsp. cornstarch dissolved in 2 tbsp. water (cold)
- 1 tbsp. oil

DIRECTIONS:
1. Sauté broccoli using 1 tbsp. oil for a few minutes then adds coconut milk.
2. Simmer for about 5 to 8 minutes Make sure broccoli softens but tender-crisp.
3. Add curry paste and whisk to combine with coconut milk.
4. Add chickpeas and bring to boil (slight) then add cornstarch. Boil for a minute.
5. Reduce heat and let the mixture to slightly cool. The sauce will thicken.
6. Serve and enjoy.

Nutrition: Calories: 506| Fat: 21.5 g | Protein: 21.1 g

102. DAIRY-FREE CHOCOLATE PUDDING

(PREP. TIME: 9 MIN | COOKING: 10 MIN | SERVING 2)

INGREDIENTS
- 3 tbsp. cornstarch
- 1/4 tbsp. vanilla extract
- 1 1/2 cups of soy milk
- 1/4 cup of cocoa powder
- ½ cup water
- 2 tbsp. Coconut sugar

DIRECTIONS:
1. Scourge water and cornstarch in a small bowl to form a paste.
2. Stir together cornstarch mixture, vanilla, soy milk, cocoa, and coconut sugar in a saucepan over medium heat
3. Cook while stirring until mixture boils and thickens then remove from heat. As the mixture cools, the pudding will continue.
4. Let the mixture cool for 5 minutes then place in a refrigerator until it cools completely.

Nutrition: Calories: 267 | Fat: 4.7 g | Protein: 8.1 g

Chapter 3. Lunch Recipes

103. CURRY SPICED LENTIL BURGERS
(Prep. Time: 4 Min | Cooking: 14 Min | Serving 6)

INGREDIENTS
- 1 cup lentils
- 3 cups water
- 3 carrots
- 1 small onion
- 3/4 cup whole-grain flour
- 2 tsp. curry powder
- 1/2 tsp. sea salt
- Pepper to taste

DIRECTIONS:
1. Boil lentils with the water, then simmer for 30 minutes
2. While cooking, toss carrots, onion, flour, curry powder, salt, and pepper.
3. Once cooked, drain, then add them to the veggies. Mash them slightly, and add more flour if you need to get the mixture to stick. Form it into a ball. Scoop up 1/4-cup portions.
4. Bake in a baking sheet lined with parchment paper at 350°F for 40 minutes

Nutrition: Calories: 114 | Fat: 1 g | Protein: 6 g

104. MAPLE DIJON BURGERS
(Prep. Time: 5 Min | Cooking: 10 Min | Serving 6)

INGREDIENTS
- 1 red bell pepper
- 1 (19 oz.) can chickpeas
- 1 cup ground almonds
- 2 tsp. Dijon mustard
- 2 tsp. maple syrup
- 1 garlic clove
- 1/2 lemon juice
- 1 tsp. dried oregano
- 1/2 tsp. dried sage
- 1 cup spinach
- 1 1/2 cups rolled oats

DIRECTIONS:
1. Preheat the oven to 350°F. Line a baking sheet with parchment paper.
2. Chop red pepper in half, remove the stem and seeds, and roast on the baking sheet cut side up in the oven.
3. Crush chickpeas, almonds, mustard, maple syrup, garlic, lemon juice, oregano, sage, and spinach. Pulse until mix. When the red pepper is softened, blend along with the oats.
4. Scoop up 1/4 cup portions and form into 12 patties, and lay them out on the baking sheet.
5. Bake for 30 minutes

Nutrition: Calories: 200 | Fat: 11 g | Fiber: 6 g | Protein: 8 g

105. CAJUN BURGERS
(Prep. Time: 5 Min | Cooking: 10 Min | Serving 3)

INGREDIENTS
For dressing:
- 1 tbsp. tahini
- 1 tbsp. apple cider vinegar
- 2 tsp. Dijon mustard
- 2 tbsp. water
- 2 garlic cloves
- 1 tsp. dried basil
- 1 tsp. dried thyme
- 1/2 tsp. dried oregano
- 1/2 tsp. dried sage
- 1/2 tsp. smoked paprika
- 1/4 tsp. cayenne pepper
- 1/4 tsp. sea salt

For burgers:
- 2 cups water
- 1 cup kasha
- 2 carrots
- Handful fresh parsley
- ½ cup buckwheat
- Sea salt to taste

DIRECTIONS:
For dressing:
1. Whisk together the tahini, vinegar, and mustard until the mixture is very thick.
2. Stir in the rest of the ingredients. Set aside.

For burgers:
1. Put the water, buckwheat, and sea salt in a medium pot. Boil for 2 minutes, then lower down heat, cover, and simmer for 15 minutes
2. Once cooked, transfer it to a large bowl. Stir the grated carrot, fresh parsley, and all the dressing into the buckwheat. Scoop up 1/4 cup portions and form into patties.
3. To bake them, put them on a baking sheet lined with parchment paper and bake at 350°F for about 30 minutes

Nutrition: Calories: 124 | Fat: 2 g | Protein: 4 g

106. Grilled AHLT
(Prep. Time: 5 Min | Cooking: 10 Min | Serving 1)

INGREDIENTS
- 1/4 cup Classic Hummus
- 2 slices whole-grain bread
- 1/4 avocado
- 1/2 cup lettuce
- 1/2 tomato, sliced
- 1 tsp. light olive oil
- Salt and pepper to taste

DIRECTIONS:
1. Layout hummus on each slice of bread. Then layer the avocado, lettuce, and tomato on one slice, sprinkle with salt and pepper, and top with the other slice.
2. Preheat the skillet to medium heat, and put 1/2 tsp. of the light olive oil just before putting the sandwich in the skillet. Cook for 3 to 5 minutes, then lift the sandwich with a spatula, drizzle the remaining 1/2 tsp. light olive oil into the skillet, and flip the sandwich to grill the other side for 3 to 5 minutes Press it down with the spatula to seal the vegetables inside.
3. Once done, remove from the skillet and slice in half to serve.

Nutrition: Calories: 322 | Fiber: 11 g | Protein: 12 g

107. Black Bean Pizza
(Prep. Time: 4 Min | Cooking: 13 Min | Serving 6)

INGREDIENTS
- 2 prebaked pizza crusts
- 1/2 cup spicy black bean dip
- 1 tomato
- 1 carrot
- 1 red onion
- 1 avocado
- Salt to taste

DIRECTIONS:
1. Prep oven to 400°F.
2. Roll out two crusts out on a large baking sheet. Lay half the Spicy Black Bean Dip on each pizza crust. Then layer on the tomato slices and season.
3. Toss grated carrot with the sea salt and lightly rub. Arrange carrot on top of the tomato, then add the onion.
4. Bake for 15 minutes
5. Top with sliced avocado and season.

Nutrition: Calories: 379 | Fiber: 15 g | Protein: 13 g

108. Mediterranean Hummus Pizza
(Prep. Time: 4 Min | Cooking: 20 Min | Serving 8)

INGREDIENTS
- 1/2 zucchini
- 1/2 red onion
- 1 cup cherry tomatoes
- 4 tbsp. black olives
- 2 prebaked pizza crusts
- 1/2 cup classic hummus
- 4 tbsp. cheesy sprinkle
- Salt to taste

DIRECTIONS:
1. Preheat the oven to 400°F.
2. Place the zucchini, onion, cherry tomatoes, and olives in a large bowl, sprinkle them with the sea salt and toss them a bit. Dash with a bit of light olive oil (if using), to seal in the flavor and keep them from drying out in the oven.
3. Lay the two crusts out on a large baking sheet. Spread half the hummus on each crust, and top with the veggie mixture and some Cheesy Sprinkle.
4. Pop the pizzas in the oven for 20 to 30 minutes, or until the veggies are soft.

Nutrition:: Calories: 500 | Fiber: 12 g | Protein: 19 g

109. Curried Mango Chickpea Wrap
(Prep. Time: 5 Min | Cooking: 0 Min | Serving 3)

INGREDIENTS
- 3 tbsp. tahini
- 1 tbsp. curry powder
- 1/4 tsp. sea salt
- 3–4 tbsp. water
- 1 (14 oz.) can chickpeas
- 1 cup diced mango
- 1 red bell pepper
- 1/2 cup fresh cilantro
- 3 large whole-grain wraps
- 2 cups lettuce
- Lime zest and juice

DIRECTIONS:
1. Scourge the tahini, lime zest and juice, curry powder, and salt until the mixture is creamy and thick. Pour 4 tbsp. water to thin it out a bit. Or you can process this all in a blender. The taste should be strong and salty, to flavor the whole salad.
2. Toss the chickpeas, mango, bell pepper, and cilantro with the tahini dressing.
3. Spoon the salad down the center of the wraps, top with shredded lettuce, and then roll up and enjoy.

Nutrition: Calories: 437| Fiber: 12 g | Protein: 15 g

110. THAI NOODLE BOWL
(PREP. TIME: 5 MIN | COOKING: 10 MIN | SERVING 2)

INGREDIENTS
- 7 oz. brown rice noodles
- 1 tsp. light olive oil
- 2 carrots
- 1 cup red cabbage
- 1 red bell pepper
- 2 scallions
- 3 tbsp. fresh mint
- 1 cup bean sprouts
- 1/4 cup peanut sauce
- 1/4 cup fresh cilantro
- 2 tbsp. roasted peanuts

DIRECTIONS:
1. Soak rice noodles into boiling water. Let sit until they soften, about 10 minutes Rinse, drain, and set aside to cool.
2. Heat up oil over medium-high, and sauté the carrots, cabbage, and bell pepper for 8 minutes Toss in the scallions, mint, and bean sprouts and cook for just a minute or two, then remove from the heat.
3. Toss the noodles with the vegetables, and mix in the Peanut Sauce.
4. Pour into bowls, and drizzle with cilantro and peanuts. Side with a lime wedge to squeeze onto the dish for a flavor boost.

Nutrition: Calories: 660 | Fiber: 10 g | Protein: 15 g

111. SUSHI BOWL
(PREP. TIME: 5 MIN | COOKING: 10 MIN | SERVING 1)

INGREDIENTS
- 1/2 cup edamame beans
- 3/4 cup brown rice
- 1/2 cup spinach
- 1/4 cup avocado
- 1/4 cup bell pepper
- 1/4 cup fresh cilantro
- 1 scallion
- 1/4 nori sheet
- 2 tbsp. tamari
- 1 tbsp. sesame seeds

DIRECTIONS:
1. Thaw or steam the edamame beans, then assemble the edamame, rice, spinach, avocado, bell pepper, cilantro, and scallions in a bowl.
2. Cut the nori with scissors into small ribbons and sprinkle on top.
3. Drizzle the bowl with tamari and top with sesame seeds.

Nutrition: Calories: 467 | Fiber: 13 g | Protein: 22 g

112. SWEET POTATO PATTIES
(PREP. TIME: 4 MIN | COOKING: 10 MIN | SERVING 4)

INGREDIENTS
- 1 cup short-grain brown rice
- 1 cup grated sweet potato
- 1/2 cup diced onion
- 1/4 cup fresh parsley
- 1 tbsp. dried dill
- 1/2 cup whole-grain flour
- 1 tsp. light olive oil
- Salt to taste

DIRECTIONS:
1. Mix rice, sweet potato, onion, and salt in a large bowl. Set aside. Stir in the parsley, dill, and nutritional yeast (if using), then add enough flour to make the batter sticky.
2. Create mixture into tight balls, and squish slightly into patties.
3. Heat a large skillet on medium, then add the oil. Cook for 8 minutes, then turnover. Cook another 5 to 7 minutes, and serve.

Nutrition: Calories: 146 | Fiber: 5 g | Protein: 6 g

113. SPRING ROLLS
(PREP. TIME: 15 MIN | COOKING: 0 MIN | SERVING 10)

INGREDIENTS
- 10 round rice roll wraps
- 1/4 cup fresh basil
- 10 palm-size lettuce leaves
- 2 carrots
- 1/2 cucumber
- 1 mango
- 3 scallions
- 1 cup bean sprouts
- 1/2 cup peanut sauce
- Water

DIRECTIONS:

1. Fill a deep plate with room-temperature water, and put a rice roll wrap in to soften. Pull it out of the water and allow it to drip for a few seconds, then place it on a dry plate.
2. Down the center of the wrap, lay 2 fresh basil leaves and a lettuce leaf, then cover with the carrots, cucumber, mango, scallions, and bean sprouts.
3. Lay on the top and bottom of the rice wrap, then fold one side over the filling and tuck it under the filling a bit. Squeeze slightly with your hands and then roll to the end of the other side. Allow the wraps to sit and stick together before serving.
4. Serve with Peanut Sauce for dipping.

Nutrition: Calories: 77 | Fiber: 1 g | Protein: 3 g

114. POTATO SKIN SAMOSAS
(PREP. TIME: 2 MIN | COOKING: 13 MIN | SERVING 8)

INGREDIENTS
- 4 small baking potatoes
- 1 tsp. coconut oil
- 1 small onion
- 2 garlic cloves
- 1 small piece of ginger
- 3 tsp. curry powder
- 2 carrots
- 1/4 cup frozen peas
- 1/4 cup fresh cilantro
- Salt and pepper to taste

DIRECTIONS:
1. Preheat the oven to 350°F.
2. Prick the potatoes with a fork, seal in aluminum foil, and bake for 30 minutes, or until soft.
3. While cooking, preheat the oil in a medium skillet and sauté the onion until it's soft, about 5 minutes. Add the garlic and ginger and sauté until they're soft as well, about 3 minutes add the curry powder, salt, and pepper, and stir to fully coat the onion. Turn off the heat.
4. Once cooked, take them and slice them in half.
5. Spoon out the flesh of the potatoes into the skillet with the onion. Add the carrots, peas, and cilantro. Stir to combine, then spoon the mixture back into the potato skins.

Nutrition: Calories: 130 | Fiber: 3 g | Protein: 3 g

115. SIMPLE SESAME STIR-FRY
(PREP. TIME: 10 MIN | COOKING: 5 MIN | SERVING 4)

INGREDIENTS
- 1 cup quinoa
- 2 cups water
- 1 head broccoli
- 2 tsp. light olive oil
- 1 cup snow peas
- 2 cups swiss chard
- 2 scallions
- 2 tbsp. water
- 1 tsp. toasted sesame oil
- 1 tbsp. tamari
- 2 tbsp. sesame seeds
- Sea salt to taste
- 2 Edamame

DIRECTIONS:
1. Boil quinoa, water, and sea salt in a medium pot, then turn to low and simmer, covered, for 20 minutes
2. Cut broccoli into bite-size florets, cutting and pulling apart from the stem. Also, chop the stem into bite-size pieces.
3. Heat a large skillet to high, and sauté the broccoli in the untoasted sesame oil, with a dash of salt to help it soften. Put the snow peas next, continuing to stir. Add the edamame until they thaw. Add the Swiss chard and scallions at the same time, tossing for only a minute to wilt. Then add 2 tbsp. of water to the hot skillet so that it sizzles and finishes the vegetables with quick steam.
4. Dress with the toasted sesame oil and tamari, and toss one last time. Remove from the heat immediately.
5. Serve a scoop of cooked quinoa, topped with stir-fry and sprinkled with some sesame seeds.

Nutrition: Calories: 334 | Fiber: 9 g | Protein: 17 g

116. SUN-DRIED TOMATO AND PESTO QUINOA
(PREP. TIME: 10 MIN | COOKING: 5 MIN | SERVING 1)

INGREDIENTS
- 1 tsp. light olive oil
- 1 cup d onion
- 1 garlic clove
- 1 cup zucchini
- 1 tomato
- 2 tbsp. sun-dried tomatoes
- 3 tbsp. Basil Pesto
- 1 cup spinach
- 2 cups cooked quinoa
- Salt to taste

DIRECTIONS:
1. Cook oil in a big skillet on medium-high, then sauté the onion, about 5 minutes Stir in garlic when the onion has softened, then add the zucchini and salt.
2. Once the zucchini is somewhat soft, about 5 minutes, turn off the heat and add the fresh and sun-dried tomatoes. Mix to combine, then toss in the pesto. Toss the vegetables to coat them.
3. Layer the spinach, then quinoa, then the zucchini mixture on a plate, topped with a bit of Cheesy Sprinkle (if using).

Nutrition: Calories: 535 | Fiber: 14 g | Protein: 20 g

117. OLIVE AND WHITE BEAN PASTA
(PREP. TIME: 10 MIN | COOKING: 5 MIN | SERVING 1)

INGREDIENTS
- 1/2 cup whole-grain pasta
- 1 tsp. light olive oil
- 1/4 cup red bell pepper
- 1/4 cup zucchini
- 1/2 cup cannellini beans
- 1/2 cup spinach
- 1 tbsp. balsamic vinegar
- 3 black olives
- 1 tbsp. nutritional yeast
- Salt to taste
- Water

DIRECTIONS:
1. Boil water, then add the pasta with the salt to cook until just tender (per the package DIRECTIONS).
2. In a big skillet, cook oil and lightly sauté the bell pepper and zucchini, 7 to 8 minutes Add the beans to warm for 2 minutes, then add the spinach last, just until it wilts. Drizzle with the vinegar at the end.
3. Serve the pasta topped or tossed with the bean mixture, and sprinkled with the olives and nutritional yeast.

Nutrition: Calories: 387 | Fiber: 19 g | Protein: 18 g

118. BBQ FRUIT SLIDERS
(PREP. TIME: 13 MIN | COOKING: 2 MIN | SERVING 5)

INGREDIENTS
- 2 (20 oz.) cans of young green jackfruit
- 1/2 cup BBQ Sauce
- 1 tsp. garlic powder
- 1 tsp. onion powder
- 6 whole-wheat slider buns
- Asian-Style Slaw with Maple-Ginger Dressing, for topping
- 3 tbsp. vegetable broth

DIRECTIONS:
1. Smash the jackfruit until it has a shredded consistency.
2. Heat a medium stockpot over medium-low heat. Put the shredded jackfruit, BBQ sauce, garlic powder, and onion powder in the pot, and stir. Cook for 10 minutes, covered, stirring once after about 5 minutes if the jackfruit begins sticking to the bottom of the pot, add in a few tbsp. vegetable broth or water.
3. Uncover and cook for 5 minutes, stirring every few minutes
4. Serve on whole-wheat slider buns with your favorite toppings.

Nutrition: Calories: 188 | Carbohydrates: 36 g | Protein: 7 g

119. HAWAIIAN LUAU BURGERS
(PREP. TIME: 5 MIN | COOKING: 10 MIN | SERVING 8)

INGREDIENTS
- 3 cups cooked black beans
- 2 cups cooked brown rice
- 1 cup quick-cooking oats
- 1/4 cup BBQ Sauce
- 1/4 cup pineapple juice
- 1 tsp. garlic powder
- 1 tsp. onion powder
- 1 pineapple
- 8 whole-wheat buns

DIRECTIONS:
1. Preheat the grill to medium-high heat.
2. Mash the black beans.
3. Incorporate rice, oats, BBQ sauce, pineapple juice, garlic powder, and onion powder to form into patties.
4. Spoon out 1/2 cup of bean mixture, and form it into a patty. Repeat.
5. Grill patties for 4 minutes on 1 side, flipping once the burgers easily release from the grill surface.
6. After grilling, cook pineapple rings for 1 to 2 minutes on each side.
7. Stack one patty and one pineapple ring with a spoonful of the BBQ sauce and buns and serve.

Nutrition: Calories: 371 | Carbohydrates: 71 g | Protein: 15 g

120. Falafel Burgers
(Prep. Time: 5 Min | Cooking: 10 Min | Serving 8)

INGREDIENTS
- 3 cups chickpeas
- 2 cups brown rice
- 1/4 cup vegetable broth
- 1/4 cup chopped fresh parsley
- 1 tbsp. lemon juice
- 2 tsp. garlic powder
- 2 tsp. onion powder
- 1 1/2 tsp. ground cumin
- 1 tsp. ground coriander
- 1/4 tsp. black pepper
- 8 whole-wheat buns

DIRECTIONS:
1. Preheat the oven to 425°F. Line a baking sheet with parchment paper.
2. Blend chickpeas, rice, broth, parsley, lemon juice, garlic powder, onion powder, cumin, coriander, and pepper on low for 40 seconds.
3. Scoop out 1/2 cup of the chickpea mixture, and form it into a patty. Place the patty on the baking sheet. Repeat.
4. Bake for 15 minutes Flip the patties, cook for 15 minutes more, and serve buns with your preferred toppings.

Nutrition: Calories: 230 | Carbohydrates: 44 g | Protein: 10 g

121. Easy Vegan Pizza Bread
(Prep. Time: 4 Min | Cooking: 10 Min | Serving 4)

INGREDIENTS
- 1 whole-wheat loaf
- 1 cup easy one-pot vegan marinara
- 1 tsp. nutritional yeast
- 1/2 tsp. onion powder
- 1/2 tsp. garlic powder

DIRECTIONS:
1. Preheat the oven to 375°F.
2. Halve the loaf of bread lengthwise. Evenly spread the marinara onto each slice of bread, then sprinkle on the nutritional yeast, onion powder, and garlic powder.
3. Situate bread on a baking sheet and bake for 20 minutes, or until the bread is a light golden brown.

Nutrition: Calories: 230 | Fiber: 7 g | Protein: 13 g

122. Baked Mac and Peas
(Prep. Time: 4 Min | Cooking: 10 Min | Serving 8)

INGREDIENTS
- 1 (16 oz.) package whole-wheat macaroni pasta
- 1 recipe Anytime "Cheese" Sauce
- 2 cups green peas

DIRECTIONS:
1. Preheat the oven to 400°F.
2. Heat up the pasta according to the package DIRECTIONS for al dente. Drain the pasta.
3. Mix pasta, sauce, and peas.
4. Bake for 30 minutes

Nutrition: Calories: 209 | Fiber: 7 g | Protein: 12 g

123. Savory Sweet Potato Casserole
(Prep. Time: 4 Min | Cooking: 11 Min | Serving 6)

INGREDIENTS
- 8 sweet potatoes
- 1/2 cup vegetable broth
- 1 tbsp. dried sage
- 1 tsp. dried thyme
- 1 tsp. dried rosemary

DIRECTIONS:
1. Preheat the oven to 375°F.
2. Peel off the skin from the cooked sweet potatoes, and put them in a baking dish. Crush sweet potatoes, then stir in the broth, sage, thyme, and rosemary.
3. Bake for 30 minutes and serve.

Nutrition: Calories: 154 | Fiber: 6 g | Protein: 3 g

124. BBQ Tofu and Mashed Potato Bowl
(Prep. Time: 3 Min | Cooking: 10 Min | Serving 4)

INGREDIENTS
- 1 (14 oz.) tofu package firm
- 1/4 cup BBQ Sauce
- 6 cups Fluffy Mashed Potatoes
- 1 recipe gravy

DIRECTIONS:
1. Remove the tofu from the water it's packaged in, and place it on a paper towel-lined plate. Allow the tofu to be pressed for a minimum of 30 minutes and up to 2 hours.

2. Slice the tofu block into 1/2-inch slices.
3. Mix the tofu slices with the BBQ sauce until the tofu is coated. Allow the tofu to marinate for 1 hour.
4. Prep the grill over high heat. Grill the tofu slices for 4 to 5 minutes, then gently flip them over and grill for 5 minutes more.
5. To serve, fill each of the 4 bowls with 1 1/2 cups of mashed potatoes, top with one-quarter of the grilled tofu, and smothered in gravy.

Nutrition: Calories: 336 | Fiber: 4 g | Protein: 15 g

125. SUNDAY SLOW ROAST
(PREP. TIME: 7 MIN | COOKING: 8 MIN | SERVING 8)

INGREDIENTS
- 6 medium white potatoes
- 6 large carrots
- 3 sweet onions
- 12 oz. green beans
- 8 oz. mushrooms
- 4 cups vegetable broth
- 1 tsp. onion powder
- 1 tsp. garlic powder
- 1 tsp. black pepper

DIRECTIONS:
1. Put the potatoes, carrots, onions, green beans, mushrooms, broth, onion powder, garlic powder, and pepper in a slow cooker. Stir together.
2. Cook for 8 hours on low.
3. Remove the lid and stir before serving.

Nutrition: Calories: 190 | Fiber: 8 g | Protein: 8 g

126. RICE-AND-VEGETABLE STIR-FRY
(PREP. TIME: 7 MIN | COOKING: 8 MIN | SERVING 5)

INGREDIENTS
- 2 cups green peas
- 2 cups green beans
- 1/4 cup vegetable broth
- 1 tsp. garlic powder
- 1 tsp. onion powder
- 4 cups brown rice

DIRECTIONS:
1. Heat a medium saucepan over medium heat.
2. Put the peas, green beans, broth, garlic powder, and onion powder in the pan, and stir. Seal and cook for 8 minutes

3. Open and stir in the cooked brown rice. Cook for an additional 5 minutes, stirring every other minute, and serve.

Nutrition: Calories: 233 | Fiber: 7 g | Protein: 8 g

127. MANGO-GINGER CHICKPEA CURRY
(PREP. TIME: 5 MIN | COOKING: 10 MIN | SERVING 6)

INGREDIENTS
- 3 cups cooked chickpeas
- 2 cups mango chunks
- 2 cups plant-based milk
- 2 tbsp. maple syrup
- 1 tbsp. curry powder
- 1 tbsp. ground ginger
- 1 tsp. ground coriander
- 1 tsp. garlic powder
- 1 tsp. onion powder
- 1/8 tsp. ground cinnamon

DIRECTIONS:
1. Heat a Dutch oven over medium heat.
2. Mix chickpeas, mango, milk, maple syrup, curry powder, ginger, coriander, garlic powder, onion powder, and cinnamon. Cover and cook for 10 minutes, stirring after about 5 minutes
3. Uncover and cook for an additional 5 minutes Serve.

Nutrition: Calories: 218 | Fiber: 9 g | Protein: 8 g

128. ITALIAN BEAN BALLS
(PREP. TIME: 3 MIN | COOKING: 10 MIN | SERVING 6)

INGREDIENTS
- 1 1/2 cups black beans
- 1 1/2 cups red kidney beans
- 1 cup brown rice
- 1 cup quick-cooking oats
- 1/4 cup Easy One-Pot Vegan Marinara
- 1 tbsp. Italian seasoning
- 1 tsp. garlic powder
- 1 tsp. onion powder
- 1/4 tsp. black pepper

DIRECTIONS:
1. Preheat the oven to 400°F. Line a baking sheet with parchment paper.
2. Crush black beans and kidney beans together.
3. Mix rice, oats, marinara, Italian seasoning, garlic powder, onion powder, and pepper.

4. Scoop out 1/4 cup of the bean mixture, and form it into a ball. Place the beanball on the baking sheet. Repeat.
5. Bake the beanballs for 30 minutes, flip once after 15 minutes

Nutrition: Calories: 144 | Fiber: 5 g | Protein: 6 g

129. CRISPY RICE-AND-BEAN TOSTADAS
(PREP. TIME: 2 MIN | COOKING: 10 MIN | SERVING 2)

INGREDIENTS
- 4 corn tortillas
- 1 cup Fat-Free Refried Beans
- 1 cup brown rice
- 1 cup black beans
- 1 lime

DIRECTIONS:
1. Preheat the oven to 400°F. Line a baking sheet with parchment paper.
2. Bake tortillas for 7 minutes
3. Evenly spread 1/4 cup of refried beans onto each crispy tortilla, then add 1/4 cup each of rice and black beans.
4. Squeeze lime juice over each tostada right before serving.

Nutrition: Calories: 422 | Fiber: 19 g | Protein: 19 g

130. STUFFED PEPPERS
(PREP. TIME: 7 MIN | COOKING: 8 MIN | SERVING 5)

INGREDIENTS
- 4 bell peppers
- 3 cups brown rice
- 1 cup black beans
- 1 cup corn
- 1 cup vegetable broth
- 2 tbsp. tomato paste
- 2 tbsp. chili powder
- 1 tsp. ground cumin

DIRECTIONS:
1. Prep the oven to 375°F.
2. Chop the tops off the bell peppers.
3. Mix rice, beans, corn, broth, tomato paste, chili powder, and cumin.
4. Scoop one-quarter of the rice mixture into each pepper. Set the peppers upright on a baking dish, and position the tops back onto the peppers.
5. Bake for 1 hour, and serve.

Nutrition: Calories: 270 | Fiber: 9 g | Protein: 11 g

131. BURRITO BOWL WITH OIL-FREE TORTILLA CHIPS
(PREP. TIME: 4 MIN | COOKING: 10 MIN | SERVING 2)

INGREDIENTS
- 4 corn tortillas
- 1 cup brown rice
- 1 cup cooked black bean
- 1 cup corn
- 2 tsp. chili powder
- 1 tsp. cumin
- 1/2 tsp. garlic powder
- 1/2 tsp. onion powder
- 2 cups shredded lettuce
- 1 avocado
- 1/4 cup salsa

DIRECTIONS:
1. Preheat the oven to 350°F. Line a baking sheet with parchment paper.
2. Cut each tortilla into 6 evenly-sized chips, and place the chips on the baking sheet. Bake for 10 minutes
3. Mix rice, black beans, corn, chili powder, cumin, garlic powder, and onion powder. Warm mixture in the microwave on high for 2 minutes
4. Divide the warm rice, bean, and corn mixture into two serving bowls, then top each with 1 cup of shredded lettuce, 1/2 avocado slices, and salsa.

Nutrition: Calories: 538 | Fiber: 21 g | Protein: 18 g

132. BAKED TAQUITOS WITH FAT-FREE REFRIED BEANS
(PREP. TIME: 5 MIN | COOKING: 9 MIN | SERVING 2)

INGREDIENTS
- 2 cups pinto beans
- 1 tsp. chili powder
- 1 tsp. ground cumin
- 1/2 tsp. garlic powder
- 1/2 tsp. onion powder
- 1/4 tsp. red pepper flakes
- 12 corn tortillas

DIRECTIONS:
1. Preheat the oven to 400°F. Line a baking sheet with parchment paper.
2 Combine the beans, chili powder, cumin, garlic powder, onion powder, and red pepper flakes in a

food processor. Pulse or blend on low for 30 seconds, set aside.
3. Heat tortillas for 2 minutes this helps soften the tortillas and makes rolling them much easier.
4. Remove the tortillas from the oven, then add a couple of heaping tbsp. of the refried beans to the bottom half of each corn tortilla. Roll the tortillas tightly, and place them back on the baking sheet, seam-side down.
5. Bake for 20 minutes, and serve.

Nutrition: Calories: 236 | Fiber: 13 g | Protein: 12 g

133. BROCCOLI AND MUSHROOM STIR-FRY

(PREP.TIME:4 MIN | COOKING:10 MIN | SERVING 4)

INGREDIENTS

- 2 cups broccoli
- 1/4 cup red onion
- 3 garlic cloves
- 2 cups mushrooms
- 1/4 tsp. crushed red pepper
- 2 tsp. fresh ginger
- 1 tbsp. light olive oil
- 1/4 cup broth
- 1/2 cup carrot
- 1/4 cup cashews
- 2 tbsp. rice wine vinegar
- 2 tbsp. soy sauce
- 1 tbsp. coconut sugar
- 1 tbsp. sesame seeds
- Water

DIRECTIONS:

1. Heat up oil over medium heat.
2. Add the broccoli, onion, garlic, mushrooms, red pepper, broth and water.
3. Cook until the veggies are soft.
4. Add the carrots, cashews, vinegar, soya, and coconut sugar. Stir well and cook for 2 minutes
5. Top with sesame seeds then serve and enjoy.

Nutrition: | Calories: 133 | Fat: 8 g | Protein: 6 g

134. SLOW COOKER CHILI

(PREP.TIME:5 MIN | COOKING:9 MIN | SERVING 12)

INGREDIENTS

- 3 cups dry pinto beans
- 1 large onion
- 3 bell peppers
- 8 large green jalapeño peppers
- 2 x 14 1/2 oz. cans tomatoes
- 1 tbsp. chili powder
- 2 tbsp. oregano flakes
- 1 tbsp. cumin powder
- 1 tbsp. garlic powder
- 3 bay leaves
- 1 tsp. ground black pepper
- Water
- Salt to taste

DIRECTIONS:

1. Soak beans with water overnight.
2. Strain and put in a 6-quart slow cooker.
3. Cover with salt and two inches of water. Cook on high for 6 hours until soft.
4. Drain the beans and add the other ingredients. Stir well to combine.
5. Close and cook for another 3 hours on high.

Nutrition: Calories: 216 | Fat: 1 g | Protein: 12 g

135. QUINOA LENTIL BURGER

(PREP. TIME: 10 MIN | COOKING: 5 MIN | SERVING 4)

INGREDIENTS

- 2 tbsp. light olive oil
- 1/4 cup diced red onion
- 1 cup cooked quinoa, cook according to package instructions
- 1 cup cooked brown lentils
- 1 x 4 oz. can dice green chilies
- 1/3 cup rolled oats
- 1/4 cup all-purpose flour
- 2 tsp. cornstarch
- 1/4 cup whole-wheat panko breadcrumbs
- 1/4 tsp. garlic powder
- 1/2 tsp. cumin
- 1 tsp. paprika
- 2 tbsp. Dijon mustard
- 3 tsp. honey

DIRECTIONS:

1. Place a skillet over medium heat and add 2 tsp. light olive oil.
2. Cook onion.
3. Grab a small bowl and add the honey and Dijon mustard.
4. Grab a large bowl and add the burger ingredients. Stir well.
5. Form into 4 patties with your hands.
6. Warm-up oil over medium heat.
7. Cook patties for 20 minutes on both sides.
8. Serve with the honey mustard and enjoy!

Nutrition: Calories: 268 | Fat: 8 g | Protein: 10 g

136. Hummus Quesadillas
(Prep. Time: 7 Min | Cooking: 8 Min | Serving 3)

INGREDIENTS
- 4 x 8-inch whole grain tortilla
- 1 cup hummus
- Extra-virgin light olive oil

DIRECTIONS:
1. Arrange tortillas on a flat surface and cover each with hummus.
2. Add the fillings (spinach, sundried tomatoes, olives, etc.) then fold over to form a half-moon shape.
3. Pop a skillet over medium heat and add a drop of oil.
4. Add the quesadillas and flip when browned.
5. Repeat with the remaining quesadillas then serve and enjoy.

Nutrition: Calories: 258 | Carbohydrates: 21 g | Fat: 9 g

137. Spaghetti Alla Puttanesca
(Prep. Time: 10 Min | Cooking: 4 Min | Serving 4)

INGREDIENTS
For Puttanesca sauce:
- 1 x 28 oz. can chunky tomato sauce
- 1/3 cup chopped Kalamata olives
- 1/3 cup capers
- 1 tbsp. Kalamata olive brine
- 1 tbsp. caper brine
- 3 garlic cloves
- 1/4 tsp. red pepper flakes
- 1 tbsp. light olive oil
- 1/2 cup chopped fresh parsley leaves
- 8 oz. whole-grain spaghetti

DIRECTIONS:
1. Grab a medium saucepan and add the tomato sauce, olives and brine, capers and brine, garlic, and red pepper flakes.
2. Simmer for 20 minutes
3. Take out from heat add the light olive oil and parsley.
4. Stir well then season.
5. Boil water over medium heat.
6. Cook spaghetti following package directions.
7. Drain and return to the pot.
8. Mix sauce over the pasta.

Nutrition: Calories: 341 | Fat: 10 g | Protein: 10 g

138. Crispy Baked Falafel
(Prep. Time: 10 Min | Cooking: 5 Min | Serving 12)

INGREDIENTS
- 1/4 cup light olive oil
- 1 cup dried garbanzo beans, soaked
- 1/2 small red onion,
- 1/2 cup packed fresh parsley
- 1/2 cup packed fresh cilantro
- 4 garlic cloves
- 1 tsp. salt
- 1/2 tsp. black pepper
- 1/2 tsp. ground cumin
- 1/4 tsp. ground cinnamon

DIRECTIONS:
1. Preheat the oven to 375°F.
2. Find a large rimmed baking sheet and add 1/4 cup light olive oil.
3. Take your food processor and blend drained garbanzo beans, onion, parsley, cilantro, garlic, salt, pepper, cumin, cinnamon, and remaining oil.
4. Create small patties and pop them into the oiled pan.
5. Cook in the oven for 30 minutes
6. Pull away from the oven then serve and enjoy.

Nutrition: Calories: 354 | Fat: 21 g | Protein: 11 g

139. Gluten-Free Mango and Black Bean Tacos
(Prep. Time: 5 Min | Cooking: 10 Min | Serving 3)

INGREDIENTS
- 2 Roma tomatoes
- 2 tbsp. red onion
- 1/4 cup orange bell pepper
- 1 tbsp. lime juice
- 2 tbsp. fresh cilantro
- 1/2 tsp. salt
- 1 x 15 oz. can black beans
- 1/4 cup vegetable broth
- 6 gluten-free corn tortillas
- 1 ripe mango
- 1 avocado

DIRECTIONS:
1. Mix tomatoes, onion, pepper, lime juice, cilantro, and salt.
2. Cover and pop to one side.
3. Take a small saucepan and add the beans and vegetable broth. Pop over medium heat, bring to a simmer, and cook for five minutes
4. Remove from the heat and mash roughly.

5. Pop the tortillas into the microwave and cook for 30 seconds.
6. Place the tortillas onto a flat surface and spread with the beans.
7. Top with the remaining **INGREDIENTS** then serve and enjoy.

Nutrition: Calories: 420 | Fat: 12 g | Protein: 14 g

140. Butternut Squash and Cranberry
(Prep. Time: 13 Min | Cooking: 7 Min | Serving 5)

INGREDIENTS
- 3 cups butternut squash
- 5 tbsp. extra-virgin light olive oil
- 2 cups cooked quinoa
- 1/2 cup dried cranberries
- 1/3 cup walnuts pieces
- 1 tbsp. basil
- 1/4 tsp. salt
- 1/4 tsp. black pepper

DIRECTIONS:
1. Grab a medium saucepan, add 3 tbsp. of the oil, and pop over medium heat.
2. Add the squash and cook until tender.
3. Grab a large bowl and toss the remaining ingredients plus the cooked squash.

Nutrition: Calories: 327 | Fat: 20 g | Protein: 6 g

141. Avocado Hummus Bowl
(Prep. Time: 10 Min | Cooking: 0 Min | Serving 4)

INGREDIENTS
- 1/2 ripe avocado
- 1/2 cup garbanzo beans
- 1/2 medium-sized cucumber
- 2/3 cup cherry tomatoes
- 1 cup baby carrots
- 10 spinach leaves
- 1/3 cup hummus
- 2 tbsp. pumpkin or shelled sunflower seeds, optional
- 1/4 tsp. sea salt
- 1/4 tsp. black pepper

DIRECTIONS:s:
1. Line bowl with the spinach leaves.
2. Add the avocado to one corner, garbanzo beans to another, tomatoes to another, and carrots to another.
3. Pop the hummus in the center and sprinkle with the seeds.
4. Season with salt and pepper well.

Nutrition: Calories: 196 | Fat: 3 g | Protein: 8 g

142. Slow Cooker Pumpkin Chili
(Prep. Time: 10 Min | Cooking: 4 Min | Serving 6)

INGREDIENTS
- 1 onion
- 2 x 14 oz. cans tomatoes
- 2 x 14 oz. cans black beans
- 1 carrot
- 1 bell pepper
- 1 jalapeno
- 2 garlic cloves
- 1 1/2 cups pumpkin puree
- 1 cups vegetable broth
- 2 tbsp. chili powder
- 1 tsp. pumpkin pie spice

DIRECTIONS:
1. Mix all **INGREDIENTS** in the slow cooker.
2. Cook on low for 5 hours.
3. Serve and enjoy!

Nutrition: Calories: 214 | Fat: 1 g | Protein: 12 g

143. Broccoli Pesto With Pasta and Cherry Tomatoes
(Prep. Time: 10 Min | Cooking: 5 Min | Serving 2)1

INGREDIENTS
For broccoli pesto:
- 2 heaped cups broccoli florets
- 1/2 cup walnuts
- 3 tbsp. nutritional yeast
- 2 garlic cloves
- 3 tbsp. light olive oil
- 1/2 cup parsley

For pasta:
- 9 oz. whole-wheat pasta, cooked
- 1 cup cherry tomatoes, cut into halves
- 1 cup cooked broccoli florets

DIRECTIONS:
1. Blend pesto ingredients and chill.
2. Mix salad ingredients into the pesto.

Nutrition: Calories: 815 | Fat: 85 g | Protein: 10 g

144. Southwest Sweet Potato Vegan Meal Prep Bowls
(Prep. Time: 10 Min | Cooking: 4 Min | Serving 4)

INGREDIENTS
- 1 large sweet potato
- 3–4 tbsp. light olive oil
- 1 tsp. southwest seasoning
- 1 x 12 oz. can sweet corn
- 1 x 19 oz. can black beans
- 1/2 lime juice
- 1/2 tsp. ground cumin
- Salt and pepper to taste

DIRECTIONS:
1. Ready the oven to 400°F and put the baking sheet with foil.
2. Place the sweet potato onto the baking sheet then sprinkle with southwest seasoning and salt and pepper.
3. Add 3 tbsp. oil and toss.
4. Bake for 25 minutes
5. Toss corn, beans, lime juice, 1 tbsp. light olive oil, cumin, salt, and pepper.
6. Transfer in storage containers and divide the potatoes between.
7. Top with the veggie mixture and add a wedge of lime to each. Chill

Nutrition: Calories: 658 | Fat: 29 g | Protein: 19 g

145. Asian Quinoa and Edamame
(Prep. Time: 13 Min | Cooking: 0 Min | Serving 4)

INGREDIENTS
- 1/2 cup dry uncooked quinoa
- 1 cup water
- 1/2 cucumber
- 1 red pepper
- 1 grated carrot
- 2 green onions
- 1 tsp. maple syrup
- 1 tsp. fresh ginger
- 2 tbsp. soy sauce
- 2 tbsp. sesame seed oil
- 2 tbsp. rice vinegar
- 1 cup edamame

DIRECTIONS:
1. Cook the quinoa following package directions then leave to cool.
2. Incorporate remaining ingredients.
3. Top with the cooled quinoa then toss. Chill.

Nutrition: Calories: 222 | Fat: 10 g | Protein: 8 g

146. Mushroom Pecan Burgers
(Prep. Time: 10 Min | Cooking: 5 Min | Serving 5)

INGREDIENTS
- 8 oz. Portobello mushrooms
- 1/4 cup red onion
- 3 tbsp. light olive oil
- 2 garlic cloves
- 1 x 15 oz. can garbanzo beans
- 1 cup pecans, diced small
- 1 1/2 cup instant oats
- 2 tbsp. hoisin sauce
- 1 tbsp. tahini

DIRECTIONS:
1. Pop a skillet over medium heat and add 1 tbsp. of the light olive oil.
2. Add the mushrooms and cook for five minutes
3. Cook onion.
4. Cook garlic for two more minutes
5. Remove from the heat.
6. Add the garbanzo beans, pecans and oats, blend.
7. Add the hoisin sauce and tahini then stir well using your hands.
8. Form into six patties.
9. Mix the rest of the light olive oil into a skillet and pop over a medium heat.
10. Fry for 5 minutes on each side.

Nutrition: Calories: 285 | Fat: 18 g | Protein: 9 g

147. Avocado Toast With White Beans
(Prep. Time: 10 Min | Cooking: 0 Min | Serving 4)

INGREDIENTS
- 1/2 cup canned white beans
- 2 tsp. tahini paste
- 2 tsp. lemon juice
- 1/2 tsp. salt
- 1/2 avocado
- 4 slices whole grain bread
- 1/2 cup grape tomatoes

DIRECTIONS:
1. Combine beans, tahini, 1/2 the lemon juice, and 1/2 the salt. Mash with a fork.
2. Crush avocado and the rest of lemon juice and salt.
3. Situate your toast onto a flat surface and add the mashed beans, spreading well.
4. Garnish with the avocado and the sliced tomatoes then serve and enjoy.

Nutrition: Calories: 140 | Fat: 5 g | Protein: 6 g

148. Veggie Spring Rolls

(Prep. Time: 9 Min | Cooking: 5 Min | Serving 4)

INGREDIENTS

- 3 cups water
- 1 (8 oz.) package thin rice noodles
- 1 (8 oz.) jar peanut sauce
- 1 large cucumber
- 2 small red bell peppers
- 8 rice wrappers

DIRECTIONS:

1. Boil water. Place the rice noodles and pour the hot water. Let sit for 3 minutes Drain, and pour the peanut sauce over the noodles. Toss; set aside.
2. Leaving the peel on the cucumber, cut it in half, and then julienne each half to create 16 (1/4-inch-wide) sticks.
3. Slice circle around the top of each red pepper. Cut off stem and seeds. Cut each into four parts, then slice into 16 strips total.
4. Dip 1 rice wrapper in warm water for 5 seconds. Place the moist rice wrapper on a work surface and let sit for 30 seconds. Add one-eighth of the noodles and sauce, 2 cucumber sticks, and 2 pepper strips. Lift one side of the rice wrapper and fold over the filling, tucking it under the filling. Crease in the sides and continue rolling until you come to the end of the wrapper. Repeat process.

Nutrition: Calories: 551 | Fiber: 6 g | Protein: 13 g

149. Smoky Coleslaw

(Prep. Time: 10 Min | Cooking: 0 Min | Serving 4)

INGREDIENTS

- 1 lb. cabbage
- 1/2 cup plain vegan yogurt
- 1/4 cup unseasoned rice vinegar
- 1 tbsp. coconut sugar
- 1/2 tsp. smoked paprika
- Salt and pepper

DIRECTIONS:

1. Puree yogurt, vinegar, coconut sugar, paprika, salt, and pepper.
2. Drizzle dressing over the cabbage and mix Cover and chill for an hour.

Nutrition: Calories: 62 | Fiber: 3 g | Protein: 2 g

150. Baked Ratatouille

(Prep. Time: 10 Min | Cooking: 3 Min | Serving 4)

INGREDIENTS

- 1 large zucchini
- 1 small eggplant
- 2 tsp. light olive oil
- 1 small red onion
- 1 (24 oz.) jar marinara sauce
- 1/2 cup basil leaves

DIRECTIONS:

1. Preheat the oven to 400°F.
2. Slice the zucchini and eggplant (peel on) into 1/4-inch rounds. Set aside.
3. Warm-up light olive oil over medium-high heat. Sauté onion. Cook marinara sauce for 3 minutes
4. Reserve 3/4 cup of the sauce and transfer the rest of it to an 8-inch square baking pan with 2-inch sides. Arrange the basil over the sauce. Place the zucchini and eggplant rounds over the basil and sauce. Dash rest 1 tsp. light olive oil over the vegetables and season Pour the reserved 3/4 cup sauce over everything.
5. Seal with foil and bake it for 20 minutes Remove then bake for 10 minutes

Nutrition: Calories: 123 | Fiber: 8 g | Protein: 5 g

151. Tasty Tabouli

(Prep. Time: 15 Min | Cooking: 0 Min | Serving 4)

INGREDIENTS

- 1/4 cup bulgur wheat
- 2 cups boiling water
- 2 large lemons, juiced
- 2 cups flat-leaf parsley leaves
- 8 oz. cherry tomatoes
- 1 cup scallions
- 1 tsp. salt
- 1/2 tsp. black pepper

DIRECTIONS:

1. Soak bulgur, over boiling water, cover for 20 minutes
2. Drain the bulgur and put it back in the bowl. Toss lemon juice, parsley, tomatoes, scallions, salt, and pepper.

Nutrition: Calories: 68 | Fiber: 5 g | Protein: 3 g

152. Skillet Seitan Stew

(Prep. Time: 2 Min | Cooking: 13 Min | Serving 4)

INGREDIENTS

- 1 (8 oz.) package cubed Seitan
- 1 tbsp. light olive oil
- 1 large carrot

- 1 cup sliced mushrooms
- 1 (14.5 oz.) can seasoned tomatoes
- 1 1/2 cups vegetable broth
- 1/2 tsp. salt
- 1/4 tsp. black pepper

DIRECTIONS:
1. Heat the Seitan and light olive oil together over medium-high heat for 5 minutes Boil carrot, mushrooms, tomatoes, broth, salt, and pepper.
2. Cover, set to medium-low, and simmer for 10 minutes

Nutrition: Calories: 297 | Fiber: 4 g | Protein: 45 g

153. Two-Alarm Chili
(Prep. Time: 5 Min | Cooking: 10 Min | Serving 2)

INGREDIENTS
- 1 tsp. light olive oil
- 1 small onion
- 2 tsp. garlic
- 1 (15 oz.) can dark red kidney beans
- 1 heaping tbsp. jalapeño pepper
- 1 (28 oz.) can fire-roasted tomatoes
- 1/2 cup water

DIRECTIONS:
1. In a pot over medium-high heat, cook the light olive oil, onion, and garlic for 3 minutes Boil beans, jalapeño, tomatoes, and water.
2. Cover, set to medium-low, and simmer for 10 minutes

Nutrition: Calories: 383 | Fiber: 20 g | Protein: 20 g

154. Basic Buddha Burrito Bowl
(Prep. Time: 4 Min | Cooking: 11 Min | Serving 4)

INGREDIENTS
- 1 cup quinoa
- 2 cups water
- 1/2 tsp. salt
- 2 tsp. light olive oil
- 1 (15 oz.) can black beans
- 16 oz. fresh spinach
- 1/2 cup salsa
- 1/4 cup vegan sour cream

DIRECTIONS:
1. In a medium saucepan, mix quinoa, water, and salt and boil over medium-high heat. Then cover, set to medium-low, and simmer for 20 minutes Remove from the heat and set aside.
2. At medium-high heat, warm up oil for 1 minute. Toss beans and spinach for 4 minutes
3. To serve, portion the quinoa and sautéed beans and spinach. Top with salsa and sour cream.

Nutrition: Calories: 355 | Fiber: 14 g | Protein: 19 g

155. Spicy Tostadas
(Prep. Time: 8 Min | Cooking: 7 Min | Serving 5)

INGREDIENTS
- 8 vegan corn tortillas
- 1 (15 oz.) can black beans
- 1 small onion
- 1 cup shredded vegan cheese
- 1/2 cup salsa

DIRECTIONS:
1. Preheat the oven to 400°F.
2. On a baking sheet, spritz tortillas with nonstick vegetable oil spray and place them oil-side down. Layout 3 tbsp. of refried beans on each tortilla. Cover each with onion slices. Sprinkle 2 tbsp. shredded vegan cheese over each.
3. Bake for 10 minutes
4. Top with salsa and serve.

Nutrition: Calories: 283 | Fiber: 9 g | Protein: 9 g

156. Red "Risotto"
(Prep. Time: 5 Min | Cooking: 9 Min | Serving 4)

INGREDIENTS
- 1 cup arborio rice
- 3 cups vegetable broth
- 1 cup jarred marinara sauce
- 1/4 cup nutritional yeast
- 1 lemon, juiced
- 1/2 tsp. salt
- 1/2 tsp. black pepper

DIRECTIONS:
1. Boil rice, broth, and marinara sauce. Cover, set heat to a low simmer for 20 minutes
2. Remove from the heat. Steam with the lid on for 10 minutes
3. While fluffing the rice with a fork, mix nutritional yeast, lemon juice, salt, and pepper, then serve.

Nutrition: Calories: 268 | Fiber: 5 g | Protein: 16 g

157. Kale Pesto Penne
(Prep. Time: 5 Min | Cooking: 10 Min | Serving 4)

INGREDIENTS
- 8 cups water
- 1 (8 oz.) package vegan penne pasta
- 3 cups kale
- 1/2 cup walnuts
- 1/4 cup lemon juice
- 1 tbsp. garlic
- 1 tsp. salt
- 1/2 tsp. black pepper
- 3 tbsp. light olive oil

DIRECTIONS:
1. Boil water and pasta for 12 minutes
2. While cooking, blend kale, walnuts, lemon juice, garlic, salt, and pepper into a food processor. If it's too thick, drizzle light olive oil.
3. Drain the pasta. Pour the pesto over the pasta. Toss and serve.

Nutrition: Calories: 390 | Fiber: 4 g | Protein: 11 g

158. Cheesy Zucchini
(Prep. Time: 4 Min | Cooking: 11 Min | Serving 5)

INGREDIENTS
- 1 large zucchini
- 1 tsp. light olive oil
- 16 oz. marinara sauce
- 2 cups vegan ricotta
- 1 tsp. black pepper

DIRECTIONS:
1. Preheat the oven to 375°F.
2. Cut zucchini lengthwise into thin strips (about 1/8 inch thick).
3. Spread the oil over the bottom of an 8-inch square baking pan with 2-inch sides. Arrange the bottom of the pan with zucchini slices, overlapping them slightly, using 3 to 4 slices. Spread over 1/2 cup of marinara sauce.
4. Dollop about 1/2 cup of vegan ricotta over the sauce. Add another layer of zucchini, 1/2 cup sauce, pepper, and 1/2 cup ricotta; repeat the layers. Pour the remaining 1/2 cup sauce over everything and top with the remaining ricotta. Season.
5. Bake, uncovered, for 15 minutes
6. Remove and put aside for 10 minutes

Nutrition: Calories: 168 | Fiber: 8 g | Protein: 16 g

159. Pea Nutty Carrot Noodles
(Prep. Time: 5 Min | Cooking: 2 Min | Serving 4)

INGREDIENTS
- 1 tsp. light olive oil
- 3 large carrots
- 1 small lime
- 1/2 tsp. salt
- 1/2 cup peanuts
- 1/2 cup chopped scallions

DIRECTIONS:
1. Over medium-high heat, heat the light olive oil. Cook carrots, cover for 2 minutes Remove from the heat, mix lime juice and salt, and toss.
2. To serve, top each with 2 tbsp. peanuts and 2 tbsp. scallions.

Nutrition: Calories: 142 | Fiber: 3 g | Protein: 5 g

160. Sweet Potato Alfredo
(Prep. Time: 3 Min | Cooking: 11 Min | Serving 4)

INGREDIENTS
- 2 tbsp. vegan butter
- 1 tsp. garlic powder
- 1/4 tsp. nutritional yeast
- 1 cup unsweetened soy milk
- 2 sweet potatoes
- 1/2 tsp. salt
- 1/2 tsp. black pepper

DIRECTIONS:
1. In medium-high heat, melt vegan butter. Whisk in the garlic powder and nutritional yeast until thick. Stir in soy milk. Let it boil.
2. Mix spiralized sweet potatoes, stirring to coat with sauce, and let it boil. Cook adjust heat to low for 10 minutes Season and serve.

Nutrition: Calories: 176 | Fiber: 7 g | Protein: 11 g

161. Chana Masala
(Prep. Time: 5 Min | Cooking: 9 Min | Serving 6)

INGREDIENTS
- 2 tsp. light olive oil
- 1 medium onion
- 1 small jalapeño or serrano pepper
- 2 tsp. garam masala
- 1 tsp. salt
- 1 tsp. black pepper
- 1 (14.5 oz.) can diced tomatoes
- 2 (15 oz.) cans of chickpeas

- 4 tbsp. water

DIRECTIONS:
1. Warm-up light olive oil at medium-high heat for 2 minutes Sauté onion and minced pepper. Sauté garam masala, salt, and pepper for 2 minutes more. Stir in the tomatoes and 1/2 cup of chickpeas.
2. Purée the mixture in the pan.
3. Boil the remainder of the chickpeas with water. Select heat to low and simmer for 10 minutes

Nutrition: Calories: 210 | Fiber: 10 g | Protein: 10 g

162. Sautéed Red Lentils and Fennel Seed
(Prep. Time: 5 Min | Cooking: 9 Min | Serving 4)

INGREDIENTS
- 1 tsp. light olive oil
- 1 cup chopped carrot
- 2 tsp. minced garlic
- 1 tsp. fennel seeds
- 1 cup dried red lentils
- 2 1/4 cups water
- 2 tbsp. lemon juice
- 1 tsp. salt

DIRECTIONS:
1. Over medium-high heat, heat the light olive oil. Sauté carrot and garlic for 3 minutes, stirring frequently. Stir fennel seeds, lentils, and water.
2. Boil, cover, set heat to medium-low or low, and simmer for 20 minutes
3. Remove from heat, stir lemon juice and salt, mash, and serve.

Nutrition: Calories: 196 | Fiber: 16 g | Protein: 13 g

163. Ratatouille
(Prep. Time: 2 Min | Cooking: 13 Min | Serving 6)

INGREDIENTS
- 8 baby eggplants
- 2 capsicums
- 4 medium tomatoes
- 4 zucchinis
- 2 onions
- 24–28 garlic cloves
- 4–6 tbsp. fresh herbs
- Virgin light olive oil for drizzling
- Salt and pepper to taste
- Balsamic vinegar

DIRECTIONS:
1. Ready the oven to 400°F and place a piece of wax baking paper on a large baking sheet.
2. If you're using baby eggplant, slice them in half lengthwise. Or, chop the full-size eggplant into roughly 1-inch bite-size pieces. Thickly slice the bell pepper/capsicum into inch-wide strips, then cut in half. Cut the tomatoes into large chunks (roughly 6 chunks per tomato). Slice the zucchini the long way and then chop it into 1/2 inch thick pieces. Likewise slice the onion in half, then into approximately half-inch thick half-moons.
3. Spread out the veggies on the baking sheet in a single layer, so none are piled up. Add the garlic cloves, not chopped—but do remember to peel them! Sprinkle the herbs atop.
4. Drizzle about 1/2 cup light olive oil over the top and tilt the baking tray from side to side, ensuring the bottoms of all the veggies are well coated. The tops are still raw and not coated in oil, which gives them a lovely crisp texture when roasting.
5. Roast for 24 minutes, then flip the mix with a spatula and roast for another 10 to 15 minutes, or until the sides now facing up have been cooked visibly.
6. Turn down the heat to about 275–300°F and roast for another 15 to 20 minutes, or until the veggie mixture has become tender and the edges begin to caramelize (look golden brown and taste sweet—you'll know that taste and smell!).
7. Season and serve immediately when hot. It serves very well with pasta, polenta, rice, balsamic vinegar, soft shell tortillas, or on a bed of fresh spring greens.

Nutrition: Calories: 147 | Fat: 9.7 g | Protein: 2.5 g

164. Peanut Coconut Curry Veggies
(Prep. Time: 3 Min | Cooking: 12 Min | Serving 5)

INGREDIENTS
- 2–5 tbsp. oil for frying
- 1 eggplant
- 1 zucchini
- 2 onions
- 2 garlic cloves
- 1-piece ginger
- 1 tsp. cumin seeds
- 1 tsp. coriander seeds
- 1 tsp. turmeric
- 1/2 tsp. chili powder
- 1 can of coconut milk
- 1 tbsp. tamarind paste

- 1 tbsp. peanut butter
- 2 tbsp. water
- Cilantro to taste

DIRECTIONS:
1. Heat 1 tbsp. oil in a pan. Cook the eggplant/aubergine in batches until golden and soft, frying it for about 3 to 5 minutes per batch.
2. Take a medium-sized soup pot. Cut onion and add it to the pot with 1–2 tbsp. oil and cook until soft and golden, somewhat translucent. Add the finely chopped garlic, zucchini, and ginger, and cook for a minute. Sprinkle the spices and cook for 2 more minutes
3. Pour in the coconut milk, tamarind paste (or simply use fresh with a couple of tbsp. warm water), and peanut butter. Simmer gently for 2 minutes
4. Add the cooked eggplant back into the pot and simmer for 15 minutes turn off the heat, stir through some finely chopped cilantro/coriander and serve with bread or rice.

Nutrition: Calories: 251 | Fat: 15.5 g | Protein: 5.5 g

165. Stuffed Portobello Mushrooms With Walnut and Thyme

(Prep. Time: 5 Min | Cooking: 8 Min | Serving 2)

INGREDIENTS
- 4 portobello mushrooms
- 4 tbsp. light olive oil
- 1 yellow onion
- 3/4 cup mushrooms
- 1 garlic clove
- 1 tsp. smoked paprika
- 1 tsp. thyme leaves
- 1 piece of day-old sourdough bread
- 2/3 cup walnuts

DIRECTIONS:
1. Prep grill to medium. Cut the large stalks of portobello mushrooms. Set aside. Rub portobello mushrooms with some frying oil on both sides, season, and grill for 6 minutes on high heat on both sides.
2. Slice onion finely. Cut mushrooms, including the portobello stems, walnuts, and toast. Crush garlic clove.
3. Get a frying pan, set in medium heat, and sauté 2 tbsp. light olive oil with the onion. Mix in the all chopped-up mushrooms and a bit of salt. Sauté.
4. Stir pressed garlic, smoked paprika, and thyme. Stir in the breadcrumbs and walnuts.
5. Scoop the mix into the middles of the portobello mushrooms. Grill again, for another 5 minutes
6. Serve. Sprinkle nut cheese.

Nutrition: Calories: 306 | Fat: 18.8 g | Protein: 11.4 g

166. Green Beans With Lemon Toasted Almonds

(Prep. Time: 5 Min | Cooking: 10 Min | Serving 3)

INGREDIENTS
- 1 lb. string beans
- 1/2 yellow onion
- 1 fresh lemon
- 1 1/2 cup almonds
- 1 tbsp. Bragg's Amino Acids
- 3 tbsp. avocado oil
- Salt and pepper to taste

DIRECTIONS:
1. After soaking the almonds overnight and letting them dehydrate/dry out, place them in a frying pan without oil on medium-low heat. Let toast for 5 to 8 minutes, stirring occasionally. Watch them carefully so they don't burn.
2. Meanwhile, trim the green beans and slice them at a steep diagonal, into bite-sized pieces. Chop the onion.
3. Take a medium-sized frying pan, put in the oil and onion, and beans. Sauté for 10 minutes, until the beans are al dente and the onion are translucent. Add the almonds, juice from the lemon (or 1/4 cup lemon juice from a bottle), Bragg's Amino Acids, and stir well, cooking for another 2 minutes
4. Serve warm as a side dish, adding salt and pepper to taste.

Nutrition: Calories: 460 | Fat: 38 g | Protein: 13.5 g

167. Mashed Cauliflower With Garlic

(Prep. Time: 5 Min | Cooking: 10 Min | Serving 9)

INGREDIENTS
- 3 heads cauliflower
- 6 tbsp. margarine
- 5–6 garlic cloves
- A pinch black pepper

- 2/6–3/4 cup unsweetened plain almond milk
- 2 inches of water
- Salt and pepper to taste
- Parsley for garnish

DIRECTIONS:
1. Cut the cauliflower into small, bite-sized pieces and place it into a large pot. Fill 2 inches of water at the bottom, to steam. Let steam for 15 to 20 minutes or until al dente.
2. While that is steaming, press the garlic and margarine into a small frying pan, and sauté over medium-low heat for 2 to 3 minutes or until the mixture has just slightly turned brown (be careful not to burn).
3. Put approximately half the cauliflower mixture into a food processor or blender or use a stick blender and mix until puréed smooth. Then, add half the garlic butter, the salt, and the pepper. Continue mixing well.
4. Feel free to add some extra almond milk to help the cauliflower purée get more watery or creamy, and less thick. You could add a couple of pinches of nutritional yeast to add some cheesy flavor if you'd like.
5. Keep the mixture warm in the oven on low heat. Repeat the blending and seasoning of the cauliflower mixture.
6. To serve, sprinkle some parsley on top. Add freshly ground pepper to taste.

Nutrition: Calories: 134 | Fat: 7.6 g | Protein: 5.5 g

168. SPICY CAULIFLOWER BURGERS
(PREP. TIME: 3 MIN | COOKING: 10 MIN | SERVING 5)

INGREDIENTS
- 8 cups cauliflower
- 1 tbsp. baking powder
- 2 tsp. dried oregano
- 1/2 tsp. garlic powder
- 2/3 cup flour
- 2 dashes of Himalayan finely ground salt
- 1/4 cup + 2 tbsp. water
- 2-3 tbsp. veggie oil

DIRECTIONS:
1. Chop the cauliflower into bite-size pieces. Fill two-inch water at the pot, and into a steamer basket if you have one. Steam the cauliflower.
2. Drain the water from the pot. Once the cauliflower has cooled, place it on a clean towel or cheesecloth. Place that over a bowl, or over the sink. Press it gently so as much water comes out of it as possible.
3. Place the cauliflower in a large bowl. Beat all the other ingredients in a separate bowl, then add those whisked-together ingredients to the cauliflower. Mash all of it very well with a spoon.
4. Shape into patties with your hands. I usually make a medium-sized "snow ball" shape, and then flatten it. To cook, fry the patties in 2–3 tbsp. veggie oil on medium heat for about 5 minutes on each side. Flip, and bake another 10 minutes

Nutrition: Calories: 83 | Fat: 0.4 g | Protein: 4.5 g

169. VIETNAMESE SUMMER ROLLS
(PREP. TIME: 4 MIN | COOKING: 10 MIN | SERVING 20)

INGREDIENTS
- 2 oz. pack of rice papers
- Dipping sauce of your choice
- 3 1/2 oz. rice vermicelli
- 1 carrot
- 1 cucumber
- 1/2 mango
- 2/3 cup cherry tomatoes
- 1/3 cup roasted peanuts
- 1 handful mint leaves
- 1 handful cilantro
- 1 fresh lime
- Water
- Basil to taste

DIRECTIONS:
1. Pour some boiling water over the rice vermicelli and leave it for a few minutes until it's rehydrated but not too soggy.
2. Cut the carrot into very thin slices or "batons," long and thin sticks. Cut the cucumber and mango the same way. Halve the cherry tomatoes and crush the roasted peanuts. Chop the fresh mint leaves and basil into long strips.
3. To make the summer roles, drain the vermicelli and then pour your dressing over the noodles and let them soak further (marinate) for about 15 minutes
4. Submerge rice paper into cold water. Set it aside with a damp, clean cloth.
5. Take rice paper and submerge it in the bowl of cold water, then place it on top of the damp cloth for 10 to 15 seconds. You want it to be moist, but not so wet that it'll tear when handling it.
6. Place the marinated noodles on one side of the rice paper, a bit off-center. Add a few slices of carrot, cucumber, mango, tomatoes, peanuts, cilantro, fresh lime, and herbs. Tuck in the shorter edges and roll.

Nutrition: Calories: 59 | Fat: 1.3 g| Protein: 0.9 g

170. CHICKPEA-FREE FALAFEL WITH CORIANDER

(PREP. TIME: 5 MIN | COOKING: 0 MIN | SERVING 4)

INGREDIENTS

- 1/2 cup sunflower seeds
- 1/3 cup pumpkin seeds
- 2 tbsp. coriander leaves
- 1/2 tsp. coriander
- 1/2 tsp. cumin
- 6 sun-dried tomatoes
- 1 garlic clove
- 1 shallot
- 1/2 cup green or black olives
- 2 pinches paprika
- 2 pinches Himalaya salt

Tahini cream:

- 3 tbsp. tahini
- 2 tsp. xylitol
- 2 tbsp. lemon juice
- A pinch of Himalaya salt
- 2 tbsp. lukewarm water

DIRECTIONS:

1. Crush all the falafel ingredients in a food processor. Form into walnut-sized balls and place directly on a mesh dehydrator sheet.
2. Set dehydrator to 115°F, or place in the oven at the lowest temperature possible, 115°.
3. To make the tahini cream, blend all the ingredients in a blender with 2 tbsp. lukewarm water.
4. Top with the falafel and drizzle over the cream.

Nutrition: Calories: 301 | Fat: 26.1 g | Protein: 9.2 g

171. HEARTY ITALIAN BEAN AND BARLEY STEW

(PREP. TIME: 5 MIN | COOKING: 8 MIN | SERVING 4)

INGREDIENTS

- 2 tbsp. light olive oil
- 1 garlic clove
- 2 carrots
- 2 celery
- 1 large leek
- 1-quart vegetable stock
- 1 tbsp. tomato purée
- 3 tbsp. pearl barley
- 1 can of beans
- 2 cups of leafy greens

DIRECTIONS:

1. Cook light olive oil in a large pan on medium heat. Cook garlic, carrots, celery, and leeks.
2. Add the soup stock or bouillon, tomato purée, and barley. Cook for 2 minutes adjust to low heat and let simmer for 15-20 minutes
3. Simmer beans and greens for 5 more minutes Serve with crusty bread. Salt and pepper to taste.

Nutrition: Calories: 196 | Fat: 7.8 g | Protein: 7.6 g

172. PEA SOUP

(PREP. TIME: 2 MIN | COOKING: 13 MIN | SERVING 3)

INGREDIENTS

- 1 onion
- 3 garlic cloves
- 1 large potato
- 2 cups of peas
- 3 quarts of vegetable broth
- 1 tbsp. vegetable oil
- 1 tbsp. lemon juice
- Fresh thyme, to taste
- Chopped peanuts, to taste
- 3 tbsp. soy cream
- Salt and pepper to taste

DIRECTIONS:

1. Finely chop the onion and garlic cloves. Then, dice the potato.
2. In a large pot, cook veggie oil or sunflower oil. Add onion and garlic, sautéing until translucent, stirring occasionally. Add diced potatoes and peas, pour in the vegetable stock, and season with Himalaya salt, freshly ground pepper and finely chopped fresh herbs to taste.
3. Simmer low heat for about 15 minutes, until the potatoes and peas are tender enough you can pierce through them with a fork. Take away from heat, stir in lemon juice and blend.
4. To serve, pour in a bit of soy cream, thyme, peanuts and stir lightly.

Nutrition: Calories: 183 | Fat: 4.5 g | Protein: 5.6 g

173. SWEET POTATO CHILI

(PREP. TIME: 8 MIN | COOKING: 7 MIN | SERVING 5)

INGREDIENTS

- 1 onion large
- 2 garlic cloves
- Light olive oil to taste
- 1 tbsp. mild chili powder

- 1 tsp. ground cumin
- 3 medium sweet potatoes
- 1 cup quinoa
- 1 can tomatoes
- 2 quarts vegetable stock
- 1 can of black beans

DIRECTIONS:
1. Take a large pot. Dice the onion. Sauté onion and garlic with light olive oil. Sprinkle chili powder and cumin, then add the sweet potatoes, quinoa, tomatoes, and stock. Let simmer for about 10 minutes, then put in the beans. Half cover the pot with a lid, letting it simmer for maybe 20 to 30 more minutes Sprinkle over the coriander you've chopped up and serve with a dollop of soured cream or yogurt if you like.

Nutrition: Calories: 388 | Fat: 5.8 g | Protein: 12.1 g

174. SPICY SWEET POTATO ENCHILADAS
(PREP. TIME: 5 MIN | COOKING: 10 MIN | SERVING 6)

INGREDIENTS
- 1 large sweet potato
- 1 red onion 1
- 1 red bell pepper
- 1 green bell pepper
- 1 tsp. cumin seed
- 1 tsp. dried chili flakes
- 3 tbsp. light olive oil
- 1 small cilantro
- 4 large tortillas
- 1 1/2 cups grated vegan cheese
- Salt and pepper to taste

Enchilada sauce:
- 1 can chopped tomatoes
- 1 tsp. smoked paprika
- 1 tsp. garlic salt
- 1 tsp. dried oregano
- 1 tsp. coconut sugar
- Coriander to taste

DIRECTIONS:
1. Prep oven to 200°C/400°F /gas mark 6. Chop all of the fresh ingredients, leaving the skins on the potatoes. Finely chop the herbs.
2. Put the potatoes, onion, bell peppers/capsicum, and spices on a non-stick baking tray or a baking sheet lined with wax parchment paper. Add the oil and lots of salt and pepper, and toss well. Cook for half an hour.
3. Stir sauce ingredients together in a blender. Take away veg off the oven and leave to cool a little. Stir through 1/2 the coriander.
4. Lay out the tortillas flat and spread out the veggie mixture evenly between them. Roll up the tortillas; you may want to look up a video on the internet for this, as it helps to watch. Place the tortillas cut-side down into an oiled baking dish.
5. Drizzle sauce and sprinkle over the cheese. Bake 20 minutes Serve with vegan sour cream, the other half of the chopped coriander, and a fresh side salad.

Nutrition: Calories: 495 | Fat: 19.4 g | Protein: 13.9 g

175. RAW NUT CHEESE
(PREP. TIME: 10 MIN | COOKING: 0 MIN | SERVING 3)

INGREDIENTS
- 3 2/3 cups raw cashews
- 1 tsp. probiotic powder
- 2 tbsp. onion powder
- 1 tbsp. garlic powder
- 4–5 tbsp. nutritional yeast
- Salt and pepper to taste

DIRECTIONS:
1. Drain the water from the overnight soaked cashews. Put them in a blender with the probiotic powder, blending until smooth.
2. Wrap mixture with plastic wrap or beeswax wrap, being careful to leave a couple of tiny spaces open for air to get in. Leave the bowl at room temperature for 8 to 12 hours, or until the cheese has risen in size.
3. Sprinkle with onion powder, garlic powder, nutritional yeast, salt, and pepper.

Nutrition: Calories: 890 | Fat: 65 g | Protein: 36 g

176. ITALIAN TOMATOES
(PREP. TIME: 7 MIN | COOKING: 3 MIN | SERVING 3)

INGREDIENTS
- 2 large, ripe tomatoes
- 1 tsp. red wine vinegar
- 4 thin slices of sourdough bread
- 1/2 garlic clove
- 1 tsp. extra virgin light olive oil
- Salt and pepper to taste

DIRECTIONS:
1. Begin toasting the bread on a hot griddle, or slightly warm the Paleo bread you've made from the recipe above it if you're following a raw diet.
2. Wash and chop the tomatoes.
3. Mix the tomatoes with vinegar, salt, and pepper.

4. Press the garlic, crushing it into a fine pulp. Spread very thinly on the toast. Top the toast with the tomatoes and add a bit of light olive oil on top of each. Consume immediately.

Nutrition: Calories: 212 | Fat: 2.8 g | Protein: 6.4 g

177. GLUTEN-FREE, RAW BREAD WITH CARAWAY ONION

(PREP. TIME: 15 MIN | COOKING: 0 MIN | SERVING 4)

INGREDIENTS

- 4 1/2 oz. sunflower seeds
- 3 oz. walnuts
- 3 celery stalks
- 2 oz. raisins
- 1 red onion
- 2 tsp. caraway seeds
- 2 tbsp. ground coriander
- 2 pinches Himalayan salt
- 3 oz. ground flaxseeds
- 4 oz. extra virgin light olive oil
- 4 tbsp. lemon juice

DIRECTIONS:

1. Submerge seeds and nuts overnight or for 4-6 hours. Drain the water. Dice the onion, celery and chop the seeds. Add all into a blender or food processor and mix very well for 2-5 minutes or until well blended. Add the rest of the ingredients.
2. Pat out flat on a baking tray lined with wax paper, or put into a dehydrator. Bake at 115°F for 6 hours.

Nutrition: Calories: 212 | Fat: 2.8 g | Protein: 6.4 g

178. FLAKY HONEY BISCUITS

(PREP. TIME: 5 MIN | COOKING: 10 MIN | SERVING 6)

INGREDIENTS

- 3 cups self-rising flour
- 1 tsp. kosher salt
- 7 tbsp. chilled coconut butter, cut into 1-tbsp. pats
- 1/4 cup honey
- 1 cup buttermilk

DIRECTIONS:

1. Preheat the oven to 425°F. Line a baking sheet with parchment paper.
2. Place the flour, salt, and coconut butter pats in the bowl of a food processor. Pulse until the coconut butter pieces are the size of peas. Alternatively, use a pastry blender to blend the coconut butter into the flour. Transfer the mixture to a large bowl.
3. Using a big spoon to form a well in the middle of the flour, and pour the honey and buttermilk into the well all at once. Use a spoon to fold the flour into the buttermilk and gently stir just until the mixture comes together to form a dough.
4. Lightly flour your clean countertop or a comparable flat workspace. Spill the dough and any loose flour bits onto the floured surface. Roll the dough to about a 1-inch thickness. Crease the dough in thirds, like a business envelope, and roll out again to a 1-inch thickness.
5. Stamp out biscuits using a biscuit cutter or round glass, and arrange them on the baking sheet about 1 inch apart.
6. Bake for 9 minutes Serve warm.

Nutrition: Calories: 97 | Fat: 3 g | Protein: 2 g

179. CURRIED APPLE CHIPS

(PREP. TIME: 5 MIN | COOKING: 10 MIN | SERVING 5)

INGREDIENTS

- 1 tbsp. freshly squeezed lemon juice
- 1/2 cup water
- 2 apples, such as Fuji or Honey crisp, cored and thinly sliced into rings
- 1 tsp. curry powder

DIRECTIONS:

1. Preheat the oven to 200°F. Prep rimmed baking sheet with parchment paper.
2. Mix the lemon juice and water together in a medium bowl. As soon as the apples are sliced, add them to the bowl to soak for 2 minutes Drain and pat dry with paper towels. Let it out in a single layer on the baking sheet.
3. Place the curry powder in a sieve or other sifter and lightly dust the apple slices.
4. Bake for 45 minutes. After 45 minutes, flip the slices over and bake for another 45 minutes, again without opening the oven.
5. For the crispiest texture, let the chips cool before eating, but they're pretty fabulous slightly warm.

Nutrition: Calories: 61 | Fat: 0.1 g | Protein: 0.2 g

180. BAKED SWEET POTATO LATKES

(PREP. TIME: 4 MIN | COOKING: 11 MIN | SERVING 7)

INGREDIENTS

- 2 medium sweet potatoes, peeled and shredded

- 1/3 cup chopped scallions, white and green parts
- 1/4 cup all-purpose flour
- 1 large egg, beaten
- 1/2 tsp. smoked paprika
- 2 tbsp. oil
- Salt and pepper to taste

DIRECTIONS:
1. Preheat oven to 400°F. Grease a baking sheet with oil.
2. Combine the sweet potatoes, scallions, flour, egg, salt, paprika, and pepper in a large bowl.
3. Scoop 1/4 cup of the sweet potato mixture and place it on the baking sheet. Press down to slightly flatten. Repeat with the remaining mixture.
4. Bake for 10 minutes, flip, and continue baking for 5 to 10 minutes more until the latkes are golden brown. Don't be concerned if the edges brown more deeply and begin to crisp.
5. Take out from the oven and serve with applesauce and/or sour cream (if using).

Nutrition: Calories: 135 | Fat: 5 g | Protein: 4 g | Sodium: 345 mg

181. Huevos Rancheros Potato Skins

(Prep. Time: 4 Min | Cooking: 11 Min | Serving 6)

INGREDIENTS
- 3 large russet potatoes
- 1 1/2 cups grated Mexican cheese mix
- 1 (15 oz.) can black beans
- 6 large eggs
- Olive oil to taste

DIRECTIONS:
1. Preheat the oven to 350°F.
2. Spike the potatoes all over using a fork and microwave on high for 12 minutes, or until softened and cooked through.
3. Halve each potato lengthwise and use a spoon to scoop out the potato flesh, leaving a 1/2-inch rim of potato intact around the edges and bottoms.
4. Brush the potatoes all over, both the outside skin and the scooped-out interior, with the light olive oil, and season generously. Place the potatoes cut-side up on a baking sheet. Layer the cheese in the bottom of each potato boat, followed by the black beans, leaving enough room for an egg.
5. Crack an egg into each potato half. It's fine if the whites run over a bit, as long as the yolks stay in place.
6. Bake the potatoes until the whites firm up and the yolks are still soft, 15 to 20 minutes, depending on how soft you prefer the yolks. Remove the potatoes from the oven and top with salsa or avocado chunks (if using).

Nutrition: Calories: 405 | Fat: 17 g | Protein: 21 g

182. Cheddar and Broccoli–Stuffed Sweet Potatoes

(Prep. Time: 8 Min | Cooking: 7 Min | Serving 4)

INGREDIENTS
- 2 medium sweet potatoes
- 1 cup broccoli florets, chopped
- 2 tbsp. thinly sliced scallions
- 1 (15 oz.) can black beans
- 1/2 cup grated Cheddar cheese, divided
- 2 inches of water
- ¼ cup Coconut butter
- Salt and pepper to taste

DIRECTIONS:
1. Preheat the oven to 400°F.
2. Prick the sweet potatoes all over using a fork. Place on a baking sheet and bake for 45 to 50 minutes, or until fork-tender. Leave the oven on.
3. Halve the sweet potatoes lengthwise and let cool slightly. Scoop out the flesh of the potatoes into a small bowl, leaving at least a 1/4-inch border around the potato skins.
4. Place a steam insert in a small pot along with 2 inches of water and bring to a boil. Stir in the broccoli to the pot, cover, and steam until tender, about 5 minutes
5. Add the steamed broccoli, scallions, black beans, and coconut butter to the bowl with the scooped-out sweet potato flesh. Stir to combine and melt the coconut butter. Stir in 1/4 cup of cheese, followed by salt and pepper.
6. Stir in the potato skins with the sweet potato mixture and drizzle with the remaining 1/4 cup of cheese. Reduce the oven temperature to 350°F. Situate the stuffed sweet potatoes on the baking sheet and bake for 15 minutes

Nutrition: Calories: 295 | Fat: 8 g | Protein: 12 g

183. Caramelized Mushrooms Over Polenta

(Prep. Time: 4 Min | Cooking: 10 Min | Serving 2)

INGREDIENTS
- 1/2 (18 oz.) tube cooked polenta
- 1 yellow onion, finely diced
- 8 oz. cremini or white mushrooms
- 2 tbsp. tamari or low-sodium soy sauce
- 2 tbsp. heavy (whipping) cream
- 5 tbsp. coconut butter

DIRECTIONS:
1. Preheat the oven to 200°F.
2. Cut the polenta into 6 (1-inch) slices.
3. Cook 1 tbsp. coconut butter in a medium skillet over medium-high heat. Add the polenta slices and cook for 3 to 4 minutes, or until golden brown. Flip and cook for another 3 minutes Situate to a baking sheet, and put in the oven to stay warm.
4. Using the same skillet, cook 2 tbsp. coconut butter over medium heat. Add the onion, mushrooms, and salt, and sauté until the vegetables begin to caramelize, about 20 minutes Move the mushroom mixture around occasionally while it cooks, but not too much.
5. Using a wooden spoon, stir in the remaining 2 tbsp. coconut butter, followed by the tamari and cream. Cook until a slightly thickened sauce forms, about 2 minutes
6. Divide the polenta slices between two shallow bowls and top with the mushrooms. Serve warm.

Nutrition: Calories: 542 | Fat: 35 g | Protein: 12 g

184. GARLIC AND PARMESAN SPAGHETTI SQUASH
(PREP. TIME: 10 MIN | COOKING: 5 MIN | SERVING 4)

INGREDIENTS
- 1 (2 to 3 lb.) spaghetti squash
- 2 tbsp. coconut butter
- 2 tbsp. chopped fresh Italian parsley
- 1/3 cup grated Parmesan cheese
- 1/4 cup Roasted Pumpkin Seeds or store-bought
- 4 garlic cloves
- Salt and pepper to taste

DIRECTIONS:
1. Preheat the oven to 375°F.
2. Pierce the squash numerous times with a knife to allow steam to escape during cooking. Put on a baking sheet and roast for 1 hour, or until the squash can be easily pierced with a sharp knife. Let cool for 10 minutes before handling.
3. Chop the squash in half lengthwise then scrape out the seeds with a spoon. With the tines of a fork, lightly scoop the flesh to create long "pasta" strands. If the flesh is still a little hard, just return the squash to the baking sheet, cut-side down, and bake until the flesh is tender. Scrape out all of the pasta strands into a medium bowl.
4. Cook coconut butter in a big skillet over medium heat. Add 4 garlic cloves and sauté until fragrant, about 2 minutes Add the parsley, cheese, salt, pepper, and spaghetti squash. Carefully toss to coat. Cook for 1 to 2 more minutes
5. Situate to a serving plate and top with the pumpkin seeds.

Nutrition: Calories: 225 | Fat: 12 g | Protein: 8 g

185. ROASTED BROCCOLI BOWL WITH AN EGG
(PREP. TIME: 4 MIN | COOKING: 11 MIN | SERVING 2)

INGREDIENTS
- 2 1/2 cups water or vegetable broth
- 1/2 cup semi-pearled faro
- 1 bunch broccoli (about 1 1/2 pounds)
- 1/3 cup coarsely grated Parmesan cheese
- 2 large eggs
- 1 1/2 tsp. salt
- 3 tbsp. light olive oil
- Black pepper to taste
- 2 tbsp. lemon juice
- 2 tbsp. coconut butter

DIRECTIONS:
1. Preheat the oven to 450°F. Prep rimmed baking sheet with parchment paper.
2. Cook water in a pot at high heat. Add the faro with 1 tsp. salt. Set the heat to low to simmer, then cook until al dente, about 30 minutes Strain any excess liquid and transfer to a large bowl.
3. Slice the ends of the broccoli and slice the stems 1/2 inch thick on the diagonal. Cut the florets into bite-size pieces. The layout on the prepared baking sheet in a single layer, drizzle with 1 tbsp. light olive oil, then sprinkle with the black pepper and remaining 1/2 tsp. salt. Roast for about 15 minutes, until the florets are browned around the edges.
4. Situate the florets to the bowl with the faro, and, if necessary, continue to roast the stems until tender.
5. Place the stems in the bowl with the florets and faro. Stir in the remaining 2 tbsp. light olive oil, lemon juice, and cheese.
6. Cook coconut butter in a small nonstick skillet over medium heat. Crash the eggs into the skillet and fry until the whites just turn opaque and firm

up. Flip and cook for no more than 10 seconds for runny yolks.
7. Divide the faro-broccoli mixture between two bowls or plates and top each with a fried egg.

Nutrition: Calories: 523 | Fat: 36 g | Protein: 27 g

186. LENTIL POTATO SALAD

(PREP. TIME: 3 MIN | COOKING: 12 MIN | SERVING 2)

INGREDIENTS

- 1/2 cup beluga lentils
- 8 fingerling potatoes
- 1 cup thinly sliced scallions
- 1/4 cup halved cherry tomatoes
- 1/4 cup lemon vinaigrette
- 2 cups of water
- Salt and pepper to taste

DIRECTIONS:

1. Simmer 2 cups of water in a small pot and add the lentils. Cover and simmer for 24 minutes Drain and set aside to cool.
2. While the lentils are cooking, get a medium pot of well-salted water to a boil and add the potatoes. Decrease the heat to simmer then cook for about 15 minutes Drain. Once cool enough to handle, slice or halve the potatoes.
3. Situate the lentils on a serving plate and top with the potatoes, scallions, and tomatoes. Drizzle with the vinaigrette and season with the salt and pepper.

Nutrition: Calories: 400 | Fat: 26 g | Protein: 7 g

187. WARM GRAIN SALAD WITH MISO BUTTER

(PREP. TIME: 6 MIN | COOKING: 9 MIN | SERVING 4)

INGREDIENTS

- 2 1/2 cups water or vegetable broth
- 1 cup semi-pearled uncooked faro or 3 cups cooked
- 1 lb. green beans
- 2 cups halved cherry tomatoes
- 1/4 cup Miso Butter, at room temperature
- 1 tsp. salt
- 1 small onion
- Olive oil to taste
- Black pepper to taste

DIRECTIONS:

1. Preheat the oven to 400°F
2. Boil broth in a small pot over medium-high heat. Add the faro and 1/2 tsp. salt. Decrease the heat to a simmer, cover then cook for 30 minutes, or until al dente. (If using cooked faro, skip this step.)
3. Place the green beans, tomatoes, and 1 small onion wedges on a rimmed baking sheet. Trickle the light olive oil then toss to coat. Spread into a single layer and sprinkle evenly with the black pepper and remaining 1/2 tsp. salt. Roast until the beans and onions are tender and very lightly crisped about 15 minutes
4. When the vegetables are roasted, toss them with the faro and miso butter right on the baking pan. The heat of the pan and vegetables will melt the butter.
5. Serve warm.

Nutrition: Calories: 182 | Fat: 9 g | Protein: 6 g

188. LEMONY KALE, AVOCADO, AND CHICKPEA SALAD

(PREP. TIME: 5 MIN | COOKING: 0 MIN | SERVING 4)

INGREDIENTS

- 1 avocado, halved
- 1 bunch curly kale stems removed and discarded, leaves coarsely chopped (about 8 cups)
- 1 (15 oz.) can chickpeas, drained and rinsed
- 2 tbsp. extra-virgin light olive oil
- 1/4 cup Roasted Pumpkin Seeds or store-bought
- 2 tbsp. lemon juice
- Pepper to taste
- 1/2 tsp. salt

DIRECTIONS:

1. Spoon flesh from one of the avocado halves out of its skin and put it in a large bowl. Add 1 tbsp. lemon juice and 1/4 tsp. salt, and pound everything together. Stir in coarsely chopped kale leaves and massage them by hand with the avocado mash until the kale becomes tender. Situate kale avocado mash on a serving plate.
2. Scrape out the flesh of the remaining avocado half from its skin and chop it into bite-size chunks. Place in the bowl that contained the kale, and stirs in chickpeas.
3. Scourge light olive oil, remaining 1 tbsp. lemon juice, remaining 1/4 tsp. salt, and pepper. Sprinkle over the chickpeas and avocado and toss to mix. Mound on top of the kale-avocado mash, and garnish with the roasted pumpkin seeds.

Nutrition: Calories: 383 | Fat: 20 g | Protein: 14 g

189. Roasted Cauliflower and Rice Bowl With Tomatoes

(Prep. Time: 8 Min | Cooking: 7 Min | Serving 4)

INGREDIENTS

- 1 cup long-grain brown rice
- 2 cups water or vegetable broth
- 4 large shallots, quartered
- 4 Roma tomatoes, halved lengthwise
- 1 small cauliflower, cut into bite-size chunks, or 1 (16 oz.) bag frozen florets
- 2 tsp. salt
- Pepper to taste
- Olive oil to taste
- Balsamic vinegar to taste

DIRECTIONS:

1. Preheat the oven to 400°F. Prep rimmed baking sheet with parchment paper.
2. Rinse the rice under cool water and strain. Bring the water and 1 tsp. salt to a boil in a medium pot over medium-high heat. Stir in rice, decrease the heat to a simmer, and cover. Cook, covered, for 45 minutes, or until tender. Muddle up the cooked rice with a fork and set it aside.
3. While the rice is cooking, arrange the shallots, tomatoes (cut-sides facing up), and cauliflower on the prepared baking sheet. Trickle with the light olive oil and toss to coat. Sprinkle everything with the remaining 1 tsp. salt and pepper.
4. Roast until the cauliflower and shallots are tender and the edges just begin to crisp about 30 minutes
5. Portion brown rice between bowls and top with the roasted vegetables. Drizzle each serving with balsamic vinegar.

Nutrition: Calories: 220 | Fat: 13 g | Protein: 5 g

190. Tomato Galettes

(Prep. Time: 5 Min | Cooking: 10 Min | Serving 2)

Ingredient:

- 1 frozen store-bought pastry round
- 5 or 6 ripe Roma tomatoes, sliced crosswise 1/4 inch thick
- 2/3 cup shredded mozzarella cheese
- 1/3 cup mayonnaise
- 1/4 cup finely chopped fresh herbs
- 1/2 tsp. salt
- 1/4 tsp. pepper

DIRECTIONS:

1. Set the oven to 425°F. Situate the rack in the center of the oven. Situate the baking sheet turned upside down on the rack while the oven preheats.
2. Situate pastry round on a sheet of parchment paper on the counter.
3. Situate tomato slices in two circles starting from the middle of the pastry, slightly overlapping the tomatoes. Sprinkle the tomatoes with 1/4 tsp. salt and 1/8 tsp. black pepper
4. Incorporate mozzarella, mayonnaise, herbs, remaining 1/4 tsp. salt, and remaining 1/8 tsp. black pepper. Situate dollops of the cheese mixture over the tomatoes.
5. Crease excess dough over the tomatoes to form a crust border. Place galette on the parchment paper to the preheated pizza stone or baking sheet. Bake for 20 to 25 minutes
6. Take out from the oven then cool for 15 minutes before cutting.

Nutrition: Calories: 419 | Fat: 30 g | Protein: 12 g

191. Taco Pizzas With Refried Beans

(Prep. Time: 5 Min | Cooking: 10 Min | Serving 2)

INGREDIENTS

- 2 large naan flatbread or 2 (12-inch) store-bought pizza crusts
- 1 (16 oz.) can refried beans
- 8–10 tortilla chips, lightly crumbled
- 4 large Roma tomatoes, finely diced
- 2 (8 oz.) packages grated Mexican cheese mix

DIRECTIONS:

1. Preheat the oven to 450°F. Situate the rack in the center of the oven and put a pizza stone turned upside down on the rack while the oven heats.
2. Bake the naan on the pizza stone or upturned baking sheet until lightly toasted, about 5 minutes if using store-bought pizza crusts, follow the DIRECTIONS on the package to bake 2 pizza crusts.
3. Divide the refried beans, tortilla chips, tomatoes, and cheese between the two flatbreads. Bake for 12 minutes
4. Cut each pizza into 8 pieces then serve with your preferred toppings as desired.

Nutrition: Calories: 1346 | Fat: 81 g | Protein: 68 g

192. Avocado Toasts With Hummus

(Prep. Time: 5 Min | Cooking: 0 Min | Serving 1)

INGREDIENTS
- 2 slices of bread
- 2 tbsp. garlic hummus
- 1/2 avocado, sliced
- 3 slices red onion
- 2 tbsp. hemp seeds
- Cilantro to taste

DIRECTIONS:
1. Spread 1 tbsp. hummus on each bread slice.
2. Put the sliced avocado, red onion, and hemp seeds on each bread slice.
3. Top with cilantro.

Nutrition: Calories: 462 | Fat: 23 g | Protein: 18 g

193. Buddha Mix
(Prep. Time: 7 Min | Cooking: 8 Min | Serving 2)

INGREDIENTS
- 1/2 cup uncooked grains (rice, barley, millet, etc.)
- 3 cups leafy greens (spinach, kale, cabbage, broccoli, bell pepper, etc.)
- 1 cup cooked legumes (any beans, chickpeas, peas, edamame, etc.)

DIRECTIONS:
1. Cook your grains.
2. Chop the greens.
3. Make a tasty dressing.
4. Combine all your ingredients and mix them thoroughly.

Nutrition: Calories: 600 | Fat: 22 g | Protein: 22 g

194. Corn Pasta With Brown Butter
(Prep. Time: 5 Min | Cooking: 10 Min | Serving 6)

INGREDIENTS
- 2 cups sweet corn kernels
- 1 cup campanile pasta
- 6 tbsp. coconut butter
- 1 cup Parmesan cheese, grated
- 1/4 cup packed fresh basil leaves
- 1/4 tsp. salt and pepper

DIRECTIONS:
1. Cook the pasta. Drain it and put it aside.
2. In a saucepan, melt the coconut butter and cook it for about 2 to 4 minutes add the corn and 1/4 tsp. salt and pepper. Cook for 2 minutes and then set aside.
3. Combine the pasta with the corn mixture. Add basil, parmesan, and salt. Stir thoroughly.

Nutrition: Calories: 495 | Fat: 40.4 g | Protein: 14 g

195. Simple Garlic Bread Snack
(Prep. Time: 5 Min | Cooking: 10 Min | Serving 2)

INGREDIENTS
- 1 long baguette-style bread
- 1/4 cup coconut butter softened
- 3 garlic cloves, minced
- 1 tbsp. fresh parsley, chopped
- 1/2 cup Parmesan cheese, grated

DIRECTIONS:
1. In a separate bowl, blend the coconut butter, minced garlic, parmesan cheese, and parsley.
2. Split your bread in half and spread the coconut butter mixture over each piece.
3. Situate in the preheated oven at 190°C.
4. Bake for 10 minutes

Nutrition: Calories: 59 | Fat: 45 g | Protein: 9 g

196. Potato Chips
(Prep. Time: 10 Min | Cooking: 5 Min | Serving 4)

INGREDIENTS
- 4 potatoes, finely sliced
- 3 tbsp. light olive oil
- Vegetable-oil cooking spray
- Salt and pepper, to taste

DIRECTIONS:
1. Put the potato slices in a bowl. Sprinkle them with light olive oil. Add salt and pepper. Mix thoroughly.
2. Cover your baking sheet with cooking spray and place the potato slices on it.
3. Put your potato slices in the oven already preheated to 190°C.
4. Bake for about 30 minutes

Nutrition: Calories: 143 | Fat: 7 g | Protein: 2 g

197. Bell Peppers
(Prep. Time: 5 Min | Cooking: 10 Min | Serving 2)

INGREDIENTS
- 1/2 cup red bell peppers, roasted
- 1/3 cup lemon juice; tahini
- 1/4 tsp. basil, chopped
- 2 garlic cloves, minced

- 1 can garbanzo beans, drained
- Salt and pepper to taste

DIRECTIONS:
1. Using an electric food processor, mix the garlic, garbanzo beans, tahini, and lemon juice. Blend until smooth. Add roasted peppers and continue processing for about 30 seconds.
2. Add salt and pepper.
3. Cover with chopped basil and serve.

Nutrition: Calories: 445 | Fat: 26.9 g | Protein: 15.9 g

198. CRUNCHY ROASTED EDAMAME
(PREP. TIME: 5 MIN | COOKING: 10 MIN | SERVING 6)

INGREDIENTS
- 1 package edamame, frozen in their pods
- 2 tbsp. extra-virgin light olive oil
- 2 garlic cloves, minced
- 1 tsp. sea salt
- 1/2 tsp. ground black pepper

DIRECTIONS:
1. In a separate bowl, drizzle the edamame with sea salt, black pepper, garlic, and light olive oil. Stir thoroughly and spread on a baking sheet.
2. Cook in the oven preheated to 190°C ovens for about 20 minutes

Nutrition: Calories: 126 | Fat: 8.4 g | Protein: 7.4 g

199. TOASTED PUMPKIN SEEDS
(PREP. TIME: 10 MIN | COOKING: 5 MIN | SERVING 6)

INGREDIENTS
- 1 1/2 cups pumpkin seeds
- 2 tsp. coconut butter, melted
- A pinch of salt

DIRECTIONS:
1. Stir the pumpkin seeds, melted coconut butter, and salt together.
2. Arrange pumpkin seeds on a baking sheet. Keep on stirring until they are golden brown. Cook for about 25 minutes

Nutrition: Calories: 105 | Fat: 9 g | Protein: 5 g

200. GRILLED CHEESE SANDWICH
(PREP. TIME: 5 MIN | COOKING: 10 MIN | SERVING 2)

INGREDIENTS

- 4 slices white bread
- 5 tbsp. coconut butter, softened and divided
- 2 slices Cheddar cheese

DIRECTIONS:
1. Put 1 tbsp. coconut butter in a skillet and heat it.
2. Get two buttered bread slices and put them butter side down on the skillet.
3. Cover the two slices of bread with cheese and top them with the remaining bread. Grill until they are lightly brown and the cheese is melted.

Nutrition: Calories: 400 | Fat: 28.3 g | Protein: 11.1 g

201. GREEK CHEESE SANDWICH
(PREP. TIME: 5 MIN | COOKING: 5 MIN | SERVING 1)

INGREDIENTS
- 1 1/2 tsp. coconut butter softened
- 2 slices whole wheat bread
- 2 tbsp. Feta cheese, crumbled
- 2 slices Cheddar cheese
- 1 tbsp. red onion, chopped
- 1/4 tomato slices

DIRECTIONS:
1. Take a non-buttered bread slice and layer Feta cheese, Cheddar cheese, 1/4 tomato slices, and red onion on it.
2. Get one slice of buttered bread and put it on the layered slice of bread.
3. Fry your sandwich for about 2 minutes on each side until it is golden brown.

Nutrition: Calories: 482 | Fat: 30.9 g | Protein: 24.6 g

202. LINGUINE WITH MUSHROOMS
(PREP. TIME: 5 MIN | COOKING: 10 MIN | SERVING 6)

INGREDIENTS
- 1 lb. linguine
- 6 tbsp. light olive oil
- 12 oz. mixed mushrooms, sliced
- 1/4 cup nutritional yeast
- 2 green onions, sliced
- Salt and pepper to taste
- 3 garlic cloves

DIRECTIONS:
1. Cook linguine according to the package instructions. Reserve 3/4 of the linguine cooking water. Drain the linguine and put it aside.

2. Add sliced mushrooms and 3 garlic cloves to the pan with olive oil and fry for 5 minutes until they are browned.
3. Put the mushrooms on the linguine. Add the nutritional yeast, reserved water, onions, salt, and pepper. Stir well and serve.

Nutrition: Calories: 430 | Fat: 15 g | Protein: 15 g

203. BAKED EGGS WITH HERBS

(PREP. TIME: 5 MIN | COOKING: 10 MIN | SERVING 2)

INGREDIENTS
- 4 eggs
- 100 g baby spinach, chopped
- 1 cup double cream
- 4 tbsp. fresh pesto
- 1 tbsp. cheese, grated
- Salt and pepper to taste

DIRECTIONS:
1. Blend the pesto, spinach, cream, salt, and pepper. Divide this mixture into 2 separate dishes. Top both with the cheese.
2. Make two hollows in each dish and break an egg into each hollow.
3. Place in the oven (preheated up to 180°C) and cook for 10 minutes

Nutrition: Calories: 579 | Fat: 54 g | Protein: 19 g

204. GREEN CHICKPEA FLOUR PANCAKES

(PREP. TIME: 5 MIN | COOKING: 5 MIN | SERVING 4)

INGREDIENTS
- 1 cup chickpea flour
- 1 cup water
- 3 spring onions, chopped
- 1 tsp. turmeric
- 1 tbsp. light olive oil
- Salt and pepper to taste

DIRECTIONS:
1. Using a blender, mix the water, chickpea flour, turmeric, salt, and pepper. Add the chopped onions and heat the oil in the pan.
2. Pour the chickpea mixture into the pan and cook for 3 minutes

Nutrition: Calories: 253 | Fat: 10.1 g | Protein: 10.1 g

Chapter 4. Dinner Recipes

205. PAD THAI BOWL
(PREP. TIME: 5 MIN | COOKING: 10 MIN | SERVING 2)

INGREDIENTS
- 7 oz. brown rice noodles
- 1 tsp. light olive oil, or 1 tbsp. vegetable broth or water
- 2 carrots, peeled or scrubbed, and julienned
- 1 cup thinly sliced Napa cabbage, or red cabbage
- 1 red bell pepper, seeded and thinly sliced
- 2 scallions, finely chopped
- 2–3 tbsp. fresh mint, finely chopped
- 1 cup bean sprouts
- 1/4 cup Peanut Sauce
- 1/4 cup fresh cilantro, finely chopped
- 2 tbsp. roasted peanuts, chopped
- Fresh lime wedges

DIRECTIONS:
1. Preparing the ingredients.
2. Situate the rice noodles in a pot, then cover them with boiling water. Let it sit until they soften for about 10 minutes Rinse, drain, and set aside to cool. Heat the oil in a large skillet to medium-high, and sauté the carrots, cabbage, and bell pepper until softened for 7 to 8 minutes Toss in the scallions, mint, and bean sprouts and cook for a minute or two, then remove from the heat.
3. Finish and serve
4. Toss the noodles with the vegetables, and mix in the peanut sauce. Transfer to bowls, and sprinkle with cilantro and peanuts. Serve with a lime wedge to squeeze onto the dish for a flavor boost.

Nutrition: Calories: 660 | Fat: 19 g | Protein: 15 g | Carbohydrates: 110 g

206. GREEN PEA RISOTTO
(PREP. TIME: 5 MIN | COOKING: 10 MIN | SERVING 4)

INGREDIENTS
- 1 tsp. vegan butter
- 4 tsp. minced garlic (about 4 cloves)
- 1 cup Arborio rice
- 2 cups vegetable broth
- 1/4 tsp. salt
- 2 tbsp. nutritional yeast
- 3 tbsp. lemon juice (about 1 1/2 small lemons)
- 2 cups fresh, canned, or frozen (thawed) green peas
- 1/4–1/2 tsp. freshly ground black pepper, to taste

DIRECTIONS:
1. Preparing the ingredients
2. Using a skillet at medium-high heat, heat the vegan butter.
3. Add the garlic and sauté for about 3 minutes
4. Add the rice, broth, and salt, and stir to combine well.
5. Bring to boil. Reduce the heat to low and simmer for about 30 minutes until the broth is absorbed and the rice is tender. Mix in the yeast and lemon juice.
6. Gently fold in the peas. Taste before seasoning with the pepper.
7. Finish and serve
8. Divide the risotto evenly among 4 single-serving containers. Let cool before sealing the lids.

Nutrition: Calories: 144 | Fat: 2 g | Protein: 10 g | Carbohydrates: 24 g

207. THREE-BEAN CHILI
(PREP. TIME: 4 MIN | COOKING: 11 MIN | SERVING 4)

INGREDIENTS
- 1 tbsp. extra-virgin light olive oil
- 1 medium yellow onion, chopped
- 3 garlic cloves, minced
- 1 (28 oz.) can crushed tomatoes
- 1 (4 oz.) can chop mild green chilies
- 1 cup water
- 3 tbsp. chili powder
- 1 canned chipotle chili in adobo, minced
- 1 tsp. ground cumin
- 1/2 tsp. dried marjoram
- 1 1/2 cup cooked or 1 (15.5 oz.) can black beans, drained and rinsed
- 1 1/2 cup cooked or 1 (15.5 oz.) can Great Northern or other white beans, drained and rinsed
- 1 1/2 cup cooked or 1 (15.5 oz.) can dark red kidney beans, drained and rinsed
- Salt and freshly ground black pepper
- 2 tbsp. Coconut sugar

DIRECTIONS:
1. Preparing the ingredients.

2. Using a saucepan, Cook oil over medium heat. Stir in the onion and garlic, cover, and cook for 7 minutes
3. Add the tomatoes, green chilies, water, chili powder, chipotle, cumin, marjoram, and coconut sugar. Stir in the black beans, Great Northern beans, and kidney beans, then season with salt and pepper. Boil, then reduce the heat to low and simmer, uncovered while stirring occasionally for 45 minutes
4. Finish and serve
5. Uncover, and cook for 13 minutes to allow flavors to develop and for the chili to thicken. Serve immediately.

Nutrition: Calories: 147 | Fat: 3 g | Protein: 11 g | Carbohydrates: 24 g

208. CHINESE BLACK BEAN CHILI
(PREP. TIME: 5 MIN | COOKING: 0 MIN | SERVING 4)

INGREDIENTS
- 1 tbsp. extra-virgin light olive oil
- 1 medium yellow onion, finely chopped
- 2 medium carrots, finely chopped
- 1 tsp. grated fresh ginger
- 2 tbsp. chili powder
- 1 tsp. brown sugar
- 1 (28 oz.) can diced tomatoes, undrained
- 1/2 cup Chinese black bean sauce
- 3/4 cup water
- 4 1/2 cups cooked black beans
- Salt and freshly ground black pepper
- 2 tbsp. minced green onion, for garnish

DIRECTIONS:
1. Preparing the ingredients.
2. Using a pot, cook the oil over medium heat. Add the onion and carrot. Cover and cook for 11 minutes
3. Stir in the ginger, chili powder, and sugar. Add the tomatoes, black bean sauce, and water. Stir in the black beans and season with salt and pepper.
4. Boil then decrease the heat to medium and simmer, covered, until the vegetables are tender for about 30 minutes
5. Finish and serve
6. Simmer for about 10 minutes longer. Serve immediately garnished with green onion.

Nutrition: Calories: 137 | Fat: 2 g | Protein: 14 g | Carbohydrates: 20 g

209. NEW WORLD CHILI
(PREP. TIME: 5 MIN | COOKING: 10 MIN | SERVING 4)

INGREDIENTS
- 1 piece small butternut squash
- 1 tbsp. extra-virgin light olive oil
- 1 medium onion, chopped
- 3 cups mild tomato salsa, homemade or store-bought
- 3 cups cooked pinto beans
- 1 cup frozen lima beans
- 1 cup fresh or frozen corn kernels
- 1 canned chipotle chili in adobo, minced
- 1 cup water
- 3 tbsp. chili powder
- 1/2 tsp. ground allspice
- 1/2 tsp. coconut sugar
- Salt and freshly ground black pepper

DIRECTIONS:
1. Preparing the ingredients.
2. Cut the squash into 1/4-inch dice and put it aside. Using a saucepan, heat the oil over medium heat. Add the onion and squash, cover, then cook until softened for about 10 minutes
3. Add the salsa, pinto beans, lima beans, corn, and chipotle chili. Stir chili powder, allspice, sugar, and salt, and black pepper into the water. Boil, then lessen the heat to medium and simmer, covered, until the vegetables are tender for about 45 minutes
4. Finish and serve
5. Uncover and simmer for about 10 minutes longer. Serve immediately.

Nutrition: Calories: 546 | Fat: 19 g | Protein: 18 g | Carbohydrates: 81 g

210. BUTTERNUT SQUASH GNOCCHI
(PREP. TIME: 3 MIN | COOKING: 12 MIN | SERVING 4)

INGREDIENTS
- 1/2 butternut squash, seeded, peeled, and diced
- 3 garlic cloves
- 1 cup vegetable broth
- 3 cups gnocchi, fresh
- 1/4 cup basil
- 1 tbsp. vegan butter

DIRECTIONS:
1. Cut butternut squash in half and peel and chop one half. It doesn't matter that much what size you cut the pieces or whether or not they're even.
2. Add the butternut squash to a large pot over medium heat with either light olive oil or a tbsp.

vegan butter. Allow it to slowly cook, uncovered, until very tender (about 30 minutes). The slower you cook the squash, the more caramelized and delicious it will become.
3. Once the squash is sufficiently creamy, add the vegetable broth, garlic, and gnocchi.
4. Boil, then reduce to a simmer. Cook for about two minutes, stirring frequently. As you stir, your butternut squash should break down, creating a creamy sauce with the gnocchi.
5. Add the basil, and vegan butter or parmesan if you would like, and stir together.
6. Remove from heat once the gnocchi is cooked (about 2 to 4 minutes total). Be careful not to overcook.
7. Serve with a dusting of vegan parmesan, salt, or some fresh basil leaves.

Nutrition: Calories: 407 | Fat: 11 g | Protein: 9 g

211. NO-COOK QUESADILLA

(PREP. TIME: 5 MIN | COOKING: 0 MIN | SERVING 2)

INGREDIENTS

- 1 avocado
- 1 cup vegan Queso
- 1/4 red onion, diced
- 2 tortillas
- 1 cup fresh salsa

DIRECTIONS:

1. Microwave the tortillas for about one minute.
2. Meanwhile, slice the avocado in half and dice the onions.
3. Smear the tortillas with as much avocado and Queso as you want and sprinkle with onions. Fold the tortillas closed when you're done.
4. Serve with salsa for dipping and some lime wedges, if desired.

Nutrition: Calories: 340 | Fat: 42 g | Protein: 17 g

212. BBQ SANDWICH

(PREP. TIME: 5 MIN | COOKING: 10 MIN | SERVING 2)

INGREDIENTS

- 1 block tofu
- 1 cup chickpeas, canned, rinsed
- 1/2 cup vegan BBQ sauce
- 2 buns
- 1 carrot, shredded
- Olive oil to taste

DIRECTIONS:

1. Crumble the tofu into pieces. If you prefer softer tofu, make bigger pieces. If you like crispy tofu, break the tofu into smaller pieces.
2. Fry the tofu in a pan with light olive oil until it reaches your desired consistency.
3. Add the chickpeas to the pan and allow them to warm up for a few minutes
4. Add the barbeque sauce to the pan with the tofu and chickpeas. Stir until evenly coated and warm, and then remove from heat.
5. Load up the buns with the mixture and top with shredded carrot.

Nutrition: Calories: 592 | Fat: 17 g | Protein: 35 g

213. CAULIFLOWER CHICKPEA SHEET PAN MEAL

(PREP. TIME: 5 MIN | COOKING: 10 MIN | SERVING 2)

INGREDIENTS

- 1 head cauliflower
- 1 head garlic
- 1 cup chickpeas, canned
- 1/4 cup tahini
- 1 lemon, juiced
- Olive oil to taste
- Salt to taste

DIRECTIONS:

1. Chop up the cauliflower and drizzle with light olive oil.
2. Cut the top off of the head of garlic, leaving the cloves exposed. Sprinkle with light olive oil and salt.
3. Place the garlic and cauliflower in a large pan and bake at 350°F for about 35 minutes, just until the cauliflower has become soft and roasted.
4. Pullout from the oven and let cool for 5 minutes
5. Squeeze the garlic out and throw away the skin. Mix the tahini, lemon juice, chickpeas, and salt with cauliflower and garlic.
6. Serve warm alone or with tortillas and guacamole.

Nutrition: Calories: 443 | Fat: 25 g |Protein: 17 g

214. MEDITERRANEAN QUESADILLA

(PREP. TIME: 10 MIN | COOKING: 5 MIN | SERVING 2)

INGREDIENTS

- 1/4 cup garlic hummus
- 1 roasted eggplant, sliced
- 1 roasted red pepper, sliced

- 2 tortillas
- Cherry tomatoes, quartered
- Olive oil to taste
- Salt to taste

DIRECTIONS:

1. Sprinkle the eggplant slices with light olive oil, sprinkle with salt, and place in a baking tray.
2. Slice the red pepper and add it to the baking tray. Roast the veggies together at 400°F for about 30 minutes, flipping the eggplant about halfway through.
3. While the veggies are cooling, heat up the tortillas in the microwave for about a minute.
4. Spread about two tbsp. of garlic hummus on the tortillas. Add the roasted eggplant and red pepper slices. Drizzle with light olive oil if you'd like. Throw on some cherry tomatoes and any other extras you might want.

Nutrition: Calories: 217 | Fat: 5 g | Protein: 8 g

215. CAULIFLOWER NACHOS
(PREP. TIME: 5 MIN | COOKING: 10 MIN | SERVING 2)

INGREDIENTS
- 1 head cauliflower
- 1 cup vegan cheddar cheese
- 1 14.5 oz. can black beans
- 1/2 cup salsa
- 1/2 cup guacamole
- Olive oil to taste

DIRECTIONS:

1. Chop the cauliflower into florets, drizzle with light olive oil (no need to overdo it), and roast at 400°F for about 25 minutes You want the cauliflower to be slightly browned.
2. Get the pan out of the oven and cover the cauliflower in vegan cheese and black beans. Situate back in the oven until the cheese is melted.
3. Serve with salsa and guacamole for dipping.

Nutrition: Calories: 276 | Fat: 6 g | Protein: 15 g

216. SIMPLE PASTA
(PREP. TIME: 4 MIN | COOKING: 11 MIN | SERVING 2)

INGREDIENTS
- 3/4 cup dry white wine (Sauvignon Blanc is a good choice; avoid Chardonnay)
- 6 oz. spaghetti
- 1/4 cup vegan parmesan (or nutritional yeast)
- 4 garlic cloves, minced
- 1 1/2 cups vegetable broth
- Olive oil to taste

DIRECTIONS:

1. Using a big pot, cook light olive oil and add the minced garlic.
2. When the garlic has become fragrant, pour in vegetable broth, wine, and spaghetti.
3. Cook until the pasta is ready. It should only take about 10 minutes you should cook this pasta like you would cook risotto. The liquid should all absorb, and you will not have to drain the pasta.
4. If you'd like to make this recipe gluten-free, opt for gluten-free spaghetti rather than zucchini noodles. The zucchini noodles won't get as creamy as spaghetti.
5. Once the pasta is ready, add some vegan parmesan and stir while still hot. This will absorb excess liquid and help to create a creamier texture.

Nutrition: Calories: 623 | Fat: 22 g | Protein: 17 g

217. SWEET AND SAVORY TOFU
(PREP. TIME: 4 MIN | COOKING: 11 MIN | SERVING 4)

INGREDIENTS
- 1 block tofu, extra firm
- 1/2 cup apple cider
- 3 tbsp. maple syrup
- 1 tsp. mustard
- 1 tsp. apple cider vinegar
- Salt and pepper to taste

DIRECTIONS:

1. Slice the tofu lengthwise to desired thickness. For sandwiches and burgers, go for about half an inch thick.
2. In a separate bowl, blend apple cider vinegar, apple cider, maple syrup, and mustard.
3. Dip the tofu in the mixture, making sure that both sides are coated evenly. Reserve some of the mixture.
4. Bake at 400°F for 30 minutes as the tofu bakes, you may need to brush it with more of the liquid mixture.
5. Serve warm or cold, with grain, alone, or on a salad. Sprinkle with salt and pepper to taste.

Nutrition: Calories: 262 | Fat: 16 g | Protein: 15 g

218. One-Pot Pumpkin Curry

(Prep. Time: 5 Min | Cooking: 10 Min | Serving 4)

INGREDIENTS

- 1 1/2 cups pumpkin, peeled and cubed
- 1 can coconut milk
- 2 cans chickpeas, rinsed and drained
- 1/4 cup curry powder
- 1 cup cauliflower

DIRECTIONS:

1. Stir in chopped pumpkin and cauliflower to a pot with coconut milk, curry powder, and salt as needed.
2. Boil then reduce to a simmer. You may need to add water as the pumpkin cooks and the liquid evaporates.
3. Once the pumpkin is cooked to your desired tenderness you can use an immersion blender to make a creamy base, or you can leave it chunky.
4. Add chickpeas to the curry and allow it to heat up.
5. Serve warm with a grain, naan, or alone.

Nutrition: Calories: 375 | Fat: 20 g | Protein: 10 g

219. Millet Stuffed Zucchini Boats

(Prep. Time: 5 Min | Cooking: 10 Min | Serving 3)

INGREDIENTS

- 4 zucchinis
- 1 1/2 cups salsa
- 2 cups millet, cooked
- 1/2 cup black olives, sliced
- 1 bell pepper, diced
- Salt and pepper to taste

DIRECTIONS:

1. Slice off the ends of the zucchini. Slice in half lengthwise. With a spoon, remove the pulp, making enough space to pack the zucchini full of goodies.
2. Bake the zucchini at 375°F for about 15 to 20 minutes, until it is tender and has released water. Drain the excess water.
3. Mix the cooked millet, black olives, salsa, and diced bell peppers in a bowl. Season with salt and pepper. Pack the zucchini boats with the millet mixture. Bake for another 15–20 minutes
4. Serve warm with any toppings you choose.

Nutrition: Calories: 439 | Fat: 5 g | Protein: 21 g

220. Meat(less) Loaf

(Prep. Time: 10 Min | Cooking: 4 Min | Serving 8)

INGREDIENTS

- 1 cup green lentils
- 1/2 cup oats
- 3 tbsp. garlic powder
- 1/4 cup ketchup
- 1 onion, diced
- Water

DIRECTIONS:

1. Stir in lentils to a large pot and cover with water. Boil then reduce heat and simmer for about 40 minutes until the lentils are thoroughly cooked. Once the lentils are finished, set aside to cool without draining.
2. With a food processor, blend about half of the lentils to help everything stick together.
3. With a spoon, mix in the onion, garlic powder, oats, and ketchup.
4. Add to a bread pan and bake for about 45 minutes

Nutrition: Calories: 213 | Fat: 1 g | Protein: 22 g

221. Tropical Protein Bowl

(Prep. Time: 15 Min | Cooking: 0 Min | Serving 4)

INGREDIENTS

- 2 cups quinoa, cooked
- 1 cup black beans, canned
- 1 ripe mango, diced
- 1 cup arugula
- 1/4 cup green goddess dressing (for the recipe, click here)
- ¼ cup mixed greens

DIRECTIONS:

1. Rinse the canned black beans and mixed greens.
2. Split the arugula between serving bowls. Top with the cooked quinoa and black beans. The quinoa should not be hot or it will wilt the greens.
3. Dice the mango and sprinkle it on top. Drizzle with green goddess dressing, mix and serve. Top with pumpkin seeds if desired.

Nutrition: Calories: 472 | Fat: 16 g | Protein: 16 g

222. Rainbow Pinwheels

(Prep. Time: 10 Min | Cooking: 0 Min | Serving 2)

INGREDIENTS

- 2 bell peppers, red, orange, or yellow
- 1 carrot, sliced

- 1/4 cup hummus
- 2 corn tortillas
- 1 cup mixed greens

DIRECTIONS:
1. Slice the carrot and bell peppers. Rinse the mixed greens if needed.
2. Slather your tortillas in hummus. Hummus provides the protein for this recipe, so don't be afraid to be generous!
3. Top the hummus with the mixed greens and veggies, arranging in rainbow color order.
4. Roll up the tortillas, and then cut them into four pieces each.

Nutrition: Calories: 200 | Fat: 5 g | Protein: 7 g

223. Spaghetti Squash With Sundried Tomato Sauce
(Prep. Time: 5 Min | Cooking: 10 Min | Serving 2)

INGREDIENTS
- 1 spaghetti squash
- 3 garlic cloves, minced
- 1/4 cup basil
- 1/2 cup sun-dried tomatoes, chopped
- 1/2 cup cashews, unsalted and soaked

DIRECTIONS:
1. Cut the spaghetti squash in half. If this is difficult, you can pop the squash in the microwave for a minute or two to soften it. Scoop out the seeds.
2. Roast in the oven at 400°F for 40 minutes
3. While the squash is cooking, incorporate soaked cashews, garlic, basil, and sun-dried tomatoes in a food processor. Blend to your desired consistency. For a chunkier sauce, leave out the tomatoes until the end.
4. When the squash is tender, spoon it out of the skin with a fork. You can throw the skin away.
5. Mix with the tomato sauce and serve topped with fresh basil, salt, or vegan parmesan.

Nutrition: Calories: 236 | Fat: 14 g | Protein: 8 g

224. Simple Stir Fry
(Prep. Time: 10 Min | Cooking: 5 Min | Serving 2)

INGREDIENTS
- 2 cups rice noodles
- 1/4 cup soy-tahini dressing (click here for recipe)
- 1 cup zucchini noodles
- 1 carrot, medium, peeled, and julienne
- 1 red bell pepper
- Water

DIRECTIONS:
1. In a large skillet, heat your chosen cooking oil. Add the veggies and reduce to medium or medium-low heat. Stir frequently to prevent burning.
2. Boil water in a pot. Mix in rice noodles and cook until tender. Drain when finished.
3. Once your veggies have reached their desired tenderness, toss them with the soy-tahini dressing and serve on top of the rice noodles. You can add more dressing to the rice noodles as needed.

Nutrition: Calories: 386 | Fat: 2 g | Protein: 4 g

225. Quinoa Lentil Burgers
(Prep. Time: 5 Min | Cooking: 10 Min | Serving 8)

INGREDIENTS
- 1/2 cup red lentils, dry
- 2–3 garlic cloves, minced
- 1 red onion, diced
- 2 flax eggs
- 1 cup quinoa, dry
- 3 cups water
- Salt to taste

DIRECTIONS:
1. Using a big pot, mix lentils and quinoa and cover with 3 cups water. Boil, then decrease the heat to simmer and cook until both are tender and all liquid has cooked away (about 15 minutes).
2. In a big bowl mix flax egg with minced garlic, chopped onions, and salt. Mix in the quinoa-and-lentil mixture.
3. Use your hands to shape burgers out of the mixture and place them an inch apart on a baking sheet. Freeze any that you would like to eat later.
4. Bake the remainder at 400°F for about 15 to 20 minutes on each side, depending on how crispy you want your burgers.
5. Serve alone, cut up in a salad, or on a bun with your favorite toppings.

Nutrition: Calories: 125 | Fat: 2 g | Protein: 6 g

226. Sage Zucchini Noodles
(Prep. Time: 5 Min | Cooking: 10 Min | Serving 2)

INGREDIENTS
- 2 zucchinis
- 1/4 cup sage, fresh
- 1/4 cup walnuts, chopped

- 1/3 cup spinach
- 3 garlic cloves, minced
- 3 tbsp. Olive oil
- Black pepper to taste

DIRECTIONS:
1. For this recipe, you'll need a vegetable spiralizer to make the zucchini noodles.
2. Once the noodles are ready, sauté the light olive oil and garlic in a pan for about 3 minutes over medium-high heat.
3. Add the sage and repeat.
4. Add the zucchini noodles and sauté for about 5 minutes
5. Remove from heat and mix with spinach, walnuts, and black pepper.

Nutrition: Calories: 267 | Fat: 24 g | Protein: 5 g

227. TWICE BAKED BUTTERNUT SQUASH
(PREP. TIME: 9 MIN | COOKING: 6 MIN | SERVING 4)

INGREDIENTS
- 1/2 butternut squash
- 1/4 cup vegan butter
- 4 garlic cloves
- 1/4 cup white wine, dry
- 2 tbsp. nutritional yeast or vegan parmesan

DIRECTIONS:
1. Chop butternut squash in half and scoop out the seeds.
2. Bake at 350°F until tender (about 45 minutes or more; the more you roast the butternut squash, the more caramelized it becomes).
3. Once tender, pull out of the oven. Spoon the soft squash out of the skin and retain the skin. Mix the squash in a bowl with vegan butter, white wine, garlic, and vegan parmesan.
4. Situate the mixture back in the skin and bake for 10 more minutes, just long enough to reduce the wine.

Nutrition: Calories: 137 | Fat: 9 g | Protein: 3 g

228. ULTRA-CRISPY ROASTED POTATOES
(PREP. TIME: 6 MIN | COOKING: 9 MIN | SERVING 4)

INGREDIENTS
- 4 potatoes
- 2–4 garlic cloves, minced
- 1 onion, diced
- 1 tbsp. paprika
- 2 tbsp. baking soda
- Water
- Olive oil to taste

DIRECTIONS:
1. Chop the potatoes to your desired size and add to a pot of boiling water with the baking soda.
2. Boil the potatoes for 21 minutes
3. In the meantime, chop the onion and mince the garlic.
4. Drain the potatoes and mix with light olive oil, onion, garlic, and paprika.
5. Bake at 400°F for 40 minutes you may want to flip them after 20 minutes Remove and serve once they have reached crispy perfection.

Nutrition: Calories: 165 | Fat: 1 g | Protein: 5 g

229. GLUTEN-FREE CAULIFLOWER FRIED "RICE"
(PREP. TIME: 5 MIN | COOKING: 10 MIN | SERVING 4)

INGREDIENTS
- 1 head cauliflower, riced
- 4 garlic cloves, minced
- 2 cups selected veggies (diced carrots or peas recommended)
- 1 tbsp. ginger, minced
- 1/4 cup tamari sauce (or soy), low-sodium

DIRECTIONS:
1. If you do not have cauliflower rice, make some yourself ahead of time. Mince the garlic and ginger, and dice any chosen veggies.
2. Over medium-high heat, sauté the garlic and ginger in the cooking oil until fragrant, then add the veggies and sauté for a few more minutes
3. Add the cauliflower and cook until tender. Drizzle a few tbsp. of naturally gluten-free tamari to taste.

Nutrition: Calories: 78 | Fat: 1 g | Protein: 6 g

230. MUSHROOM CAULIFLOWER RISOTTO
(PREP. TIME: 10 MIN | COOKING: 5 MIN | SERVING 4)

INGREDIENTS
- 1 head of cauliflower, grated
- 1 cup vegetable stock
- 9 oz. mushrooms, chopped
- 1 cup coconut cream
- 2 tbsp. coconut butter

DIRECTIONS:

1. Fill in stock into a saucepan and bring it to a boil. Set it aside.
2. Melt coconut butter in a skillet and add mushrooms to the sauté until golden brown.
3. Stir in grated cauliflower and stock.
4. Bring the mixture to a simmer. Add cream.
5. Cook until liquid is absorbed and cauliflower is al dente.
6. Serve.

Nutrition:: Calories: 186 | Fat: 17.1 g | Fiber: 2.4 g

231. HALLOUMI BURGER
(PREP. TIME: 10 MIN | COOKING: 0 MIN | SERVING 4)

INGREDIENTS
- 15 oz. halloumi cheese
- Coconut butter or coconut oil to taste
- 6 2/3 tbsp. sour cream
- 6 2/3 tbsp. mayonnaise
- Sliced vegetables, of your choice

DIRECTIONS:
1. Mix sour cream with mayonnaise in a bowl and cover the bowl. Refrigerate until further use.
2. Melt coconut butter in a skillet and add halloumi cheese to cook until soft and light brown.
3. Place the cheese on the platter and top it with the mayo mixture and vegetables.
4. Serve.

Nutrition:: Calories: 534 | Fat: 45.1 g | Protein: 23.8 g

232. CREAMY GREEN CABBAGE
(PREP. TIME: 5 MIN | COOKING: 10 MIN | SERVING 4)

INGREDIENTS
- 2 oz. coconut butter
- 1 1/2 lbs. green cabbage, shredded
- 1 1/4 cups coconut cream
- Salt and pepper
- 8 tbsp. fresh parsley, finely chopped

DIRECTIONS:
1. Heat coconut butter in a skillet and add cabbage to the sauté until golden brown.
2. Stir in cream and bring it to a simmer.
3. Add salt and pepper for seasoning.
4. Garnish with parsley.
5. Serve warm.

Nutrition: Calories: 432 | Fat: 42.3 g | Protein: 4.2 g

233. CHEESY BROCCOLI AND CAULIFLOWER
(PREP. TIME: 4 MIN | COOKING: 10 MIN | SERVING 4)

INGREDIENTS
- 8 oz. cauliflower, chopped
- 1 lb. broccoli, chopped
- 5 1/3 oz. shredded cheese
- 2 oz. coconut butter
- 4 tbsp. sour cream

DIRECTIONS:
1. Melt coconut butter in a big skillet then stir in all the vegetables.
2. Sauté over medium-high heat until golden brown.
3. Add all the remaining ingredients to the vegetables.
4. Mix well then serve.

Nutrition: Calories 244 | Fat 20.4 g | Protein 12.3 g

234. GREEN BEANS WITH ROASTED ONIONS
(PREP. TIME: 4 MIN | COOKING: 10 MIN | SERVING 6)

INGREDIENTS
- 1 yellow onion, sliced into rings
- 1/2 tsp. salt
- 1/2 tsp. onion powder
- 2 tbsp. coconut flour
- 1 1/3 lbs. fresh green beans, trimmed and chopped
- Oil to taste

DIRECTIONS:
1. Mix salt with onion powder and coconut flour in a large bowl.
2. Add onion rings and mix well to coat.
3. Spread the rings in the baking sheet, lined with parchment paper.
4. Top them with some oil and bake for 10 minutes at 400°F.
5. Meanwhile, parboil the green beans for 3 to 5 minutes in the boiling water.
6. Drain and serve the beans with baked onion rings.
7. Serve.

Nutrition: Calories: 214 | Fat: 19.4 g | Protein: 8.3 g

235. EGGPLANT FRIES
(PREP. TIME: 10 MIN | COOKING: 5 MIN | SERVING 8)

INGREDIENTS
- 2 eggplants, peeled and cut into French Fry shape

- 2 cups almond flour
- Salt and pepper
- 2 eggs
- 2 tbsp. coconut oil spray

DIRECTIONS:
1. Prep your oven to 400°F (200°C).
2. Combine almond flour with salt and black pepper in a bowl.
3. Beat eggs in another bowl until frothy
4. Soak the eggplant pieces into the egg then coat them with a flour mixture.
5. Add another layer of egg and flour.
6. Arrange these pieces on a greased baking sheet and top them with the coconut oil on top.
7. Bake for about 15 minutes until crispy.
8. Serve warm.

Nutrition: Calories: 212 | Fat: 15.7 g | Protein: 8.5 g

236. GARLIC FOCACCIA
(PREP. TIME: 3 MIN | COOKING: 12 MIN | SERVING 8)

INGREDIENTS
- 1 1/2 cups shredded mozzarella cheese
- 2 tbsp. cream cheese
- 1 egg
- 3/4 cup almond flour
- Salt to taste
- 1 garlic clove

DIRECTIONS:
1. Prep the oven to 400°F (200°C).
2. Heat cream cheese with mozzarella in a small pan until soft. Mix well.
3. Stir in all the remaining ingredients to the pan. Mix again.
4. Add water if the mixture is too thick, to attain a dough-like consistency.
5. Place this dough into an 8inch round baking pan lined with parchment paper
6. Pierce some holes in the bread using a fork.
7. Bake for 12 minutes
8. Serve with melted coconut butter on top or as desired.
9. Enjoy.

Nutrition: Calories: 135 | Fat: 9.9 g | Protein: 8.6 g

237. PORTOBELLO MUSHROOMS
(PREP. TIME: 3 MIN | COOKING: 10 MIN | SERVING 4)

INGREDIENTS
- 12 cherry tomatoes
- 2 oz. scallions
- 4 portabella mushrooms, stems removed
- 4 1/4 oz. light olive oil
- Salt and pepper to taste

DIRECTIONS:
1. Cook light olive oil in a big skillet over medium heat.
2. Stir in mushrooms and sauté for 3 minutes
3. Stir in cherry tomatoes and scallions.
4. Sauté for about 5 minutes
5. Adjust seasoning with salt and pepper.
6. Sauté until vegetables are soft
7. Serve warm and enjoy.

Nutrition: Calories: 154 | Fat: 10.4 g | Protein: 6.7 g

238. BUTTER-FRIED GREEN CABBAGE
(PREP. TIME: 5 MIN | COOKING: 11 MIN | SERVING 4)

INGREDIENTS
- 1 1/2 lbs. shredded green cabbage
- 3 oz. vegan butter
- Salt to taste
- Freshly ground black pepper, to taste
- 1 dollop, whipped cream

DIRECTIONS:
1. Melt vegan butter in a large skillet.
2. Stir in cabbage and sauté for about 15 minutes until golden brown.
3. Season with salt and pepper.
4. Serve warm with a dollop of cream.

Nutrition: Calories: 199 | Fat: 17.4 g | Protein: 2.4 g

239. ASIAN GARLIC TOFU
(PREP. TIME: 10 MIN | COOKING: 4 MIN | SERVING 4)

INGREDIENTS
- 1 package super firm tofu
- 1/4 cup Hoisin sauce
- 1 tsp. ginger garlic paste
- 1/4 tsp. red pepper flakes
- 1 tsp. sesame oil

DIRECTIONS:
1. Pull out tofu from packaging. Situate about 4 paper towels on a plate.
2. Place tofu on top of the plate and cover with more paper towels.
3. Situate heavy cast iron pan on top. Let sit 30 minutes

4. Incorporate all the remaining **INGREDIENTS** in a bowl and set them aside.
5. Slice the tofu into small cubes and transfer them to the marinade.
6. Mix well and marinate for 30 minutes
7. Cook oil in a skillet and add tofu to the sauté until golden brown from all sides.
8. Garnish with green onions.
9. Serve warm.

Nutrition: Calories: 467 | Fat: 28.5 g | Protein: 45.9 g

240. STUFFED MUSHROOMS
(PREP. TIME: 4 MIN | COOKING: 10 MIN | SERVING 4)

INGREDIENTS
- 4 Portobello mushrooms
- 1 cup crumbled blue cheese
- Fresh thyme to taste
- 2 tbsp. extra virgin light olive oil
- Salt to taste

DIRECTIONS:
1. Preheat the oven to 350°F.
2. Cut off the stems from the mushrooms and chop them into small pieces.
3. Mix stems pieces with blue cheese, thyme and salt in a bowl.
4. Stuff each mushroom with the prepared cheese filling.
5. Drizzle some oil on top and place the mushrooms on a baking sheet.
6. Bake for 15 to 20 minutes
7. Serve warm.

Nutrition: Calories: 124 | Fat: 22.4 g | Fiber: 2.8 g

241. CREAMY LEEKS
(PREP. TIME: 4 MIN | COOKING: 11 MIN | SERVING 6)

INGREDIENTS
- 1 1/2 lb. leeks, trimmed and chopped into 4-inch pieces
- 2 oz. vegan butter
- 1 cup coconut cream
- 3 1/2 oz. cheddar cheese
- Salt and pepper to taste

DIRECTIONS:
1. Prep the oven to 400°F (200°C).
2. Cook vegan butter in a skillet over medium heat.
3. Add leeks to sauté for 5 minutes
4. Spread the leeks in a greased baking dish.
5. Boil cream in a saucepan then reduces the heat to low.
6. Stir in cheese, salt, and pepper.
7. Pour this sauce over the leeks.
8. Bake for about 15 to 20 minutes
9. Serve warm.

Nutrition: Calories: 204 | Fat: 15.7 g | Protein: 6.3 g

242. PARMESAN CROUTONS
(PREP. TIME: 10 MIN | COOKING: 4 MIN | SERVING 8)

INGREDIENTS
- 1 1/2 cups almond flour
- 2 tsp. baking powder
- 1 tsp. sea salt
- 1 1/4 cups boiling water
- 3 egg whites
- Parmesan cheese totaste

DIRECTIONS:
1. Prep the oven to 350°F (175°C).
2. Mix almond flour with salt and baking powder in a bowl.
3. Whisk egg whites and add to the dry mixture.
4. Mix well with water until it forms a smooth dough.
5. Prepare 8 flat pieces of dough using moist hands.
6. Layout the flattened dough on a baking sheet some distance apart.
7. Bake them for about 40 minutes
8. Drizzle parmesan cheese on top and bake for 5 minutes
9. Serve and enjoy.

Nutrition: Calories: 156 | Fat: 11.7 g | Protein: 8.1 g

243. QUESADILLAS
(PREP. TIME: 10 MIN | COOKING: 4 MIN | SERVING 4)

INGREDIENTS
- 4 low carb tortillas cut into small pieces
- 5 oz. grated Mexican cheese
- 1 oz. leafy greens
- 1 tbsp. light olive oil, for frying
- Salt and pepper to taste

DIRECTIONS:
1. Cook oil in a pan over medium heat.
2. Spread half of the tortilla pieces in the pan and top them with half of the cheese and leafy greens.
3. Drizzle salt and pepper and the remaining cheese on top and add another layer of tortillas.
4. Cook for 1 minute then flip to cook for another minute.

5. Slice it into eatable chunks.
6. Serve.

Nutrition: Calories: 238 | Fat: 16.9 g | Protein: 10.8 g

244. Cheesy Cauliflower
(Prep. Time: 10 Min | Cooking: 5 Min | Serving 3)

INGREDIENTS
- 1 cauliflower head
- 1/4 cup vegan butter, cut into small pieces
- 1 tsp. mayonnaise
- 1 tbsp. prepared mustard
- 1/2 cup Parmesan cheese, grated

DIRECTIONS:
1. Preheat your oven to 390°F.
2. Combine mayonnaise and mustard in a bowl.
3. Add cauliflower to the mayonnaise mixture. Mix well.
4. Spread the cauliflower in a baking dish and top it with vegan butter.
5. Sprinkle with cheese on top and bake for about 25 minutes
6. Serve warm.

Nutrition: Calories: 228 | Fat: 20.2 g | Fiber: 2.4 g

245. Parmesan Roasted Bamboo Sprouts
(Prep. Time: 10 Min | Cooking: 5 Min | Serving 3)

INGREDIENTS
- 1 lb. bamboo sprouts
- 2 tbsp. vegan butter
- 1 cup parmesan cheese, grated
- 1/4 tsp. paprika

DIRECTIONS:
1. Set oven to 350 degrees F then grease a baking dish then set it aside
2. Mix vegan butter, paprika, parmesan cheese, salt, and black pepper in a bowl.
3. Add bamboo sprouts to the vegan butter marinade and mix well. Marinate for 1 hour.
4. Situate the mixture to the baking dish and bake for 15 minutes
5. Serve.

Nutrition: Calories: 193 | Fat: 15.8 g | Protein: 12.6 g

246. Brussels Sprout With Lemon
(Prep. Time: 10 Min | Cooking: 0 Min | Serving 4)

INGREDIENTS
- 1 lb. Brussels sprouts, trimmed and shredded
- 8 tbsp. light olive oil
- 1 lemon, juice, and zest
- Salt and pepper to taste
- 2/5–3/4 cup spicy almond & seed mix or your own choice of nuts and seeds

DIRECTIONS:
1. Mix lemon juice with salt, pepper, and olive in a bowl.
2. Stir in shredded Brussels sprouts. Mix well. Keep aside for 10 minutes
3. Add nuts mixture to the sprouts.
4. Serve.

Nutrition: Calories: 382 | Fat: 36.5 g | Protein: 6.3 g

247. Cauliflower Hash Browns
(Prep. Time: 10 Min | Cooking: 3 Min | Serving 4)

INGREDIENTS
- 1 lb. cauliflower, trimmed and grated
- 3 eggs
- 1/2 yellow onion, grated
- Salt and black pepper to taste
- 4 oz. vegan butter, for frying

DIRECTIONS:
1. Scourge eggs in a bowl and mix in onion, cauliflower, salt, and pepper.
2. Heat vegan butter in the skillet over medium heat.
3. Stir batter spoon by spoon to the vegan butter and spread the batter into a 3 to 4-inch diameter circle
4. Cook for 4 minutes per side.
5. Use the entire batter to repeat the process.
6. Serve warm.

Nutrition: Calories: 284 | Fat: 26.4 g | Protein: 6.8 g

248. Cauliflower Parmesan
(Prep. Time: 10 Min | Cooking: 5 Min | Serving 4)

INGREDIENTS
- 1 1/2 lb. cauliflower, trimmed and sliced
- 2 tbsp. light olive oil
- salt to taste
- Black pepper, to taste
- 4 oz. grated parmesan cheese

DIRECTIONS:

1. Set oven to 400°F
2. Layout the cauliflower slices on a baking sheet lined with parchment paper.
3. Drizzle salt, pepper, light olive oil, and parmesan cheese on top.
4. Bake for about 20 to 25 minutes
5. Serve warm.

Nutrition: Calories: 278 | Fat: 20.7 g | Protein: 6.4 g

249. CAULIFLOWER MASH
(PREP. TIME: 10 MIN | COOKING: 5 MIN | SERVING 4)

INGREDIENTS
- 1 lb. cauliflower, cut into florets
- 3 oz. whipped heavy cream
- 4 oz. vegan butter
- 1/2 lemon, juice, and zest
- Light olive oil (optional)
- Water
- Salt to taste

DIRECTIONS:
1. Boil water along with salt in a saucepan.
2. Add cauliflower to the water and cook until soft.
3. Drain and transfer the cauliflower to a blender.
4. Add all the remaining **INGREDIENTS** and blend until smooth.
5. Serve.

Nutrition: Calories: 337 | Fat: 34.5 g | Protein: 3 g

250. MILLET PILAF
(PREP. TIME: 5 MIN | COOKING: 10 MIN | SERVING 4)

INGREDIENTS
- 1 cup millet, uncooked
- 8 dried apricots, chopped
- 1/4 cup shelled pistachios, chopped
- 1 1/2 tbsp. light olive oil
- 1 lemon, juiced
- 1 3/4 cup water
- 3/4 tsp. salt
- 1/2 tsp. ground black pepper
- Parsley to taste

DIRECTIONS:
1. Switch on the instant pot, place millet and 1 3/4 cup water in the inner pot, and stir until mixed.
2. Secure instant pot with its lid in the sealed position, then press the manual button, adjust cooking time to 10 minutes, select high-pressure cooking, and let cook until instant pot buzz.
3. Instant pot will take 10 minutes or more to build pressure, and when it buzzes, press the cancel button and do natural pressure release for 10 minutes or more until the pressure knob drops down.
4. Then carefully open the instant pot, add remaining ingredients, season with 3/4 tsp. salt and 1/2 tsp. ground black pepper, and stir until mixed.
5. Garnish with parsley and serve straight away.

Nutrition: Calories: 308 | Fat: 11 g | Protein: 7 g

251. SPICED QUINOA AND CAULIFLOWER RICE BOWLS
(PREP. TIME: 5 MIN | COOKING: 10 MIN | SERVING 8)

INGREDIENTS
- 12 oz. tofu, extra-firm, drained, and 1/2 inch cubes
- 1 cup quinoa, uncooked
- 2 medium red bell peppers, chopped
- 1 large white onion, peeled and chopped
- 4 cups cauliflower rice
- 1 tbsp. light olive oil
- 1 tsp. minced garlic
- 1 tsp. salt
- 1/2 tsp. ground black pepper
- 1 tsp. ground turmeric
- 1 tsp. ground cumin
- 1 tsp. ground coriander
- 2 cups + 2 tbsp. vegetable broth
- Cilantro to taste
- Almonds to taste
- Lemon juice to taste

DIRECTIONS:
1. Switch on the instant pot, grease the inner pot with 1 tbsp. light olive oil, press the sauté/simmer button, then adjust the cooking time to 5 minutes and let preheat.
2. Add onion, cook for 3 minutes, and then add 1 tsp. minced garlic, and quinoa and cook for 2 minutes
3. Then season quinoa with 1 tsp. salt, 1/2 tsp. ground black pepper, 1 tsp. ground turmeric, 1 tsp. ground cumin, and 1 tsp. ground coriander, stir until mixed, and cook for 1 minute or until fragrant.
4. Stir in 2 tbsp. vegetable broth, add tofu and red bell pepper, pour in 2 cups vegetable broth and stir until just mixed.
5. Press the cancel button, secure instant pot with its lid in the sealed position, then press the manual button, adjust cooking time to 1 minute, select high-pressure cooking, and let cook until instant pot buzz.

6. Instant pot will take 10 minutes or more to build pressure, and when it buzzes, press the cancel button, do natural pressure release for 5 minutes and then do quick pressure release until pressure knob drops down.
7. Then carefully open the instant pot, add cauliflower rice along with remaining ingredients, reserving lemon juice, cilantro, and almonds, and stir until mixed.
8. Shut instant pot with the lid and let the mixture sit for 5 minutes or until cauliflower rice is tender-crisp.
9. Garnish with cilantro and almonds, drizzle with lemon juice and serve.

Nutrition: Calories: 211 | Fat: 8.2 g | Protein: 11.2 g

252. Black Beans and Rice
(Prep. Time: 10 Min | Cooking: 4 Min | Serving 8)

INGREDIENTS
- 1 1/2 cup brown rice
- 1 1/2 cup dried black beans
- 1/2 medium white onion, peeled and chopped
- 2 tbsp. minced garlic
- 2 tsp. light olive oil
- 1 3/4 tsp. salt
- 2 tsp. red chili powder
- 1 1/2 tsp. paprika
- 2 tsp. ground cumin
- 1 1/2 tsp. dried oregano
- 3 cups water
- 3 cups vegetable broth

DIRECTIONS:
1. Switch on the instant pot, grease the inner pot with 2 tsp. light olive oil, press the sauté/simmer button, then adjust the cooking time to 5 minutes and let preheat.
2. Add onion, cook for 3 minutes, then add garlic, season with 1 3/4 tsp. salt, 2 tsp. red chili powder, 1 1/2 tsp. paprika, 2 tsp. ground cumin, and 1 1/2 tsp. dried oregano and cook for 1 minute or until fragrant.
3. Add beans and rice, pour in 3 cups water and 3 cups vegetable broth, and stir until mixed.
4. Press the cancel button, secure instant pot with its lid in the sealed position, then press the manual button, adjust cooking time to 30 minutes, select high-pressure cooking, and let cook until instant pot buzz.
5. Instant pot will take 10 minutes or more to build pressure, and when it buzzes, press the cancel button and do natural pressure release for 10 minutes or more until pressure knob drops down.
6. Then carefully open the instant pot, fluff the rice with a fork, drizzle with lime juice, and serve with salsa.

Nutrition: Calories: 268 | Fat: 9 g | Protein: 10.3 g

253. Chickpea Curry
(Prep. Time: 10 Min | Cooking: 5 Min | Serving 6)

INGREDIENTS
- 30 oz. cooked chickpeas
- 1 cup corn, frozen
- 14.5 oz. diced tomatoes
- 1 medium white onion, peeled and diced
- 1 cup kale leaves
- 2 tbsp. light olive oil
- 1 bell pepper
- 1 tbsp. minced garlic
- 1 tbsp. curry powder
- 1 tsp. sea salt
- 1/4 tsp. ground black pepper
- 1/2 cup tomato juice
- 1 cup vegetable broth
- Lime juice to taste
- Cilantro to taste

DIRECTIONS:
1. Switch on the instant pot, grease the inner pot with 2 tbsp. light olive oil, press the sauté/simmer button, then adjust the cooking time to 5 minutes and let preheat.
2. Add onion, cook for 4 minutes or until softened, then add bell pepper and 1 tbsp. minced garlic, and cook for 2 minutes
3. Season with 1 tbsp. curry powder, 1 tsp. sea salt, and 1/4 tsp. ground black pepper, continue cooking for 30 seconds, then add remaining ingredients, pour in 1/2 cup tomato juice and 1 cup vegetable broth, and stir until mixed.
4. Press the cancel button, secure the instant pot with its lid in the sealed position, then press the manual button, adjust cooking time to 5 minutes, select high-pressure cooking, and let cook until instant pot buzz.
5. Instant pot will take 10 minutes or more to build pressure, and when it buzzes, press the cancel button and do natural pressure release for 10 minutes or more until the pressure knob drops down.
6. Then carefully open the instant pot, stir the curry, then drizzle with lime juice, and top with cilantro.
7. Serve straight away.

Nutrition: Calories: 119 | Fat: 5 g | Protein: 2 g

254. VEGETABLE PEA SOUP
(PREP. TIME: 4 MIN | COOKING: 10 MIN | SERVING 4)

INGREDIENTS
- 2 cups yellow split peas, uncooked
- 1 medium white onion, peeled and diced
- 2 stalks celery, sliced
- 3 medium carrots, sliced
- 1 1/2 tsp. minced garlic
- 1 tbsp. light olive oil
- 1 tsp. salt
- 1 tsp. ground cumin
- 1/2 tsp. ground coriander
- 2 tsp. curry powder
- 2 cups water
- 4 cups vegetable broth
- Parsley to taste

DIRECTIONS:
1. Switch on the instant pot, grease the inner pot with 1 tbsp. light olive oil, press the sauté/simmer button, then adjust the cooking time to 5 minutes and let preheat.
2. Stir in onion, cook for a minute. Mix in carrot, garlic, and celery and cook for 2 minutes or until sauté.
3. Season vegetables with peas, 1 tsp. salt, 1 tsp. ground cumin, 1/2 tsp. ground coriander, and 2 tsp. curry powder, stir until mixed, and pour in 2 cups water and 4 cups vegetable broth.
4. Press the cancel button, secure the instant pot with its lid in the sealed position, then press the manual button, adjust cooking time to 10 minutes, select high-pressure cooking, and let cook until instant pot buzz.
5. Instant pot will take 10 minutes or more to build pressure, and when it buzzes, press the cancel button and do natural pressure release for 10 minutes or more until the pressure knob drops down.
6. Then carefully open the instant pot, stir the soup, garnish with parsley and serve.

Nutrition: Calories: 158 | Fat: 2.8 g | Protein: 8.3 g

255. SPANISH RICE
(PREP. TIME: 10 MIN | COOKING: 5 MIN | SERVING 6)

INGREDIENTS
- 1 1/2 cups white rice, rinsed
- 1 small onion, peeled and chopped
- 1 1/2 cups mixed bell pepper, diced
- 1 medium tomato, seeded and diced
- 6 oz. tomato paste
- 1 tbsp. light olive oil
- 1 tsp. minced garlic
- 3/4 tsp. salt
- 1/2 tsp. red chili powder
- 1/4 tsp. ground cumin
- 2 cups vegetable broth
- Parsley to taste

DIRECTIONS:
1. Switch on the instant pot, grease the inner pot with 1 tbsp. light olive oil, press the sauté/simmer button, then adjust the cooking time to 5 minutes and let preheat.
2. Add rice, onion, 1 tsp. minced garlic, tomato, tomato paste, and all the pepper, cook for 3 minutes, then season with 3/4 tsp. salt, 1/2 tsp. red chili powder, and 1/4 tsp. ground cumin, pour in 2 cups vegetable broth, and stir until mixed.
3. Press the cancel button, secure the instant pot with its lid in the sealed position, then press the manual button, adjusts cooking time to 10 minutes, select high-pressure cooking, and let cook until instant pot buzz.
4. Instant pot will take 10 minutes or more to build pressure, and when it buzzes, press the cancel button and do natural pressure release for 10 minutes or more until pressure knob drops down.
5. Then carefully open the instant pot, fluff the rice with a fork, sprinkle with parsley, and serve.

Nutrition: Calories: 211 | Fat: 3.6 g | Protein: 4.6 g

256. SPICED BROWN RICE
(PREP. TIME: 10 MIN | COOKING: 5 MIN | SERVING 3)

INGREDIENTS
- 1 1/2 cups brown rice
- 1/2 cup chopped apricots, dried
- 1/2 cup cashews, roasted
- 1/2 cup raisins
- 2 tsp. grated ginger
- 1/2 tsp. cinnamon
- 1/8 tsp. ground cloves
- 3 cups water
- Cashews to taste

DIRECTIONS:
1. Switch on the instant pot, place all the ingredients in the inner pot, sprinkle with 2 tsp. grated ginger, 1/2 tsp. cinnamon, and 1/8 tsp. ground cloves, pour in 3 cups water and stir until mixed.

2. Secure instant pot with its lid in the sealed position, then press the manual button, adjust cooking time to 22 minutes, select high-pressure cooking, and let cook until instant pot buzz.
3. Instant pot will take 10 minutes or more to build pressure, and when it buzzes, press the cancel button and do natural pressure release for 10 minutes or more until the pressure knob drops down.
4. Then carefully open the instant pot, fluff the rice with a fork and garnish with cashews.
5. Serve straight away.

Nutrition: Calories: 216 | Fat: 2 g | Protein: 5 g

257. Salsa Brown Rice and Kidney Beans

(Prep. Time: 8 Min | Cooking: 7 Min | Serving 4)

INGREDIENTS

- 1 1/2 cup brown rice, uncooked
- 1 1/4 cup red kidney beans, uncooked
- 1/2 bunch of cilantro, chopped
- 1 cup tomato salsa
- 2 cups water
- 3 cups vegetable stock

DIRECTIONS:

1. Switch on the instant pot, add brown rice and beans in the inner pot, pour in 2 cups water and 3 cups vegetable stock, and then add salsa and chopped cilantro stems, don't stir.
2. Secure instant pot with its lid in the sealed position, then press the manual button, adjust cooking time to 25 minutes, select high-pressure cooking, and let cook until instant pot buzz.
3. Instant pot will take 10 minutes or more to build pressure, and when it buzzes, press the cancel button and do natural pressure release for 10 minutes or more until the pressure knob drops down.
4. Then carefully open the instant pot, stir the beans-rice mixture, garnish with cilantro and serve.

Nutrition: Calories: 218.2 | Fat: 4.3 g | Protein: 10.4 g

258. Walnut Lentil Tacos

(Prep. Time: 10 Min | Cooking: 5 Min | Serving 12)

INGREDIENTS

- 1 cup brown lentils, uncooked
- 1 medium white onion, peeled and diced
- 15 oz. diced tomatoes, fire-roasted
- 3/4 cup chopped walnuts
- 1 tbsp. light olive oil
- 1/2 tsp. minced garlic
- 1/2 tsp. salt
- 1/4 tsp. ground black pepper
- 1/4 tsp. oregano
- 1 tbsp. red chili powder
- 1/2 tsp. paprika
- 1/4 tsp. red pepper flakes
- 1 1/2 tsp. ground cumin
- 2 1/4 cups vegetable broth
- 12 tortillas
- Lettuce to taste
- Jalapeno to taste

DIRECTIONS:

1. Switch on the instant pot, grease the inner pot with 1 tbsp. light olive oil, press the sauté/simmer button, then adjust the cooking time to 5 minutes and let preheat.
2. Add lentils, onion, and 1/2 tsp. minced garlic, cook for 4 minutes, then season with 1/2 tsp. salt, 1/4 tsp. ground black pepper, 1/4 tsp. oregano, 1 tbsp. red chili powder, 1/2 tsp. paprika, tomatoes, 1/4 tsp. red pepper flakes, walnuts, 1 1/2 tsp. ground cumin and stir until mixed.
3. Pour in 2 1/4 cups vegetable broth, press the cancel button, secure instant pot with its lid in the sealed position, then press the manual button, adjust cooking time to 15 minutes, select high-pressure cooking, and let cook until instant pot buzz.
4. Instant pot will take 10 minutes or more to build pressure, and when it buzzes, press the cancel button, do natural pressure release for 5 minutes and then do quick pressure release until pressure knob drops down.
5. Then carefully open the instant pot, stir the lentils, then spoon in the tortillas, top with lettuce and jalapeno, and serve.

Nutrition: Calories: 157.5 | Fat: 4 g | Protein: 6.5 g

259. Citrusy Black Beans

(Prep. Time: 7 Min | Cooking: 8 Min | Serving 4)

INGREDIENTS

- 2 1/2 cups black beans, uncooked
- 1 medium white onion, peeled and chopped
- 2 tsp. minced garlic
- 1 lime, juiced
- 1 tsp. salt
- 1 tsp. red chili flakes
- 1 tsp. dried mint

- 1 tsp. ground cumin
- 1 tsp. coriander
- 3 cups vegetable stock
- Lime juice to taste

DIRECTIONS:

1. Switch on the instant pot, add all the ingredients to the inner pot, season with 1 tsp. salt, 1 tsp. red chili flakes, 1 tsp. dried mint, 1 tsp. ground cumin, and coriander, pour in 3 cups vegetable stock and stir until mixed.
2. Secure instant pot with its lid in the sealed position, then press the manual button, adjust cooking time to 25 minutes, select high-pressure cooking, and let cook until instant pot buzz.
3. Instant pot will take 10 minutes or more to build pressure, and when it buzzes, press the cancel button and do natural pressure release for 10 minutes or more until the pressure knob drops down.
4. Then carefully open the instant pot, stir the beans, drizzle with lime juice, and serve.

Nutrition: Calories: 227 | Fat: 1 g | Protein: 15 g

260. TOFU CURRY
(PREP. TIME: 5 MIN | COOKING: 10 MIN | SERVING 4)

INGREDIENTS

- 14 oz. extra-firm and drained tofu, cut into cubes
- 3 tbsp. green curry paste
- 1 medium green bell pepper, cored and 1-inch cubed
- 1 cup broccoli florets
- 1 medium carrot, peeled and sliced
- 2 tbsp. light olive oil
- 2 cups coconut milk
- Lemon juice to taste
- Basil leaves to taste

DIRECTIONS:

1. Switch on the instant pot, grease the inner pot with 2 tbsp. light olive oil, press the sauté/simmer button, then adjust the cooking time to 5 minutes and let preheat.
2. Add green curry paste, cook for 30 seconds or until fragrant, then pour in 2 cups coconut milk and stir until mixed.
3. Add remaining ingredients, stir until mixed and press the cancel button.
4. Secure instant pot with its lid in the sealed position, then press the manual button, adjust cooking time to 2 minutes, select low-pressure cooking and let cook until instant pot buzz.
5. Instant pot will take 10 minutes or more to build pressure, and when it buzzes, press the cancel button and do quick pressure release until pressure knob drops down.
6. Then carefully open the instant pot, stir the curry, then drizzle with lemon juice and garnish with basil leaves.
7. Serve straight away.

Nutrition: Calories: 418 | Fat: 36.8 g | Protein: 11 g

261. PUMPKIN WALNUT CHILI
(PREP. TIME: 5 MIN | COOKING: 10 MIN | SERVING 4)

INGREDIENTS

- 2 cups red lentils, uncooked
- 28 oz. cooked black beans
- 28 oz. fire-roasted tomatoes
- 1 1/2 tsp. minced garlic
- 2 cups walnuts, chopped
- 3 chopped chipotle pepper
- 2 chopped poblano pepper
- 1 1/2 tsp. minced garlic
- 1 tbsp. salt
- 2 tbsp. red chili powder
- 1 tbsp. smoked paprika
- 6 cups water
- 1 1/2 cup pumpkin puree

DIRECTIONS:

1. Switch on the instant pot, grease the inner pot, add all the ingredients, then add 3 chopped chipotle pepper, 2 chopped poblano pepper, 1 1/2 tsp. minced garlic, season with 1 tbsp. salt, 2 tbsp. red chili powder, 1 tbsp. smoked paprika, and stir until mixed.
2. Pour in 6 cups water, except for pumpkin puree and beans, and stir until mixed.
3. Secure instant pot with its lid in the sealed position, then press the soup button, adjust cooking time to 30 minutes, select high-pressure cooking and let cook until instant pot buzz.
4. Instant pot will take 10 minutes or more to build pressure, and when it buzzes, press the cancel button and do natural pressure release for 10 minutes or more until pressure knob drops down.
5. Then carefully open the instant pot, stir the chili, then add beans and 1 1/2 cup pumpkin puree and stir until well mixed.
6. Serve straight away.

Nutrition: Calories: 333 | Fat: 14 g | Protein: 13.5 g

262. Lentil Curry

(Prep. Time: 10 Min | Cooking: 5 Min | Serving 5)

INGREDIENTS

- 1 1/2 cups green lentil, uncooked
- 3 tbsp. ginger
- 1 small shallot, peeled and chopped
- 14 oz. coconut milk
- 1 cup and 1 tbsp. water, divided
- 1/2 tbsp. coconut oil
- 2 tbsp. minced garlic
- 1 tbsp. oil
- 1 tsp. salt
- 1/4 tsp. cayenne pepper
- 1/2 tbsp. coconut sugar
- 3/4 tsp. ground turmeric
- 1 tbsp + 1 tsp. curry powder
- Lemon juice to taste
- Cilantro to taste

DIRECTIONS:

1. Switch on the instant pot, grease the inner pot with 1/2 tbsp. coconut oil, press the sauté/simmer button, then adjust the cooking time to 5 minutes and let preheat.
2. Add shallots, 3 tbsp. grated ginger, 2 tbsp. minced garlic, and 1 tbsp. oil, cook for 2 minutes, then season with 1 tsp. salt, 1/4 tsp. cayenne pepper, 1/2 tbsp. coconut sugar, 3/4 tsp. ground turmeric, 1 tbsp. and 1 tsp. curry powder, and stir until well combined.
3. Cook for 1 minute, then add lentils, pour in the milk and water, and stir well.
4. Press the cancel button, secure the instant pot with its lid in the sealed position, then press the manual button, adjusts cooking time to 15 minutes, select high-pressure cooking, and let cook until instant pot buzz.
5. Instant pot will take 10 minutes or more to build pressure, and when it buzzes, press the cancel button and do natural pressure release for 10 minutes or more until the pressure knob drops down.
6. Then carefully open the instant pot, stir in lemon juice and sprinkle with cilantro.
7. Serve curry with brown rice.

Nutrition: Calories: 315 | Fat: 12 g | Protein: 7 g

263. Pasta Puttanesca

(PREP. TIME: 4 MIN | COOKING: 11 MIN | SERVING 4)

INGREDIENTS

- 4 cups penne pasta, whole-grain
- 1/2 cup Kalamata olives, sliced
- 1 tbsp. capers
- 4 cups pasta sauce
- 3 cups water
- 1 1/2 tsp. minced garlic
- 1 1/2 tsp. salt
- 1/4 tsp. red pepper flakes
- 1 tsp. ground black pepper

DIRECTIONS:

1. Switch on the instant pot, grease the inner pot, press the sauté/simmer button, then adjust the cooking time to 5 minutes and let preheat.
2. Add 1 1/2 tsp. minced garlic, cook for 1 minute or until fragrant, then season with 1 1/2 tsp. salt, 1/4 tsp. red pepper flakes, and 1 tsp. ground black pepper, add remaining ingredients and stir until mixed.
3. Press the cancel button, secure the instant pot with its lid in the sealed position, then press the manual button, adjusts cooking time to 5 minutes, select high-pressure cooking, and let cook until instant pot buzz.
4. Instant pot will take 10 minutes or more to build pressure, and when it buzzes, press the cancel button and do natural pressure release for 5 minutes and then do quick pressure release until pressure knob drops down.
5. Then carefully open the instant pot, stir the pasta, and serve.

Nutrition: Calories: 504 | Fat: 4 g | Protein: 18 g

264. BBQ Meatballs

(Prep. Time: 5 Min | Cooking: 10 Min | Serving 4)

INGREDIENTS

- 2 lb. vegan meatballs, frozen
- 1 1/2 cups barbeque sauce, unsweetened
- 14 oz. can whole berry cranberry sauce
- 1 tbsp. cornstarch
- 1/4 cup and 1 tbsp. water

DIRECTIONS:

1. Switch on the instant pot, pour 1/4 cup water in the inner pot, then add meatballs and cover with BBQ sauce and cranberry sauce.
2. Secure instant pot with its lid in the sealed position, then press the manual button, adjust cooking time to 5 minutes, select high-pressure cooking, and let cook until instant pot buzz.
3. Instant pot will take 10 minutes or more to build pressure, and when it buzzes, press the cancel button and do natural pressure release for 5 minutes, then do quick pressure release until pressure knob drops down.

4. Then carefully open the instant pot, gently stir the meatballs, whisk together cornstarch and remaining water until smooth, and add into the instant pot.
5. Press the sauté/simmer button, adjust the cooking time to 5 minutes and cook until the sauce thickens to the desired level.
6. Serve straight away.

Nutrition: Calories: 232.7 | Fat: 15.2 g | Protein: 7.3 g

265. LENTIL SLOPPY JOES
(PREP. TIME: 3 MIN | COOKING: 12 MIN | SERVING 8)

INGREDIENTS
- 1 cup brown lentils, uncooked
- 1 small white onion, peeled and diced
- 28 oz. crushed tomatoes
- 1 1/2 cups vegetable broth
- 2 tbsp. tomato paste
- 1 tbsp. light olive oil
- 1 1/2 tsp. minced garlic
- 1 tsp. salt
- 1/2 tsp. ground black pepper
- 1 tbsp. chili powder
- 1 tsp. paprika
- 2 tsp. dried oregano
- 1 1/2 cup vegetable broth

DIRECTIONS:
1. Switch on the instant pot, grease the inner pot with 1 tbsp. light olive oil, press the sauté/simmer button, then adjust the cooking time to 5 minutes and let preheat.
2. Add onion, cook for 2 minutes or until sauté, then add 1 1/2 tsp. minced garlic and cook for 2 minutes
3. Season lentils and onions with 1 tsp. salt, 1/2 tsp. ground black pepper, 1 tbsp. chili powder, 1 tsp. paprika, and 2 tsp. dried oregano, add tomatoes and tomato paste, pour in 1 1/2 cup vegetable broth, and stir until mixed.
4. Press the cancel button, secure the instant pot with its lid in the sealed position, then press the manual button, adjusts cooking time to 12 minutes, select high-pressure cooking, and let cook until instant pot buzz.
5. Instant pot will take 10 minutes or more to build pressure, and when it buzzes, press the cancel button and do natural pressure release for 10 minutes or more until the pressure knob drops down.
6. Then carefully open the instant pot, stir the lentils mixture, and serve with rolls.

Nutrition: Calories: 166 | Fat: 1 g | Protein: 9 g

266. GREEN COCONUT CURRY
(PREP. TIME: 10 MIN | COOKING: 5 MIN | SERVING 4)

INGREDIENTS
- 3 medium potatoes, peeled and cubed
- 2 cups cauliflower florets and broccoli
- 1/2 sliced red bell pepper
- 1 cup peas, frozen
- 1/2 cup vegetable stock

Curry:
- 1 tsp. salt
- 2 tbsp. green curry paste
- 2 cups vegetable stock
- 1 cup coconut milk

DIRECTIONS:
1. Switch on the instant pot, add potatoes in the inner pot along with cauliflower and broccoli florets, red pepper, peas, and pour in 1/2 cup vegetable stock.
2. Secure instant pot with its lid in the sealed position, then press the manual button, adjust the cooking time to 3 minutes, select high-pressure cooking, and let cook until instant pot buzz.
3. Instant pot will take 10 minutes or more to build pressure, and when it buzzes, press the cancel button and do natural pressure release for 10 minutes or more until the pressure knob drops down.
4. Carefully open the instant pot, stir the mixture, then season the curry with 1 tsp. salt and 2 tbsp. green curry paste, pour in 2 cups vegetable stock and 1 cup coconut milk and stir until mixed.
5. Press the soup button, adjust cooking time to 10 minutes and cook until curry is thoroughly heated.
6. Serve straight away.

Nutrition: Calories: 145.1 | Fat: 6.5 g | Protein: 5.6 g

267. POTATO CARROT MEDLEY
(PREP. TIME: 6 MIN | COOKING: 9 MIN | SERVING 6)

INGREDIENTS
- 1 medium white onion, peeled and diced
- 4 lb. potatoes, peeled and cut into bite-size pieces
- 2 lb. carrots, peeled and diced
- 1 1/2 cup vegetable broth
- 2 tbsp. chopped parsley
- 2 tbsp. light olive oil
- 1 1/2 tsp. minced garlic
- 1 tsp. spike original seasoning

- 1 tsp. Italian seasoning
- 1 1/2 cup vegetable broth

DIRECTIONS:
1. Switch on the instant pot, grease the inner pot with 2 tbsp. light olive oil, press the sauté/simmer button, then adjust the cooking time to 5 minutes and let preheat.
2. Add onion and potatoes, cook for 5 minutes or until sauté, then add carrots and cook for another 5 minutes
3. Add 1 1/2 tsp. minced garlic, then season with 1 tsp. spike original seasoning and 1 tsp. Italian seasoning, pour in 1 1/2 cup vegetable broth, and stir well.
4. Press the cancel button, secure the instant pot with its lid in the sealed position, then press the manual button, adjusts cooking time to 5 minutes, select high-pressure cooking, and let cook until instant pot buzz.
5. Instant pot will take 10 minutes or more to build pressure, and when it buzzes, press the cancel button and do natural pressure release for 10 minutes or more until the pressure knob drops down.
6. Then carefully open the instant pot, stir the medley and garnish with parsley.
7. Serve straight away.

Nutrition: Calories: 356 | Fat: 6 g | Protein: 9 g

268. JACKFRUIT CURRY
(PREP. TIME: 4 MIN | COOKING: 11 MIN | SERVING 2)

INGREDIENTS
- 1 small white onion, peeled and chopped
- 20 oz. green Jackfruit, drained
- 1 1/2 cups tomato puree
- 1/2 tsp. cumin seeds
- 1/2 tsp. mustard seeds
- 1 tsp. light olive oil
- 2 1/2 tsp. minced garlic
- 1 1/2 tbsp. grated ginger
- 3/4 tsp. salt
- 1 tsp. coriander powder
- 1/2 tsp. turmeric
- 1/4 tsp. ground black pepper
- 1 cup water

DIRECTIONS:
1. Switch on the instant pot, grease the inner pot with 1 tsp. light olive oil, press the sauté/simmer button, then adjust the cooking time to 5 minutes and let preheat.
2. Add all the seeds, cook for 1 minute or until sizzles, then add 2 red chilies and cook for 30 seconds.
3. Add onion along with green Jackfruit, tomato puree, 2 1/2 tsp. minced garlic, and 1 1/2 tbsp. grated ginger, season with 3/4 tsp. salt, 1 tsp. coriander powder, 1/2 tsp. turmeric, and 1/4 tsp. ground black pepper and cook for 5 minutes or until translucent.
4. Pour in 1 cup water, stir until mixed and press the cancel button.
5. Secure instant pot with its lid in the sealed position, then press the manual button, adjust cooking time to 8 minutes, select high-pressure cooking, and let cook until instant pot buzz.
6. Instant pot will take 10 minutes or more to build pressure, and when it buzzes, press the cancel button and do natural pressure release for 10 minutes or more until the pressure knob drops down.
7. Then carefully open the instant pot, shred jackfruits with two forks and garnish with cilantro.
8. Serve straight away.

Nutrition: Calories: 369 | Fat: 3 g | Protein: 4 g

269. POTATO CURRY
(PREP. TIME: 9 MIN | COOKING: 6 MIN | SERVING 5)

INGREDIENTS
- 5 cups baby potatoes cut into large chunks
- 2 cups green beans cut into bite-sized pieces
- 1 medium white onion, peeled and chopped
- 2 cups + 4 tbsp. water
- 1 2/3 cups coconut milk
- 1 tbsp. light olive oil
- 1 garlic cloves
- 2 tbsp. minced garlic
- 2 tsp. salt
- 1 tsp. black pepper
- 1 tbsp. coconut sugar
- 1 tsp. red chili flakes
- 2 tbsp. curry powder
- 2 cups water
- 1 2/3 cup milk
- Arrowroot powder to taste

DIRECTIONS:
1. Switch on the instant pot, grease the inner pot with 1 tbsp. light olive oil, press the sauté/simmer button, then adjust the cooking time to 5 minutes and let preheat.
2. Add onion, cook for 5 minutes, add garlic, cook for 1 minute, then add potatoes, 2 tbsp. minced garlic,

season with 2 tsp. salt, 1 tsp. black pepper, 1 tbsp. coconut sugar, 1 tsp. red chili flakes, and 2 tbsp. curry powder, pour in 2 cups water and 1 2/3 cup milk, and stir well.
3. Press the cancel button, secure instant pot with its lid in the sealed position, then press the manual button, adjusts cooking time to 20 minutes, select high-pressure cooking, and let cook until instant pot buzz.
4. Instant pot will take 10 minutes or more to build pressure, and when it buzzes, press the cancel button and do natural pressure release for 10 minutes or more until pressure knob drops down.
5. Then carefully open the instant pot, stir the mixture, stir arrowroot powder and 4 tbsp. water until combined, add into the instant pot and stir until combined.
6. Add beans, stir well, press the sauté/simmer button, then adjust cooking time to 5 minutes and until beans are tender and gravy reaches to desired consistency.
7. Serve immediately.

Nutrition: Calories: 258 | Fat: 5 g | Protein: 7 g

270. SQUASH AND CUMIN CHILI
(PREP. TIME: 9 MIN | COOKING: 6 MIN | SERVING 4)

INGREDIENTS
- 1 medium butternut squash
- 1 large pinch of chili flakes
- 1 tbsp. light olive oil
- 1–1/2 oz. pine nuts
- 1 small bunch of fresh coriander, chopped
- Nuts to taste

DIRECTIONS:
1. Take the squash and slice it
2. Remove seeds and cut them into smaller chunks
3. Take a bowl and add chunked squash, spice, and oil
4. Mix well
5. Pre-heat your Fryer to 360°F and add the squash to the cooking basket
6. Roast for 20 minutes. Ensure to shake the basket from time to time to avoid burning
7. Take a pan and place it over medium heat, add pine nuts to the pan, and dry toast for 2 minutes
8. Sprinkle nuts on top of the squash and serve
9. Enjoy!

Nutrition: Calories: 414 | Fat: 15 g | Protein: 16 g

271. FRIED-UP AVOCADOS
(PREP. TIME: 5 MIN | COOKING: 10 MIN | SERVING 6)

INGREDIENTS
- 1/2 cup almond meal
- 1/2 tsp. salt
- 1 Hass avocado, peeled, pitted and sliced
- Aquafaba from 1 bean can (bean liquid)

DIRECTIONS:
1. Take a shallow bowl and add almond meal, salt
2. Pour Aquafaba in another bowl, dredge avocado slices in Aquafaba, and then into the crumbs to get a nice coating
3. Assemble them in a single layer in your Air Fryer cooking basket, don't overlap
4. Cook for 10 minutes at 390°F, give the basket a shake, and cook for 5 minutes more
5. Serve and enjoy!

Nutrition: Calories: 356 | Fat: 14 g | Protein: 23 g

272. HEARTY GREEN BEANS
(PREP. TIME: 5 MIN | COOKING: 10 MIN | SERVING 6)

INGREDIENTS
- 1 lb. green beans washed and de-stemmed
- 1 lemon
- A pinch of salt and pepper
- 1/4 tsp. oil

DIRECTIONS:
1. Add beans to your Air Fryer cooking basket
2. Squeeze a few drops of lemon
3. Season with salt and pepper
4. Drizzle light olive oil on top
5. Cook for 11 minutes at 400°F
6. Once done, serve and enjoy!

Nutrition: Calories: 84 | Fat: 5 g | Protein: 2 g

273. PARMESAN CABBAGE WEDGES
(PREP. TIME: 5 MIN | COOKING: 10 MIN | SERVING 4)

INGREDIENTS
- 1/2 a head cabbage
- 2 cups parmesan
- 4 tbsp. vegan butter
- Salt and pepper to taste

DIRECTIONS:
1. Preheat your Air Fryer to 380°F.
2. Take a container and add melted vegan butter, and season with salt and pepper.

3. Cover cabbages with your melted vegan butter.
4. Coat cabbages with parmesan.
5. Transfer the coated cabbages to your Air Fryer and bake for 20 minutes
6. Serve with cheesy sauce and enjoy!

Nutrition: Calories: 108 | Fat: 7 g | Protein: 2 g

274. Extreme Zucchini Fries
(Prep. Time: 4 Min | Cooking: 11 Min | Serving 4)

INGREDIENTS
- 3 medium zucchinis, sliced
- 2 egg whites
- 1/2 cup seasoned almond meal
- 2 tbsp. grated parmesan cheese
- 1/4 tsp. garlic powder
- Cooking spray
- Salt and pepper to taste

DIRECTIONS:
1. Pre-heat your Fryer to 425°F.
2. Take the Air Fryer cooking basket and place a cooling rack.
3. Coat the rack with cooking spray.
4. Take a bowl, add egg whites, beat it well, and season with some pepper and salt.
5. Take another bowl and add garlic powder, cheese, and almond meal
6. Take the Zucchini sticks and dredge them in the egg and finally breadcrumbs.
7. Transfer the Zucchini to your cooking basket and spray a bit of oil.
8. Bake for 20 minutes and serve with Ranch sauce.
9. Enjoy!

Nutrition: Calories: 367 | Fat: 28 g | Protein: 4 g

275. Easy Fried Tomatoes
(Prep. Time: 5 Min | Cooking: 10 Min | Serving 3)

INGREDIENTS
- 1 green tomato
- 1/4 tbsp. Creole seasoning
- Salt and pepper to taste
- 1/4 cup almond flour
- 1/2 cup buttermilk

DIRECTIONS:
1. Add flour to your plate and take another plate and add buttermilk
2. Slice tomatoes then sprinkle with salt and pepper
3. Make a mix of creole seasoning and crumbs
4. Take tomato slice and cover with flour, place in buttermilk and then into crumbs
5. Repeat with all tomatoes
6. Preheat your fryer to 400°F
7. Cook the tomato slices for 5 minutes
8. Serve with basil and enjoy!

Nutrition: Calories: 166 | Fat: 12 g | Protein: 3 g

276. Roasted Up Brussels
(Prep. Time: 10 Min | Cooking: 5 Min | Serving 4)

INGREDIENTS
- 1 block Brussels sprouts
- 1/2 tsp. garlic
- 2 tsp. light olive oil
- 1/2 tsp. pepper
- Salt as needed

DIRECTIONS:
1. Preheat your Fryer to 390°F.
2. Remove leaves off the chokes, leaving only the head.
3. Wash and dry the sprouts well.
4. Make a mixture of light olive oil, salt, and pepper with garlic.
5. Cover sprouts with the marinade and let them rest for 5 minutes
6. Transfer coated sprouts to Air Fryer and cook for 15 minutes
7. Serve and enjoy!

Nutrition: Calories: 43 | Fat: 2 g | Protein: 2 g

277. Roasted Brussels and Pine Nuts
(Prep. Time: 10 Min | Cooking: 5 Min | Serving 6)

INGREDIENTS
- 15 oz. Brussels sprouts
- 1 tbsp. light olive oil
- 1–3/4 ounces raisins, drained
- Juice of 1 orange
- 1–3/4 ounces toasted pine nuts
- Water

DIRECTIONS:
1. Take a pot of boiling water, then add sprouts and boil them for 4 minutes
2. Transfer the sprouts to cold water and drain them well.
3. Place them in a freezer and cool them.

4. Take your raisins and soak them in orange juice for 20 minutes
5. Warm your Air Fryer to a temperature of 392°F.
6. Take a pan and pour oil, and stir the sprouts.
7. Take the sprouts and transfer them to your Air Fryer.
8. Roast for 15 minutes
9. Serve the sprouts with pine nuts, orange juice, and raisins!

Nutrition: Calories: 260 | Fat: 20 g | Protein: 7 g

278. Low-Calorie Beets Dish
(Prep. Time: 4 Min | Cooking: 10 Min | Serving 2)

INGREDIENTS
- 4 whole beets
- 1 tbsp. balsamic vinegar
- 1 tbsp. light olive oil
- Salt and pepper to taste
- 2 springs rosemary

DIRECTIONS:
1. Wash your beets and peel them
2. Cut beets into cubes
3. Take a bowl and mix in rosemary, pepper, salt, vinegar
4. Cover beets with the prepared sauce
5. Coat the beets with light olive oil
6. Pre-heat your Fryer to 400°F
7. Transfer beets to Air Fryer cooking basket and cook for 10 minutes
8. Serve with your cheese sauce and enjoy!

Nutrition: Calories: 149 | Fat: 1 g | Protein: 30 g

279. Broccoli and Parmesan Dish
(Prep. Time: 5 Min | Cooking: 10 Min | Serving 4)

INGREDIENTS
- 1 fresh head broccoli
- 1 tbsp. light olive oil
- 1 lemon, juiced
- Salt and pepper to taste
- 1 oz. parmesan cheese, grated

DIRECTIONS:
1. Wash broccoli thoroughly and cut them into florets.
2. Add the listed **INGREDIENTS** to your broccoli and mix well.
3. Preheat your fryer to 365°F.
4. Air fry broccoli for 20 minutes
5. Serve and enjoy!

Nutrition: Calories: 114 | Fat: 6 g Protein: 7 g

280. Fried-Up Pumpkin Seeds
(Prep. Time: 4 Min | Cooking: 10 Min | Serving 2)

INGREDIENTS
- 1–1/2 cups pumpkin seeds
- Light olive oil as needed
- 1–1/2 tsp. salt
- 1 tsp. smoked paprika
- 2-quarter of water

DIRECTIONS:
1. Cut pumpkin and scrape out seeds and flesh
2. Separate flesh from seeds and rinse the seeds under cold water
3. Bring two-quarter of salted water to boil and add seeds, boil for 10 minutes
4. Drain seeds and spread them on a kitchen towel
5. Dry for 20 minutes
6. Preheat your fryer to 350°F
7. Take a bowl and add seeds, smoked paprika, and light olive oil
8. Season with salt and transfer to your Air Fryer cooking basket
9. Cook for 35 minutes

Nutrition: Calories: 237 | Fat: 21 g | Protein: 12 g

281. Jalapeno Poppers
(Prep. Time: 5 Min | Cooking: 10 Min | Serving 4)

INGREDIENTS
- 10 jalapeno poppers halved and deseeded
- 8 oz. cashew cream
- 1/4 cup fresh parsley
- 3/4 cup almond meal

DIRECTIONS:
1. Take a bowl and mix 1/2 of almond meal and cashew cream
2. Add parsley and stuff the pepper with the mixture
3. Press the top gently with remaining crumbs and make an even topping
4. Transfer to Air Fryer cooking basket and cook for 8 minutes at 370°F
5. Let it cool and enjoy!

Nutrition: Calories: 456 | Fat: 60 g | Protein: 15 g

282. Air Fried Olives
(Prep. Time: 5 Min | Cooking: 8 Min | Serving 4)

INGREDIENTS
- 1 (5 1/2 oz./156 g) jar pitted green olives
- 1/2 cup all-purpose flour
- Salt and pepper, to taste
- 1/2 cup bread crumbs
- 1 egg
- Cooking spray

DIRECTIONS:
1. Set the air fryer oven to 400°F (204°C).
2. Take away the olives from the jar and dry thoroughly with paper towels.
3. In a small bowl, combine the flour with salt and pepper to taste. Place the bread crumbs in another small container. In a third small bowl, beat the egg.
4. Spray the basket with cooking spray.
5. Drench the olives in the flour, then the egg, and then the bread crumbs.
6. Place the breaded olives in the air fryer basket. It is okay to stack them. Spray the olives with cooking spray.
7. Place the air fryer basket onto the warming pan.
8. Slide into Rack Position 2.
9. Select Air Fry and set the time to 6 minutes
10. Flip the olives and air fry for an additional 2 minutes, or until brown and crisp.
11. Cool for 5 minutes before serving.

Nutrition: Calories: 188 | Fat: 6.8 g | Protein: 30.3 g

283. BREADED ARTICHOKE HEARTS
(PREP. TIME: 5 MIN | COOKING: 8 MIN | SERVING 14)

INGREDIENTS
- 14 whole artichoke hearts, packed in water
- 1 egg
- 1/2 cup all-purpose flour
- 1/3 cup panko bread crumbs
- 1 tsp. Italian seasoning
- Cooking spray

DIRECTIONS:
1. Preheat the air fryer oven to 380°F
2. Squash excess water from the artichoke hearts then situate them on paper towels to dry.
3. Stir the egg.
4. In another small bowl, stir in the flour.
5. With a third small bowl, blend the bread crumbs and Italian seasoning and stir.
6. Spritz the air fryer basket by means of cooking spray.
7. Drench the artichoke hearts in the flour, then the egg, then the bread crumb mixture.
8. Situate breaded artichoke hearts in the air fryer basket. Spray them with cooking spray.
9. Place the air fryer basket onto the baking pan.
10. Slide into Rack Position 2, select Air Fry, and set time to 8 minutes you may wait until the artichoke hearts have browned and are crisp. Flip once halfway through the cooking time.
11. Let cool for 5 minutes before serving.

Nutrition: Calories: 149 | Fat: 1 g | Protein: 30 g

284. BRUSCHETTA WITH BASIL PESTO
(PREP. TIME: 10 MIN | COOKING: 5 MIN | SERVING 4)

INGREDIENTS
- 8 slices French bread, 1/2 inch thick
- 2 tbsp. softened vegan butter
- 1 cup shredded Mozzarella cheese
- 1/2 cup basil pesto
- 1 cup chopped grape tomatoes
- 1 cup green onions

DIRECTIONS:
1. Preheat the air fryer oven to 350°F (177°C).
2. Spread the bread with the vegan butter and position butter-side up in a baking pan.
3. Slide the baking pan into Rack Position 1, select Convection Bake, set time to 4 minutes, or wait until the bread is light golden brown.
4. Remove the bread from the oven and top each piece with some of the cheese.
5. Back to the oven and bake for 1 to 3 minutes more, or until the cheese melts.
6. In the meantime, combine the pesto, tomatoes, and green onions in a small bowl.
7. When the cheese has melted, take away the oven's bread and put it on a serving platter. Top each slice utilizing some of the pesto mixtures and serve.

Nutrition:: Calories: 251 | Fat: 19 g | Protein: 17 g

285. CAJUN ZUCCHINI CHIPS
(PREP. TIME: 9 MIN | COOKING: 6 MIN | SERVING 4)

INGREDIENTS
- 2 large zucchinis cut into 1/8-inch-thick slices
- 2 tsp. Cajun seasoning
- Cooking spray

DIRECTIONS:
1. Preheat the air fryer oven to 370°F (188°C).

2. Spray the air fryer basket lightly with cooking spray.
3. Put the zucchini slices in a medium bowl and spray them generously with cooking spray.
4. Sprinkle the Cajun seasoning over the zucchini and stir to make sure they are evenly coated with oil and seasoning.
5. Position the slices in a single layer in the air fryer basket, making sure not to overcrowd.
6. Place the air fryer basket onto the baking pan.
7. Slide into Rack Position 2
8. Select Air Fry and set the time to 8 minutes
9. Flip the slices over and air fry for an additional 7 to 8 minutes, or until they are as crunchy and brown as you prefer.
10. Serve immediately.

Nutrition: Calories: 367 | Fat: 28 g | Protein: 4 g

286. CHEESY APPLE ROLL-UPS
(PREP. TIME: 5 MIN | COOKING: 5 MIN | SERVING 8)

INGREDIENTS
- 8 slices whole wheat sandwich bread
- 4 oz. (113 g) Colby Jack cheese, grated
- 1/2 small apple, chopped
- 2 tbsp. vegan butter, melted

DIRECTIONS:
1. Preheat the air fryer oven to 390°F (199°C).
2. Take away the crusts from the bread and flatten the slices with a rolling pin. Don't be gentle. Press hard so that the bread will be fragile.
3. Top bread slices with cheese and chopped apple, dividing the ingredients evenly.
4. Roll up each slice tightly and secure each with one or two toothpicks.
5. Brush outside of rolls with melted vegan butter. Place them in the air fryer basket.
6. Place the air fryer basket onto the baking pan.
7. Slide into Rack Position 2, select Air Fry, and set time to 5 minutes you may also wait until the outside is crisp and nicely browned.
8. Serve hot.

Nutrition: Calories: 147 | Fat: 9.5 g | Protein: 1.9 g

287. CHEESY JALAPEÑO POPPERS
(PREP. TIME: 5 MIN | COOKING: 10 MIN | SERVING 4)

INGREDIENTS
- 8 jalapeño peppers
- 1/2 cup whipped cream cheese
- 1/4 cup shredded Cheddar cheese

DIRECTIONS:
1. Preheat the air fryer oven to 360°F (182°C).
2. Practice a paring knife to carefully cut off the jalapeño tops, then scoop out the ribs and seeds. Set aside.
3. In a medium bowl, combine the whipped cream cheese and shredded Cheddar cheese. Place the mixture in a sealable plastic bag, and using a pair of scissors, cut off one corner from the bag. Gently squeeze some cream cheese mixture into each pepper until almost full.
4. Place a piece of parchment paper on the bottom of the air fryer basket and place the poppers on top, distributing evenly.
5. Place the air fryer basket onto the baking pan.
6. Slide into Rack Position 2, select Air Fry, and set time to 10 minutes
7. Allow the poppers to cool for 5 to 10 minutes before serving.

Nutrition: Calories: 456 | Fat: 60 g | Protein: 15 g

288. CHEESY STEAK FRIES
(PREP. TIME: 5 MIN | COOKING: 20 MIN | SERVING 5)

INGREDIENTS
- 1 (28 oz./794 g) bag frozen steak fries
- Cooking spray
- 1/2 cup beef gravy
- 1 cup shredded Mozzarella cheese
- 2 scallions, green parts only, chopped
- Salt and pepper to taste

DIRECTIONS:
1. Set the air fryer oven to 400°F (204°C).
2. Place the frozen steak fries in the air fryer basket.
3. Place the air fryer basket onto the baking pan.
4. Slide into Rack Position 2, select Air Fry, and set time to 10 minutes
5. Shake the basket and spritz the fries with cooking spray. Sprinkle with salt and pepper. Air fry for an additional 8 minutes
6. Pour the beef gravy into a medium, microwave-safe bowl—microwave for 30 seconds, or until the sauce is warm.
7. Sprinkle the fries with the cheese. Air fry for an additional 2 minutes until the cheese is melted.
8. Transfer the fries to a serving dish. Drizzle the fries with gravy and sprinkle the scallions on top for a green garnish. Serve warm.

Nutrition: Calories: 536 | Fat: 23.7 g | Protein: 13.4 g

289. CRISPY CAJUN DILL PICKLE CHIPS

(PREP. TIME: 5 MIN | COOKING: 5 MIN | SERVING 16)

INGREDIENTS
- 1/4 cup all-purpose flour
- 1/2 cup panko bread crumbs
- 1 large egg, beaten
- 2 tsp. Cajun seasoning
- 2 large dill pickles, sliced into eight rounds each
- Cooking spray

DIRECTIONS:
1. Preheat the air fryer oven to 390ºF (199ºC).
2. Place the all-purpose flour, panko bread crumbs, and egg into three separate shallow bowls, then stir the Cajun seasoning into the flour.
3. Dredge each pickle chip in the flour mixture, then the egg, and finally the bread crumbs. Shake off any excess, and then place each coated pickle chip on a plate.
4. Spritz the air fryer basket by means of cooking spray, and then place the pickle chips in the basket.
5. Place the air fryer basket onto the baking pan.
6. Slide into Rack Position 2, select Air Fry, set time to 5 minutes, or wait until crispy and golden brown.
7. Remove the chips and allow them to slightly cool on a wire rack before serving.

Nutrition: Calories: 367 | Fat: 28 g | Protein: 4 g

290. SUMMER ROLLS WITH PEANUT SAUCE

(PREP. TIME: 15 MIN | COOKING: 0 MIN | SERVING 4-6)

INGREDIENTS
- 6–8 Vietnamese/Thai round rice paper wraps
- 1 (13 oz.) package organic, extra-firm smoked or plain tofu, drained, cut into long, thin slices
- 1 cucumber, cored, cut into matchsticks (about 1 cup)
- 1 cup carrot, cut into matchsticks
- 1 cup mung bean or soybean sprouts
- 4–6 cups of spinach
- 12–16 basil leaves
- 3–4 mint sprigs
- Sweet peanut dressing for serving
- Water

DIRECTIONS:
1. Place the rice paper wrap under running water or in a large bowl of water for a moment, then set it on a plate or cutting board to absorb the water for 30 seconds. The wrap should be transparent and pliable.
2. Place your desired amount of filling on each wrap, being careful not to overfill because they will be hard to close.
3. Tightly fold the bottom of the wraps over the ingredients and then fold on each side. Continue rolling each wrap onto itself to form the rolls. Enjoy your rolls dipped in sweet peanut dressing.

Nutrition: Calories: 216 | Fat: 6 g | Protein: 13 g | Carbohydrates: 32 g

291. CHEESY WHITE BEAN CAULIFLOWER SOUP

(PREP. TIME: 5 MIN | COOKING: 10 MIN | SERVING 6)

INGREDIENTS
- 1 tbsp. light olive oil
- 1 onion, chopped
- 2 celery stalks, chopped
- 2 carrots, chopped
- 3 garlic cloves, minced
- 1 tsp. turmeric
- 1 head cauliflower, chopped into florets (about 5 cups)
- 4 cups vegetable broth
- 1 cup unsweetened nondairy milk
- 1/4 cup nutritional yeast
- 1 tsp. onion powder
- 1/2 tsp. salt
- Juice of 1/2 lemon
- 2 (14 oz.) cans of white navy or cannellini beans, drained and rinsed
- Freshly ground black pepper to taste

DIRECTIONS:
1. In a large stockpot, warm the oil over medium heat. Add the onion, celery, and carrots. Cook until the onions become slightly translucent, within 5 minutes add the garlic and turmeric and cook for 1 minute more.
2. Add the cauliflower and broth, cover, and bring to a boil. Once boiling, reduce the heat and simmer, covered, until the cauliflower has softened, about 10 minutes Pour in the milk, yeast, onion powder, and salt, and stir it.
3. Remove the pot and either use an immersion blender to purée the soup or transfer it to a blender and process it until smooth.
4. Once a smooth consistency is reached, return the soup to heat and add the lemon juice and beans. Stir and taste it; add extra salt and black pepper, if desired. Enjoy this soup with hot sauce.

Nutrition: Calories: 238 | Fat: 4 g | Protein: 15 g | Carbohydrates: 37 g

292. Split Pea Soup

(Prep. Time: 15 Min | Cooking: 60 Min | Serving 6)

INGREDIENTS

- 2 tbsp. light olive oil
- 1 medium onion, coarsely chopped
- 2 carrots, coarsely chopped
- 2 celery stalks, coarsely chopped
- A pinch + 2 tsp. salt, divided
- 2 cups yellow split peas, rinsed & drained
- 8 cups of water
- 1 bay leaf
- 1 tsp. paprika
- Freshly ground black pepper to taste
- 6 cups spinach, chopped
- 2 vegan sausages or spicy store-bought, chopped (optional)

DIRECTIONS:

1. In a large stockpot, warm the oil over medium heat. Add the onion, carrots, celery, and a pinch of salt and cook until the onions start to soften.
2. Add the split peas, water, bay leaf, paprika, the remaining 2 tsp. of salt, and pepper. Bring to a boil.
3. Adjust the heat to low, then simmer, occasionally stirring, until the split peas are soft and the soup is thick about 50 minutes
4. Remove and discard the bay leaf. Stir in the spinach and sausage (if using) and cook for a couple of minutes more—taste, adjust seasonings with salt and pepper.

Nutrition: Calories: 362 | Fat: 10 g | Protein: 25 g | Carbohydrates: 46 g

293. Quinoa and Chickpea Tabbouleh

(Prep. Time: 15 Min | Cooking: 0 Min | Serving 6)

INGREDIENTS

- 1 cup quinoa, cooked
- 1 cup tomato, chopped
- 1 cup cucumber, chopped
- 1 cup scallions, chopped
- 1 cup fresh parsley, chopped
- 1 (14 oz.) can chickpeas, drained and rinsed
- 2 garlic cloves, minced
- 1/4 cup chopped mint/1 tbsp. dried mint
- 2 tbsp. light olive oil
- Juice of 1 lemon
- 1/2 tsp. salt
- Freshly ground black pepper to taste

DIRECTIONS:

1. Mix the quinoa, tomato, cucumber, scallions, parsley, chickpeas, garlic, and mint in a large bowl.
2. Pour the light olive oil plus lemon juice over the quinoa mixture and then stir in the salt and as much pepper as you'd like. Stir until everything is well combined. Enjoy immediately.

Nutrition: Calories: 170 | Fat: 6 g | Protein: 6 g | Carbohydrates: 25 g

294. Cauliflower Caesar Salad With Chickpea Croutons

(Prep. Time: 5 Min | Cooking: 10 Min | Serving 4)

INGREDIENTS

- 1 head cauliflower, chopped (about 8 cups)
- 3 tbsp. oil, divided
- A few pinches salt + 1/4 tsp., divided
- 1 (14 oz.) can chickpeas, drained and rinsed
- 1 tsp. oregano
- 1/4 tsp. garlic powder
- 1/4 tsp. onion powder
- 2 heads romaine lettuce, chopped
- 1/4 cup tofu Caesar dressing for serving

DIRECTIONS:

1. Preheat the oven to 450°F. Prepare two baking sheets lined using parchment paper or silicone liners.
2. Mix the cauliflower, 2 tbsp. of light olive oil, and a few big pinches of salt in a large bowl. Mix to ensure the cauliflower is well coated with oil. Spread the cauliflower out evenly on one of the baking sheets.
3. In a medium bowl, combine the chickpeas, the remaining 1 tbsp. of light olive oil, oregano, garlic powder, onion powder, and the remaining 1/4 tsp. of salt. Spread the chickpeas out evenly on the other baking sheet.
4. Place the sheets in the oven and bake for 20 minutes; then give the sheet with the chickpeas a bit of a shake to ensure they aren't sticking or burning. Continue baking for 20 minutes more or until the cauliflower is soft and the chickpeas are crunchy.
5. To serve, divide the lettuce among 4 bowls and top each with even portions of the cauliflower, chickpeas, and about 1/4 cup of Caesar dressing.

Nutrition: Calories: 365 | Fat: 20 g | Protein: 16 g| Carbohydrates: 37 g

295. Vegetable Rose Potato

(Prep. Time: 6 Min | Cooking: 9 Min | Serving 4)

INGREDIENTS

- 4 red rose potatoes
- 6 leaves Lacinato kale, stemmed, chopped
- 2 tbsp. light olive oil
- 1 onion, chopped
- 1 green bell pepper, diced
- 1 tsp. smoked paprika
- 1 tsp. seasoning, salt-free
- Ground pepper and salt to taste

DIRECTIONS:

1. Microwave your potatoes until done, but still firm. Finely chop them when cool.
2. Preheat oil in a skillet over medium heat. Sauté onion until translucent. Add potatoes and bell pepper and sauté, stirring constantly over medium-high heat until golden-brown.
3. Stir in the kale and seasoning, then cook, stirring constantly until the mixture is a bit browned. Occasionally add water to prevent sticking if necessary. Sprinkle with pepper and salt to taste. Serve hot.

Nutrition: Calories: 337 | Fat: 7.4 g | Protein: 8 g | Carbohydrates: 63 g

296. Rice Arugula Salad

(Prep. Time: 5 Min | Cooking: 8 Min | Serving 2)

INGREDIENTS

- 1 cup wild rice, cooked
- 1 handful arugula, washed
- 3/4 cup almonds
- 6 sun-dried tomatoes in oil, chopped
- 3 tbsp. light olive oil
- 1 onion
- Pepper and salt to taste

DIRECTIONS:

1. Put your frying pan over low heat and roast the almonds for 3 minutes Transfer to a salad bowl.
2. Sauté onions in 1/3 light olive oil for 3 minutes on low heat. Add dried tomatoes and cook for about 2 minutes Transfer to a bowl.
3. Add the remaining light olive oil to the pan and fry the bread until crunchy. Sprinkle with pepper and salt. Set aside.
4. Add arugula to the bowl containing sautéed tomato mixture. Add wild rice and toss to combine. Season with pepper, salt.

Nutrition: Calories: 688 | Fat: 37.7 g | Protein: 19 g | Carbohydrates: 56 g

297. Tomato Salad

(Prep. Time: 15 Min | Cooking: 0 Min | Serving 4)

INGREDIENTS

- 1 head romaine lettuce, washed, chopped
- 1 avocado, sliced
- 24 cherry tomatoes
- 1/2 cup cilantro, chopped
- Fresh lime juice for dressing

DIRECTIONS:

1. Divide all the ingredients between 4 plates and drizzle with lime juice dressing. Toss well to combine. Enjoy immediately.

Nutrition: Calories: 203 | Fat: 16.2 g | Protein: 6 g | Carbohydrates: 12 g

298. Kale Apple Roasted Root Vegetable Salad

(Prep. Time: 5 Min | Cooking: 9 Min | Serving 6)

INGREDIENTS

- 1 (1/2) cups parsnips, turnips, and red rose potatoes, diced
- 8 cups kale, chopped
- 1/2 cup apple chunks
- 2 tbsp. apple cider vinegar
- 1/2 tsp. cinnamon
- 1/2 tsp. turmeric
- 4 tbsp. light olive oil, divided
- Salt and pepper to taste

DIRECTIONS:

1. Place a skillet over medium heat. Add vinegar, apple, cinnamon, turmeric, and salt. Bring the mixture to a boil and set aside.
2. Preheat the oven to 350°F. Preheat oil in a cast-iron pan over medium heat. Add parsnips, turnips and red rose potatoes and cook for about 5 minutes
3. Transfer to the oven and roast for about 10 minutes Place a skillet over medium heat. Add the remaining light olive oil. To the skillet, add the kale and apples and cook for about 4 minutes
4. Add the parsnips, turnips, red rose potatoes, and vinegar mixture to the skillet. Cook for about 5 minutes Add salt and pepper to taste. Serve while hot and enjoy!

Nutrition: Calories: 128 | Fat: 16 g | Protein: 3 g | Carbohydrates: 32 g

299. RICE ARUGULA SALAD WITH SESAME GARLIC DRESSING
(PREP. TIME: 15 MIN | COOKING: 0 MIN | SERVING 4)

INGREDIENTS
- 1 cup wild rice, cooked
- 1/8 tsp. cumin
- 1/2 bunch arugula, chopped
- 2 tbsp. parsley, chopped
- 2 tbsp. basil, chopped
- Salt and black pepper to taste

For the dressing:
- 1 head garlic, roasted and peeled
- 1/2 cup apple juice
- 1/4 cup lemon juice
- 1/4 cup tahini
- 1/4 cup virgin light olive oil
- Salt to taste
- ¼ cup Olives

DIRECTIONS:
1. Fill in the dressing ingredients in a blender and blend until the mixture is creamy and smooth. Set aside.
2. Place a stockpot over medium-high heat. Season rice with cumin and salt. Pour half of the dressing on top and mix well. Set aside to chill for about 10 minutes
3. To the bowl add arugula, parsley, basil, olives, salt, and pepper. Serve and enjoy!

Nutrition: Calories: 447 | Fat: 44.4 g | Protein: 19 g | Carbohydrates: 43 g

300. ROASTED LEMON ASPARAGUS WATERCRESS SALAD
(PREP. TIME: 9 MIN | COOKING: 5 MIN | SERVING 4)

INGREDIENTS
- 2 cups asparagus, ends trimmed
- 2 cups watercress
- 2 cups baby spinach
- 1 lemon, sliced, seeded
- 1 onion, sliced
- 1/8 tsp. cayenne
- 2 tbsp. light olive oil
- Salt and pepper to taste

DIRECTIONS:
1. Preheat 1 tbsp. oil in a skillet over medium heat. Add the asparagus and cook for about 5 minutes Set aside. Return the skillet to medium-low heat. Add the remaining light olive oil.
2. Add onion and lemon slices and cook for about 5 minutes remove from heat and season with salt, cayenne, and pepper.
3. Add the baby spinach to a large bowl. Add cooked onion, watercress, and lemon slices on top. Finally, add the asparagus. Serve and enjoy!

Nutrition: Calories: 129 | Fat: 7 g | Protein: 5 g | Carbohydrates: 11 g

301. PUMPKIN AND BRUSSELS SPROUTS MIX
(PREP. TIME: 5 MIN | COOKING: 10 MIN | SERVING 8)

INGREDIENTS
- 1 lb. Brussels sprouts, halved
- 1 pumpkin, peeled, cubed
- 4 garlic cloves, sliced
- 2 tbsp. fresh parsley, chopped
- 2 tbsp. balsamic vinegar
- 1/3 cup light olive oil
- Salt and pepper to taste
- Cooking spray

DIRECTIONS:
1. Warm oven to 400°F. Prepare a baking dish and coat with cooking spray. Mix sprouts, pumpkin, balsamic vinegar, salt, pepper, and garlic in a bowl. Add oil and toss well to coat the vegetables.
2. Transfer to the baking dish and cook for 35–40 minutes Stir once halfway. Serve topped with parsley.

Nutrition: Calories: 152 | Fat: 9 g | Protein: 4 g | Carbohydrates: 17 g

302. ALMOND AND TOMATO SALAD
(PREP. TIME: 4 MIN | COOKING: 10 MIN | SERVING 4)

INGREDIENTS
- 1 cup arugula/rocket
- 7 oz. fresh tomatoes, sliced or chopped
- 2 tsp. light olive oil
- 2 cups kale
- 1/2 cup almonds

DIRECTIONS:

1. Put oil into your pan and heat it on medium heat. Add tomatoes into the pan and fry for about 10 minutes once cooked, allow it to cool. Combine all the salad ingredients in a bowl and serve.

Nutrition: Calories: 355 | Fat: 19.1 g | Protein: 33 g | Carbohydrates: 8.3 g

303. STRAWBERRY SPINACH SALAD
(PREP. TIME: 15 MIN | COOKING: 0 MIN | SERVING 4)

INGREDIENTS
- 5 cups baby spinach
- 2 cups strawberries, sliced
- 2 tbsp. lemon juice
- 1/2 tsp. Dijon mustard
- 1/4 cup light olive oil
- 3/4 cup toasted almonds, chopped
- 1/4 red onion, sliced
- Salt and pepper to taste
- Vegan cheese to taste

DIRECTIONS:
1. Take a large bowl and mix Dijon mustard with lemon juice in it, and slowly add light olive oil and combine. Season the mixture with black pepper and salt.
2. Now, mix spinach, strawberries, 1/2 cup of almonds, and sliced onion in a bowl. Pour the dressing on top and toss to combine. Serve the salad topped with almonds and vegan cheese.

Nutrition: Calories: 116 | Fat: 3 g | Protein: 6 g | Carbohydrates: 13 g

304. APPLE SPINACH SALAD
(PREP. TIME: 15 MIN | COOKING: 0 MIN | SERVING 4)

INGREDIENTS
- 5 oz. fresh spinach
- 1/4 red onion, sliced
- 1 apple, sliced
- 1/4 cup sliced toasted almonds

For the dressing:
- 3 tbsp. red wine vinegar
- 1/3 cup light olive oil
- 1 minced garlic clove
- 2 tsp. Dijon mustard
- Salt and pepper to taste

DIRECTIONS:
1. Combine red wine vinegar, light olive oil, garlic, and Dijon mustard in a bowl. Season with black pepper and salt.
2. In a separate bowl mix fresh spinach, apple, onion, toasted almonds. Pour the dressing on top and toss to combine. Serve

Nutrition: Calories: 232 | Fat: 20.8 g | Protein: 3 g | Carbohydrates: 10 g

305. KALE POWER SALAD
(PREP. TIME: 5 MIN | COOKING: 10 MIN | SERVING 2)

INGREDIENTS
- 1 bunch kale, ribs removed and chopped
- 1/2 cup quinoa
- 1 tbsp. light olive oil
- 1/2 lime, juiced
- 1/2 tsp. salt
- 1 tbsp. light olive oil
- 1 red rose potato, cut into small cubes
- 1 tsp. ground cumin
- 3/4 tsp. salt
- 1/2 tsp. smoked paprika
- 2 lime, juiced
- 1 avocado, sliced into long strips
- 1 tbsp. light olive oil
- 1 tbsp. cilantro leaves
- 1 jalapeno, deseeded, membranes removed, and chopped
- Salt to taste
- 1/4 cup pepitas
- 2 cups of water

DIRECTIONS:
1. Rinse quinoa in running water for 2 minutes Mix 2 cups water and rinsed quinoa in a pot, reduce the heat to simmer, and cook for 15 minutes
2. Remove quinoa from heat and let rest, covered, for 5 minutes uncover the pot, drain excess water, and fluff quinoa with a fork. Let cool.
3. Warm-up light olive oil in a pan over medium heat. Add chopped red rose potatoes and toss. Add smoked paprika, cumin, and salt. Mix to combine.
4. Add 1/4 cup water once the pan is sizzling. Cover the pan then adjust heat to low. Cook for 10 minutes, stirring occasionally. Open the pan, raise heat to medium and cook for 7 minutes. Set aside to cool.
5. Transfer kale to a bowl and add salt to it and massage with hands. Scrunch handfuls of kale in your hands. Repeat until kale is darker.
6. Mix 2 tbsp. light olive oil, 1/2 tsp. of salt, and 1 lime juice in a bowl. Add over the kale and toss to coat.
7. Add 2 avocados, 2 lime juices, 2 tbsp. of light olive oil, jalapeno, cilantro leaves, and salt in a blender. Blend well and season the avocado sauce.

8. Toast pepitas in a skillet over medium-low heat for 5 minutes, stirring frequently. Add quinoa to the kale bowl and toss to combine well.
9. Divide kale and quinoa mixture into 4 bowls. Top with red rose potatoes, avocado sauce, and pepitas. Enjoy!

Nutrition: Calories: 250 | Fat: 11 g | Protein: 9 g | Carbohydrates: 25 g

306. Falafel Kale Salad With Tahini Dressing

(Prep. Time: 15 Min | Cooking: 0 Min | Serving 4)

INGREDIENTS

- 12 balls vegan falafels
- 6 cups kale, chopped
- 1/2 red onion, thinly sliced
- 2 slices pita bread, cut into squares
- 1 jalapeno, chopped
- Tahini dressing for serving
- 1–2 lemons, juiced

DIRECTIONS:

1. In a mixing bowl, combine kale and lemon juice and toss well to mix. Place into the refrigerator. Divide kale among four bowls.
2. Top with three Falafel balls, red onion, jalapeno, and pita slices. Top with tahini dressing and serve.

Nutrition: Calories: 178 | Fat: 2.8 g Protein: 4 g | Carbohydrates: 16 g

Chapter 5. Salad and Soup Recipes

307. TOMATO GAZPACHO
(PREP. TIME: 8 MIN | COOKING: 7 MIN | SERVING 6)

INGREDIENTS
- 2 tbsp. red wine vinegar
- 1/2 tsp. pepper
- 1 tsp. sea salt
- 1 avocado,
- 1/4 cup basil, fresh, and chopped
- 3 tbsp. light olive oil
- 1 garlic clove, crushed
- 1 red bell pepper
- 1 cucumber
- 2 1/2 lb. large tomatoes

DIRECTIONS:
1. Place half of your cucumber, bell pepper, and 1/4 cup of each tomato in a bowl, covering. Set it in the fried.
2. Puree your remaining tomatoes, cucumber, and bell pepper with garlic, three tbsp. oil, two tbsp. of vinegar, sea salt, and black pepper into a blender, blending until smooth. Situate into a bowl, and chill for two hours.
3. Chop the avocado, adding it to your chopped vegetables, adding your remaining oil, vinegar, salt, pepper, and basil.
4. Ladle your tomato puree mixture into bowls, and serve with chopped vegetables as a salad.

Nutrition: Calories: 148 | Protein: 7 g | Fiber: 6 g

308. TOMATO PUMPKIN SOUP
(PREP. TIME: 5 MIN | COOKING: 9 MIN | SERVING 4)

INGREDIENTS
- 2 cups pumpkin
- 1/2 cup tomato
- 1/2 cup onion
- 1 1/2 tsp. curry powder
- 1/2 tsp. paprika
- 2 cups vegetable stock
- 1 tsp. light olive oil
- 1/2 tsp. garlic

DIRECTIONS:
1. Using a saucepan, stir in oil, garlic, and onion and sauté for 3 minutes over medium heat.
2. Stir in the remaining INGREDIENTS into the saucepan and bring to boil.
3. Lessen heat and cover and simmer for 10 minutes
4. Puree the soup with a blender.
5. Mix well and serve warm.

Nutrition: Calories: 180 | Protein: 10 g | Fiber: 5 g

309. CAULIFLOWER SPINACH SOUP
(PREP. TIME: 6 MIN | COOKING: 9 MIN | SERVING 5)

INGREDIENTS
- 1/2 cup unsweetened coconut milk
- 5 oz. fresh spinach, chopped
- 5 watercress, chopped
- 8 cups vegetable stock
- 1 lb. cauliflower, chopped
- Salt to taste

DIRECTIONS:
1. Fill in stock and cauliflower in a large saucepan and bring to boil over medium heat for 15 minutes
2. Stir in spinach and watercress and cook for 11 minutes
3. Pull away from heat and blend the soup by using a blender.
4. Add coconut milk and stir well. Season with salt.
5. Stir well and serve hot.

Nutrition: Calories: 163 | Protein: 10 g | Fiber: 3 g

310. AVOCADO MINT SOUP
(PREP. TIME: 5 MIN | COOKING: 10 MIN | SERVING 2)

INGREDIENTS
- 1 medium avocado
- 1 cup coconut milk
- 2 romaine lettuce leaves
- 20 fresh mint leaves
- 1 tbsp. fresh lime juice
- 1/8 tsp. salt

DIRECTIONS:
1. Incorporate all ingredients into the blender
2. Transfer into the serving bowls and chill for 10 minutes
3. Mix well and serve chilled.

Nutrition: Calories: 187 | Protein: 11 g | Fiber: 9 g

311. Creamy Squash Soup

(Prep. Time: 7 Min | Cooking: 8 Min | Serving 8)

INGREDIENTS
- 3 cups butternut squash
- 1 1/2 cups coconut milk
- 1 tbsp. coconut oil
- 1 tsp. dried onion flakes
- 1 tbsp. curry powder
- 4 cups water
- 1 garlic clove
- 1 tsp. kosher salt

DIRECTIONS:
1. Incorporate squash, coconut oil, onion flakes, curry powder, water, garlic, and salt into a large saucepan. Bring to boil over high heat.
2. Select heat to medium and simmer for 20 minutes
3. Puree the soup using a blender. Put the soup back to the saucepan and stir in coconut milk and cook for 2 minutes
4. Stir well and serve hot.

Nutrition: Calories: 180 | Protein: 9 g | Fiber: 7 g

312. Zucchini Soup

(Prep. Time: 8 Min | Cooking: 7 Min | Serving 8)

INGREDIENTS
- 2 1/2 lb. zucchini
- 1/3 cup basil leaves
- 4 cups vegetable stock
- 4 garlic cloves
- 2 tbsp. light olive oil
- 1 medium onion
- Salt and pepper to taste

DIRECTIONS:
1. Cook light olive oil in a pan over medium-low heat.
2. Sauté zucchini and onion. Add garlic and sauté for a minute.
3. Simmer vegetable stock for 15 minutes
4. Remove from heat. Stir in basil and puree the soup using a blender until smooth and creamy. Season with pepper and salt.
5. Stir well and serve.

Nutrition: Calories: 153 | Protein: 7 g | Fiber: 5 g

313. Creamy Celery Soup

(Prep. Time: 4 Min | Cooking: 11 Min | Serving 4)

INGREDIENTS
- 6 cups celery
- 1/2 tsp. dill
- 2 cups water
- 1 cup coconut milk
- 1 onion, chopped
- A pinch of salt

DIRECTIONS:
1. Add all ingredients into the electric pot and stir well.
2. Cover the electric pot with the lid and select soup setting.
3. Release pressure using a quick-release method then open the lid.
4. Mash soup using an immersion blender.
5. Stir well and serve warm.

Nutrition: Calories: 183 | Protein: 12 g | Fiber: 7 g

314. Avocado Cucumber Soup

(Prep. Time: 4 Min | Cooking: 11 Min | Serving 3)

INGREDIENTS
- 1 large cucumber
- 3/4 cup water
- 1/4 cup lemon juice
- 2 garlic cloves
- 6 green onion
- 2 avocados, pitted
- 1/2 tsp. black pepper
- 1/2 tsp. pink salt

DIRECTIONS:
1. Position all ingredients into the blender and blend until smooth and creamy.
2. Place in refrigerator for 30 minutes
3. Stir well and serve chilled.

Nutrition: Calories: 163 | Protein: 7 g | Fiber: 4 g

315. Creamy Garlic Onion Soup

(Prep. Time: 8 Min | Cooking: 7 Min | Serving 4)

INGREDIENTS
- 1 onion
- 4 cups vegetable stock
- 1 1/2 tbsp. light olive oil
- 1 shallot
- 2 garlic cloves
- 1 leek

DIRECTIONS:
1. Boil stock and light olive oil in a saucepan.
2. Stir the remaining ingredients well.
3. Close and simmer for 25 minutes

4. Mash soup with an immersion blender until smooth.
5. Stir well and serve warm.

Nutrition: Calories: 177 | Protein: 11 g | Fiber: 6 g

316. AVOCADO BROCCOLI SOUP
(PREP. TIME: 10 MIN | COOKING: 5 MIN | SERVING 4)

INGREDIENTS
- 2 cups broccoli florets
- 5 cups vegetable broth
- 2 avocados
- Salt and pepper to taste

DIRECTIONS:
1. Boil broccoli for 5 minutes Strain well.
2. Blend broccoli, vegetable broth, avocados, pepper, and salt until smooth.
3. Stir well and serve warm.

Nutrition: Calories: 183 | Protein: 9 g | Fiber: 5 g

317. GREEN SPINACH KALE SOUP
(PREP. TIME: 10 MIN | COOKING: 5 MIN | SERVING 6)

INGREDIENTS
- 2 avocados
- 8 oz. spinach
- 8 oz. kale
- 1 fresh lime juice
- 1 cup water
- 3 1/3 cup coconut milk
- 3 oz. light olive oil
- 1/4 tsp. pepper
- 1 tsp. salt

DIRECTIONS:
1. Warm-up light olive oil in a pan at medium heat.
2. Sauté kale and spinach to the saucepan for 2 to 3 minutes Remove saucepan from heat. Stir coconut milk, spices, avocado, and water well.
3. Blend soup with an immersion blender. Add fresh lime juice and stir well.
4. Serve and enjoy.

Nutrition: Calories: 183 | Protein: 10 g | Fiber: 5 g

318. CAULIFLOWER ASPARAGUS SOUP
(PREP. TIME: 5 MIN | COOKING: 10 MIN | SERVING 4)

INGREDIENTS
- 20 asparagus spears
- 4 cups vegetable stock
- 1/2 cauliflower head
- 2 garlic cloves
- 1 tbsp. coconut oil
- Salt and pepper

DIRECTIONS:
1. Cook coconut oil in a huge saucepan over medium heat.
2. Add garlic and sauté until softened.
3. Add cauliflower, vegetable stock, pepper, and salt. Stir well and bring to boil.
4. Decrease the heat to low then simmer for 20 minutes
5. Add chopped asparagus and cook until softened.
6. Crush soup using an immersion blender until smooth and creamy.
7. Stir well and serve warm.

Nutrition: Calories: 163 | Protein: 12 g | Fiber: 7 g

319. AFRICAN PINEAPPLE PEANUT STEW
(PREP. TIME: 5 MIN | COOKING: 10 MIN | SERVING 4)

INGREDIENTS
- 4 cups kale
- 1 cup onion
- 1/2 cup peanut butter
- 1 tbsp. hot pepper sauce
- 2 minced garlic cloves
- 1/2 cup chopped cilantro
- 2 cups pineapple
- 1 tbsp. vegetable oil
- Salt to taste

DIRECTIONS:
1. In a saucepan sauté the garlic and onions in the oil until the onions are lightly browned, approximately 10 minutes, stirring often.
2. Wash the kale, till the time the onions are sautéed.
3. Get rid of the stems. Mound the leaves on a cutting surface and slice crosswise into slices (preferably 1-inch thick).
4. Now put the pineapple and juice to the onions and bring to a simmer. Stir the kale in, cover, and simmer until just tender, stirring frequently, for approximately 5 minutes
5. Mix in the hot pepper sauce, peanut butter, cilantro, and simmer for more than 5 minutes
6. Add salt according to your taste.

Nutrition: Calories: 193 | Protein: 10 g | Fiber: 7 g

320. CABBAGE AND BEET STEW
(PREP. TIME: 5 MIN | COOKING: 10 MIN | SERVING 4)

INGREDIENTS

- 2 tbsp. light olive oil
- 3 cups vegetable broth
- 2 tbsp. lemon juice, fresh
- 1/2 teaspoon garlic powder
- 1/2 cup carrots
- 2 cups cabbage
- 1 cup beets
- dill for garnish
- 1/2 teaspoon onion powder

DIRECTIONS:

1. Heat oil in a pot, and then sauté your vegetables.
2. Pour your broth in, mixing in your seasoning. Simmer then tops with dill and lemon juice.

Nutrition: Calories: 173 | Protein: 8 g | Fiber: 6 g

321. Basil Tomato Soup

(Prep. Time: 5 Min | Cooking: 10 Min | Serving 6)

INGREDIENTS

- 28 oz. can tomato
- 1/4 cup basil pesto
- 1/4 tsp. dried basil leaves
- 1 tsp. apple cider vinegar
- 2 tbsp. erythritol
- 1/4 tsp. garlic powder
- 1/2 tsp. onion powder
- 2 cups water
- 1 1/2 tsp. kosher salt

DIRECTIONS:

1. Add tomatoes, garlic powder, onion powder, water, and salt in a saucepan.
2. Bring to boil over medium heat. Reduce heat and simmer for 2 minutes
3. Pull out saucepan from heat and mash soup using a blender until smooth.
4. Stir well pesto, dried basil, vinegar, and erythritol.

Nutrition: Calories: 163 | Protein: 12 g | Fiber: 5 g

322. Hearty Chickpea Soup

(Prep. Time: 4 Min | Cooking: 10 Min | Serving 7)

INGREDIENTS

- 2 carrots
- 4 celery stalks
- 6 cups economical vegetable broth
- 8 cups water
- 8 oz. spaghetti or thin brown rice noodles
- 1 1/2 cups cooked chickpeas
- 1 tsp. dried herbs
- 1/4–1/2 tsp. salt
- Pepper to taste

DIRECTIONS:

1. In a huge soup pot, mix carrots, celery, vegetable broth, and water. Bring to a boil over medium heat, then add the spaghetti, chickpeas, dried herbs, 1/4 tsp. salt (or 1/2 tsp. if your broth is unsalted), and a few grinds of pepper. Cook for 9 minutes

Nutrition: Calories: 173 | Protein: 8 g | Fiber: 6 g

323. Cream of Tomato Soup

(Prep. Time: 5 Min | Cooking: 5 Min | Serving 2)

INGREDIENTS

- 1 (28 oz.) can of tomatoes
- 2 tsp. dried herbs
- 3 tsp. onion powder
- 1 cup unsweetened nondairy milk
- Salt and pepper to taste

DIRECTIONS:

1. Fill tomatoes and their juices into a large pot and bring them to near-boiling over medium heat. Add the dried herbs, onion powder (if using), milk, salt, and pepper to taste. Stir to combine.
2. Mix tomatoes, use a hand blender to purée the soup.

Nutrition: Calories: 90 | Protein: 4 g | Fiber: 4 g

324. Creamy Mushroom

(Prep. Time: 2 Min | Cooking: 13 Min | Serving 3)

INGREDIENTS

- 2 tsp. light olive oil
- 1 onion
- 2 garlic cloves
- 2 cups mushrooms
- 2 tbsp. all-purpose flour
- 1 tsp. dried herbs
- 4 cups economical vegetable broth
- 1 1/2 cups nondairy milk
- Salt and pepper to taste

DIRECTIONS:

1. Cook light olive oil over medium-high heat. Stir in onion, garlic, mushrooms, and salt.
2. Toss flour over the ingredients in the pot. Cook for 2 minutes to toast the flour.
3. Sprinkle dried herbs, vegetable broth, milk, and pepper. Select heat to low, and simmer. Cook for 10 minutes

Nutrition: Calories: 127 | Protein: 4 g | Fiber: 3 g

325. Tofu Miso Soup

(Prep. Time: 8 Min | Cooking: 5 Min | Serving 2)

INGREDIENTS
- 7 oz. firm tofu
- 4 cups water
- 1/4 cup miso paste
- 2 scallions

DIRECTIONS:
1. Press your tofu before you start: Put it between several layers of paper towels. Let stand for 30 minutes Discard. Slice tofu into 1/2-inch cubes.
2. In a pot at medium heat, allow water to just below boiling. Stir the miso paste into the water until dissolved. Add the tofu and scallions and serve.

Nutrition: Calories: 204 | Protein: 19 g | Fiber: 4 g

326. Hot and Sour Tofu Soup

(Prep. Time: 2 Min | Cooking: 13 Min | Serving 3)

INGREDIENTS
- 7 oz. firm tofu
- 1 tsp. light olive oil
- 1 cup sliced mushrooms
- 1 cup finely chopped cabbage
- 1 garlic clove, minced
- 1/2-inch piece fresh ginger
- 4 cups water
- 2 tbsp. rice vinegar
- 2 tbsp. soy sauce
- 1 tsp. toasted sesame oil
- 1 tsp. coconut sugar
- 1 scallion
- A pinch of salt
- Red pepper flakes to taste

DIRECTIONS:
1. Press your tofu before you start: Put it between several layers of paper towels. Set aside for 30 minutes Chop tofu into 1/2-inch cubes.
2. In a big soup pot, cook light olive oil over medium-high heat. Add the mushrooms, cabbage, garlic, ginger, and a pinch of salt. Sauté for 7 to 8 minutes, until the vegetables are softened.
3. Add the water, vinegar, soy sauce, sesame oil, sugar, red pepper flakes, and tofu. Boil, then select heat to low. Simmer the soup for 5 to 10 minutes Serve with the scallion sprinkled on top.

Nutrition: Calories: 161 | Protein: 13 g | Fiber: 3 g

327. Creamy Cauliflower Soup

(Prep. Time: 3 Min | Cooking: 12 Min | Serving 5)

INGREDIENTS
- 1 tsp. light olive oil
- 1 onion
- 3 cups cauliflower
- 2 potatoes
- 6 cups water
- 2 tbsp. dried herbs
- 1–2 scallions
- Salt and pepper to taste

DIRECTIONS:
1. Cook light olive oil in a soup pot over medium-high heat. Add the onion and cauliflower, and sauté for about 5 minutes
2. Add the potatoes, water, and dried herbs, and season to taste with salt and pepper. Boil soup, reduce the heat to low and cover the pot. Simmer for 17 minutes using a hand blender, purée the soup until smooth. Stir in the scallions and serve.

Nutrition: Calories: 80 | Protein: 2 g | Fiber: 3 g

328. Pumpkin Soup

(Prep. Time: 4 Min | Cooking: 11 Min | Serving 3)

INGREDIENTS
- 1 tsp. light olive oil
- 1 onion
- 1 tsp. ground ginger
- 1 pear
- 1 tsp. curry powder
- 1/2 tsp. pumpkin pie spice
- 1/2 tsp. smoked paprika
- 4 cups water
- 3 cups canned pumpkin purée
- 1–2 tsp. salt
- 1/2 cup canned coconut milk
- 4 tbsp. nutritional yeast
- Pepper to taste

DIRECTIONS:
1. Cook oil in a pot over medium heat. Add the onion, ginger, and pear and sauté for about 5 minutes, until soft. Sprinkle in any optional spices and stir to combine.
2. Add the water, pumpkin, salt, and pepper, and stir until smooth and combined. Cook until just bubbling, about 10 minutes
3. Mix in the coconut milk (if using) and nutritional yeast (if using), and remove the soup from the heat.

Nutrition: Calories: 90 | Protein: 2 g | Fiber: 3 g

329. Wild Rice Stew

(Prep. Time: 4 Min | Cooking: 11 Min | Serving 5)

INGREDIENTS
- 2 tsp. light olive oil
- 2 cups mushrooms
- 1 tsp. salt
- 1 onion
- 4 garlic cloves
- 1 tbsp. dried herbs
- 3/4 cup white rice
- 1/4 cup wild rice
- 3 cups water
- 3 cups economical vegetable broth
- 4 tbsp. balsamic vinegar
- 1 cup frozen peas, thawed
- 1 cup unsweetened nondairy milk
- 2 cups chopped greens

DIRECTIONS:
1. Warm-up light olive oil in a large soup pot over medium-high heat. Sauté mushrooms and a pinch of salt for 4 minutes Cook onion and garlic for 2 minutes more.
2. Stir in the dried herbs (plus the onion powder, if using), white rice, wild rice, water, vegetable broth, vinegar (if using), and season. Boil, place heat to low, and cover. Simmer for 15 minutes
3. Put off the heat and mix the peas, milk (if using), and greens. Let the greens wilt before serving.

Nutrition: Calories: 201 | Protein: 6 g | Fiber: 4 g

330. Black-Eyed Pea and Sweet Potato Soup

(Prep. Time: 4 Min | Cooking: 10 Min | Serving 4)

INGREDIENTS
- 1 tsp. light olive oil
- 3 cups sweet potato
- 1/2 onion
- 1 garlic clove
- 2 cups water
- 1 (15 oz.) can black-eyed peas
- 2 tbsp. lime juice
- 1 tbsp. coconut sugar
- 1 tsp. paprika
- A pinch cayenne pepper
- 3 cups shredded cabbage
- 1 cup corn kernels
- A pinch of salt

DIRECTIONS:
1. Cook up light olive oil in a big soup pot over medium-high heat. Place the sweet potato, onion, garlic, and a pinch of salt. Sauté for 3 to 4 minutes
2. Add the water, black-eyed peas, lime juice, sugar, paprika, cayenne pepper, and salt to taste. Boil for 15 minutes
3. Add the cabbage and corn to the pot, stirring to combine, and cook for 5 minutes more. Turn off the heat, let cool for a few minutes, and serve.

Nutrition: Calories: 224 | Protein: 9 g | Fiber: 10 g

331. Creamy Garlic-Spinach Rotini Soup

(Prep. Time: 4 Min | Cooking: 10 Min | Serving 4)

INGREDIENTS
- 1 tsp. light olive oil
- 1 cup mushrooms
- 1/4 tsp. salt
- 4 garlic cloves
- 2 peeled carrots
- 6 cups vegetable broth
- 1 cup rotini or gnocchi
- 3/4 cup unsweetened nondairy milk
- 1/4 cup nutritional yeast
- 2 cups fresh spinach
- 1/4 cup pitted black olives
- Pepper to taste

DIRECTIONS:
1. Heat the light olive oil in a huge soup pot over medium-high heat. Situate the mushrooms and a pinch of salt. Sauté for about 4 minutes Add the garlic (if using fresh) and carrots, sauté for 1 minute more.
2. Add the vegetable broth, remaining 1/4 tsp. of salt, and pepper (plus the garlic powder, if using). Boil and add the pasta. Cook for about 10 minutes
3. Turn down the heat and mix in the milk, nutritional yeast, spinach, and olives. Top with croutons (if using).

Nutrition: Calories: 207 | Protein: 11 g | Fiber: 7 g

332. Tuscan White Bean Soup

(Prep. Time: 5 Min | Cooking: 10 Min | Serving 4)

INGREDIENTS
- 2 tsp. light olive oil
- 1 onion
- 4 garlic cloves
- 2 carrots
- 1 tbsp. dried herbs
- 4 cups vegetable broth
- 2 (15 oz.) cans of white beans
- 2 tbsp. lemon juice

- 2 cups chopped greens
- A pinch of salt
- Black pepper to taste
- Red pepper flakes to taste

DIRECTIONS:
1. Cook light olive oil in a pot at medium-high heat. Place onion, garlic (if using fresh), carrots, and a pinch of salt. Sauté for about 5 minutes, stirring occasionally. Sprinkle in the dried herbs (plus the garlic powder, if using), black pepper, and red pepper flakes, and toss to combine.
2. Add the vegetable broth, beans, and another pinch of salt, and bring the soup to a low simmer to heat through. If you like, make the broth a bit creamier by puréeing 1 to 2 cups of soup in a countertop blender and returning it to the pot.
3. Stir in the lemon juice and greens, and let the greens wilt into the soup before serving.

Nutrition: Calories: 145 | Protein: 7 g | Fiber: 6 g

333. MINESTRONE
(PREP. TIME: 4 MIN | COOKING: 10 MIN | SERVING 10)

INGREDIENTS
- 2 tsp. light olive oil
- 2 carrots
- 1 onion
- 4 garlic cloves
- 4 potatoes
- 1 cup green beans
- 1 (28 oz.) can of tomatoes
- 2 (15 oz.) cans navy beans
- 6 cups economical vegetable broth
- 6 cups water
- 1 tbsp. dried herbs
- 2 cups small pasta
- 1 zucchini
- 3 cups greens
- A pinch of salt

DIRECTIONS:
1. Cook up oil in the soup pot over medium-high heat. Mix in carrots, onion (if using fresh), garlic (if using fresh), and a pinch of salt. Sauté for about 5 minutes
2. Add the potatoes, green beans, tomatoes with their juices, beans, vegetable broth, water, and dried herbs (plus the onion powder and/or garlic powder, if using). Boil, turn down the heat and cover. Simmer for 20 minutes.
3. Add the pasta and zucchini to the pot. Simmer for 10 minutes turn off the heat, stir in the chopped greens, and let them wilt into the soup before serving.

Nutrition: Calories: 207 | Protein: 9 g | Fiber: 7 g

334. ITALIAN WEDDING SOUP
(PREP. TIME: 4 MIN | COOKING: 11 MIN | SERVING 4)

INGREDIENTS
- 1 tsp. light olive oil
- 2 carrots
- 1/2 onion
- 4 garlic cloves
- 8 cups water
- 1 cup orzo
- 1 tbsp. dried herbs
- 1 recipe quinoa meatballs
- 2 cups chopped greens
- A pinch of salt

DIRECTIONS:
1. Cook light olive oil in a large soup pot over medium-high heat. Stir in carrots, onion, garlic (if using fresh), and a pinch of salt. Sauté for 3 to 4 minutes
2. Add the water, orzo, and dried herbs (plus the garlic powder, if using). Season well and boil. Decrease the heat to low then simmer for 10 minutes
3. Add the meatballs and greens, and stir until the greens are wilted. Season well.

Nutrition: Calories: 168 | Protein: 9 g | Fiber: 6 g

335. CORN CHOWDER
(PREP. TIME: 3 MIN | COOKING: 10 MIN | SERVING 4)

INGREDIENTS
- 1 tsp. light olive oil
- 1 onion
- 2 garlic cloves
- 1 tsp. salt
- 2 potatoes
- 3 cups water
- 3 cups economical vegetable broth
- 4 cups frozen corn kernels
- Chopped scallion to taste
- Pepper to taste

DIRECTIONS:
1. Cook oil in a big pot over medium-high heat. Position onion, garlic, and a pinch of salt, and sauté for 2 to 3 minutes
2. Add the potatoes, water, vegetable broth, 1 tsp. salt, and pepper to taste. Boil and turn the heat to low. Simmer for 15 to 20 minutes

3. Heat up corn. Using a hand blender, purée as much of the soup as you like in the pot. Serve topped with chopped scallion.

Nutrition: Calories: 225 | Protein: 6 g | Fiber: 5 g

336. COCONUT CURRY SOUP
(PREP. TIME: 5 MIN | COOKING: 10 MIN | SERVING 5)

INGREDIENTS
- 1 tsp. light olive oil
- 1 onion
- 1-inch piece fresh ginger
- 2 tbsp. red curry paste
- 2 tbsp. coconut sugar
- 1 tsp. salt
- 3 cups sweet potato
- 3 cups cauliflower florets
- 1 cup canned coconut milk
- 3 cups water

DIRECTIONS:
1. Cook oil in a huge pot at medium heat. Add the onion and ginger, and stir-fry for about 3 minutes Stir fry the curry paste, sugar, and salt for 3 minutes more. Add the potato, cauliflower, coconut milk, and water. Simmer for 20 minutes
2. Using a hand blender, purée the soup until smooth, then transfer it to a countertop blender. Serve hot.

Nutrition: Calories: 288 | Protein: 5 g | Fiber: 4 g

337. RUBY GRAPEFRUIT AND RADICCHIO SALAD
(PREP. TIME: 10 MIN | COOKING: 0 MIN | SERVING 4)

INGREDIENTS
For the salad:
- 1 large ruby grapefruit
- 1 small head radicchio
- 2 cups green leaf lettuce
- 2 cups baby spinach
- 1 bunch watercress
- 6 radishes, sliced paper-thin

For the dressing:
- Juice of 1 lemon
- 2 tsp. agave
- 1 tsp. white wine vinegar
- 1/2 tsp. sea salt
- 1/2 tsp. black pepper
- 1/4 cup light olive oil

DIRECTIONS:
For salad:
1. Cut both ends off of the grapefruit, stand it on a cutting board on one of the flat sides, and, using a sharp knife, cut away the peel and all of the white pith. Remove the individual segments by slicing between the membrane and fruit on each side of each segment, dropping the fruit into a large salad bowl as you go.
2. Add the radicchio, lettuce, spinach, watercress, and radishes to the bowl and toss well.

For dressing:
1. Whisk together the lemon juice, agave, vinegar, salt, and pepper. Slowly whisk in the light olive oil and mix.
2. Toss the salad with the dressing.

Nutrition: Calories: 148 | Protein: 5 g | Fiber: 4 g

338. APPLE AND GINGER SLAW
(PREP. TIME: 10 MIN | COOKING: 0 MIN | SERVING 4)

INGREDIENTS
- 2 tbsp. light olive oil
- 1 lemon juice
- 1 tsp. ginger
- 2 apples
- 4 cups red cabbage
- Salt to taste

DIRECTIONS:
1. Scourge light olive oil, lemon juice, ginger, and salt and set aside.
2. Mix the apples and cabbage. Toss with the vinaigrette and serve immediately.

Nutrition: Calories: 190 | Protein: 10 g | Fiber: 4 g

339. SPINACH AND POMEGRANATE SALAD
(PREP. TIME: 10 MIN | COOKING: 0 MIN | SERVING 4)

INGREDIENTS
- 10 oz. baby spinach
- 1 pomegranate's seed
- 1 cup fresh blackberries
- 1/4 red onion
- 1/2 cup pecans
- 1/4 cup balsamic vinegar
- 3/4 cup light olive oil
- 1/2 tsp. salt
- 1/2 tsp. black pepper

DIRECTIONS:
1. Mix spinach, pomegranate seeds, blackberries, red onion, and pecans.

2. Scourge together the vinegar, light olive oil, salt, and pepper. Toss with the salad and serve immediately.

Nutrition: Calories: 218 | Protein: 9 g | Fiber: 6 g

340. PEAR VEGGIE SALAD
(PREP. TIME: 7 MIN | COOKING: 8 MIN | SERVING 3)

INGREDIENTS
- 1/4 cup pecans
- 10 oz. arugula
- 2 pears
- 1 tbsp. shallot
- 2 tbsp. champagne vinegar
- 2 tbsp. light olive oil
- 1/4 tsp. salt
- 1/4 tsp. black pepper
- 1/4 tsp. Dijon mustard

DIRECTIONS:
1. Preheat the oven to 350°F. Arrange pecans in 1 layer on a baking sheet. Toast in the preheated oven until fragrant, about 6 minutes Remove from the oven and let cool.
2. Toss the pecans, arugula, and pears.
3. Scourge together the shallot, vinegar, light olive oil, salt, pepper, and -mustard. Toss with the salad and serve immediately.

Nutrition: Calories: 198 | Protein: 10 t | Fiber: 2 g

341. APPLE AND FENNEL SALAD
(PREP. TIME: 15 MIN | COOKING: 0 MIN | SERVING 8)

INGREDIENTS
- 5 apples
- 1/2 lemon juice
- 2 fennel bulbs
- 2 stalks celery
- 1/2 bunch fresh parsley
- 2 tbsp. fennel fronds
- 2 tbsp. apple cider vinegar
- 1/4 cup light olive oil
- 1/4 tsp. sea salt
- 1/4 tsp. black pepper

DIRECTIONS:
1. Throw the apples with lemon juice. Add the sliced fennel, celery, and parsley and toss to combine.
2. Blend together the fennel fronds, vinegar, light olive oil, salt, and pepper. Toss with the salad and serve immediately.

Nutrition: Calories: 208 | Protein: 11 g | Fiber: 5 g

342. GERMAN POTATO SALAD
(PREP. TIME: 7 MIN | COOKING: 8 MIN | SERVING 8)

INGREDIENTS
- 8 red potatoes
- 3 tsp. salt
- 1 red onion
- 1/4 cup light olive oil
- 2 tbsp. Dijon mustard
- 2 tbsp. red wine vinegar
- 1/2 tsp. black pepper
- 3 tbsp. chives
- Water

DIRECTIONS:
1. Mix the potatoes, water, and 2 tsp. of salt. Boil until the potatoes are tender, about 10 minutes Situate in a bowl with the red onion.
2. Over medium heat, whisk together the light olive oil, mustard, -vinegar, the remaining 1 tsp. salt, and pepper.
3. Heat until warm, then remove from heat. Toss with the potatoes and onion. Stir in the chives and serve warm.

Nutrition: Calories: 197 | Protein: 13 g | Fiber: 6 g

343. TABBOULEH
(PREP. TIME: 7 MIN | COOKING: 8 MIN | SERVING 5)

INGREDIENTS
- 2 cups couscous
- 2 cups vegetable stock
- 1 tomato
- 1 cucumber
- 1/4 cup light olive oil
- 2 tbsp. lemon juice
- 2 tbsp. basil
- 2 tbsp. parsley
- 1 tbsp. mint
- 1/2 tsp. salt
- 1/4 tsp. black pepper

DIRECTIONS:
1. In a saucepan at medium-high heat, bring the vegetable stock to a boil. Add the couscous and remove it from the heat. Cover and keep aside for 5 minutes let cool completely.
2. Mix the cooled couscous with the tomato and cucumber.
3. Blend together the light olive oil, lemon juice, basil, parsley, mint, salt, and pepper. Toss with the couscous and vegetables. Serve immediately.

Nutrition: Calories: 209 | Protein: 12 g | Fiber: 7 g

344. Kale and Root Vegetable Salad

(Prep. Time: 15 Min | Cooking: 0 Min | Serving 4)

INGREDIENTS
- 1 1/2 lb. kale
- 2 carrots
- 1 turnip
- 4 radishes
- 3 green onions
- 2 tbsp. light olive oil
- 1 tbsp. lemon juice
- Zest of 1/2 lemon
- 2 tsp. agave
- 1/2 tsp. sea salt
- 1/4 tsp. black pepper

DIRECTIONS:
1. Mix the kale, carrots, turnip, radishes, and green onions.
2. Combine together the light olive oil, lemon juice, lemon zest, agave, salt, pepper, and cayenne, if using. Toss with the kale mixture and serve immediately.

Nutrition: Calories: 215 | Protein: 13 g | Fiber: 4 g

345. Brown Rice and Pepper Salad

(Prep. Time: 15 Min | Cooking: 0 Min | Serving 4)

INGREDIENTS
- 2 cups prepared brown rice
- 1/2 red onion
- 1 red bell pepper
- 1 orange bell pepper
- 1 carrot
- 1/4 cup light olive oil
- 2 tbsp. unseasoned rice vinegar
- 1 tbsp. soy sauce
- 1 garlic clove
- 1 tbsp. fresh ginger
- 1/4 tsp. salt
- 1/4 tsp. black pepper

DIRECTIONS:
1. Mix the rice, onion, bell peppers, and carrot.
2. Blend together the light olive oil, rice vinegar, soy sauce, garlic, ginger, salt, and pepper. Toss with the rice mixture and serve immediately.

Nutrition: Calories: 218 | Protein: 10 g | Fiber: 6 g

346. Three-Bean Salad

(Prep. Time: 10 Min | Cooking: 0 Min | Serving 4)

INGREDIENTS
- 1 (15 oz.) can of chickpeas
- 1 (15 oz.) can of kidney beans
- 1 (15 oz.) can of cannellini beans
- 1 red onion
- 1 cup fresh parsley
- 1/3 cup white wine vinegar
- 2 tbsp. agave
- 1/4 cup light olive oil
- 1 tsp. rosemary
- 1 tsp. sea salt
- 1/4 tsp. black pepper

DIRECTIONS:
1. Mix beans, onion, and parsley and toss to mix.
2. Incorporate together the vinegar, agave, light olive oil, rosemary, salt, -pepper, and cayenne, if using. Toss with the bean mixture. Chill for few hours

Nutrition: Calories: 211 | Protein: 11 g | Fiber: 6 g

347. Satsuma, Fruit Salad

(Prep. Time: 15 Min | Cooking: 0 Min | Serving 5)

INGREDIENTS
- 10 pieces of Satsuma oranges
- Seeds of 1 pomegranate
- 1 pink grapefruit
- Juice of 1 orange

DIRECTIONS:
1. Incorporate the oranges, pomegranate seeds, and grapefruit. Drizzle orange juice over the top and toss to combine. Refrigerate for 2 hours to allow the flavors to blend before serving.

Nutrition: Calories: 198 | Protein: 9 g | Fiber: 5 g

348. Quinoa Pilaf

(Prep. Time: 10 Min | Cooking: 5 Min | Serving 4)

INGREDIENTS
- 1 cup quinoa
- 2 cups vegetable stock
- 1/4 cup pine nuts
- 2 tbsp. light olive oil
- 1/2 onion
- 1/3 cup parsley
- Salt and pepper to taste

DIRECTIONS:
1. In a pot, boil quinoa and vegetable stock over medium-high heat, stirring occasionally. Reduce to a simmer. Cover and cook for 15 minutes
2. Preheat sauté pan over medium-high heat. Toast pine nuts to the dry hot pan for 3 minutes keep aside.

3. Fill light olive oil in the same pan and heat until it shimmers. Cook onion for 5 minutes
4. When the quinoa is soft and all the liquid is absorbed, remove it from the heat and fluff it with a fork. Stir in the pine nuts, onion, and parsley. Season with salt and -pepper. Serve hot.

Nutrition: Calories: 188 | Protein: 10 g | Fiber: 3 g

349. Lemon and Thyme Couscous
(Prep. Time: 5 Min | Cooking: 10 Min | Serving 6)

INGREDIENTS
- 2 3/4 cups vegetable stock
- Juice and zest of 1 lemon
- 2 tbsp. thyme
- 1 1/2 cups couscous
- 1/4 cup parsley
- Salt and pepper to taste

DIRECTIONS:
1. In a medium pot, boil together vegetable stock, lemon juice, and thyme. Stir in the couscous, cover, and remove from the heat. Keep aside for 5 minutes Fluff with a fork.
2. Stir in the lemon zest and parsley. Season with salt and pepper. Serve hot.

Nutrition: Calories: 288 | Protein: 5 g | Fiber: 4 g

350. Spicy Picnic Beans
(Prep. Time: 5 Min | Cooking: 10 Min | Serving 6)

INGREDIENTS
- 1 jalapeño
- 1 red bell pepper
- 1 green bell pepper
- 1 onion
- 5 garlic cloves
- 2 (15 oz.)cans of pinto beans
- 1 (15 oz.) can of kidney beans
- 1 (15 oz.) can of chickpeas
- 1 (18 oz.) bottle of barbecue sauce
- 1/2 tsp. chipotle powder
- Salt and pepper to taste

DIRECTIONS:
1. In a food processor, blend jalapeño, bell peppers, onion, and garlic for ten 1-second pulses, stopping halfway through to scrape down the sides.
2. In a large pot, combine the processed mixture with the beans, barbecue sauce, chickpeas, and chipotle powder. Simmer over medium-high heat, stirring frequently to blend the flavors, about 15 minutes

3. Season with salt and pepper. Serve hot.

Nutrition: Calories: 178 | Protein: 11 g | Fiber: 5 g

351. Chickpeas with Lemon and Spinach
(Prep. Time: 8 Min | Cooking: 7 Min | Serving 3)

INGREDIENTS
- 3 tbsp. light olive oil
- 1 (15 oz.) can of chickpeas
- 10 oz. baby spinach
- 1/2 tsp. sea salt
- Juice and zest of 1 lemon
- Pepper to taste

DIRECTIONS:
1. In a huge sauté pan, preheat light olive oil over medium-high heat until it shimmers. Cook chickpeas for 5 minutes
2. Cook spinach for 5 minutes Add the salt, lemon juice, lemon zest, and pepper and stir to combine. Serve immediately.

Nutrition: Calories: 208 | Protein: 11 g | Fiber: 7 g

352. Spicy Chickpeas
(Prep. Time: 3 Min | Cooking: 12 Min | Serving 6)

INGREDIENTS
- 1/4 cup light olive oil
- 1/2 tsp. cayenne pepper
- 2 (15 oz.) chickpeas
- 3/4 tsp. paprika
- 1 tsp. sea salt
- 1/2 tsp. chili powder
- 1/2 tsp. onion powder
- 1/2 tsp. cumin
- 3/4 tsp. garlic powder

DIRECTIONS:
1. Ready oven to 425°F. Strain chickpeas and let them dry in a towel-lined dish for 10 to 15 minutes Transfer the chickpeas onto a lined baking sheet and spread them out in a single layer.
2. Pour light olive oil over the chickpeas and sprinkle with salt. Bake them in the oven for 23 to 25 minutes or until they are golden brown, stirring frequently.
3. Once baked, stir in the remaining spices and toss well. Next, season and taste, adding more salt and pepper as needed. Serve and enjoy.

Nutrition: Calories: 224 | Protein: 13 g | Fat: 10 g

353. Coleslaw Salad

(Prep. Time: 7 Min | Cooking: 8 Min | Serving 3)

INGREDIENTS
- 4 scallions
- 10 oz. pasta
- 1 lb. carrot
- 1 lb. white cabbage

For the dressing:
- 1 tsp. sea salt
- 1/2 cup vegan mayonnaise
- 1/2 tsp. black pepper
- 2 tbsp. maple syrup
- 1/2 cup hummus
- Juice of 1/2 of 1 lemon
- 2 tbsp. Dijon mustard

DIRECTIONS:
1. Cook pasta following the package's instructions. Cook until al dente then drains. After that, make the dressing by placing all the ingredients in a medium bowl until combined well.
2. Incorporate pasta along with the remaining ingredients. Spoon the dressing over it and toss well. Serve and enjoy.

Nutrition: Calories: 524 | Protein: 17 g | Carbohydrates: 85 g

354. Corn Avocado Salad

(Prep. Time: 5 Min | Cooking: 10 Min | Serving 4)

INGREDIENTS
- 1 cup edamame
- 2 avocadoes
- 1 medium shallot
- 2 cups cherry tomatoes
- 2 cups sweet corn kernels

For the dressing:
- Juice of 1 lime
- 1/4 tsp. chili powder
- 1 tsp. sea salt
- 1 tsp. extra virgin light olive oil
- 1/4 cup fresh cilantro
- Water

DIRECTIONS:
1. Boil water in a medium-sized saucepan over medium-high heat. Once it starts boiling, stir in the corn and simmer them for 6 to 8 minutes or until cooked. Tip: Make sure to not overcook. Drain.
2. Set aside to cool. Mix all the dressing ingredients.
3. Incorporate the rest of the **INGREDIENTS** along with dressing in the mixing bowl and toss well. Season well. Serve and enjoy.

Nutrition: Calories: 375 | Protein: 14 g | Carbohydrates: 43 g

355. Couscous With Chickpeas Salad

(Prep. Time: 5 Min | Cooking: 10 Min | Serving 4)

INGREDIENTS
For the couscous:
- 1 cup couscous
- 1 1/2 cup water

For the salad:
- 12 oz. tofu, extra-firm
- 1 medium shallot
- 1 cup chickpeas
- 1/2 tsp. turmeric powder
- 1 tbsp. light olive oil
- 1 cucumber, diced
- 1/2 tsp. turmeric powder
- 4 tbsp. pine nuts
- 1 cup dill

For the dressing:
- Dash of pepper, ground
- 1 tbsp. Dijon mustard
- 1 tsp. sea salt
- 1/2 cup orange juice

DIRECTIONS:
1. Boil water in a pot at medium-high heat.
2. When it starts boiling, pour the hot water into a large heatproof bowl with couscous in it.
3. Cover the heatproof bowl with a lid and allow it to sit for 14 minutes
4. Fluff the couscous with a fork.
5. Heat a skillet and spoon in 1/3 of the oil into it.
6. Then, stir in the sliced shallot and cook them for 3 minutes or until transparent. Set aside on a plate.
7. Fry tofu along with the remaining oil for 9 minutes
8. To this, add the turmeric powder and mix again.
9. Mix in all the dressing ingredients.
10. Incorporate couscous, salad ingredients, and dressing.

Nutrition: Calories: 408 | Protein: 18 g | Carbohydrates: 54 g

356. Black and White Bean Salad

(Prep. Time: 5 Min | Cooking: 10 Min | Serving 4)

INGREDIENTS
For salad:
- 1/4 cup red onion
- 1/3 cup quinoa
- 1 cup cucumber
- 19 oz. drained black beans
- 1 jalapeno pepper
- 19 oz. drained navy beans
- 1/4 cup fresh coriander
- 3/4 cup of water

For dressing:
- 1/4 tsp. pepper
- 1/4 cup vegetable oil
- 1/4 tsp. salt
- 2 tbsp. lime juice
- 1/2 tsp. chili powder
- 1 tsp. coriander
- 1 tbsp. cider vinegar
- 1/2 tsp. oregano
- 1 garlic clove

DIRECTIONS:
1. Cook the quinoa for 11 minutes in a shallow saucepan filled with 3/4 cup of water.
2. Incorporate all the dressing ingredients.
3. Toss all the salad ingredients into a large mixing bowl and stir in the cooked quinoa and dressing.

Nutrition: Calories: 573 | Protein: 26.7 g | Carbohydrates: 83.5 g

357. CAESAR SALAD
(PREP. TIME: 15 MIN | COOKING: 0 MIN | SERVING 5)

INGREDIENTS
- 1/2 cup chickpeas
- 1 cup romaine lettuce
- 1 cup baby spinach
- 1 tsp. organic garlic minced
- 1 cup organic croutons
- 1 tsp. organic Dijon mustard
- 4 tsp. lemon juice
- 1/4 cup organic lite unsweetened coconut milk

DIRECTIONS:
1. Wash the lettuce and baby spinach leaves.
2. Toss them into a salad bowl.
3. Add croutons and chickpeas and toss the salad.
4. In a mixing bowl, mix together garlic, Dijon mustard, coconut milk, and lemon juice. Whisk it together until it forms a cream sauce.
5. Season the dressing to taste.
6. Dish the salad up into salad bowls and add a generous amount of the creamy salad dressing.

Nutrition: Calories: 102 | Fat: 3.1 g | Carbohydrates: 15 g

358. RED CABBAGE SALAD
(PREP. TIME: 15 MIN | COOKING: 0 MIN | SERVING 5)

INGREDIENTS
- 1 small red cabbage
- 3 pickling onions
- 1 jalapeño pepper
- 2 medium-sized mangoes
- 1 lime
- 2 large oranges
- 2 tsp. tahini
- 2 tsp. organic honey
- 2 tsp. freshly squeezed orange juice
- Salt and pepper to taste

DIRECTIONS:
1. With a cheese grater to shred the red cabbage; place shredded cabbage in a salad bowl.
2. Peel the oranges and grate the skins into fine orange zest right into a small mixing bowl.
3. Squeeze 2 tsp. juice from oranges, remove any pips, chop them into chunks, and put them into the salad bowl.
4. Grid the peel of the lemon into the bowl of orange zest.
5. Squeeze the rest of the lemon to make 2 tsp. lemon juice and add to the orange juice mix.
6. Peel mangoes and cut them into bite-sized cubes then add them to the salad bowl.
7. Toss together the cabbage, mango, and orange in the salad bowl.
8. Peel and finely chop the pickling onions before adding them to the cabbage salad bowls; mix them in well.
9. De-seed and chop the jalapeño pepper finely, then add it to the salad. Toss the salad well.
10. In a mixing bowl add together the tahini, honey, lemon, and orange juice along with the lemon-orange zest and blend together until completely combined.
11. Add salt and pepper to the dressing to taste.
12. Dish salad into salad bowls, drizzle with the zesty salad dressing and serve.

Nutrition: Calories: 211 | Fat: 2.1 g | Carbohydrates: 48.8 g

359. SPICY ROASTED CHICKPEAS
(PREP. TIME: 0 MIN | COOKING: 15 MIN | SERVING 4)

INGREDIENTS
- 15 oz. can of chickpeas with no added salt
- 1 tsp. Cajun spice
- 1/2 tsp. cayenne pepper
- 1 tsp. turmeric
- 1 tsp. dried mixed herbs
- 2 tbsp. extra virgin light olive oil

DIRECTIONS:
1. Preheat the oven to 375°F.
2. Prepare a baking sheet with pam vegan cooking spray.
3. Drain the chickpeas and pat them dry, place them in a medium-sized mixing bowl.

4. Toss cayenne pepper, Cajun spice, extra virgin light olive oil, mixed herb, and turmeric over the chickpeas.
5. Give the bowl a good toss to ensure all the chickpeas are coated with oil and spices.
6. Lay the chickpeas out flat at the bottom of the baking sheet.
7. Situate the baking sheet in the oven for 20 to 25 minutes or until the chickpeas are crisp and golden brown.
8. Remove from oven and let it cool.

Nutrition: Calories: 92 | Fat: 1.4 g | Fiber: 3.2 g

360. Fresh Salsa and Peachy Mango Chutney on the Side

(Prep. Time: 15 Min | Cooking: 0 Min | Serving 8)

INGREDIENTS
- 3 large tomatoes
- 1 white onion
- 4 spring onions
- 3 tsp. organic garlic minced
- 2 large mangoes
- 3 large peaches
- 3 tsp. fresh basil leaves
- 2 tsp. organic honey
- 3 tbsp. organic white grape vinegar
- 3 tbsp. organic balsamic vinegar
- 1 tsp. cayenne pepper
- Salt and pepper to taste

DIRECTIONS:
1. Wash the peaches and tomatoes.
2. Chop the peaches and the tomatoes into small salsa-sized chunks.
3. Mix chopped tomatoes and peaches in a medium-sized bowl.
4. Chop white onion into chunks to add to the tomatoes and peaches.
5. Chop the spring onion and place it in the bowl with the tomatoes and peaches.
6. Peel mangoes and cut them into bite-sized chunks before adding them to the tomatoes and peaches mixture.
7. In a mixing bowl, whisk together the garlic, balsamic vinegar, honey, white grape vinegar, finely chopped basil leaves, and cayenne pepper.
8. Mix the vinegar mixture together well before pouring it over the salsa-chutney mixture.
9. Blend the vinegar mixture in well, add salt and pepper to taste.
10. Cover the salsa-chutney and put it in the refrigerator to soak for at least 20 minutes

Nutrition: Calories: 80 | Fat: 0.5 g | Protein: 1.9 g

361. Spicy Sweet Potato Tofu Scramble

(Prep. Time: 10 Min | Cooking: 5 Min | Serving 2)

INGREDIENTS
- 3/4 lb. extra-firm tofu
- 1/2 small white onion
- 1 small sweet potato
- 1/2 cup fresh cherry tomatoes
- 1/2 cup fresh rocket
- 2 tbsp. vegan Parmesan
- 1/4 tsp. cayenne pepper
- 1/4 tsp. garlic powder
- Pam vegan cooking spray
- Water

DIRECTIONS:
1. Wash the sweet potato well.
2. Cut the sweet potato into bite-sized cubes.
3. Place some water into a pot on the stove and bring it to a boil before turning the stove to medium heat.
4. Place the sweet potato into the boiling water and allow them to simmer for 6 minutes Drain the water off them after 5 to 6 minutes and put them to one side.
5. Spray a medium-sized skillet with PAM vegan cooking spray.
6. Slice the onion finely and add it to the skillet on the stove. Cook until the onion is soft and glassy.
7. While cooking, crush the tofu into a bowl, and add garlic powder and cayenne pepper. Mix the spices through the tofu, you can add 1/4 tsp. turmeric if desired.
8. Once onions are soft mix the tofu to them and cook for up to 10 minutes
9. Chop the cherry tomatoes in half.
10. After 10 minutes stir in sweet potato and chopped cherry tomatoes. Simmer at medium heat for 5 to 6 minutes.
11. Top with fresh rocket and shredded vegan Parmesan.

Nutrition: Calories: 256 | Fat: 11.1 g | Protein: 20.8 g

362. Avocado Salad Collard Wrap

(Prep. Time: 15 Min | Cooking: 0 Min | Serving 4)

INGREDIENTS

- 1 medium avocado
- 1 fresh lime or lemon
- 1 red bell pepper
- 1 yellow bell pepper
- 4 large collard leaves
- 4 tbsp. alfalfa sprouts
- 1 tbsp. chickpeas with no added salt
- 1 tbsp. chia seeds
- 1 tbsp. sunflower seeds
- 1 tbsp. sesame seeds
- 1 tbsp. organic balsamic vinegar
- 1/2 tsp. organic garlic minced
- 1/2 tsp. ground ginger
- 1 tsp. tahini
- Water

DIRECTIONS:
1. Wash collard leaves and cut off the stem of each leaf.
2. Place the collard leaves in warm water with 2 tbsp. of freshly squeezed lime juice and soak for 13 minutes
3. While the collard is soaking peel and slice the avocado lengthwise into thin slices enough to fit 3 slices into 4 wraps.
4. Wash, de-seed, and chop the red as well as yellow bell peppers into small chunks.
5. Place the tahini, ground ginger, balsamic vinegar, chia seeds, chickpeas, and garlic into a blender and blend until the mixture combines into a chunky texture.
6. Take the collard leaves out of the lime water, pat them dry with a clean towel, and place them on a serving plate.
7. Squeeze some fresh lime juice onto each leaf and spread it around the leaf.
8. Place a layer of avocado onto the center of each leaf, then top the avocado with red pepper, yellow peppers, alfalfa sprouts, and drizzle a bit more lime juice over the mixture.
9. Add the tahini mixture, spreading it over the avocado, peppers, and alfalfa sprouts. Sprinkle with sesame and sunflower seeds.
10. Fold the four corners of the collard leaf over each other as you would do to a tortilla wrap and serve.

Nutrition: Calories: 200 | Fat: 15.4 g | Protein: 5.3 g

363. ARTICHOKE, RADISH, CARROT, AND STRAWBERRY BOWLS

(PREP. TIME: 15 MIN | COOKING: 0 MIN | SERVING 4)
INGREDIENTS
- 4 organic marinated baby artichoke hearts
- 4 red radishes
- 1 large horseradish
- 2 large carrots
- 1 cup fresh strawberries
- 1 small kiwi fruit
- 2 cups mixed salad leaves
- 2 tsp. fresh basil leaves
- 2 tsp. fresh chopped dill
- 2 tsp. sesame seeds
- 4 tbsp. non-dairy feta cheese
- 4 tbsp. organic balsamic vinegar
- 1 tbsp. tahini
- 2 tbsp. non-dairy plain yogurt
- 3 tsp. organic honey
- Salt and pepper to taste

DIRECTIONS:
1. Chop the baby artichokes into bite-sized chunks and place them in a salad bowl.
2. Wash, peel, and finely grate the horseradish, place the grated horseradish into the salad bowl.
3. Wash and slice the red radishes into thin rounds.
4. Peel and julienne the carrots into long thin slices, place them into the salad bowl.
5. Peel and chop the kiwi fruit into small cubes and place it in the salad bowl.
6. Slice strawberries in half and mix them in the salad bowl with the rest of the ingredients.
7. Mix the ingredients in the salad bowl together, giving them a good toss.
8. Add crumbled feta over the top of the salad.
9. Finely chop the dill and basil leaves.
10. Blend the yogurt, tahini, balsamic vinegar, honey, and dill, basil, and sesame seeds.
11. Add salt and pepper to the yogurt mix to taste and then blend it together into a fine mixture.
12. Use 4 round bowls and place a handful of salad leaves at the bottom of each bowl.
13. Dish up a healthy portion of the salad into each bowl, drizzle with salad dressing and serve.

Nutrition: Calories: 231 | Fat: 10.8 g | Protein: 9.9 g

364. TOFU STIR FRY

(PEP. TIME: 5 MIN | COOKING: 10 MIN | SERVING 2)

INGREDIENTS
- 6 oz. extra firm tofu
- 3 1/2 oz. dried rice noodles
- 1/2 tsp. fresh root ginger
- 1 tsp. organic garlic minced
- 4 spring onions
- 5 oz. Choi
- 1 fresh red bell pepper
- 1 yellow bell pepper
- 3 oz. mange tout
- 4 tbsp. beansprouts

- 1 tbsp. chopped fresh basil
- 2 tsp. sunflower seeds
- 2 tsp. sesame seeds
- 2 tsp. organic coconut oil
- 2 tsp. smooth hot sauce
- 2 tsp. low sodium soy sauce
- 1 tsp. organic honey
- 6 tbsp. organic low sodium vegetable stock

DIRECTIONS:
1. Cook the noodles per instructions on the packet.
2. Chop up the tofu.
3. Mix together soy sauce, honey, and chili sauce in a small bowl.
4. Peel all the vegetables then chop them into bite-sized chunks. This does not include mange tout, ginger, or beansprouts.
5. Grate the fresh root ginger.
6. Heat the coconut oil in a teflon-coated or non-stick wok or skillet.
7. Cook ginger, garlic, and onions.
8. Sauté chopped tofu for 4 to 5 minutes
9. Incorporate all the rest of the vegetables and cook until the tofu starts to turn golden brown.
10. Add the honey soy mix and stir the mixture until it coats the **INGREDIENTS** in the wok.
11. Cook for extra 7 minutes before adding the cooked noodles.
12. Cook the noodles with vegetables for 3 to 4 minutes before removing the stir-fry from the stove.
13. Dish into serving bowls, garnish with fresh basil, sesame seeds, and sunflower seeds.

Nutrition: Calories: 127 | Fat: 5.5 g | Protein: 6.1 g

365. MACARONI AND CHEESE
(PREP. TIME: 5 MIN | COOKING: 10 MIN | SERVING 4)

INGREDIENTS
- 2 tbsp. dried whole grain bread crumbs
- 5 oz. macaroni
- 1 large leek
- 8 oz. vegan mozzarella
- 1/2 tsp. organic mustard powder
- 3 oz. organic low sodium vegetable stock
- Water
- Salt and black pepper to taste

DIRECTIONS:
1. Place the macaroni in a pot of water on the stove to cook.
2. Finely chop the leek and place it with the macaroni to cook.
3. The macaroni is ready when it is tender.
4. When the macaroni is done remove it from the stove, drain off excess water, and place it in an oven dish.
5. Mix together mustard powder, vegetable stock, and 3/4 of the mozzarella cheese.
6. Flavor the mustard mixture with low sodium salt and ground black pepper to taste.
7. Dust bread crumbs on top of the macaroni in the baking dish and spoon over the cheese sauce.
8. Mix the cheese sauce into the macaroni so it is blended through.
9. Use the last 1/4 of the mozzarella cheese to sprinkle over the top of the dish.
10. Place it under a hot grill for 5 minutes

Nutrition: Calories: 520 | Fat: 14 g | Protein: 15.1 g

366. BERRY FRUIT SALAD WITH CHOCOLATE COCONUT WHIPPED CREAM
(PREP. TIME: 15 MIN | COOKING: 0 MIN | SERVING 6)

INGREDIENTS
- 1 cup frozen pomegranate seeds
- 1 cup mixed berries fresh or frozen
- 1 large banana
- 1 cup watermelon fresh or frozen
- 2 large plums
- 1 tbsp. fresh mint leaves
- 4 blocks dark non-dairy chocolate
- 2 tbsp. organic maple syrup
- 4 tbsp. whipped coconut cream
- 2 tsp. organic unsweetened cocoa powder
- 1/4 tsp. mixed spice

DIRECTIONS:
1. Mix the berries and pomegranate seeds.
2. Peel and cut bananas into thin rounds then place in the salad bowl with the berries and pomegranate seeds.
3. Wash and chop the 2 large plums into bite-sized cubes then place them in the salad bowl with the rest of the fruit.
4. Toss the fruit salad well.
5. Grate the dark chocolate into a mixing bowl and put it to one side.
6. Finely chop the mint leaves.
7. Place the whipped coconut cream into a mixing bowl and add 3/4 of finely chopped mint leaves.
8. Mix the mint leaves into the whipped cream and add the cocoa powder.
9. Drizzle the maple syrup over the fruit in the salad bowl and mix it in well along with the mixed spice.
10. Dish the fruit salad up into dessert bowls, top with whipped cream, and sprinkle the remaining

chopped mint leaves over the contents of the bowl.
11. Top with grated dark chocolate and serve.

Nutrition: Calories: 236 | Fat: 7 g | Protein: 2.5 g

367. ALOO GOBI
(PREP. TIME: 10 MIN | COOKING: 5 MIN | SERVING 4)

INGREDIENTS
- 1 large cauliflower
- 1 large russet potato
- 1 medium yellow onion
- 1 cup canned diced tomatoes
- 1 cup frozen peas
- 1/4 cup water
- 1 (2-inch) piece fresh ginger
- 1 1/2 tsp. garlic
- 1 jalapeño
- 1 tbsp. cumin seeds
- 1 tbsp. garam masala
- 1 tsp. ground turmeric
- 1 heaping tbsp. fresh cilantro

DIRECTIONS:
1. Combine the cauliflower, potato, onion, diced tomatoes, peas, water, ginger, garlic, jalapeño, cumin seeds, garam masala, and turmeric.
2. Cook low for 5 hours in the slow cooker. Garnish with the cilantro, and serve.

Nutrition: Calories: 115 | Protein: 6 g | Fiber: 6 g

368. JACKFRUIT CARNITAS
(PREP. TIME: 7 MIN | COOKING: 8 MIN | SERVING 4)

INGREDIENTS
- 2 (20 oz.) cans of jackfruit
- 3/4 cup Very Easy Vegetable Broth
- 1 tbsp. ground cumin
- 1 tbsp. dried oregano
- 1 1/2 tsp. ground coriander
- 1 tsp. minced garlic
- 1/2 tsp. ground cinnamon
- 2 bay leaves

DIRECTIONS:
1. Combine the jackfruit, vegetable broth, cumin, oregano, coriander, garlic, cinnamon, and bay leaves in a slow cooker. Stir to combine.
2. Cook on low for 8 hours. Shred jackfruit apart.
3. Remove the bay leaves. Serve with your favorite taco fixings.

Nutrition: Calories: 286 | Protein: 6 g | Fiber: 5 g

369. BAKED BEANS
(PREP. TIME: 9 MIN | COOKING: 6 MIN | SERVING 4)

INGREDIENTS
- 2 (15 oz.) cans of white beans
- 1 (15 oz.) can tomato sauce
- 1 medium yellow onion
- 1 1/2 tsp. garlic
- 3 tbsp. brown sugar
- 2 tbsp. molasses
- 1 tbsp. prepared yellow mustard
- 1 tbsp. chili powder
- 1 tsp. soy sauce

DIRECTIONS:
1. Mix beans, tomato sauce, onion, garlic, brown sugar, molasses, mustard, chili powder, and soy sauce into a slow cooker.
2. Cook it on low for 6 hours. Season.

Nutrition: Calories: 468 | Protein: 25 g | Fiber: 20 g

370. BRUSSELS SPROUTS CURRY
(PREP. TIME: 7 MIN | COOKING: 8 MIN | SERVING 4)

INGREDIENTS
- 3/4 lb. Brussels sprouts
- 1 can full-fat coconut milk
- 1 cup Very Easy Vegetable Broth
- 1 medium onion
- 1 medium carrot
- 1 medium red or Yukon potato
- 1 1/2 tsp. garlic
- 1 (1-inch) piece fresh ginger
- 1 small serrano chili
- 2 tbsp. peanut butter
- 1 tbsp. rice vinegar
- 1 tbsp. cane sugar
- 1 tbsp. soy sauce
- 1 tsp. curry powder
- 1 tsp. ground turmeric

DIRECTIONS:
1. Mix Brussels sprouts, coconut milk, vegetable broth, onion, carrot, potato, garlic, ginger, serrano chili, peanut butter, vinegar, cane sugar, soy sauce, curry powder, and turmeric in a slow cooker.
2. Cook it low for 7 hours. Season. Serve

Nutrition: Calories: 404 | Protein: 10 g | Fiber: 8 g

371. JAMBALAYA
(PREP. TIME: 7 MIN | COOKING: 8 MIN | SERVING 4)

INGREDIENTS

- 2 cups Very Easy Vegetable Broth
- 1 large yellow onion
- 1 green bell pepper
- 2 celery stalks, chopped
- 1 1/2 tsp. garlic
- 1 (15 oz.) can dark red kidney beans
- 1 (15 oz.) can black-eyed peas
- 1 (15 oz.) can diced tomatoes
- 2 tbsp. Cajun seasoning
- 2 tsp. dried oregano
- 2 tsp. dried parsley
- 1 tsp. cayenne pepper
- 1 tsp. smoked paprika
- 1/2 tsp. dried thyme

DIRECTIONS:
1. Mix vegetable broth, onion, bell pepper, celery, garlic, kidney beans, black-eyed peas, diced tomatoes, Cajun seasoning, oregano, parsley, cayenne pepper, smoked paprika, and dried thyme in a slow cooker.
2. Close and cook it low for 6 hours. Serve

Nutrition: Calories: 428 | Protein: 28 g | Fiber: 19 g

372. Mushroom-Kale Stroganoff
(Prep. Time: 9 Min | Cooking: 6 Min | Serving 4)

INGREDIENTS
- 1 lb. mushrooms
- 1 1/2 cups Very Easy Vegetable Broth
- 1 cup kale
- 1 small yellow onion
- 2 garlic cloves
- 2 tbsp. all-purpose flour
- 2 tbsp. ketchup
- 2 tsp. paprika
- 1/2 cup vegan sour cream
- 1/4 cup chopped fresh parsley

DIRECTIONS:
1. Incorporate mushrooms, vegetable broth, kale, onion, garlic, flour, ketchup or tomato paste, and paprika in a slow cooker.
2. Seal and cook on low for 6 hours. Stir in the sour cream and parsley.

Nutrition: Calories: 146 | Protein: 8 g | Fiber: 3 g

373. Sloppy Joe Filling
(Prep. Time: 7 Min | Cooking: 8 Min | Serving 4)

INGREDIENTS
- 3 cups textured vegetable protein
- 3 cups water
- 2 (6 oz.) cans tomato paste
- 1 medium yellow onion
- 1/2 medium green bell pepper
- 2 tsp. garlic
- 4 tbsp. vegan Worcestershire sauce
- 3 tbsp. brown sugar
- 3 tbsp. apple cider vinegar
- 3 tbsp. prepared yellow mustard
- 1 tbsp. salt
- 1 tsp. chili powder

DIRECTIONS:
1. Blend textured vegetable protein, water, tomato paste, onion, bell pepper, garlic, Worcestershire sauce, brown sugar, vinegar, mustard, hot sauce (if using), salt, and chili powder.
2. Close and cook at low for 8 hours in the slow cooker. Serve.

Nutrition: Calories: 452 | Protein: 75 g | Fiber: 11 g

374. Hoppin' John
(Prep. Time: 11 Min | Cooking: 4 Min | Serving 4)

INGREDIENTS
- 3 (15 oz.) cans of black-eyed peas
- 1 (14.5 oz.) can Cajun-style stewed tomatoes
- 2 cups hot water
- 1 cup kale
- 3/4 cup red bell pepper
- 1/2 cup scallions
- 1 medium jalapeño pepper
- 1 tsp. minced garlic
- 1 1/2 tsp. hot sauce
- 1 vegetable bouillon cube

DIRECTIONS:
1. Stir black-eyed peas, tomatoes, hot water, kale, bell pepper, scallions, jalapeño, garlic, hot sauce, and bouillon cube in a slow cooker.
2. Cover and cook in low for 4 hours. Serve

Nutrition: Calories: 164 | Protein: 10 g | Fiber: 8 g

375. African Sweet Potato Stew
(Prep. Time: 8 Min | Cooking: 7 Min | Serving 4)

INGREDIENTS
- 4 cups sweet potatoes
- 1 (15 oz.) can red kidney beans
- 1 (14.5 oz.) can of tomatoes
- 1 cup red bell pepper
- 2 cups very easy vegetable broth
- 1 medium yellow onion
- 1 (4.5 oz.) can green chili
- 1 tsp. minced garlic
- 1 1/2 tsp. ground ginger

- 1 tsp. ground cumin
- 4 tbsp. creamy peanut butter

DIRECTIONS:
1. Combine the sweet potatoes, kidney beans, diced tomatoes, bell pepper, vegetable broth, onion, green chilies, garlic, ginger, and cumin in a slow cooker.
2. Cook at low for 7 hours.
3. Ladle a little of the soup and mix in the peanut butter, then pour the mixture back into the stew.
4. Season. Mix well and serve.

Nutrition: Calories: 514 | Protein: 22 g | Fiber: 17 g

376. SWEET-AND-SOUR TEMPEH
(PREP. TIME: 8 MIN | COOKING: 7 MIN | SERVING 4)

INGREDIENTS
For sauce:
- 3/4 cup pineapple chunks
- 1/2 cup tomatoes
- 1/2 cup water
- 1/4 cup onion
- 1/4 cup soy sauce
- 2 tbsp. rice vinegar
- 1/4 tsp. red pepper flakes
- 1 (1/2-inch) piece fresh ginger

For tempeh:
- 2 (8 oz.) packages of tempeh
- 2 cups diced bell pepper
- 1 1/2 cups diced pineapple
- 1/2 cup diced onion

DIRECTIONS:
For sauce:
1. Put the pineapple chunks, crushed tomatoes, water, onion, soy sauce, rice vinegar, red pepper flakes, and ginger in a blender; blend until smooth.

For tempeh:
1. Blend sauce, tempeh, bell pepper, diced pineapple, and onion in a slow cooker. Cook in low for 7 hours.

Nutrition: Calories: 324 | Protein: 24 g | Fiber: 4 g

377. JACKFRUIT COCHINITA PIBIL
(PREP. TIME: 7 MIN | COOKING: 8 MIN | SERVING 8)

INGREDIENTS
- 2 (20 oz.) cans of jackfruit
- 2/3 cup lemon juice
- 1/3 cup orange juice
- 2 habanero peppers
- 2 tbsp. achiote paste
- 2 tsp. ground cumin
- 2 tsp. smoked paprika
- 2 tsp. chili powder
- 2 tsp. ground coriander
- 8 tortillas

DIRECTIONS:
1. Incorporate jackfruit, lemon juice, orange juice, habanero peppers, achiote paste, cumin, smoked paprika, chili powder, and coriander
2. Using the slow cooker, cook on low for 8 hours.
3. Shred jackfruit. Season.
4. Heat tortillas directly over a gas fire. Spoon the jackfruit into the tortillas and serve.

Nutrition: Calories: 297 | Protein: 5 g | Fiber: 6 g

378. DELIGHTFUL DAL
(PREP. TIME: 6 MIN | COOKING: 9 MIN | SERVING 4)

INGREDIENTS
- 3 cups red lentils
- 6 cups water
- 1 (28 oz.) can diced tomatoes
- 1 small yellow onion
- 2 1/2 tsp. garlic
- 1 (1-inch) piece fresh ginger
- 1 tbsp. ground turmeric
- 2 tsp. ground cumin
- 1 1/2 tsp. ground cardamom
- 1 1/2 tsp. whole mustard seeds
- 1 tsp. fennel seeds
- 1 bay leaf
- 1 tsp. salt
- 1/4 tsp. black pepper

DIRECTIONS:
1. Mix lentils, water, diced tomatoes, onion, garlic, ginger, turmeric, cumin, cardamom, mustard seeds, fennel seeds, bay leaf, salt, and pepper.
2. With the slow cooker, cook on low for 9 hours. Remove the bay leaf, and serve.

Nutrition: Calories: 585 | Protein: 40 g | Fiber: 48 g

379. MOROCCAN CHICKPEA STEW
(PREP. TIME: 9 MIN | COOKING: 6 MIN | SERVING 4)

INGREDIENTS
- 1 small butternut squash
- 3 cups Very Easy Vegetable Broth
- 1 medium yellow onion
- 1 bell pepper
- 1 (15 oz.) can chickpeas
- 1 (14.5 oz.) can tomato sauce

- 3/4 cup brown lentils
- 1 1/2 tsp. garlic
- 1 1/2 tsp. ground ginger
- 1 1/2 tsp. ground turmeric
- 1 1/2 tsp. ground cumin
- 1 tsp. ground cinnamon
- 3/4 tsp. smoked paprika
- 1/2 tsp. salt
- 1 (8 oz.) package fresh udon noodles

DIRECTIONS:
1. Incorporate butternut squash, vegetable broth, onion, bell pepper, chickpeas, tomato sauce, brown lentils, garlic, ginger, turmeric, cumin, cinnamon, smoked paprika, and salt in a slow cooker. Mix well.
2. Cover and cook 6 hours on low. Stir in noodles. Season and serve.

Nutrition: Calories: 427 | Protein: 26 g | Fiber: 24 g

380. Tex-Mex Taco Filling
(Prep. Time: 8 Min | Cooking: 7 Min | Serving 6)

INGREDIENTS
- 2 cups Very Easy Vegetable Broth
- 1 cup green lentils
- 1/2 cup uncooked quinoa
- 1/4 cup yellow onion
- 1 1/2 tsp. garlic
- 2 tsp. ground cumin
- 1 tsp. chili powder
- 1/2 tsp. smoked paprika

DIRECTIONS:
1. Blend vegetable broth, lentils, quinoa, onion, garlic, cumin, chili powder, and smoked paprika in a slow cooker.
2. Cook in low for 7 hours. Season. Serve with your choice of toppings.

Nutrition: Calories: 283 | Protein: 14 g | Fiber: 17 g

381. Cauliflower Bolognese
(Prep. Time: 6 Min | Cooking: 9 Min | Serving 4)

INGREDIENTS
- 1/2 head cauliflower
- 1 (10 oz.) container button mushrooms
- 1 small yellow onion
- 2 medium carrots
- 2 cups eggplant chunks
- 2 1/2 tsp. garlic
- 2 (28 oz.) cans of tomatoes
- 2 tbsp. tomato paste
- 2 tbsp. cane sugar
- 2 tbsp. balsamic vinegar
- 2 tbsp. nutritional yeast
- 1 1/2 tbsp. dried oregano
- 1 1/2 tbsp. dried basil
- 1 1/2 tsp. fresh rosemary leaves

DIRECTIONS:
1. In a food processor, blend cauliflower, mushrooms, onion, carrots, eggplant, and garlic. Transfer to a slow cooker.
2. Add the crushed tomatoes, tomato paste, cane sugar, balsamic vinegar, nutritional yeast, oregano, basil, and rosemary to the slow cooker; mix well.
3. Cover and cook in low for 9 hours. Season and serve.

Nutrition: Calories: 281 | Protein: 17 g | Fiber: 10 g

382. Delectable Dal
(Prep. Time: 5 Min | Cooking: 10 Min | Serving 4)

INGREDIENTS
- 1 tsp. light olive oil
- 1 cup chopped carrot
- 2 tsp. minced garlic
- 1 tsp. fennel seeds
- 1 cup dried red lentils
- 2 1/4 cups water
- 2 tbsp. lemon juice
- 1 tsp. salt

DIRECTIONS:
1. Over medium-high heat, heat the light olive oil. Sauté carrot and garlic for 3 minutes, stirring frequently. Stir fennel seeds, lentils, and water.
2. Boil, cover, set heat to medium-low or low, and simmer for 20 minutes
3. Remove from heat, stir lemon juice and salt, mash, and serve.

Nutrition: Calories: 196 | Protein: 13 g | Fiber: 16 g

383. Almond Roasted Veggies Salad
(Prep. Time: 4 Min | Cooking: 10 Min | Serving 4)

INGREDIENTS
- 1 cup carrots
- 1 cup broccoli
- 1 cup cauliflower
- 1 tbsp. light olive oil
- 1 cup whole almonds
- Salt and pepper to taste

For the dressing:
- 2 zest and juice lemon

- 2 tbsp. Mirin
- 1 garlic clove crushed
- 2 tbsp. extra-virgin light olive oil

DIRECTIONS:
1. Bake all the vegetables on the baking tray, sprinkle salt and pepper, brush with light olive oil for 20 minutes
2. Prep the dressing by mixing all the ingredients except oil and combine it slowly at the end whisking to gain the correct consistency
3. Add vegetables to the tray and pour dressing and almonds from the top and serve

Nutrition: Calories: 309 | Protein: 9.7 g | Fat: 25 g

384. Apple Almond
(Prep. Time: 8 Min | Cooking: 7 Min | Serving 3)

INGREDIENTS
- 4 apple
- 1 cup grated almond
- 1 juice lime
- 1/2 tsp. sea salt
- Coconut yogurt to serve

DIRECTIONS:
1. Incorporate all the ingredients well
2. Now serve it with some coconut yogurt if you desire

Nutrition: Calories: 395 | Protein: 7.5 g | Fat: 18.3 g

385. Asian Cabbage
(Prep. Time: 9 Min | Cooking: 6 Min | Serving 7)

INGREDIENTS
- 1 small red cabbage
- 4 cm piece of ginger shredded
- 2 bird's-eye chilies
- 50 g caster sugar
- 100 ml vinegar
- 2 tsp. sesame oil
- 2 tsp. black sesame seeds
- 100 ml water
- 1 tsp. salt

DIRECTIONS:
1. Take a cabbage
2. Remove the sagging outer leaves and quarter the cabbage
3. Remove the core and put the remaining in a bowl along with ginger and some slit chilies
4. Dissolved the sugar in the mixture of vinegar then pour 100 ml water along with 1 tsp. salt
5. Marinate the cabbage for 2 hours
6. Drain the cabbage well and pour some sesame seeds and oil

Nutrition: Calories: 53 | Protein: 1.6 g | Fat: 1.7 g

386. Avocado Chat
(Prep. Time: 10 Min | Cooking: 5 Min | Serving 4)

INGREDIENTS
- 4 avocado
- 2 tsp. Chaat masala
- 1 juiced lime
- 1/2 tsp. sea salt

DIRECTIONS:
1. Combine all the ingredients well
2. Now serve it with some coconut yogurt if you desire

Nutrition: Calories: 234 | Protein: 2.9 g | Fat: 21 g

387. Avocado Protein Salad
(Prep. Time: 0 Min | Cooking: 15 Min | Serving 2)

INGREDIENTS
- 400 g can of kidney beans
- 1 avocado
- 1 red chili
- 1 tsp. cumin seeds
- 1/2 tsp. salt
- 1/2 red onion
- 3 roasted red peppers
- 2 handfuls rocket
- 2 warmed pitta bread
- 2 tbsp. light olive oil
- Lime juice to taste

DIRECTIONS:
1. Mix onion, avocado, peppers, beans, and chili in a bowl
2. Whisk 2 tbsp. light olive oil and lime juice while adding seasoning and cumin seeds
3. Put it in the bowl and mix well
4. Add the bean mixture to the rocket pile into 2 plates
5. Best served with warm pittas

Nutrition: Calories:536 | Protein: 19.3 g | Fat: 28.4 g

388. Beetroot Hummus
(Prep. Time: 5 Min | Cooking: 10 Min | Serving 4)

INGREDIENTS
- 400 g tin chickpeas

- 160 g cooked beetroots
- 3 tbsp. tahini
- 1 garlic clove
- 1 1/2 juiced lemon
- 3 tbsp. extra-virgin light olive oil
- Salt to taste

DIRECTIONS:
1. Blend beetroot, chickpeas, tahini, light olive oil, salt, and garlic together in a blender
2. Add in lemon juice and mix
3. Drizzle with extra light olive oil

Nutrition: Calories: 245 | Protein: 7.8 g | Fat: 16.7 g

389. BEANS SALAD

(PREP. TIME: 8 MIN | COOKING: 17 MIN | SERVING 5)

INGREDIENTS
- 1 cup can beans
- 1 onion
- 1 avocado
- 2 tbsp. lemon juice
- 2 tsp. Harissa
- 1 tbsp. light olive oil
- 1 garlic clove
- 2 tbsp. flat-leaf parsley
- Salt to taste

DIRECTIONS:
1. Add garlic, lemon juice, harissa, and light olive oil in a bowl and whisk
2. Take a serving bowl and add beans, onion, avocado, salt, and the sauce you made
3. Add parsley from the top and serve

Nutrition: Calories: 332 | Protein: 10.45 g | Fat: 18.1 g

390. BROCCOLI ROASTED TOASTS

(PREP. TIME: 10 MIN | COOKING: 5 MIN | SERVING 4)

INGREDIENTS
- 2 cups broccoli
- 2 tbsp. light olive oil
- 1 cup cherry tomatoes
- 6 sprigs thyme
- 4 thick slices of onion
- 4 toasted sourdough
- Salt to taste

DIRECTIONS:
1. Preheat the oven to medium heat
2. Add broccoli to the bowl having thyme, light olive oil, and salt
3. Bake for 25 minutes
4. Remove from the oven and spread on the toasted sourdough
5. Top with cherry tomatoes and onion slices and serve

Nutrition: Calories: 268 | Protein: 9.5 g | Fat: 8.6 g

391. BUTTERNUT SQUASH HUMMUS

(PREP. TIME: 5 MIN | COOKING: 10 MIN | SERVING 4)

INGREDIENTS
- 2 cups can of chickpeas
- 1 cup butternut squash
- 3 tbsp. tahini
- 1 garlic clove
- 2 tbsp. lemon
- 3 tbsp. extra-virgin light olive oil
- Salt to taste

DIRECTIONS:
1. Blend butternut squash, chickpeas, tahini, light olive oil, salt, and garlic together in a blender
2. Add in lemon juice and mix
3. Dash with extra light olive oil

Nutrition: Calories: 240 | Protein: 7.8 g | Fat: 12.6 g

392. BUTTERNUT SQUASH WITH VEGAN YOGURT

(PREP. TIME: 10 MIN | COOKING: 5 MIN | SERVING 2)

INGREDIENTS
- 1 tbsp. light olive oil
- 2 cups butternut squash
- Salt to taste
- 1/2 tsp. smoked paprika
- 1/2 cup vegan yogurt

DIRECTIONS:
1. Take a pan and heat light olive oil
2. Take a bowl and add butternut squash, salt, paprika and mix well and add to the pan
3. Fry on low heat for 20 minutes and turn in between
4. Allow it to cool a bit and mix with yogurt
5. Serve as a salad with the main dish

Nutrition: Calories: 162.5 | Protein: 3.2 g | Fat: 8.27 g

393. CAULIFLOWER AND SQUASH MIX

(PREP. TIME: 10 MIN | COOKING: 5 MIN | SERVING 2)

INGREDIENTS

- 2 tbsp. light olive oil
- 2 cups cut in big florets cauliflower
- 2 cups butternut squash
- 1 tbsp. rice vinegar
- 1 tsp. dried oregano
- 1/2 tsp. dried chili flakes
- Salt and pepper to taste

DIRECTIONS:
1. Take a pan and heat light olive oil
2. Take a bowl and add cauliflower, butternut squash, salt, pepper, and rice vinegar and mix well
3. Fry on low heat for 20 minutes and turn in between
4. When done sprinkle chili flakes and oregano on the top

Nutrition: Calories: 249 | Protein: 4.2 g | Fat: 14.5 g

394. CHICKPEAS AVOCADO SALAD
(PREP. TIME: 10 MIN | COOKING: 5 MIN | SERVING 2)

INGREDIENTS
- 1 avocado
- 1 cup chickpeas
- 1 red onion
- 3 roasted red peppers
- 1 red chili
- 1 tsp. cumin seeds
- 2 tbsp. light olive oil
- 2 handfuls rocket
- Lime juice to taste

DIRECTIONS:
1. Mix onion, avocado, peppers, chickpeas, and chili in a bowl
2. Blend two tbsp. of light olive oil and lime juice though adding seasoning and cumin seeds
3. Put it in the bowl and mix well
4. Add the chickpeas mixture to the rocket pile into 2 plates

Nutrition: Calories: 416 | Protein: 10.4 g | Fat: 26.8 g

395. CHICKPEAS CUCUMBER SALAD
(PREP. TIME: 10 MIN | COOKING: 5 MIN | SERVING 2)

INGREDIENTS
- 1 cup chickpeas
- 2 cups cucumber
- 1 cup onion
- 2 tbsp. lemon juice
- 2 tsp. rose harissa
- 2 tbsp. light olive oil
- 2 tbsp. flat-leaf parsley
- 1 garlic clove

DIRECTIONS:
1. Add garlic, lemon juice, harissa, and light olive oil in a bowl and whisk
2. Take a serving bowl and combine chickpeas, onion, cucumber, and the sauce you made
3. Add parsley from the top and serve

Nutrition: Calories: 344 | Protein: 9.25 g | Fat: 16.3 g

396. CRUNCHY POMEGRANATE FLOWER SPROUTS
(PREP. TIME: 10 MIN | COOKING: 5 MIN | SERVING 2)

INGREDIENTS
- 3 tbsp. pomegranate molasses
- 150 g flower sprouts
- Vegetable oil for deep-frying
- A pinch of sea salt flakes
- A pinch of Pul Biber:

DIRECTIONS:
1. Preheat oil in the pan and when enough heated add flower sprouts
2. Just fry them for 30 seconds
3. Mix with other ingredients.
4. Serve right away

Nutrition: Calories: 202 | Protein: 3.4 g | Fat: 11.3 g

Chapter 6. Snack Recipes

397. Cinnamon Baked Apple Chips
(Prep. Time: 13 Min | Cooking: 2 Min | Serving 2)

INGREDIENTS
- 1 tsp. cinnamon
- 1–2 apples

DIRECTIONS:
1. Preheat your oven to 200°F
2. Take a sharp knife and slice apples into thin slices
3. Discard seeds
4. Prep baking sheet with parchment paper and arrange apples on it
5. Make sure they do not overlap
6. Once done, sprinkle cinnamon over apples
7. Bake in the oven for 1 hour
8. Flip and bake for an hour more until no longer moist
9. Serve and enjoy!

Nutrition: Calories: 147 | Carbohydrates: 39 g | Protein: 1 g

398. Acorn Squash with Mango Chutney
(Prep. Time: 10 Min | Cooking: 5 Min | Serving 4)

INGREDIENTS
- 1 large acorn squash
- 1/4 cup mango chutney
- 1/4 cup flaked coconut
- Salt and pepper as needed

DIRECTIONS:
1. Chop squash into quarters and remove the seeds, discard the stringy pulp.
2. Spray your cooker with light olive oil.
3. Transfer the squash to the slow cooker
4. Take a bowl and add coconut, salt, pepper, and chutney, mix well and divide the mixture into the center of the Squash.
5. Season well.
6. Close and cook on low for 2 to 3 hours.
7. Enjoy!

Nutrition: Calories: 226 | Fat: 6 g | Carbohydrates: 24 g

399. Carrot Chips
(Prep. Time: 4 Min | Cooking: 11 Min | Serving 3)

INGREDIENTS
- 3 cups carrots, sliced into paper-thin rounds
- 2 tbsp. light olive oil
- 2 tsp. ground cumin
- 1/2 tsp. smoked paprika
- A pinch of salt

DIRECTIONS:
1. Preheat your oven to 400°F
2. Slice carrot into paper-thin shaped coins using a peeler
3. Toss with oil and spices
4. Layout the slices onto a parchment paper-lined baking sheet in a single layer
5. Sprinkle salt
6. Transfer to oven and bake for 8-10 minutes
7. Remove and serve
8. Enjoy!

Nutrition: Calories: 434 | Fat: 35 g | Carbohydrates: 32 g

400. Brussels and Pistachio
(Prep. Time: 8 Min | Cooking: 7 Min | Serving 5)

INGREDIENTS
- 1 lb. brussels sprouts, tough bottom trimmed and halved lengthwise
- 4 shallots, peeled and quartered
- 1 tbsp. extra-virgin light olive oil
- Sea salt to taste
- Freshly ground black pepper to taste
- 1/2 cup roasted pistachios, chopped
- Zest of 1/2 lemon
- Juice of 1/2 lemon

DIRECTIONS:
1. Preheat your oven to 400°F
2. In baking sheet and line, it with aluminum foil
3. Keep it on the side
4. Take a large bowl and add Brussels and shallots and dress them with light olive oil
5. Season well and spread veggies onto a sheet
6. Bake for 15 minutes until slightly caramelized
7. Remove the oven and transfer to a serving bowl
8. Toss with lemon zest, lemon juice, and pistachios
9. Serve and enjoy!

Nutrition: Calories: 126 | Fat: 7 g | Carbohydrates: 14 g

401. Buffalo Cashews
(Prep. Time: 10 Min | Cooking: 5 Min | Serving 4)

INGREDIENTS
- 2 cups raw cashews
- 3/4 cup red hot sauce
- 1/3 cup avocado oil
- 1/2 tsp. garlic powder
- 1/4 tsp. turmeric

DIRECTIONS:
1. Mix wet ingredients in a bowl and stir in seasoning
2. Add cashews to the bowl and mix
3. Soak cashews in hot sauce mix for 2 to 4 hours
4. Preheat your oven to 325°F
5. Spread cashews onto a baking sheet
6. Bake for 35 to 55 minutes, turn every 10 to 15 minutes
7. Let them cool and serve!

Nutrition: Calories: 268 | Fat: 16 g | Carbohydrates: 20 g

402. Morning Peach
(Prep. Time: 10 Min | Cooking: 5 Min | Serving 4)

INGREDIENTS
- 6 small peaches, cored and cut into wedges
- 1/4 cup of coconut sugar
- 2 tbsp. coconut butter
- 1/4 tsp. almond extract

DIRECTIONS:
1. Take a small pan and add peaches, sugar, butter, and almond extract
2. Toss well
3. Cook over medium-high heat for 5 minutes, divide the mix into bowls, and serve
4. Enjoy!

Nutrition: Calories: 198 | Fat: 2 g | Carbohydrates: 11 g

403. Mango Rice
(Prep. Time: 7 Min | Cooking: 8 Min | Serving 3)

INGREDIENTS
- 1/2 cup coconut sugar
- 1 mango
- 14 oz. coconut milk
- 1/2 cup basmati rice

DIRECTIONS:
1. Cook the rice following the package's instructions, stir 1/2 sugar. Ensure to alternate half of the required water with coconut milk
2. In different skillet and boil rest of coconut milk with sugar, once thick stir in rice
3. Topped with mango slices and serve

Nutrition: Calories: 550 | Fat: 30 g | Carbohydrates: 70 g

404. Pecan Fruity Crumble
(Prep. Time: 9 Min | Cooking: 6 Min | Serving 5)

INGREDIENTS
- 14 oz. blueberries
- 1 tbsp. lemon juice
- 2 tsp. stevia powder
- 3 tbsp. chia seeds
- 2 cups almond flour
- 1/4 cup pecans
- 5 tbsp. coconut oil
- 2 tbsp. cinnamon

DIRECTIONS:
1. Incorporate blueberries, stevia, chia seeds, and lemon juice and stir
2. Preheat iron skillet stir in mixture
3. Combine the rest of the ingredients, pour mixture over blueberries
4. Preheat your oven to 400°F
5. Bake it for 30 minutes

Nutrition: Calories: 380 | Fat: 32 g | Carbohydrates: 20 g

405. Healthy Rice Pudding
(Prep. Time: 8 Min | Cooking: 7 Min | Serving 3)

INGREDIENTS
- 1 cup of brown rice
- 1 tsp. vanilla extract
- 1/2 tsp. salt
- 1/2 tsp. cinnamon
- 1/4 tsp. nutmeg
- 3 egg substitutes
- 3 cups coconut milk
- 2 cups brown rice

DIRECTIONS:
1. Stir all ingredients well
2. Prep oven to 300°F
3. Situate into baking dish
4. Bake for 1 hour and 30 minutes

Nutrition: Calories: 330 | Fat: 10 g | Carbohydrates: 52 g

406. Oatmeal Cookies
(Prep. Time: 10 Min | Cooking: 5 Min | Serving 4)

INGREDIENTS
- 1/4 cup applesauce
- 1/2 tsp. cinnamon
- 1/3 cup raisins
- 1/2 tsp. vanilla extract, pure
- 1 cup ripe banana, mashed
- 2 cups oatmeal

DIRECTIONS:

1. Set oven to 350°F
2. Incorporate everything until you have a gooey mixture
3. Fill batter into an ungreased baking sheet drop by drop and press them using a tbsp.
4. Bake for 15 minutes

Nutrition: Calories: 80 | Carbohydrates: 16 g | Protein: 2 g

407. Apple Slices

(Prep. Time: 8 Min | Cooking: 12 Min | Serving 5)

INGREDIENTS
- 1 cup coconut oil
- 1/4 cup date paste
- 2 tbsp. cinnamon
- 4 granny smith apples

DIRECTIONS:
1. In a huge-sized skillet and heat over medium heat
2. Cook oil.
3. Sprinkle cinnamon and date paste into the oil
4. Stir in sliced apples and cook for 7 minutes

Nutrition: Calories: 368 | Carbohydrates: 44 g | Protein: 1 g

408. The Garbanzo Bean Extravaganza

(Prep. Time: 10 Min | Cooking: 0 Min | Serving 5)

INGREDIENTS
- 1 can of garbanzo beans
- 1 tbsp. light olive oil
- 1 tsp. sunflower seeds
- 1 tsp. garlic powder
- 1/2 tsp. paprika

DIRECTIONS:
1. Preheat your oven to 375°F
2. In a baking sheet lined with silicone baking mat
3. Drain and rinse garbanzo beans, dry, and put into a large bowl
4. Toss with light olive oil, sunflower seeds, garlic powder, paprika and mix well
5. Spread over a baking sheet
6. Cook for 20 minutes at 190°C
7. Turn chickpeas so they are roasted well
8. Return in the oven for 25 minutes at 190°C
9. Let them cool and enjoy!

Nutrition: Calories: 395 | Carbohydrates: 52 g | Protein: 35 g

409. Roasted Onions and Green Beans

(Prep. Time: 10 Min | Cooking: 5 Min | Serving 6)

INGREDIENTS
- 1 yellow onion, sliced into rings
- 1/2 tsp. onion powder
- 2 tbsp. coconut flour
- 1–1/3 lb. fresh green beans, trimmed and chopped
- Oil to taste
- Water

DIRECTIONS:
1. Take a large bowl and mix sunflower seeds with onion powder and coconut flour
2. Add onion rings
3. Mix well to coat
4. Spread the rings on the baking sheet, lined with parchment paper
5. Drizzled with some oil
6. Bake for 10 minutes at 400°F
7. Parboil the green beans for 3 to 5 minutes in the boiling water
8. Drain and serve the beans with baked onion rings
9. Eat warm and enjoy!

Nutrition: Calories: 214 | Carbohydrates: 3.7 g | Protein: 8.3 g

410. Lemony Sprouts

(Prep. Time: 11 Min | Cooking: 0 Min | Serving 3)

INGREDIENTS
- 1 lb. Brussels
- 8 tbsp. light olive oil
- 1 lemon juice
- 3/4 cup spicy almond and seed mix
- Salt and pepper to taste

DIRECTIONS:
1. Take a bowl and mix in lemon juice, salt, pepper and light olive oil
2. Mix well
3. Stir in shredded Brussels and toss
4. Let it sit for 10 minutes
5. Add nuts and toss
6. Serve and enjoy!

Nutrition: Calories: 382 | Carbohydrates: 9 g | Protein: 7 g

411. Hummus Without Oil

(Prep. Time: 5 Min | Cooking: 0 Min | Serving 6)

INGREDIENTS
- 2 tbsp. lemon juice

- 1 (15 oz.) can of chickpeas
- 2 tbsp. tahini
- 2 garlic cloves
- ½ cup Red pepper hummus
- 2 tbsp. of almond milk pepper

DIRECTIONS:
1. Cleanse chickpeas and process them in a high-speed blender with garlic until breaking into fine pieces.
2. Add the other ingredients and blend everything. Pour in some water if you want a less thick consistency.

Nutrition: Calories: 202| Carbohydrates: 35 g | Protein: 11 g

412. Tempting Quinoa Tabbouleh

(Prep. Time: 4 Min | Cooking: 10 Min | Serving 6)

INGREDIENTS
- 1 cup quinoa
- 1 garlic clove
- 1/2 tsp. salt
- 1/2 cup of extra virgin light olive oil
- 2 tbsp. lemon juice
- 2 Persian cucumbers
- 2 scallions
- 1-pint cherry tomatoes
- 1/2 cup fresh mint
- 2/3 cup parsley
- 1 1/4 cups of water

DIRECTIONS:
1. Boil the quinoa over high heat mixed with salt in 1 1/4 cups of water. Adjust heat to medium-low, then simmer for 10 minutes Remove and rest for 5 minutes Fluff it with a fork.
2. Whisk the garlic with the lemon juice. Add the light olive oil gradually. Season.
3. On a baking sheet, lay over the quinoa and set aside. Mix 1/4 of the dressing.
4. Add the tomatoes, scallions, herbs, and cucumber. Toss and season. Add the remaining dressing.

Nutrition: Calories: 292 | Fat: 20 g | Protein: 5 g

413. Quick Peanut Butter Bars

(Prep. Time: 8 Min | Cooking: 0 Min | Serving 2)

INGREDIENTS
- 20 soft-pitted Medjool dates
- 1 cup raw almonds
- 1 1/4 cup pretzels
- 1/3 cup natural peanut butter

DIRECTIONS:
1. Crush almonds in a food processor.
2. Blend the peanut butter and the dates until a thick dough
3. Crush the pretzels. Mix with the rest of the ingredients.
4. Line square pan with parchment paper. Press the dough onto the pan.
5. Freeze for 2 hours.
6. Once set, cut it into bars.

Nutrition: Calories: 343 | Fat: 23 g | Protein: 5 g

414. Healthy Cauliflower Popcorn

(Prep. Time: 3 Min | Cooking: 12 Min | Serving 2)

INGREDIENTS
- 2 heads cauliflower

Spicy sauce:
- 1/2 cup water
- 1/2 tsp. turmeric
- 1 cup dates
- 2–3 tbsp. nutritional yeast
- 1/4 cup sun-dried tomatoes
- 2 tbsp. raw tahini
- 1–2 tsp. cayenne pepper
- 2 tsp. onion powder
- 1 tbsp. apple cider vinegar
- 2 tsp. garlic powder

DIRECTIONS:
1. Chop the cauliflower into small pieces.
2. Incorporate all the ingredients for the spicy sauce in a blender.
3. Coat well the cauliflower florets.
4. Stir in the spicy florets in a dehydrator tray.
5. Sprinkle some salt and your favorite herb if you want.
6. Dehydrate the cauliflower for 12 hours at 115°F until it is crunchy.

Nutrition: Calories: 69 | Fat: 2.4 g | Protein: 3.1 g

415. Hummus Made With Sweet Potato

(Prep. Time: 5 Min | Cooking: 10 Min | Serving 4)

INGREDIENTS
- 2 cups cooked chickpeas
- 2 medium sweet potatoes
- 3 tbsp. tahini
- 3 tbsp. light olive oil
- 3 garlic gloves
- Juice 1 lemon
- 1/4 tsp. cumin

- Zest 1 lemon
- 1/2 tsp. smoked paprika
- 1 1/2 tsp. cayenne pepper
- Sesame seeds to taste

DIRECTIONS:
1. Prep the oven to 400°F. Situate sweet potatoes on the middle rack of the oven and bake for 45 minutes Set aside.
2. In a food processor, incorporate all the other ingredients.
3. Peel off sweet potato skin.
4. Blend in sweet potatoes with the rest of the ingredients.
5. Once mash, sprinkle some sesame seeds and cayenne pepper!

Nutrition: Calories: 33.6 | Fat: 0.9 g | Protein: 1 g

416. CRISP BALLS MADE WITH PEANUT BUTTER

(PREP. TIME: 15 MIN | COOKING: 0 MIN | SERVING 16)

INGREDIENTS
- 1/4 cup wheat germ
- 1/2 cup natural peanut butter
- 1/3 cup rolled oats
- 1/4 cup unsweetened flaked coconut
- 1/4 cup quick oats
- 1/2 tsp. ground cinnamon
- 1/4 cup brown rice crisp cereal
- 1 tbsp. maple syrup
- 1/4 cup apple cider vinegar

DIRECTIONS:
1. Incorporate all the ingredients apart from the rice cereal.
2. Create 16 balls in 1-inch diameter.
3. Roll each ball on the rice cereal. Coat well.

Nutrition: Calories: 79 | Fat: 4.8 g | Protein: 3.5 g

417. HEALTHY PROTEIN BARS

(PREP. TIME: 15 MIN | COOKING: 0 MIN | SERVING 12)

INGREDIENTS
- 1 large banana
- 1 cup of rolled oats
- 1 serving vegan vanilla protein powder

DIRECTIONS:
1. In a food processor, mix protein powder and rolled oats for 1 minute.
2. Mix in the banana and form a pliable and coarse dough.
3. Form into bars and store them in a container.

Nutrition: Calories: 47 | Fat: 0.7 g | Protein: 2.7 g

418. TEMPEH BACON-SMOKED

(PREP. TIME: 5 MIN | COOKING: 10 MIN | SERVING 10)

INGREDIENTS
- 3 tbsp. maple syrup
- 8 oz. packages tempeh
- 1/4 cup soy sauce
- 2 tsp. liquid smoke

DIRECTIONS:
1. Steam the block of tempeh.
2. Incorporate tamari, maple syrup, and liquid smoke.
3. When the tempeh cools down, chop into strips and add to the prepared marinade.
4. Cook the tempeh at medium-high heat with a dash of the marinade. Cook both sides.
5. You can pour some more marinade to cook the tempeh for 5 minutes for each side.

Nutrition: Calories: 130 | Carbohydrates: 17 g | Protein: 12 g

419. DELICIOUS QUICHE MADE WITH CAULIFLOWER AND CHICKPEA

(PREP. TIME: 5 MIN | COOKING: 10 MIN | SERVING 2-4)

INGREDIENTS
- 1/2 tsp. salt
- 1 cup grated cauliflower
- 1 cup chickpea flour
- 1/2 tsp. baking powder
- 1/2 zucchini
- 1 tbsp. flax meal
- 1 cup water
- 1 sprig of fresh rosemary
- 1/2 tsp. Italian seasoning
- 1/2 freshly red onion
- 1/4 tsp. baking powder

DIRECTIONS:
1. Combine all the dry ingredients.
2. Chop the onion and zucchini.
3. Grid the cauliflower and mix it with the dry ingredients. Mix in water.
4. Add the zucchini, onion, and rosemary to make a clumpy and thick mixture.
5. Now put the mixture in the tin or silicone and press it down lightly.
6. Bake at 350°F for 30 minutes

Nutrition: Calories: 156 | Fat: 8.6 g | Carbohydrates: 8.1 g

420. Carrot Cake with Oatmeal
(Prep. Time: 5 Min | Cooking: 10 Min | Serving 2)

INGREDIENTS
- 1 cup of water
- 1/2 tsp. of cinnamon
- 1 cup of rolled oats
- Salt to taste
- 1/4 cup of raisins
- 1/2 cup of shredded carrots
- 1 cup of non-dairy milk
- 1/4 tsp. of allspice
- 1/2 tsp. of vanilla extract

Toppings:
- 1/4 cup of chopped walnuts
- 2 tbsp. maple syrup
- 2 tbsp. shredded coconut

DIRECTIONS:
1. Situate the pot on low heat and let non-dairy milk, oats, and water to a simmer.
2. Mix in carrots, vanilla extract, raisins, salt, cinnamon, and allspice.
3. Transfer the thickened dish to bowls. Dash maple syrup on top or top them with coconut or walnuts.

Nutrition: Calories: 210 | Fat: 11.48 g | Carbohydrates: 10.3 g

421. Tasty Oatmeal Muffins
(Prep. Time: 5 Min | Cooking: 10 Min | Serving 12)

INGREDIENTS
- 1/2 cup of hot water
- 1/2 cup of raisins
- 1/4 cup of ground flaxseed
- 2 cups of rolled oats
- 1/4 tsp. of sea salt
- 1/2 cup of walnuts
- 1/4 tsp. of baking soda
- 1 banana
- 2 tbsp. cinnamon
- 1/4 cup of maple syrup
- Water

DIRECTIONS:
1. Scourge the flaxseed with water and allow the mixture to sit for about 5 minutes
2. Using a food processor, process all the ingredients along with the flaxseed mix. Blend everything for 30 seconds. To make it rough-textured cookies, you need to have a semi-coarse batter.
3. Situate the batter in cupcake liners and put them in a muffin tin. Bake for 25 minutes at 350°F.

Nutrition: Calories: 133 | Fat: 2 g | Protein: 3 g

422. Omelet with Chickpea Flour
(Prep. Time: 5 Min | Cooking: 10 Min | Serving 1)

INGREDIENTS
- 1/2 tsp. of onion powder
- 1/4 tsp. of black pepper
- 1 cup of chickpea flour
- 1/2 tsp. garlic powder
- 1/2 tsp. baking soda
- 1/4 tsp. white pepper
- 1/3 cup of nutritional yeast
- 3 finely chopped green onions
- 4 oz. sautéed mushrooms
- 1 cup of water

DIRECTIONS:
1. Stir onion powder, white pepper, chickpea flour, garlic powder, black and white pepper, baking soda, and nutritional yeast. Pour in 1 cup of water and create a smooth batter.
2. At medium heat, position a frying pan and add the batter just like the way you would cook pancakes. On the batter, drizzle some green onion and mushrooms. Turn the omelet and cook evenly on both sides.
3. When both sides are cooked, serve the omelet with spinach, tomatoes, hot sauce, and salsa.

Nutrition: Calories: 150 | Fat: 1.9 g | Protein: 10.2 g

423. A Toast to Remember
(Prep. Time: 5 Min | Cooking: 10 Min | Serving 4)

INGREDIENTS
- 1 can of black beans
- A pinch of sea salt
- 2 pieces of whole-wheat toast
- 1/4 tsp. chipotle spice
- A pinch of black pepper
- 1 tsp. garlic powder
- 1 freshly juiced lime
- 1 freshly diced avocado
- 1/4 cup of corn
- 3 tbsp. finely diced onion
- 1/2 freshly diced tomato
- Fresh cilantro to taste

DIRECTIONS:
1. Mix the chipotle spice with the beans, salt, garlic powder, and pepper. Stir in the lime juice. Boil all of these until you have a thick and starchy mix.
2. In a bowl, mix the corn, tomato, avocado, red onion, cilantro, and juice from the rest of the lime. Add some pepper and salt.
3. Toast the bread and first spread the black bean mixture followed by the avocado mix.

Nutrition: Calories: 290 | Fat: 9 g | Protein: 12 g

424. TASTY PANINI
(PREP. TIME: 5 MIN | COOKING: 0 MIN | SERVING 1)

INGREDIENTS
- 1/4 cup of hot water
- 1 tbsp. cinnamon
- 1/4 cup of raisins
- 2 tsp. cacao powder
- 1 ripe banana
- 2 slices of whole-grain bread
- 1/4 cup of natural peanut butter

DIRECTIONS:
1. In a bowl, mix the cinnamon, hot water, raisins, and cacao powder.
2. Spread the peanut butter on the bread.
3. Chop bananas and put them on the toast.
4. Mix the raisin mixture in a blender and spread it on the sandwich.

Nutrition: Calories: 850 | Fat: 34 g | Protein: 27 g

425. CHICKPEA AND TOMATO
(PREP. TIME: 5 MIN | COOKING: 10 MIN | SERVING 3-4)

INGREDIENTS
- 1 freshly chopped red pepper
- 2 cups of cooked chickpeas
- 1/3 cup of freshly chopped parsley
- 5 freshly chopped spring onions
- 1 cup of rinsed baby spinach leaves
- 1/2 a lemon, juiced
- 5 freshly chopped medium tomatoes
- 1 tbsp. balsamic vinegar
- 2 tbsp. sesame seeds
- 1/2 thinly sliced hot pepper
- 2 tbsp. light olive oil
- 2 tbsp. flax seeds

DIRECTIONS:
1. Thoroughly clean and chop all the vegetables. Do not chop the baby spinach.
2. Toss the chickpeas, onions, tomatoes, peppers, spinach, and parsley.
3. Toss with the sesame seeds and sprinkle the flax seeds.
4. Drizzle with light olive oil, lemon juice, and balsamic vinegar.
5. Season and serve this summer staple. It is fresh and healthy, and you cannot say no to this delicious salad.

Nutrition: Calories: 138 | Fat: 4.1 g | Protein: 4.5 g

Chapter 7. Dessert Recipes

426. Banana Chocolate Cupcakes
(Prep. Time: 5 Min | Cooking: 10 Min | Serving 12)

INGREDIENTS
- 3 medium bananas
- 1 cup non-dairy milk
- 2 tbsp. coconut butter
- 1 tsp. apple cider vinegar
- 1 tsp. pure vanilla extract
- 1 1/4 cups whole-grain flour
- 1/2 cup rolled oats
- 1/4 cup coconut sugar (optional)
- 1 tsp. baking powder
- 1/2 tsp. baking soda
- 1/2 cup unsweetened cocoa powder
- 1/4 cup chia seeds, or sesame seeds
- 1/4 cup dark chocolate chips, dried cranberries, or raisins (optional)
- Salt to taste

DIRECTIONS:
1. Preheat the oven to 350°F. Lightly grease the cups of 2–6 cups muffin tins.
2. Put the bananas, milk, coconut butter, vinegar, and vanilla in a blender and purée until smooth.
3. Put the flour, oats, sugar (if using), baking powder, baking soda, cocoa powder, chia seeds, salt, and chocolate chips in another large bowl, and stir to combine. Mix together the wet and dry ingredients, stirring as little as possible. Portion into muffin cups, and bake for 20 to 25 minutes

Nutrition: Calories: 215 | Fiber: 9 g | Protein: 6 g

427. Minty Fruit Salad
(Prep. Time: 10 Min | Cooking: 5 Min | Serving 4)

INGREDIENTS
- 1/4 cup lemon juice
- 4 tsp. maple syrup
- 2 cups chopped pineapple
- 2 cups chopped strawberries
- 2 cups raspberries
- 1 cup blueberries
- 8 fresh mint leaves

DIRECTIONS:
1. Incorporate ingredients in this order:
2. A tbsp. of lemon juice, 1 tsp. of maple syrup, 1/2 cup of pineapple, 1/2 cup of strawberries, 1/2 cup of raspberries, 1/4 cup of blueberries, and 2 mint leaves.
3. Repeat to fill 3 more jars. Close the jars tightly with lids.

Nutrition: Calories: 138 | Fat: 1 g | Protein: 2 g

428. Mango Coconut Cream Pie
(Prep. Time: 10 Min | Cooking: 0 Min | Serving 8)

INGREDIENTS
For crust:
- 1/2 cup rolled oats
- 1 cup cashews
- 1 cup soft pitted dates

For filling:
- 1 cup canned coconut milk
- 1/2 cup water
- 2 large mangos
- 1/2 cup unsweetened shredded coconut

DIRECTIONS:
1. Situate all the crust ingredients in a food processor and pulse until it holds together. Press the mixture down firmly into an 8-inch pie or springform pan.
2. Put the all-filling ingredients in a blender and purée until smooth (about 1 minute).
3. Position filling into the crust, use a rubber spatula to smooth the top, and freeze for 30 minutes once frozen, it should be set out for about 15 minutes to soften before serving.
4. Top with a batch of coconut whipped cream scooped on top of the pie once it's set. Topped off with a sprinkling of toasted shredded coconut.

Nutrition: Calories: 427 | Fat: 28 g | Protein: 8 g

429. Cherry-Vanilla Rice Pudding
(Prep. Time: 5 Min | Cooking: 0 Min | Serving 6)

INGREDIENTS
- 1 cup short-grain brown rice
- 1 3/4 cups nondairy milk
- 1 1/2 cups water
- 4 tbsp. pure maple syrup
- 1 tsp. vanilla extract
- A pinch of salt
- 1/4 cup dried cherries

DIRECTIONS:
1. In your electric pressure cooker's cooking pot, combine the rice, milk, water, maple syrup, vanilla, and salt.

2. High pressure for 30 minutes Seal, and select high pressure for 30 minutes
3. Pressure release. Once complete, allow pressure release naturally, about 20 minutes Unlock and remove the lid. Stir in the cherries and put the lid back on loosely for about 10 minutes Serve, adding more milk or sugar, as desired.

Nutrition: Calories: 177 | Fiber: 2 g | Protein: 3 g

430. Mint Chocolate Chip Sorbet
(Prep. Time: 5 Min | Cooking: 0 Min | Serving 1)

INGREDIENTS
- 1 frozen banana
- 1 tbsp. coconut butter
- 2 tbsp. fresh mint
- 1/4 cup or less non-dairy milk
- 3 tbsp. non-dairy chocolate chips
- 3 tbsp. goji berries

DIRECTIONS:
1. Put the banana, coconut butter, and mint in a food processor or blender and purée until smooth.
2. Add the non-dairy milk if needed to keep blending. Pulse the chocolate chips and goji berries (if using) into the mix so they're roughly chopped up.

Nutrition: Calories: 212 | Fiber: 4 g | Protein: 3 g

431. Peach-Mango Crumble
(Prep. Time: 10 Min | Cooking: 0 Min | Serving 5)

INGREDIENTS
- 3 cups peaches
- 3 cups mangos
- 4 tbsp. coconut sugar
- 1 cup gluten-free rolled oats
- 1/2 cup shredded coconut
- 2 tbsp. coconut oil
- 2 cups of water

DIRECTIONS:
1. In a 6- to 7-inch round baking dish, toss together the peaches, mangos, and 2 tbsp. sugar. In a food processor, mix oats, coconut, coconut oil, and the remaining 2 tbsp. sugar.
2. Drizzle oat mixture over the fruit mixture.
3. Cover the dish with aluminum foil. Put a trivet in the bottom of the electric pressure cooker's cooking pot and pour 2 cups of water. Using a foil sling or silicone helper handles, lower the pan onto the trivet.
4. High pressure for 6 minutes Close, and select high pressure for 6 minutes

5. Pressure release. When the cooking time is complete, quickly release the pressure. Unlock.
6. Set aside for few minutes before carefully lifting out the dish with oven mitts or tongs. Scoop out portions to serve.

Nutrition: Calories: 321 | Fiber: 7 g | Protein: 4 g

432. Zesty Orange-Cranberry Energy Bites
(Prep. Time: 15 Min | Cooking: 0 Min | Serving 12)

INGREDIENTS
- 2 tbsp. coconut butter
- 2 tbsp. maple syrup
- 3/4 cup cooked quinoa
- 1/4 cup sesame seeds
- 1 tbsp. chia seeds
- 1/2 tsp. almond extract
- Zest of 1 orange
- 1 tbsp. dried cranberries
- 1/4 cup ground almonds

DIRECTIONS:
1. In a bowl, combine the nut or seed butter and syrup until smooth and creamy. Mix in the rest of the ingredients, and mix to make sure the consistency is holding together in a ball. Form the mix into 12 balls.
2. Situate on a baking sheet lined with parchment or waxed paper and put in the fridge to set for about 15 minutes
3. Add more nut or seed butter mixed with syrup until it all sticks together.

Nutrition: Calories: 109 | Fiber: 3 g | Protein: 3 g

433. Almond-Date Energy Bites
(Prep. Time: 10 Min | Cooking: 0 Min | Serving 24)

INGREDIENTS
- 1 cup dates
- 1 cup unsweetened coconut
- 1/4 cup chia seeds
- 3/4 cup ground almonds
- 1/4 cup cocoa nibs

DIRECTIONS:
1. Place everything in a food processor until crumbly and sticking together, pushing down the sides whenever necessary to keep it blending.
2. Form the mix into 24 balls and place them on a baking sheet lined with parchment or waxed paper. Chill for 15

minutes Uses the softest dates you can find. Medjool dates are the best for this purpose.

Nutrition: Calories: 152 | Fiber: 5 g | Protein: 3 g

434. PUMPKIN PIE CUPS
(PREP. TIME: 5 MIN | COOKING: 0 MIN | SERVING 5)

INGREDIENTS
- 1 cup canned pumpkin purée
- 1 cup nondairy milk
- 6 tbsp. coconut sugar
- 1/4 cup spelled flour or all-purpose flour
- 1/2 tsp. pumpkin pie spice
- Salt to taste

DIRECTIONS:
1. Scourge pumpkin, milk, sugar, flour, pumpkin pie spice, and salt. Pour the mixture into 4 heatproof ramekins. Drizzle a bit more sugar on the top of each, if you like. Put a trivet at the bottom of your electric pressure cooker's cooking pot and fill in a cup of water. Place the ramekins onto the trivet, stacking them if needed
2. High pressure for 5 minutes Seal, and click high pressure for 6 minutes
3. Pressure release. Once complete, quickly release the pressure. Remove the lid. Set aside for few minutes before carefully lifting out the ramekins with oven mitts or tongs.

Nutrition: Calories: 129 | Fiber: 3 g | Protein: 3 g

435. COCONUT AND ALMOND TRUFFLES
(PREP. TIME: 15 MIN | COOKING: 0 MIN | SERVING 8)

INGREDIENTS
- 1 cup pitted dates
- 1 cup almonds
- 1/2 cup sweetened cocoa powder
- 1/2 cup unsweetened coconut
- 1/4 cup pure maple syrup
- 1 tsp. vanilla extract
- 1 tsp. almond extract
- 1/4 tsp. sea salt

DIRECTIONS:
1. In a food processor, blend all the ingredients. Chill the mixture for about 1 hour.
2. Form mixture into balls and then roll the balls in cocoa powder to coat.
3. Serve immediately or keep chilled until ready to serve.

Nutrition: Calories: 139 | Fiber: 3 g | Protein: 4 g

436. FUDGY BROWNIES
(PREP. TIME: 10 MIN | COOKING: 0 MIN | SERVING 6)

INGREDIENTS
- 3 oz. dairy-free dark chocolate
- 1 tbsp. coconut oil
- 1/2 cup applesauce
- 2 tbsp. coconut sugar
- 1/3 cup all-purpose flour
- 1/2 tsp. baking powder
- 1 cup or 2of water.
- Salt to taste

DIRECTIONS:
1. Put a trivet in your electric pressure cooker's cooking pot and pour in 1 cup or 2of water. Select sauté or simmer. In a large heatproof glass or ceramic bowl, combine the chocolate and coconut oil. Place the bowl over the top of your pressure cooker, as you would a double boiler.
2. Stir rarely, then turn off the pressure cooker. Stir the applesauce and sugar into the chocolate mixture. Mix flour, baking powder, and salt. Pour the batter into 3 heat-proof ramekins. Put them in a heat-proof dish and cover them with aluminum foil. Using a foil sling or silicone helper handles, lower the dish onto the trivet.
3. High pressure for 5 minutes Cover, and press high pressure for 5 minutes
4. Pressure release. When done, quickly release the pressure. Open lid.
5. Let cool for a few minutes before carefully lifting out the dish, or ramekins, with oven mitts or tongs. Let cool for a few minutes more before serving.
6. Top with fresh raspberries and an extra drizzle of melted chocolate.

Nutrition: Calories: 316 | Fiber: 5 g | Protein: 5 g

437. CHOCOLATE MACAROONS
(PREP. TIME: 5 MIN | COOKING: 10 MIN | SERVING 8)

INGREDIENTS
- 1 cup unsweetened coconut
- 2 tbsp. cocoa powder
- 2/3 cup coconut milk
- 1/4 cup agave

DIRECTIONS:
1. Preheat the oven to 350°F. Line a baking sheet with parchment paper. In a medium saucepan, cook all the ingredients over -medium-high heat until a firm dough is formed. Scoop the dough into balls and place it on the baking sheet.
2. Bake for 15 minutes, remove from the oven and let cool on the baking sheet.

3. Serve cooled macaroons or store in a tightly sealed container for up to

Nutrition: Calories: 119 | Fiber: 4 g | Protein: 5 g

438. CHOCOLATE PUDDING
(PREP. TIME: 7 MIN | COOKING: 0 MIN | SERVING 2)

INGREDIENTS
- 1 banana
- 2 to 4 tbsp. nondairy milk
- 2 tbsp. unsweetened cocoa powder
- 2 tbsp. coconut sugar
- 1/2 ripe avocado

DIRECTIONS:
1. In a small blender, combine the banana, milk, cocoa powder, sugar (if using), and avocado (if using). Purée until smooth.

Nutrition: Calories: 244 | Fiber: 8 g | Protein: 4 g

439. LIME AND WATERMELON
(PREP. TIME: 15 MIN | COOKING: 0 MIN | SERVING 5)

INGREDIENTS
- 8 cups seedless-watermelon chunks
- Juice of 2 limes
- 1/2 cup coconut sugar
- Strips of lime zest, for garnish

DIRECTIONS:
1. In a blender or food processor, combine the watermelon, lime juice, and sugar and process until smooth. You may have to do this in two batches. After processing, stir well to combine both batches.
2. Pour the mixture into a 9-by-13-inch glass dish. Freeze for 2 to 3 hours. Remove from the freezer and use a fork to scrape the top layer of ice. Leave the shaved ice on top and return to the freezer.
3. In another hour, remove from the freezer and repeat. Do this a few more times until all the ice is scraped up. Serve frozen, garnished with strips of lime zest.

Nutrition: Calories: 124 | Fiber: 3 g | Protein: 8 g

440. COCONUT-BANANA PUDDING
(PREP. TIME: 4 MIN | COOKING: 5 MIN | SERVING 4)

INGREDIENTS
- 3 bananas
- 1 (13.5 oz.) can full-fat coconut milk
- 1/4 cup organic cane sugar
- 1 tbsp. cornstarch
- 1 tsp. vanilla extract
- 2 pinches of salt
- 6 drops natural yellow food coloring
- Ground cinnamon to taste

DIRECTIONS:
1. Combine 1 banana, coconut milk, sugar, cornstarch, vanilla, food coloring, and salt in a blender. Blend until smooth and creamy.
2. Transfer to a saucepot and bring to a boil over medium-high heat. Immediately reduce to a simmer and whisk for 3 minutes
3. Transfer the mixture to a container and allow it to cool for 1 hour. Cover and refrigerate overnight to set. When you're ready to serve, slice the remaining 2 bananas and build individual servings as follows: pudding, banana slices, pudding, and so on until a single-serving dish is filled to the desired level. Sprinkle with ground cinnamon.

Nutrition: Calories: 190 | Fiber: 4 g | Protein: 8 g

441. BEETS BARS WITH DRY FRUITS
(PREP. TIME: 5 MIN | COOKING: 10 MIN | SERVING 4)

INGREDIENTS
- 1 tbsp. flax seed
- 3 tbsp. water
- 5 oz. whole wheat flour
- 8 oz. beetroot
- 3 tbsp. dates
- 3 tbsp. figs
- 4 tbsp. honey
- 4 tbsp. light olive oil
- 1 tsp. baking powder
- 1 tsp. baking soda
- 1 tsp. pure vanilla extract
- 1/4 tsp. salt

DIRECTIONS:
1. Preheat oven to 300°F.
2. Soak the flaxseed with water for 10 minutes
3. Grease a baking sheet with light olive oil; set aside.
4. Place the wheat flour along with all remaining ingredients into a food processor.
5. Process until all ingredients are combined well.
6. Place the mixture into the prepared baking sheet and bake for 35 to 40 minutes
7. Remove the baking sheet from the oven, and let it cool completely.
8. Cut into squares and serve.
9. Store into a container and refrigerate for up to 4 days.

Nutrition: Calories: 247 | Fiber: 1.8 g | Protein: 3.1 g

442. COCOA, AVOCADO, AND CHIA CREAM

(PREP. TIME: 15 MIN | COOKING: 0 MIN | SERVING 4)

INGREDIENTS
- 3 tbsp. cocoa powder
- 2 ripe avocados
- 3 tbsp. coconut oil melted
- 3/4 cup honey strained
- 1 tsp. ground chia seeds
- 1 tsp. pure vanilla extract
- Chopped nuts to taste

DIRECTIONS:
1. Combine all ingredients in a high-speed blender and blend until smooth and well combined.
2. Divide mixture among cups and refrigerate for at least 2 hours before serving
3. Sprinkle with chopped nuts and serve.

Nutrition: Calories: 503 | Fiber: 10.7 g | Protein: 3.8 g

443. COCONUT BALLS WITH LEMON RINDS

(PREP. TIME: 10 MIN | COOKING: 0 MIN | SERVING 6)

INGREDIENTS
- 1 cup coconut butter
- 1 cup coconut milk canned
- 1 cup coconut shreds
- 1/2 cup ground almonds (without salt)
- 1/2 tsp. cinnamon
- 1 tsp. pure vanilla extract
- 1/2 tsp. nutmeg
- 2 tbsp. honey or maple syrup

Coating and serving:
- 1 cup coconut shreds for coating
- 2 lemon zest (finely grated fresh)

DIRECTIONS:
1. Add all ingredients into the food processor; process until creamy.
2. Pour the mixture into a refrigerator for 2 hours.
3. Form the mixture into balls, and roll them in coconut shreds.
4. Arrange balls on a plate, sprinkle with lemon rinds and refrigerate until firm.

Nutrition: Calories: 427.96 | Fiber: 2.5 g | Protein: 3.2 g

444. COCONUT RICE PUDDING WITH CARDAMOM

(PREP. TIME: 5 MIN | COOKING: 10 MIN | SERVING 6)

INGREDIENTS
- 9 oz. Arborio
- 2 1/4 cups water
- 2 1/4 cups coconut milk
- 1 1/2 cups coconut butter
- 1 cup coconut sugar
- 1/4 tsp. ground cardamom
- 1 tsp. cinnamon seeds

DIRECTIONS:
1. Add rice, water, coconut milk, and coconut butter in a saucepan, and bring to boil.
2. Add sugar, cardamom, and cinnamon seeds; give a good stir.
3. Reduce the heat to medium-low and simmer for 20 to 25 minutes, stirring constantly.
4. Once the rice has started to thicken, remove the saucepan from heat, cover, and let it rest for 5 minutes
5. Sprinkle with cinnamon on top and serve warm or cold.

Nutrition: Calories: 629 | Fiber: 2.51 g | Protein: 7 g

445. NUTTY CAKE

(PREP. TIME: 3 MIN | COOKING: 12 MIN | SERVING 7)

INGREDIENTS
- 1/2 lb. coconut butter
- 3/4 cup coconut sugar
- 1/4 lb. ground walnuts
- 1/2 cup coconut flour
- 2 tbsp. cornflour
- 1 tbsp. arrowroot powder
- 1 tsp. baking powder

DIRECTIONS:
1. Preheat your oven to 360°F/180°C.
2. Add all ingredients into a food processor.
3. Process until combined well and get a uniform texture.
4. Pour the mixture into a large mold and place it in the oven.
5. Bake for about 12 to 15 minutes
6. Let sit for 10 minutes, remove from mold, and serve.

Nutrition: Calories: 538 | Fiber: 3.45 g | Protein: 6.71 g

446. Dark Honey Hazelnut Cookies
(Prep. Time: 5 Min | Cooking: 10 Min | Serving 12)

INGREDIENTS
- 1 tbsp. light olive oil
- 1/2 cup ground hazelnuts
- 1/2 tsp. baking soda
- 1 1/2 cups of hazelnut flour
- 2 tbsp. of coconut flour
- 1/2 tsp. cinnamon
- 1 medium banana mashed
- 2 tbsp. coconut oil melted
- 4 tbsp. dark honey strained
- 1 tsp. pure vanilla extract
- Salt to taste

DIRECTIONS:
1. Preheat oven to 340°F.
2. Grease a baking sheet with light olive oil; set aside.
3. Combine together ground hazelnuts, baking soda, hazelnut flour, coconut flour, cinnamon, and salt in a bowl.
4. In a separate bowl, whisk mashed banana, coconut oil, dark honey, and vanilla extract.
5. Combine the hazelnut flour mixture with the banana mixture; beat with the electric mixer
6. Shape the dough into 12 balls; place in a prepared baking sheet.
7. Bake for about 17 to 18 minutes
8. Remove from the oven; leave to cool for 15 minutes and serve.

Nutrition: Calories: 99 | Fiber: 1 g | Protein: 1.8 g

447. Energy Dried Figs Brownies
(Prep. Time: 15 Min | Cooking: 0 Min | Serving 4)

INGREDIENTS
- 1 cup dried figs
- 2 tbsp. cocoa powder
- 1 cup almonds chopped
- 2 tbsp. extracted honey
- 1 scoop protein powder
- 2 tbsp. of water

DIRECTIONS:
1. Add all ingredients to a food processor.
2. Process until combined well.
3. Transfer the mixture into a bowl, and knead with your hands.
4. Lay a mixture on a working surface and roll dough into about 1/3 of an inch-thick sheet.
5. Cut the mixture into the square.
6. Refrigerate for one hour before serving.

Nutrition: Calories: 347 | Fiber: 8.5 g | Protein: 10.31 g

448. Hearty Apple Bran Muffins
(Prep. Time: 5 Min | Cooking: 10 Min | Serving 12)

INGREDIENTS
- 1 cup all-purpose flour
- 1/3 cup brown sugar (packed)
- 2 tsp. baking powder
- 1/4 tsp. salt
- 1/4 tsp. ground cinnamon
- 1/4 tsp. ground nutmeg
- 1 cup tart apple
- 3/4 cup water
- 1/2 cup soy milk
- 1/4 cup canola oil
- 1/2 mashed banana
- 2 cups bran flake cereal

DIRECTIONS:
1. Preheat oven to 400°F.
2. Grease with oil 12 muffin cups; set aside.
3. In a bowl, combine together flour, brown sugar, baking powder, salt, cinnamon, and nutmeg
4. In a separate bowl, whisk together apple, water, dry milk, vegetable oil, and banana in a small bowl; add to flour mixture and stir until moistened.
5. Finely, add in bran cereals and stir well.
6. Spoon mixture into prepared muffin cups, filling 2/3 full.
7. Bake for 12 to 15 minutes
8. Your muffins are ready when the wooden pick inserted in the center comes out clean.
9. Remove muffins to a wire rack and cool slightly.
10. Store muffins in an airtight container for up to 4 days.

Nutrition: Calories: 137 | Fiber: 1.81 g | Protein: 2.12 g

449. Honey Raisins Crispy Balls
(Prep. Time: 15 Min | Cooking: 0 Min | Serving 15)

INGREDIENTS
- 1/2 cup coconut sugar
- 1/2 cup honey
- 1/2 cup peanut butter
- 1-1/2 cups crispy rice cereal
- 1/2 cup raisins

DIRECTIONS:
1. Place a sheet of waxed paper on a cookie sheet.
2. Combine sugar, honey, and peanut butter in a medium bowl.
3. Stir until mixed well. Stir in cereal and raisins.
4. Shape the mixture into 1-inch balls.
5. Refrigerate for 2 hours or until firm.
6. Keep stored in a tightly covered container in the refrigerator.

Nutrition: Calories: 56 | Fiber: 0.3 g | Protein: 1.27 g

450. PROTEIN BANANA CREAM
(PREP. TIME: 13 MIN | COOKING: 0 MIN | SERVING 3)

INGREDIENTS
- 1 cup almond milk
- 2 ripe bananas
- 2 tbsp. coconut butter
- 1 tbsp. pure vanilla extract
- 1 scoop vegan protein powder

DIRECTIONS:
1. Add all ingredients into a high-speed blender.
2. Blend until smooth and creamy.
3. If the cream is too thick, add some more almond milk.
4. Pour the mixture into a glass jar or container and chill for 2 hours.
5. Serve! Enjoy!

Nutrition: Calories: 327 | Fiber: 5.18 g | Protein: 5.14 g

451. PROTEIN CARROT MACAROONS
(PREP. TIME: 10 MIN | COOKING: 5 MIN | SERVING 8)

INGREDIENTS
- 2 large carrots grated
- 1/4 cup water
- 1/2 cup sesame oil
- 2 cups coconut flakes
- 1 tbsp. protein powder
- 3/4 cup rice flour
- 1 tsp. pure vanilla extract
- 3 tbsp. agave syrup

DIRECTIONS:
1. Preheat oven to 350°F/175°C.
2. Grease a baking sheet with sesame oil; set aside.
3. Knead all ingredients together in a large bowl until well combined.
4. Shape the mixture into balls.
5. Arrange balls on a prepared baking sheet and bake for 30 minutes, rotating once.
6. Remove the macaroons from the pan and allow them to cool completely.

Nutrition: Calories: 289 | Fiber: 3.2 g | Protein: 3.19 g

452. RAW LEMON "CHEESECAKE"
(PREP. TIME: 6 MIN | COOKING: 0 MIN | SERVING 10)

INGREDIENTS
For crust:
- 2 cups raw almonds ground
- 2 tbsp. coconut flakes
- 1/4 tsp. vanilla extract
- 1/4 cup date paste
- 1/4 tsp. sea salt

For filling:
- 3/4 cup coconut oil, melted
- 1 cup Lemon juice
- 1 cup almond milk
- 1 1/2 cups ground nuts
- 3/4 cup extracted honey
- 1 tsp. vanilla extract

DIRECTIONS:
1. Add all ingredients for the crust into your food processor or high-speed blender.
2. Blend/process until smooth and combined well.
3. Pour the mixture into the round pan and refrigerate for 2 hours.
4. Combine all ingredients for filling into a blender and beat about 30 to 45 seconds.
5. Pour the mixture evenly over the cake crust.
6. Freeze cheesecake for 4 hours.

Nutrition: Calories: 414 | Fiber: 5.8 g | Protein: 8.42 g

453. SEMOLINA CAKE WITH BROWN SUGAR SYRUP
(PREP. TIME: 5 MIN | COOKING: 10 MIN | SERVING 14)

INGREDIENTS
- 1 tbsp. light olive oil or non-stick cooking spray

For cake:
- 1 1/2 cup fine semolina
- 1 1/2 cup coarse semolina
- 1 1/2 cup coconut sugar
- 2 1/2 cups coconut milk
- 2 tsp. baking powder
- 1 tsp. pure vanilla extract

For syrup:
- 1 1/2 cup water
- 2 1/2 cup brown sugar

DIRECTIONS:
1. Preheat oven to 360°F.
2. Grease a baking dish with oil or cooking spray; set aside.
3. Combine all ingredients for the cake in a mixing bowl; beat with an electric mixer until combined well.
4. Pour the batter into a prepared baking dish.
5. Bake for 1 hour and 15 minutes
6. Remove the cake from the oven and cut diagonally with a warm knife
7. In a saucepan, cook water and sugar over medium heat for about 6 minutes

8. Pour hot syrup evenly over the cake.
9. Let cool on room temperature and serve.

Nutrition: Calories: 410 | Fiber: 1.4 g | Protein: 5 g

454. Strawberries, Quinoa and Silk Tofu Dessert

(Prep. Time: 5 Min | Cooking: 10 Min | Serving 3)

INGREDIENTS
- 1 cup strawberries
- 4 tbsp. brown sugar—(packed)
- 1/2 cup cooked quinoa
- 1 cup silken tofu
- 1 fresh juice of half a lemon
- 1/2 tsp. pure vanilla extract
- 1 cup of water

DIRECTIONS:
1. Add strawberries and sugar in a bowl, cover, and set aside for half an hour.
2. In the meantime, cook quinoa in 1 cup of water for about 15 to 20 minutes or until water is absorbed.
3. Remove from the heat, uncover and mash with a fork.
4. Place strawberries, quinoa, and all remaining **INGREDIENTS** into a blender and blend until combined well without lumps.
5. Taste and adjust sugar to taste.
6. Refrigerate mixture for one hour before serving.

Nutrition: Calories: 233 | Fiber: 3.12 g | Protein: 8 g

455. Strawberry and Banana Ice Cream

(Prep. Time: 4 Min | Cooking: 0 Min | Serving 8)

INGREDIENTS
- 2 large frozen bananas
- 3 cups chopped strawberries
- 2 1/2 cups coconut milk
- 1 cup coconut sugar
- 2 tsp. strawberry extract

DIRECTIONS:
1. Put all ingredients in a blender and blend until soft.
2. Place the mixture in a freezer-safe container and freeze for at least 4 hours or overnight.
3. Transfer the frozen mixture to a bowl and beat with a mixer until smooth to break up the ice crystals; repeat the process at least 4 times.
4. Let the ice cream at room temperature for 15 minutes before serving.

Nutrition: Calories: 220 | Fiber: 1.91 g | Protein: 1.8 g

456. Strawberry Coconut Ice Cream

(Prep. Time: 10 Min | Cooking: 0 Min | Serving 4)

INGREDIENTS
- 4 cups frouncesen strawberries
- 1 vanilla bean, seeded
- 28 oz. coconut cream
- 1/2 cup maple syrup

DIRECTIONS:
1. Place cream in a food processor and pulse for 1 minute until soft peaks come together.
2. Then tip the cream in a bowl, add remaining ingredients in the blender and blend until thick mixture comes together.
3. Add the mixture into the cream, fold until combined, and then transfer ice cream into a freezer-safe bowl and freeze for 4 hours until firm, whisking every 20 minutes after 1 hour.
4. Serve straight away.

Nutrition: Calories: 100 | Fat: 100 g | Protein: 100 g

457. Chocolaty Oat Bites

(Prep. Time: 15 Min | Cooking: 0 Min | Serving 6)

INGREDIENTS
- 2/3 cup creamy peanut butter
- 1 cup old-fashioned oats
- 1/2 cups unsweetened vegan chocolate chips
- 1/2 cups ground flaxseeds
- 2 tbsp. maple syrup

DIRECTIONS:
1. Incorporate all the ingredients and mix until well combined.
2. Refrigerate for about 20 to 30 minutes
3. With your hands make equal-sized balls from the mixture.
4. Arrange the balls onto a parchment paper-lined baking sheet in a single layer.
5. Refrigerate to set for about 15 minutes before serving.

Nutrition: Calories: 310 | Fat: 19 g | Protein: 14 g

458. Peanut Butter Mousse

(Prep. Time: 15 Min | Cooking: 0 Min | Serving 5)

INGREDIENTS
- 3 tbsp. agave nectar
- 14 ounces coconut milk, unsweetened, chilled

- 4 tbsp. creamy peanut butter, salted

DIRECTIONS:
1. Separate coconut milk and its solid, then add solid from coconut milk into the bowl and beat for 45 seconds until fluffy.
2. Then place the remaining ingredients until smooth, refrigerate for 45 minutes and serve.

Nutrition: Calories: 270 | Fat: 20 g | Protein: 5 g

459. SALTED COCONUT-ALMOND FUDGE
(PREP. TIME: 5 MIN | COOKING: 10 MIN | SERVING 12)

INGREDIENTS
- 3/4 cup creamy coconut butter
- 1/2 cup maple syrup
- 1/3 cup coconut oil, softened or melted
- 6 tbsp. fair-trade unsweetened cocoa powder
- 1 tsp. coarse or flaked sea salt

DIRECTIONS:
1. Preparing the ingredients.
2. Prep loaf pan with a double layer of plastic wrap. Place one layer horizontally in the pan with a generous amount of overhang, and the second layer vertically with a generous amount of overhang.
3. In a medium bowl, gently mix together the coconut butter, maple syrup, and coconut oil until well combined and smooth. Drizzle cocoa powder and gently stir it into the mixture until well combined and creamy.
4. Fill in the mixture into the prepared pan and sprinkle with sea salt. Bring the overflowing edges of the plastic wrap over the top of the fudge to completely cover it. Situate pan in the freezer for at least 1 hour or overnight, or until the fudge is firm.
5. Finish and Serve
6. Pull away the pan from the freezer and lift the fudge out of the pan using the plastic-wrap overhangs to pull it out. Situate to a cutting board and cut into 1-inch pieces.

Nutrition: Calories: 319 |Fat: 16 g | Protein: 18 g

460. PEANUT BUTTER FUDGE
(PREP. TIME: 10 MIN | COOKING: 5 MIN | SERVING 8)

INGREDIENTS
- 1/2 cup peanut butter
- 2 tbsp. maple syrup
- 1/4 tsp. salt
- 2 tbsp. coconut oil, melted
- 1/4 tsp. vanilla extract, unsweetened

DIRECTIONS:
1. Take a heatproof bowl, place all the ingredients in it, microwave for 15 seconds, and then stir until well combined.
2. Take a freezer-proof container, line it with parchment paper, pour in fudge mixture, spread evenly, and freeze for 40 minutes until set and harden.
3. When ready to eat, let fudge set for 5 minutes, then cut it into squares and serve.

Nutrition: Calories: 96 |Fat: 3.6 g | Protein: 1.5 g

461. COCONUT BARS WITH CHOCOLATE CHIPS
(PREP. TIME: 9 MIN | COOKING: 6 MIN | SERVING 16)

INGREDIENTS
- 1/4 cup coconut oil
- 1 cup shredded coconut
- 1/4 cup pure date sugar
- 2 tbsp. agave syrup
- 1 cup vegan chocolate chips

DIRECTIONS:
1. Grease a dish with coconut oil. Set aside. In a bowl, mix the coconut, sugar, agave syrup, and coconut oil. Spread the mixture onto the dish, pressing down.
2. Situate the chocolate chips in a heatproof bowl and microwave for 1 minute. Stir and heat 30 seconds more until the chocolate is melted. Pour over the coconut and let harden for 20 minutes Chop into 16 bars.

Nutrition: Calories: 319 | Fat: 24 g | Protein: 11 g

462. COCONUT RICE WITH MANGOS
(PREP. TIME: 9 MIN | COOKING: 6 MIN | SERVING 6)

INGREDIENTS
- 2 cups coconut milk
- 1 1/2 cups coconut flakes
- 1/4 cup maple syrup
- 1 mango sliced

DIRECTIONS:
1. Heat saucepan over high heat.
2. Fill in coconut milk and bring it to a boil.
3. Stir in coconut flakes and maple syrup.
4. Cover then cook on low heat for about 15 minutes
5. Pour coconut rice on a plate.
6. Serve with mango slice and enjoy.

Nutrition: Calories: 75 | Fat: 69 g | Protein: 3 g

463. SPICED APPLE CHIA PUDDING
(PREP. TIME: 10 MIN | COOKING: 5 MIN | SERVING 1)

INGREDIENTS
- 1/2 cup unsweetened applesauce
- 1/4 cup non-dairy milk or canned coconut milk
- 1 tbsp. chia seeds
- 1 1/2 tsp. coconut sugar
- A pinch ground cinnamon or pumpkin pie spice

DIRECTIONS:
1. Preparing the ingredients.
2. Scourge applesauce, milk, chia seeds, coconut sugar, and cinnamon. Enjoy as is, or let sit for 30 minutes so the chia seeds soften and expand.

Nutrition: Calories: 153 | Fat: 5 g | Protein:: 3 g

464. FUDGE
(PREP. TIME: 9 MIN | COOKING: 6 MIN | SERVING 18)

INGREDIENTS
- 1 cup vegan chocolate chips
- 1/2 cup soy milk

DIRECTIONS:
1. Line an 8-inch portion skillet with wax paper. Set aside.
2. Heat up chocolate chips and soy milk in a double boiler or add chocolate and almond spread to a medium, microwave-safe bowl. Heat up it in the microwave in 20-second increments until chocolate melts. In between each 20-second burst, stir the chocolate until it is smooth.
3. Empty the melted chocolate mixture into the lined skillet. Tap the sides of the skillet to make sure the mixture spreads into an even layer. Alternatively, use a spoon to make swirls on top.
4. Move the skillet to the refrigerator until it is firm. Remove the skillet from the refrigerator and cut fudge into 18 squares.

Nutrition: Calories: 388 |Fat: 29 g | Protein: 24 g

465. DARK CHOCOLATE RASPBERRY ICE CREAM
(PREP. TIME: 10 MIN | COOKING: 0 MIN | SERVING 2)

INGREDIENTS
- 2 Frouncesen bananas, sliced
- 1/4 cup fresh raspberries
- 2 tbsp. cocoa powder, unsweetened
- 2 tbsp. raspberry jelly

DIRECTIONS:
1. Situate all the ingredients in a food processor, except for berries, and pulse for 2 minutes until smooth.
2. Distribute the ice cream mixture between two bowls, stir in berries until combined, and then serve immediately.

Nutrition: Calories: 104 |Fat: 0.9 g | Protein: 0.4 g

466. COCONUT AND CHOCOLATE CAKE
(PREP. TIME: 9 MIN | COOKING: 6 MIN | SERVING 4)

INGREDIENTS
- 2/3 cup toasted almond flour
- 1/4 cup unsalted plant butter, melted
- 2 cups chocolate bars, cubed
- 2 1/2 cups coconut cream
- Fresh berries for topping
- 2 tbsp. Maple syrup

DIRECTIONS:
1. Lightly grease a 9-inch springform pan with some plant butter and set it aside.
2. Mix the almond flour and plant butter in a medium bowl and pour the mixture into the springform pan. Use the spoon to spread and press the mixture into the bottom of the pan. Place in the refrigerator to firm for 30 minutes
3. Meanwhile, pour the chocolate in a safe microwave bowl and melt for 1 minute stirring every 30 seconds. Remove from the microwave and mix in the coconut cream and maple syrup.
4. Remove the cake pan from the oven, pour the chocolate mixture on top making too sure to shake the pan and even the layer. Chill further for 4 to 6 hours. Take out the pan from the fridge, release the cake and garnish with the raspberries or strawberries. Slice and serve.

Nutrition: Calories: 299 | Fat: 28 g | Protein: 15 g

467. TAMARI TOASTED ALMONDS
(PREP. TIME: 7 MIN | COOKING: 8 MIN | SERVING 4)

INGREDIENTS
- 1/2 cup raw almonds, or sunflower seeds
- 2 tbsp. tamari, or soy sauce
- 1 tsp. toasted sesame oil

DIRECTIONS:
1. Preparing the ingredients.

2. Heat a dry skillet to medium-high heat, then add the almonds, stirring very frequently to keep them from burning. Once the almonds are toasted, 7 to 8 minutes for almonds, or 3 to 4 minutes for sunflower seeds, pour the tamari and sesame oil into the hot skillet and stir to coat.
3. You can turn off the heat, and as the almonds cool the tamari mixture will stick to and dry on the nuts.

Nutrition: Calories: 89 | Fat: 8 g | Protein: 4 g

468. Express Coconut Flax Pudding
(Prep. Time: 9 Min | Cooking: 6 Min | Serving 4)

INGREDIENTS
- 1 tbsp. coconut oil softened
- 1 tbsp. coconut cream
- 2 cups coconut milk canned
- 3/4 cup ground flax seed
- 4 tbsp. coconut palm sugar (or to taste)

DIRECTIONS:
1. Press the sauté button on your Instant Pot
2. Add coconut oil, coconut cream, coconut milk, and ground flaxseed.
3. Stir about 5 to 10 minutes
4. Seal lid into place and set on the manual setting for 5 minutes
5. When the timer beeps, press "Cancel" and carefully flip the Quick Release valve to let the pressure out.
6. Add the palm sugar and stir well.
7. Taste and adjust sugar to taste.
8. Allow pudding to cool down completely.
9. Situate the pudding in an airtight container and refrigerate for up to 2 weeks.

Nutrition: Calories: 210 |Fat: 16 g | Protein: 12 g

469. Mango Coconut Chia Pudding
(Prep. Time: 10 Min | Cooking: 0 Min | Serving 1)

INGREDIENTS
- 1 medium mango, peeled, cubed
- 1/4 cup chia seeds
- 2 tbsp. coconut flakes
- 1 cup coconut milk, unsweetened
- 1 1/2 tsp. maple syrup

DIRECTIONS:
1. Take a bowl, place chia seeds in it, whisk in milk until combined, and then stir in maple syrup.
2. Cover the bowl with a plastic wrap; it should touch the pudding mixture and refrigerate for 2 hours until the pudding has set.
3. Then puree mango until smooth, top it evenly over pudding, sprinkle with coconut flakes, and serve.

Nutrition: Calories: 159 |Fat: 9 g | Protein: 3 g

470. Cacao Nut Bites
(Prep. Time: 9 Min | Cooking: 6 Min | Serving 4)

INGREDIENTS
- 3 1/2 oz. dairy-free dark chocolate
- 1/2 cup mixed nuts
- 2 tbsp. roasted coconut chips
- 1 tbsp. sunflower seeds
- Sea salt

DIRECTIONS:
1. Pour the chocolate into a safe microwave bowl and melt in the microwave for 1 to 2 minutes
2. Into 10 small cupcake liners (2-inches in diameters) share the chocolate. Drop in the nuts, coconut chips, sunflower seeds, and sprinkle with some salt. Chill in the refrigerator until firm.

Nutrition: Calories: 301 | Fat: 29 g | Protein: 14 g

471. Avocado-Based Chocolate Mousse
(Prep. Time: 10 Min | Cooking: 0 Min | Serving 3)

INGREDIENTS
- 4 ripe avocados
- 1 cup agave syrup, divided
- 1 cup cacao, divided
- 1/4 tsp. salt
- 1/4 tsp. vanilla extract

DIRECTIONS:
1. Prepare the avocados and place the pulp in a food processor. Process until smooth.
2. Add half the agave syrup, half the cacao, the salt, and the vanilla; process until smooth.
3. Taste to see if it needs more agave syrup or cacao and add anything that's lacking.
4. Refrigerate for at least two hours, or overnight, before serving.

Nutrition: Calories: 311 | Fat: 16 g | Protein: 10 g

472. Oatmeal and Peanut Butter Bar

(Prep. Time: 10 Min | Cooking: 5 Min | Serving 8)

INGREDIENTS
- 1 1/2 cups date, pit removed
- 1/2 cup peanut butter
- 1/2 cup old-fashioned rolled oats

DIRECTIONS:
1. Grease and line an 8-inch x 8-inch baking tin with parchment and pop to one side.
2. Grab your food processor, add the dates, and whizz until chopped.
3. Add the peanut butter and the oats and pulse.
4. Scoop into the baking tin then pop into the fridge or freezer until set and serve.

Nutrition: Calories: 318 | Fat: 19 g | Protein: 19 g

473. Maple-Pumpkin Cookies

(Prep. Time: 10 Min | Cooking: 0 Min | Serving 12)

INGREDIENTS
- 2 lb. pumpkin, sliced
- 3 tbsp. melted coconut oil, divided
- 1 tbsp. maple syrup
- 1 cup whole-wheat flour
- 2 tsp. baking powder
- Sea salt to taste

DIRECTIONS:
1. Preheat oven to 360°F.
2. Place the pumpkin in a greased tray and bake for 45 minutes until tender. Let cool before mashing it.
3. Mix the mashed pumpkin, 1 1/2 tbsp. coconut oil and maple syrup in a bowl.
4. Combine the flour, salt, and baking powder in another bowl. Fold in the pumpkin mixture and whisk with a fork until smooth.
5. Divide the mixture into balls. Arrange spaced out on a lined with parchment paper baking sheet; flatten the balls until a cookie shape is formed. Brush with the remaining melted coconut oil. Bake for 10 minutes, until they rise and become gold. Serve cooled.

Nutrition: Calories: 324 | Fat 27 g | Protein: 14 g

474. Coconut Chocolate Truffles

(Prep. Time: 8 Min | Cooking: 7 Min | Serving 12)

INGREDIENTS
- 1 cup raw cashews, soaked overnight
- 3/4 cup pitted cherries
- 2 tbsp. coconut oil
- 1 cup shredded coconut
- 2 tbsp. cocoa powder

DIRECTIONS:
1. Line a baking sheet with parchment paper and set it aside.
2. Blend the cashews, cherries, coconut oil, half of the shredded coconut, and cocoa powder in a food processor until ingredients are evenly mixed. Spread the remaining shredded coconut on a dish. Mold the mixture into 12 truffle shapes. Roll the truffles in the coconut dish, shaking off any excess, then arrange on the prepared baking sheet. Refrigerate for 1 hour.

Nutrition: Calories: 317 | Fat: 17 g | Protein: 7 g

475. Avocado Toasts

(Prep. Time: 5 Min | Cooking: 0 Min | Serving 5)

INGREDIENTS
- 5 whole-grain crackers
- 1/4 avocado, mashed
- 1 tbsp. black olives, sliced
- 1/4 cup tomatoes, chopped

DIRECTIONS:
1. Arrange whole-grain crackers in a food container.
2. Spread each cracker with mashed avocado.
3. Top with black olives and tomatoes.
4. Refrigerate until ready to eat.
5. Toast in the oven before serving.

Nutrition: Calories: 211 | Fat: 13 g | Protein: 4 g

476. Sweet and Spicy Snack Mix

(Prep. Time: 5 Min | Cooking: 10 Min | Serving 20)

INGREDIENTS
- 4 cups mixed vegetable sticks
- 2 cups corn square cereal; oatmeal
- 1 3/4 cups pretzel sticks
- 1 tsp. packed brown sugar; paprika
- 1/2 tsp. ground cumin; cayenne pepper, chili
- 1/2 cup almonds
- Cooking spray

DIRECTIONS:
1. Preheat your oven to 300°F.
2. In a roasting pan, add the vegetable sticks, 1/2 cup almonds, corn and oat cereals, and pretzel sticks.
3. In a bowl, mix the rest of the ingredients.
4. Coat the cereal mixture with cooking spray.
5. Sprinkle spice mixture on top of the cereals.

6. Bake in the oven for 18 minutes
7. Store in an airtight container for up to 7 days.

Nutrition: Calories: 92 | Fat: 3 g | Protein: 2 g

477. MELON DESSERT
(PREP. TIME: 5 MIN | COOKING: 0 MIN | SERVING 6)

INGREDIENTS
- 4 cups melon balls
- 1/2 cup sparkling water (berry flavor)
- 3 tbsp. white balsamic vinegar
- 1 lemon zest

DIRECTIONS:
1. Mix sparkling water and vinegar in a bowl.
2. Toss melon balls in the mixture.
3. Transfer to a glass jar with a lid.
4. Cover and refrigerate until ready to serve.
5. Garnish with lemon zest before serving.

Nutrition: Calories: 47 | Fat: 0.6 g | Protein: 1 g

478. MANGO AND STRAWBERRY ICE CREAM
(PREP. TIME: 10 MIN | COOKING: 0 MIN | SERVING 4)

INGREDIENTS
- 12 oz. mango cubes
- 8 oz. strawberry slices
- 1 tbsp. freshly squeezed lime juice

DIRECTIONS:
1. Put all the ingredients in a food processor.
2. Blend until smooth.
3. Store in the freezer for up to 3 months.
4. Let it soften a little for 30 minutes before serving.

Nutrition: Calories: 70 | Fat: 0.4 g | Protein: 1 g

479. WATERMELON PIZZA
(PREP. TIME: 10 MIN | COOKING: 0 MIN | SERVING 8)

INGREDIENTS
- 1/4 tsp. vanilla extract
- 1/2 cup coconut-milk yogurt; blackberries
- 2 large round slices of watermelon from the center
- 2/3 cup strawberries, sliced
- 2 tbsp. unsweetened coconut flakes, toasted
- 1 tsp. maple

DIRECTIONS:
1. Mix vanilla, 1 tsp. maple and yogurt in a bowl.
2. Spread mixture on top of each watermelon slice.
3. Cut into 8 slices.
4. Top with blackberries and strawberries.
5. Sprinkle coconut flakes on top.

Nutrition: Calories: 70 | Fat: 2 g | Protein: 1 g

480. ROASTED MANGO AND COCONUT
(PREP. TIME: 5 MIN | COOKING: 10 MIN | SERVING 4)

INGREDIENTS
- 2 mangoes, cubed
- 2 tbsp. coconut flakes
- 2 tsp. orange zest
- 2 tsp. crystallized ginger, chopped

DIRECTIONS:
1. Preheat your oven to 350°F.
2. Put the mango cubes in custard cups.
3. Top with coconut flakes, orange zest, and ginger.
4. Bake in the oven for 10 minutes

Nutrition: Calories: 89 | Fat: 2 g | Protein: 1 g

481. FRUIT COMPOTE
(PREP. TIME: 7 MIN | COOKING: 8 MIN | SERVING 10)

INGREDIENTS
- 3/4 cup dried apricots, sliced into quarters
- 3 tbsp. orange juice concentrate
- 15 oz. pineapple chunks; 3 pears
- 1 tbsp. quick-cooking tapioca
- 1/2 tsp. ground ginger
- 2 cups dark sweet cherries
- 1/4 cup coconut flakes

DIRECTIONS:
1. In a slow cooker, add all the ingredients except the 2 cups dark sweet cherries and 1/4 cup coconut flakes.
2. Cover the pot and cook on a low setting for 8 hours.
3. Stir in the cherries.
4. Transfer to food containers.
5. Sprinkle with coconut flakes.
6. Refrigerate and serve when ready to eat.

Nutrition: Calories: 124 | Fat: 1 g | Protein: 1 g

482. CREAMY CASHEW SAUCE
(PREP. TIME: 5 MIN | COOKING: 0 MIN | SERVING 8)

INGREDIENTS
- 3/4 cup raw cashews
- 1/2 cup water

- 1/4 cup parsley leaves
- 1 tbsp. cider vinegar
- 1/2 tsp. low sodium tamari

DIRECTIONS:
1. Put all the ingredients in a blender.
2. Puree until smooth.
3. Refrigerate for up to 4 days until ready to use.

Nutrition: Calories: 76 | Fat: 6 g | Protein: 2 g

483. CHOCO PEANUT BUTTER
(PREP. TIME: 5 MIN | COOKING: 10 MIN | SERVING 8)

INGREDIENTS
- 1 1/4 cups unsalted peanut
- 1/3 cup chopped dark chocolate chips, melted
- 2 tbsp. pure maple syrup
- 1 tbsp. peanut oil
- 1/2 tsp. vanilla extract

DIRECTIONS:
1. Preheat your oven to 350°F.
2. Arrange peanuts in a single layer on a baking sheet.
3. Bake for 10 minutes
4. Transfer to a food processor and add the rest of the ingredients.
5. Blend until smooth.
6. Store for up to 1 month.

Nutrition: Calories: 201 | Fat: 15 g | Protein: 6 g

484. GINGER CRANBERRY SAUCE
(PREP. TIME: 5 MIN | COOKING: 10 MIN | SERVING 10)

INGREDIENTS
- 1/2 cup maple syrup; water
- 2 tbsp. lime juice
- 1/3 cup coconut sugar
- 1 tsp. fresh ginger, chopped
- 3 cups cranberries

DIRECTIONS:
1. In a saucepan over medium-high heat, add the maple syrup, water, lime juice, and sugar.
2. Bring to a boil.
3. Stir to dissolve the sugar.
4. Reduce heat and simmer for 3 minutes
5. Add ginger and cranberries.
6. Simmer for 5 minutes
7. Store in a glass jar in the refrigerator for up to 3 days.
8. Bring to room temperature for half an hour before serving.

Nutrition: Calories: 83 | Fat: 0.6 g | Protein: 0.2 g

485. AVOCADO PANCAKES
(PREP. TIME: 5 MIN | COOKING: 10 MIN | SERVING 4)

INGREDIENTS
- 2 tbsp. flaxseed meal
- 1 cup mashed ripe avocado
- 1 tsp. vanilla extract; oil
- 1 1/2 tsp. baking powder
- 1 cup all-purpose flour
- 5 tbsp. water
- 1 cup almond milk
- 2 tbsp. coconut sugar
- 1/4 tsp. salt
- 1 tsp. the lemon zest
- Blueberries to taste

DIRECTIONS:
1. Put flaxseed meal in a bowl.
2. Stir in 5 tbsp. water.
3. Let sit for 5 minutes
4. Add 1 cup almond milk, 2 tbsp. coconut sugar, avocado, vanilla extract, 1/4 tsp. salt and 1 tsp. the lemon zest in a blender.
5. Blend until smooth.
6. Transfer the mixture to a bowl and add the flaxseed mixture.
7. Stir in baking powder and flour.
8. In a pan over medium heat, add the oil.
9. Pour a small amount of the batter.
10. Flip once the surface starts to bubble.
11. Cook for 4 minutes per side.
12. Place in a food container and top with blueberries.

Nutrition: Calories: 258 | Fat: 7 g | Protein: 5 g

486. OATMEAL WITH PEARS
(PREP. TIME: 5 MIN | COOKING: 5 MIN | SERVING 1)

INGREDIENTS
- 1/4 cup rolled oats, cooked
- 1/4 tsp. ground ginger
- 1/4 tsp. ground cinnamon
- 1/4 cup pear, sliced

DIRECTIONS:
1. Transfer cooked oats to a glass jar with a lid.
2. Stir in the ginger and cinnamon.
3. Top with pear slices.

Nutrition: Calories: 108 | Fat: 2 g | Protein: 3 g

487. Thai Oatmeal
(Prep. Time: 10 Min | Cooking: 5 Min | Serving 1)

INGREDIENTS
- 1 tbsp. peanut butter; cilantro
- 1/2 cup coconut milk; rolled oats
- 1/2 tsp. curry powder
- 2 tbsp. tomatoes, chopped
- 1/4 cup spinach, cooked and chopped
- 1 tsp. tamari

DIRECTIONS:
1. Place oats, peanut butter, milk, curry powder, and 1 tsp. tamari in a jar.
2. Mix well.
3. Refrigerate overnight.
4. Top with tomatoes, spinach, and cilantro before serving.

Nutrition: Calories: 307 | Fat: 14 g | Protein: 10 g

488. Tropical Oats
(Prep. Time: 10 Min | Cooking: 5 Min | Serving 1)

INGREDIENTS
- 1/2 cup rolled oats, cooked
- 1 tbsp. dried mango, chopped
- 1/4 cup pineapple, diced
- 1 1/2 tsp. chia seeds
- 1 1/2 tsp. shredded coconut (unsweetened)
- 3/4 cup coconut milk

DIRECTIONS:
1. Add layers of oats, 3/4 cup coconut milk, mango, pineapple, and chia seeds in a glass jar with a lid.
2. Seal the jar and refrigerate until ready to eat.
3. Top with the coconut shreds before serving.

Nutrition: Calories: 281 | Fat: 10 g | Protein: 7 g

489. Sweet Potato Hash Browns
(Prep. Time: 10 Min | Cooking: 5 Min | Serving 6)

INGREDIENTS
- 1 garlic clove, grated
- 1/4 cup shallot, chopped
- 5 cups sweet potato, shredded
- 3 tbsp. light olive oil, divided
- Salt and pepper to taste

DIRECTIONS:
1. Put the garlic, shallot, sweet potato, 1 tbsp. light olive oil, salt, and pepper in a bowl.
2. Add 1 tbsp. oil to a pan over medium heat.
3. Pour a half cup of the sweet potato patty into the pan. Flatten using a spatula.
4. Cook the patty for 3 minutes per side.
5. Cook the remaining patties with the remaining oil.

Nutrition: Calories: 103 | Fat: 7 g | Protein: 1 g

490. Apple, Pecans, and Cinnamon Oatmeal
(Prep. Time: 5 Min | Cooking: 10 Min | Serving 1)

INGREDIENTS
- 1/2 cup rolled oats; apple
- 1/2 tbsp. chia seeds
- 1 tsp. maple syrup
- 1/2 cup (unsweetened) almond milk
- 2 tbsp. pecans, toasted
- Salt to taste

DIRECTIONS:
1. Layer the oats, maple syrup, 1/4 tsp. cinnamon, chia seeds, and almond milk in a glass jar.
2. Season with a little bit of salt.
3. Cover the jar and refrigerate.
4. Top with apples and pecans before serving.

Nutrition: Calories: 215 | Fat: 4 g | Protein: 6 g

491. Pumpkin Oats
(Prep. Time: 5 Min | Cooking: 0 Min | Serving 1)

INGREDIENTS
- 1/2 cup rolled oats; soy milk
- 2 tsp. maple syrup
- 3 tbsp. pumpkin puree
- 1/2 tsp. vanilla extract
- 1/4 tsp. ground cinnamon
- A pinch of salt

DIRECTIONS:
1. Mix the oats, soy milk, maple syrup, pumpkin puree, vanilla extract, and cinnamon in a glass jar with a lid.
2. Season with a pinch of salt.
3. Seal the jar and refrigerate.
4. Top with pumpkin seeds before serving.

Nutrition: Calories: 182 | Fat: 4 g | Protein: 6 g

492. Melon Muesli
(Prep. Time: 10 Min | Cooking: 5 Min | Serving 2)

INGREDIENTS
- 1/2 cup muesli cereal (uncooked)
- 1/2 cup almond milk (unsweetened)

- 1/2 cup water
- 1/2 cup fresh cantaloupe, chopped
- 1 pinch ground cinnamon

DIRECTIONS:
1. In a heat-proof bowl, mix the cereal, milk, and water.
2. Microwave in high power for 5 minutes
3. Top with the cantaloupe and season with cinnamon before serving.

Nutrition: Calories: 96 | Fat: 2 g | Protein: 3 g

493. Citrus Vinaigrette
(Prep. Time: 5 Min | Cooking: 0 Min | Serving 12)

INGREDIENTS
- 1 orange
- 2 limes
- 2 tbsp. Dijon mustard
- 4 garlic cloves, peeled
- 1/4 cup light olive oil

DIRECTIONS:
1. Squeeze juice from the orange and limes.
2. Add the fruits and their juices to the blender.
3. Add the other ingredients.
4. Blend until smooth.
5. Serve with salad or steamed veggies.

Nutrition: Calories: 45 | Fat: 5 g | Protein: 0.4 g

494. Lemon Garlic Tahini Sauce
(Prep. Time: 10 Min | Cooking: 0 Min | Serving 8)

INGREDIENTS
- 3 tbsp. tahini
- 3 tbsp. warm water
- 2 tbsp. lemon juice
- 1 tbsp. light olive oil
- 1 garlic clove, grated

DIRECTIONS:
1. Combine all the ingredients in a glass jar with a lid.
2. Shake to blend well.
3. Cover and refrigerate until ready to use.

Nutrition: Calories: 50 | Fat: 5 g | Protein: 1 g

495. No-Carb Cereal Bars
(Prep. Time: 15 Min | Cooking: 0 Min | Serving 8)

INGREDIENTS
- 1 cup pumpkin and sunflower seeds
- 1 cup almonds; hazelnut
- 1 flax egg (see recipe)
- 1/4 cup coconut butter; cocoa butter
- 1 tsp. stevia powder

DIRECTIONS:
1. Set oven to 350°F/175°C, and line a shallow baking dish with parchment paper.
2. Transfer all the listed ingredients to a blender or food processor. Blend it into a chunky mixture.
3. Situate the mixture onto the baking dish and spread it out evenly into a flat chunk on the parchment paper.
4. Bake this chunk for about 15 minutes
5. Get the baking dish out of the oven and let cool down for about 10 minutes
6. Cut the chunk into the desired number of bars while it's still a bit warm.

Nutrition: Calories: 223 |Fat: 20.3 g | Protein: 7.2 g

496. Nutty Chocolate Bombs
(Prep. Time: 14 Min | Cooking: 0 Min | Serving 6)

INGREDIENTS
Nut butter bottom:
- 1/2 cup peanut butter; coconut oil
- 1/2 cup almonds; hazelnut
- 1/2 tbsp. pumpkin spice

Chocolate top:
- 1/4 cup cocoa butter
- 2 tbsp. cocoa powder
- 1/2 tsp. stevia powder

DIRECTIONS:
1. Line a muffin tray with muffin liners.
2. Pour coconut oil and peanut butter into a small bowl. Heat the bowl in the microwave for 10 seconds, or until the oil and butter have melted. Make sure it doesn't get too hot.
3. Transfer the melted ingredients and the remaining nut butter bottom ingredients to a food processor or blender. Blend everything into a chunky mix.
4. Transfer 1 tbsp. of the mixture from the blender into each muffin liner.
5. Repeat this process until the blender container is empty, making sure that all 12 muffin liners are evenly filled.
6. Situate the muffin tray in the freezer for about 30 minutes, until the bottom layers are firm.
7. Warm up the cocoa butter in a small saucepan over low heat until it's completely melted.
8. Stir in the cocoa powder and 1/2 tsp. stevia powder. Make sure the chocolate top ingredients are well incorporated.
9. Get the muffin tray out of the freezer and divide the chocolate top mixture over the muffins. Use a

tsp. and make sure the chocolate top mixture gets evenly distributed.
10. Put the muffin tray with the covered cups back in the freezer for another 30 minutes, until the nutty chocolate bombs are firm and ready to serve.

Nutrition: Calories: 253 |Fat: 24.7 g | Protein: 4.8 g

497. No-Bake Hazelnut Chocolate Bars

(Prep. Time: 15 Min | Cooking: 0 Min | Serving 8)

INGREDIENTS
- 1/2 cup coconut oil
- 2 cups hazelnuts
- 1/4 cup almonds; walnuts; cocoa powder
- 1 tbsp. pure vanilla extract
- 1 tsp. stevia powder

DIRECTIONS:
1. Prep shallow baking dish with parchment paper.
2. Transfer all the listed ingredients to a food processor or blender. Blend the ingredients into a chunky mixture.
3. Situate the mixture onto the baking dish and spread it out evenly into a flat chunk.
4. Wrap the baking dish and put it in the freezer for 45 minutes, until the chunk is firm.
5. Take the baking dish out of the freezer, cut up the chunk into the desired number of bars, and store, or serve and share.

Nutrition: Calories: 185 | Fat: 18 g | Protein: 3.4 g

498. Coconut Chocolate Balls

(Prep. Time: 15 Min | Cooking: 0 Min | Serving 12)

INGREDIENTS
- 1 cup macadamia nuts; coconut butter
- 1/2 cup cocoa butter; coconut oil
- 6 tbsp. cocoa powder
- 1 tbsp. vanilla extract
- 1 tsp. stevia powder
- 1 cup shredded coconut flakes

DIRECTIONS:
1. Transfer all the listed ingredients—except the 1 cup shredded coconut flakes—to a food processor or blender. Blend the ingredients into a smooth mixture.
2. Prep the baking tray with parchment paper to prevent the balls from sticking to the plate.
3. Scoop out a tbsp. of the chocolate and coconut mixture and roll it into a firm ball by using your hands.
4. Repeat the same for the other 23 balls. Coat each ball with the shredded coconut flakes and then transfer them to the baking tray.
5. Situate the baking tray in the freezer for 45 minutes, until all balls are solid.
6. Take the baking dish out of the freezer and store the coconut balls, or, serve them right away. Share the coconut chocolate balls with others and enjoy!
7. Alternatively, store the chocolate balls in the fridge, using an airtight container and consume them within 6 days.

Nutrition: Calories: 210 | Fat: 20.8 g | Protein: 3.5 g

499. Raspberry Cheesecake Fudge

(Prep. Time: 15 Min | Cooking: 0 Min | Serving 12)

INGREDIENTS
- 1 cup raw cashews (unsalted)
- 1/2 cup macadamia nuts (unsalted)
- 1/2 cup vegan protein powder (vanilla flavor); coconut cream
- 2 tsp. nutritional yeast
- 2 tbsp. freeze-dried raspberry powder

DIRECTIONS:
1. Prep a deep baking dish with parchment paper.
2. Transfer all the listed ingredients to a food processor or blender. Blend the ingredients into a smooth mixture.
3. Transfer the mixture onto the deep baking dish and spread it out into an even layer.
4. Put the baking dish in the freezer for 45 minutes, until the fudge chunk is firm.
5. Take the baking dish out of the freezer, cut the chunk into the desired number of fudge servings, and enjoy right away!

Nutrition: Calories: 178 | Fat: 12.7 g | Protein: 10.9 g

500. Blueberry Lemon Choco Cups

(Prep. Time: 15 Min | Cooking: 0 Min | Serving 12)

INGREDIENTS
- 1/2 cup cocoa butter; coconut oil
- 2 tbsp. organic lemon zest
- 1/4 cup fresh lemon juice; cocoa powder
- 1/2 tsp. stevia powder
- 20 blueberries

DIRECTIONS:

1. Situate cocoa butter and coconut oil in a medium bowl. Heat this bowl in the microwave for 10 seconds, until the butter and oil have melted. Make sure it doesn't get too hot.
2. Pull the bowl out of the microwave then mix in all the remaining ingredients. Make sure everything is well incorporated.
3. Line a muffin tray with muffin liners.
4. Scoop the soft mixture out of the bowl with a tbsp. into the muffin liners. If the mixture isn't soft enough to be transferred, heat it again in the microwave for 10 seconds.
5. Fill all the muffin liners evenly, 1 tbsp. at a time.
6. Refrigerate the cups for 45 minutes, until firm. Take the cups out, serve and enjoy!

Nutrition: Calories: 178 | Fat: 18.7 g | Protein: 0.8 g

501. CREAMY COCONUT VANILLA CUPS
(PREP. TIME: 15 MIN | COOKING: 0 MIN | SERVING 12)

INGREDIENTS
1. 1/4 cup coconut cream
2. 1/2 cup coconut flakes (unsweetened); coconut butter
3. 1/4 cup coconut oil
4. 1 tbsp. vanilla extract
5. 1 tsp. stevia powder

DIRECTIONS:
1. Put the coconut butter, coconut cream, and coconut oil in a small saucepan. Heat the pan over medium-low heat while whisking the ingredients until molten and mixed together.
2. Pull the pan off the heat then set it aside. Let the mixture cool down.
3. Transfer the mixture into a medium-sized bowl and mix in the remaining ingredients.
4. Line a muffin tray with muffin liners.
5. Scoop the soft mixture out of the bowl with a tbsp. into the muffin liners.
6. Fill all the muffin liners evenly, 1 tbsp. at a time.
7. Refrigerate the cups for 45 minutes, until the coconut cups are firm.
8. Serve and enjoy, or, store the creamy coconut vanilla cups in the fridge, using an airtight container, and consume within 6 days.

Nutrition: Calories: 139 | Fat: 13.5 g | Protein: 2.6 g

502. PEANUT BUTTER POWER BARS
(PREP. TIME: 15 MIN | COOKING: 0 MIN | SERVING 16)

INGREDIENTS
- 1/2 cup peanut butter; coconut oil
- 1/4 cup sunflower seeds; walnuts
- 1/4 cup hemp seeds; coconut butter
- 1 tbsp. vanilla extract
- 1 tsp. stevia powder

DIRECTIONS:
1. Put the coconut butter, peanut butter, and coconut oil in a small saucepan. Heat the saucepan over medium-low heat and whisk the ingredients until everything is molten and fully incorporated.
2. Pull the pan off the heat then set the mixture aside to cool down.
3. Line a baking dish with parchment paper.
4. Fill in the contents of the saucepan into a medium-sized bowl and mix in the remaining ingredients.
5. Situate mixture onto the baking dish and spread it out into an even layer.
6. Put the baking dish in the freezer for 45 minutes, until the chunk is firm.
7. Take the baking dish out freezer and cut the chunk into the desired number of bars.

Nutrition: Calories: 178 | Fat: 16.8 g | Protein: 4.6 g

503. DARK CHOCOLATE MINT CUPS
(PREP. TIME: 15 MIN | COOKING: 0 MIN | SERVING 16)

INGREDIENTS
- 1/2 cup coconut butter; cocoa butter
- 1/4 cup coconut oil
- 1/4 cup cocoa powder (unsweetened)
- 1 tsp. mint extract; stevia powder
- 1 tbsp. vanilla extract

DIRECTIONS:
1. Put the cocoa butter, coconut butter, and coconut oil in a small saucepan. Heat the saucepan over medium-low heat. Incorporate the ingredients using a whisk, add the cocoa powder, and whisk again until all ingredients are fully incorporated.
2. Pull the saucepan off the heat and set it aside to cool down.
3. Line a baking dish with parchment paper.
4. Fill in the mixture from the saucepan into a medium-sized bowl and mix in all the remaining ingredients. Make sure all ingredients are fully incorporated.
5. Transfer a tbsp. of the mixture from the bowl into each muffin liner.
6. Repeat this process until the bowl is empty, making sure that all 16 muffin liners are evenly filled.

7. Refrigerate the cups for 45 minutes, until the coconut cups are firm.
8. Take the cups out of the freezer, serve, and enjoy them right away.
9. Alternatively, store the chocolate mint cups in the fridge, using an airtight container, and consume within 6 days.

Nutrition: Calories: 151 | Fat: 15 g | Protein: 2.3 g

504. LOW-CARB PISTACHIO GELATO

(PREP. TIME: 15 MIN | COOKING: 0 MIN | SERVING 16)

INGREDIENTS
- 2 cups raw cashews (unsalted)
- 4 cups full-fat coconut milk
- 1/2 cup coconut oil
- 1 tsp. almond extract; stevia powder
- 2 tsp. tapioca starch
- Water
- 1 cup of pistachios

DIRECTIONS:
1. Cover the cashews in a small bowl filled with water, and let sit for 4 to 6 hours. Rinse and drain the cashews after soaking. Make sure no water is left.
2. Add 1 cup of pistachios to a blender or food processor, or, alternatively, use a coffee grinder; blend or grind the pistachios into a fine powder.
3. Keep or add the pistachio powder into the blender or food processor. Add the soaked nuts and the other ingredients except for the remaining pistachios. Blend the ingredients into a smooth mixture.
4. Situate the mixture in an ice cream maker and make the gelato according to the appliance's instructions. Alternatively, mix the leftover pistachios into half of the ice cream mixture and freeze it for about 4 hours. Keep the rest in the fridge for this time.
5. Further blend both mixtures in the blender or food processor into the desired gelato consistency.
6. Situate gelato in an airtight container and put it in the freezer for about 3 hours.
7. Let the gelato thaw for 15 minutes before serving. Enjoy!
8. The pistachio gelato can be stored, using an airtight container, for a maximum of 12 months. Thaw for about 5 minutes before serving.

Nutrition: Calories: 320 |Fat: 29.95 g | Protein: 5.8 g

505. TOASTED CASHEWS WITH NUT FLAKES

(PREP. TIME: 4 MIN | COOKING: 11 MIN | SERVING 3)

INGREDIENTS
- 1 cup cashews (unsalted)
- 1/4 cup toasted coconut flakes
- 4 tbsp. almond flakes; water
- 1 tbsp. liquid monk sweetener
- 1/2 tsp. vanilla extract
- 1/2 tbsp. cinnamon
- Salt to taste

DIRECTIONS:
1. Put a medium-sized frying pan or skillet over medium heat.
2. Add the liquid monk sweetener, 1/2 tbsp. cinnamon, salt, water, and vanilla extract. Stir the ingredients until everything is combined.
3. Then add the cashew nuts while constantly stirring. Make sure to coat all the nuts evenly in the liquid mixture.
4. Keep stirring while the liquid starts to crystalize on the nuts.
5. Transfer the toasted cashews to a plate and allow them to cool down.
6. Add the toasted coconut flakes and almond flakes, and then enjoy them right away.

Nutrition: Calories: 338 | Fat: 27.9 g | Protein: 10.3 g

506. CHOCOLATE AND YOGURT ICE CREAM

(PREP. TIME: 15 MIN | COOKING: 0 MIN | SERVING 1)

INGREDIENTS
- 2/3 cup low-fat Greek yogurt
- 1 scoop organic soy protein (vanilla or chocolate flavor)
- 1 tbsp. cocoa powder (unsweetened)
- 1 cup unsweetened almond milk
- 4 tbsp. almonds (crushed, alternatively use almond flakes)
- 6 drops of stevia sweetener

DIRECTIONS:
1. Take a medium-sized bowl and add the Greek yogurt, protein powder, cocoa powder, almond milk, and 6 drops of stevia sweetener. With a whisk, combine the ingredients together.
2. Put the bowl into the freezer for an hour.
3. Stir the ice cream and put it back in the freezer for 30 minutes repeat this step.

4. After 2 hours, ice cream is ready. Allow it to soften for 5 minutes, top it with the crushed almonds, serve, and enjoy!
5. The ice cream can be stored, using an airtight container, for a maximum of 12 months. Thaw for about 5 minutes before serving.

Nutrition: Calories: 355 | Fat: 17.9 g | Protein: 36.7 g

507. CHOCO CHIP ICE-CREAM WITH MINT
(PREP. TIME: 15 MIN | COOKING: 0 MIN | SERVING 8)

INGREDIENTS
- 2 cups heavy whipping cream (use coconut cream for vegan ice cream)
- 1/2 scoop organic soy protein (chocolate flavor)
- 1/2 tbsp. instant coffee powder; agar-agar
- 1 tsp. salt
- 6 tbsp. dark chocolate (85% cocoa or higher, use chunks or crush a chocolate bar)
- Water
- 1/4 tsp. stevia powder
- 3 tsp. vanilla extract
- 4 tsp. peppermint oil

DIRECTIONS:
1. Put the heavy whipping cream in a large bowl and freeze it for at least 20 minutes
2. Take out the cream and use a whisk to whip it for up to 10 minutes Transfer the bowl back to the freezer.
3. In a medium-sized pan, add the agar-agar and water. Stir until the agar-agar has dissolved in the water, and then blend in the 1/4 tsp. stevia powder.
4. Stir in the instant coffee powder and salt. Put the pan over medium heat. Stir constantly while heating the mixture, and make sure that no lumps remain.
5. Get the pan off the heat then stir in the protein powder. Set the mixture aside to cool down.
6. Take the whipped cream and add the 3 tsp. vanilla extract and 4 tsp. peppermint oil. Use more of both for a stronger taste.
7. Add the vegan gelatin mixture from the pan to the cream. Incorporate both mixtures by using a whisk or an electric mixer. This process is best done by working with multiple batches.
8. Taste the mixture and add more stevia, vanilla, and/or peppermint, depending on desired taste.
9. Freeze the mixture for 15 minutes Stir it and freeze for another 10 minutes
10. Top the ice cream with the dark chocolate chunks and freeze for at least 2 hours.
11. Allow defrosting 5 minutes before serving. Top with some additional dark chocolate, chopped mint, and enjoy!
12. The ice cream can be stored in an airtight container for a maximum of 12 months. Thaw for about 5 minutes before serving.

Nutrition: Calories: 275 | Fat: 27.2 g | Protein: 3.7 g

508. CRISPY CHEESE SNACKS
(PREP. TIME: 4 MIN | COOKING: 11 MIN | SERVING 4)

INGREDIENTS
- 2 medium organic eggs
- 1/2 cup cheddar cheese; almond flour
- 1/4 cup parmesan cheese (shredded)
- 1 8-oz. package tempeh
- 1 tsp. paprika powder

DIRECTIONS:
1. Prep the oven to 400°F and line a baking tray with parchment paper.
2. Take a medium-sized bowl and mix the 2 eggs, cheeses, flour, and spices in it by using a spoon. Make sure that no lumps remain.
3. Divide the mixture into 8 even portions.
4. Cut the tempeh into 8 chunks.
5. Cover each piece of tempeh with a piece of the cheese mixture.
6. Transfer the snacks to the baking tray. Bake for 12 minutes
7. Allow the snacks to cool down before serving and enjoy!
8. Alternatively, store the cheese snacks in the fridge in an airtight container, and consume them within 5 days.

Nutrition: Calories: 248 | Fat: 15.9 g | Protein: 21.6 g

509. CRÈME BRULE
(PREP. TIME: 5 MIN | COOKING: 10 MIN | SERVING 4)

INGREDIENTS
- 2 cups heavy cream
- 6 large organic egg yolks
- 1 tbsp. grass-fed butter; brandy
- 1/4 tsp. vanilla extract
- 1 tsp. stevia sweetener

DIRECTIONS:
1. Preheat the oven to 350°F
2. Fill a large oven dish or pan with a layer of hot water. Grease 4 ramekins with the butter and

place these in the water. The water should cover the ramekins halfway.
3. In a medium bowl, scourge egg yolks using a whisk. Add the stevia sweetener and vanilla extract and stir.
4. Take a medium-sized saucepan, add the heavy cream, and heat it over medium heat while continuously stirring.
5. Slowly stir in egg yolk mixture to the saucepan while continuously stirring.
6. Add the brandy, stir, and take the saucepan off the heat.
7. Portion the mixture into the 4 ramekins and put the dish or pan into the oven.
8. Bake the crème Brule in the oven for about 30 minutes, until the top is golden brown.
9. Pull the dish or pan out of the oven and cool the ramekins in a layer of cold water.
10. Refrigerate the ramekins for up to 8 hours, serve, and enjoy!

Nutrition: Calories: 529 | Fat: 53 g | Protein: 7.4 g

510. AVOCADO CHOCOLATE PUDDING
(PREP. TIME: 10 MIN | COOKING: 9 MIN | SERVING 4)

INGREDIENTS
- 4 large Hass avocados (peeled, pitted, sliced)
- 1/4 cup full-fat coconut milk; dark chocolate
- 4 tbsp. pure cocoa powder (unsweetened)
- 1 tsp. stevia sweetener; cinnamon powder
- 2 tsp. vanilla extract

DIRECTIONS:
1. Add all required ingredients—including the optional lemon juice and zest if desired—to a blender or food processor and blend for up to 3 minutes, until everything is combined. Scrape the sides of the blender or food processor if necessary.
2. Make sure that the pudding is creamy and blend for an additional minute if necessary.
3. Transfer the pudding into one or two bowls, cover, and refrigerate for at least 8 hours.
4. Serve the pudding with the optional mint leaves on top if desired, and enjoy!

Nutrition: Calories: 398 | Fat: 35.5 g | Protein: 7.7 g

511. BLACK OLIVE AND THYME CHEESE SPREAD
(PREP. TIME: 6 MIN | COOKING: 9 MIN | SERVING 16)

INGREDIENTS
- 1 cup macadamia nuts; pine nuts
- 1 tsp. thyme; rosemary
- 2 tsp. nutritional yeast 1 tsp. Himalayan salt
- 10 black olives (pitted, finely chopped)

DIRECTIONS:
1. Set the oven to 350°F, then prep a baking sheet with parchment paper.
2. Put the nuts on a baking sheet, and spread them out so they can roast evenly. Situate the baking sheet to the oven and roast the nuts for about 8 minutes, until slightly browned.
3. Pull the nuts out of the oven then set aside for about 4 minutes, allowing them to cool down.
4. Stir in all ingredients to a blender and process until everything combines into a smooth mixture. With a spatula to scrape down the sides of the blender container in between blending to make sure everything gets mixed evenly.
5. Serve, share, and enjoy!

Nutrition: Calories: 118 | Fat: 11.9 g | Protein: 2 g

512. EGG MUFFINS
(PREP. TIME: 4 MIN | COOKING: 9 MIN | SERVING 9)

INGREDIENTS
- 9 large organic eggs
- 1/2 cup scallions (finely chopped)
- 1 cup broccoli florets; mushroom
- 4 tbsp. sugar-free sweet hot sauce
- 1/4 cup fresh parsley (chopped)
- Salt and pepper to taste

DIRECTIONS:
1. Prep oven to 375°F and line a 9-cup muffin tray with muffin liners.
2. Take a large bowl, crack the eggs in it, and whisk while adding salt and pepper to taste.
3. Stir in all the remaining ingredients to the bowl and stir thoroughly.
4. Fill each muffin liner with the egg mixture. Repeat this for all 9 muffins.
5. Situate tray to the oven and bake for about 30 minutes, or until the muffins have risen and browned on top.
6. Pull the tray out of the oven then let the muffins cool down for about 2 minutes; serve and enjoy.
7. Alternatively, store the muffins in an airtight container in the fridge, and consume them within 3 days.

Nutrition: Calories: 76 | Fat: 4.9 g | Protein: 6.9 g

513. Chia Pudding With Blueberries
(Prep. Time: 7 Min | Cooking: 6 Min | Serving 2)

INGREDIENTS
- 12 tbsp. chia seeds
- 3 cups unsweetened almond milk
- 1 cup water
- 4-6 drops stevia sweetener
- 1/4 cup blueberries

DIRECTIONS:
1. Situate all the ingredients in a medium-sized bowl and stir. Alternatively, put all ingredients in a mason jar, close tightly, and shake.
2. Let the pudding sit for 5 minutes, then give it another stir (or shake).
3. Transfer the bowl or Mason jar to the fridge. Cool the pudding for at least 1 hour.
4. Give the pudding another stir, top it with the blueberries, and then serve and enjoy!

Nutrition: Calories: 256 | Fat: 19.8 g | Protein: 9.6 g

514. Papaya Smoothie
(Prep. Time: 4 Min | Cooking: 0 Min | Serving 2)

INGREDIENTS
- 2-3 frozen broccoli florets
- 1 cup orange juice
- 1 small ripe avocado, peeled, cored, and diced
- 1 cup papaya
- 1 cup fresh strawberries

DIRECTIONS:
1. Combine all ingredients in a high-speed blender and blend until smooth.

Nutrition: Calories: 52 | Fat: 8 g | Protein: 4 g

Chapter 8. Appetizer Recipes

515. Veggie Salad
(Prep. Time: 15 Min | Cooking: 0 Min | Serving 2)

INGREDIENTS
- 4 medium organic eggs
- 4 cups baby spinach leaves
- 2 medium shallots (finely minced)
- 1 tbsp. lemon juice
- 1 1/2 tbsp. light olive oil
- Water

DIRECTIONS:
1. Situate eggs in a saucepan filled with water. Bring the water to a boil over medium heat.
2. When the water boils, set the heat down to low and cover the saucepan. Allow the eggs to sit in simmering water for 6 to 12 minutes (6 minutes for a soft yolk, and up to 12 minutes for a thoroughly cooked yolk).
3. Take the saucepan off the heat, drain the hot water, and rinse the eggs with cold water. Peel the eggs and set them aside.
4. Situate eggs to a medium bowl and add the lemon juice, 1 tbsp. of light olive oil, minced shallots, and season well.
5. Mash everything together with a potato masher into a chunky egg salad.
6. Serve the salad over baby spinach leaves, and sprinkle it with half a tbsp. of light olive oil.
7. Toss the salad to mix everything together, serve, and enjoy!

Nutrition: Calories: 275 | Fat: 22.2 g | Protein: 13.7 g

516. Baked Kale Chips
(Prep. Time: 4 Min | Cooking: 11 Min | Serving 4)

INGREDIENTS
- 1 bunch large curly or dinosaur (Tuscan) kale
- 1 tbsp. extra-virgin light olive oil
- 1 tsp. paprika (optional)
- 1/4 tsp. salt

DIRECTIONS:
1. Preheat the oven to 300°F. Prep two large baking sheets using parchment paper.
2. Rinse and dry the kale, making sure there is no moisture left. Cutaway the center spine from each kale leaf and discard. This will leave you with 2 pieces. Cut both pieces in half, so each leaf has been cut into quarters.
3. In a large bowl, combine the salt, oil, and all the spices you are using. Add the kale and massage the oil mixture into the kale with your hands to coat evenly.
4. Situate the kale pieces in a single layer on the baking sheets and bake until they are crisp, 25 to 30 minutes

Nutrition: Calories: 159 | Fat: 7 g | Protein: 6 g

517. White Bean Dip With Olives
(Prep. Time: 12 Min | Cooking: 0 Min | Serving 4)

INGREDIENTS
- 2 (15.5 oz.) cans white beans, drained, rinsed, and coarsely chopped
- 1 cup pitted mixed olives, coarsely chopped
- 1/4 cup coarsely chopped fresh parsley
- 3 to 4 tbsp. fresh lemon juice
- Zest of 1 lemon, divided
- 2 tbsp. Oil

DIRECTIONS:
1. In a medium bowl, toss the beans, olives, parsley, oil, lemon juice, and most of the lemon zest. Reserve 1 tsp. of zest for a garnish.
2. Season well and drizzle lemon juice if desired.
3. Top with the remaining tsp. of lemon zest to serve.

Nutrition: Calories: 264 | Fat: 8 g | Protein: 12 g

518. Roasted Eggplant Dip
(Prep. Time: 9 Min | Cooking: 6 Min | Serving 4)

INGREDIENTS
- 2 medium eggplants
- 1/2 cup tahini
- 4 tsp. pomegranate molasses
- 3 tbsp. fresh lemon juice
- 6 tbsp. chopped fresh parsley
- 2 tbsp. water
- 2 garlic cloves
- Salt and pepper to taste

DIRECTIONS:
1. Situate the rack in the middle of the oven and turn the oven on broil. Line a baking sheet with foil.
2. Prick the eggplants with a sharp knife in a few places. Put them on the parchment paper-lined baking sheet and place them on the middle rack under the broiler. Broil for 45 minutes to 1 hour,

turning them every 10 minutes the eggplants need to deflate completely and the skin should burn and break. Pull out the eggplants from the oven and set them aside to cool.
3. Once cool enough to handle, cut lengthwise down the center of each eggplant and scoop out the flesh, avoiding the blackened skin, and place in a fine-mesh colander. Leave over a bowl to drain and cool for 40 minutes
4. Chop the eggplant roughly and transfer it to a medium mixing bowl. Add the tahini, 2 tbsp. water, pomegranate molasses, lemon juice, parsley, 2 garlic cloves, salt, and pepper. Mix well.
5. Taste and season with more salt, pepper, garlic, or lemon juice.
6. Serve with toasted pita bread.

Nutrition: Calories: 273 | Fat: 17 g | Protein: 8 g

519. Stuffed Dates with Cashew Cream and Roasted Almonds
(Prep. Time: 3 Min | Cooking: 11 Min | Serving 4)

INGREDIENTS
- 1 cup shelled, raw, unsalted almonds
- 2 cups raw unsalted cashews
- 1 1/2 tbsp. pure maple syrup
- 1/2 tsp. vanilla extract, or more to taste
- 12 fresh dates
- Water

DIRECTIONS:
1. Preheat the oven to 350°F. Prep rimmed baking sheet with parchment paper.
2. Layout almonds in a single layer and roast for 10 to 12 minutes
3. In a food processor, add the drained cashews, maple syrup, vanilla, and half of the water. Mix until smooth, adding more water if needed.
4. Slice open one side of each date and remove the pit with your fingers. Stuff each date with some cashew cream.
5. Serve with roasted almonds.

Nutrition: Calories: 646 | Fat: 44 g | Protein: 19 g

520. Crunchy Vegetable Spring Rolls
(Prep. Time: 15 Min | Cooking: 0 Min | Serving 4)

INGREDIENTS
- 8 (8-inch) dried rice paper wrappers
- 4 cups julienned thin crunchy vegetables of your choice, like red bell pepper, carrots, or cucumbers
- 2 small avocados, sliced
- 1 small bunch of fresh mint, stemmed
- Water

DIRECTIONS:
1. Work with the rice paper 1 wrapper at a time. Fill hot water into a shallow dish and immerse the rice paper sheet to soften for about 15 seconds. Remove from the water and pat both sides dry with a paper towel or clean kitchen towel. Lay on a cutting board.
2. To the bottom third of the wrapper situate a small handful of the julienned vegetables, a slice of avocado, and 4 or 5 mint leaves. Gently fold up and over once, then tuck in the edges and continue rolling tightly until the seam is sealed. Situate the roll on a platter, seam side down, and cover with a damp kitchen towel.
3. Repeat with the remaining wrappers and ingredients. Serve immediately.

Nutrition: Calories: 294 | Fat: 14 g | Protein: 5 g

521. Coconut Bacon
(Prep. Time: 6 Min | Cooking: 9 Min | Serving 4)

INGREDIENTS
- 1 1/2 tsp. smoked paprika
- 1 1/2 tbsp. low-sodium, gluten-free soy sauce or tamari
- 1 tbsp. pure maple syrup
- 1/2 tbsp. water
- 3 1/2 cups unsweetened flaked coconut
- Pepper to taste

DIRECTIONS:
1. Preheat the oven to 325°F. Prep a big baking sheet with parchment paper.
2. Combine the paprika, soy sauce, maple syrup, pepper, and water in a large bowl.
3. Pour in the flaked coconut and use a wooden spoon to gently toss the coconut in the liquid. When the coconut is evenly coated, pour it onto the baking sheet.
4. Bake for 20 to 25 minutes, using a spatula to flip the bacon about every 5 minutes so it cooks evenly. Remove when everything is crispy and golden brown.

Nutrition: Calories: 204 | Fat: 18 g | Protein: 2 g

522. Portobello Bacon
(Prep. Time: 8 Min | Cooking: 6 Min | Serving 4)

INGREDIENTS
- 5 large Portobello mushrooms, stemmed and gills removed
- 1/4 cup gluten-free low-sodium soy sauce or tamari
- 2 tsp. smoked paprika
- 3 tbsp. pure maple syrup
- Pepper to taste

DIRECTIONS:
1. Cut the mushrooms into 1/4-inch slices.
2. Using a small bowl, scourge soy sauce, paprika, and maple syrup. Season with pepper.
3. Place the mushrooms into a shallow glass dish and pour the marinade over them. Toss to make sure that all the mushroom slices are fully covered. Let the mushrooms marinate overnight covered in the refrigerator.
4. Preheat the oven to 275°F. Line a baking sheet with parchment paper.
5. Lay each mushroom slice on the baking sheet, avoiding overlapping. You may need 2 baking sheets. Bake for 60 minutes

Nutrition: Calories: 76 | Fat: 0 g | Protein: 5 g

523. ROASTED CARROTS AND CHICKPEAS
(PREP. TIME: 11 MIN | COOKING: 3 MIN | SERVING 4)

INGREDIENTS
- 10 carrots, peeled and cut into 1 1/2-inch matchsticks
- 1/4 tsp. cayenne pepper or paprika
- 1 1/2 cups cooked chickpeas
- 2 tsp. pure maple syrup
- 1 tbsp. lemon juice
- 3 tsp. oil

DIRECTIONS:
1. Prep the oven to 400°F. Line a big baking sheet using parchment paper.
2. Spread out the carrot sticks on the baking sheet and roast for 10 minutes
3. Meanwhile, in a medium bowl, combine 1 tbsp. lemon juice, 2 tsp. oil, and the cayenne pepper. Toss the chickpeas with the lemon juice mixture.
4. Add to the baking sheet with the carrots and roast for 20 to 30 minutes more, or until the carrots are tender-crisp and lightly brown and the chickpeas are crunchy.
5. Meanwhile, whisk together the remaining 1 tbsp. lemon juice, maple syrup, and 1 tsp. oil in a small bowl.
6. Put the carrots and chickpeas in a serving bowl while still warm and toss with the dressing.

Nutrition: Calories: 204 | Fat: 5 g | Protein: 7 g

524. CAULIFLOWER BUFFALO WINGS
(PREP. TIME: 8 MIN | COOKING: 7 MIN | SERVING 4)

INGREDIENTS
- 2 tbsp. extra-virgin light olive oil
- 2 tbsp. soy sauce
- 2 tbsp. rice vinegar
- 1–2 tbsp. Sriracha sauce
- 1 cauliflower head, leaves removed, cut into florets

DIRECTIONS:
1. Set oven to 400°F. Prep a big baking sheet using parchment paper
2. Blend oil, soy sauce, vinegar, and sriracha sauce
3. Gently stir in the cauliflower to the bowl and toss to coat with the marinade.
4. Spread cauliflower on a baking sheet then roast for 15 minutes. Flip and roast for an extra 10 to 15 minutes, or until tender.
5. Garnish with fresh cilantro and serve.

Nutrition: Calories: 123 | Fat: 7 g | Protein: 5 g

525. CRISPY CRUNCHY COCONUT TOFU
(PREP. TIME: 5 MIN | COOKING: 10 MIN | SERVING 4)

INGREDIENTS
- 1 (14 oz.) package extra-firm tofu
- 4 tbsp. cornstarch
- 1/4 tsp. baking powder
- 1/2 cup panko breadcrumbs
- 3/4 cup unsweetened shredded coconut
- Water
- Salt and pepper to taste

DIRECTIONS:
1. Set the oven to 400°F. Line a big baking sheet using parchment paper.
2. Squeeze the tofu using a clean kitchen towel to drain, then cut it into 2-inch cubes. Do the batter by combining the cornstarch, baking powder, salt, and water in a mixing bowl.
3. Put the breadcrumbs, salt, pepper, and shredded coconut on a large plate and use your hands to combine them.
4. Soak each piece of tofu in the batter, then lift to let the excess runoff. Dip in the coconut panko breadcrumbs and roll to cover completely. Transfer to the baking sheet.
5. Bake 27 minutes, or until golden brown.

Nutrition: Calories: 223 | Fat: 13 g | Protein: 11 g

526. Sweet Potato Latkes

(Prep. Time: 6 Min | Cooking: 9 Min | Serving 4)

INGREDIENTS
- 2 sweet potatoes (about 1 1/2 lb. total), peeled
- 2 russet potatoes (about 1 1/2 lb. total), peeled
- 1 small red or white onion
- 2 flax eggs
- 3 tbsp. rice flour
- 2 cups water
- Salt and pepper to taste
- 3 tbsp. oil

DIRECTIONS:
1. Using the big shredding blade of a food processor, grate the sweet potatoes, potatoes, and onion into a large bowl.
2. Wrap everything in a clean dish towel and twist tightly over the sink to wring out as much water as possible.
3. Put the potatoes back in the large bowl and season with salt and pepper. Fold in the flax eggs and rice flour. Incorporate using your hands until thoroughly combined.
4. Situate a big nonstick skillet over medium heat. Add the oil and heat until hot.
5. Working in batches, spoon about 1/4 cup of the potato mixture into the pan, pressing lightly with a spatula to form 5-inch pancakes that are about 1/4-inch thick. Cook for 8 minutes, turning once about halfway through.
6. Transfer the cooked latkes to the oven to keep warm as you cook more.

Nutrition: Calories: 318 | Fat: 3 g | Protein: 6 g

527. Italian-Style Spaghetti Squash

(Prep. Time: 9 Min | Cooking: 6 Min | Serving 4)

INGREDIENTS
- 1 large spaghetti squash (about 2 1/2 lb.), halved lengthwise, seeded and membranes removed
- 2 tbsp. extra-virgin light olive oil
- 1/4 cup pine nuts
- 2 cups tomato sauce
- Pepper to taste

DIRECTIONS:
1. Preheat the oven to 425°F. Prep 9-x13-inch baking dish using parchment paper.
2. Mix the flesh of the squash with oil and season with pepper. If you are oil-free, omit the oil. Place the squash in the baking dish cut-side down and roast until golden and tender when pierced with a knife, about 45 minutes
3. Meanwhile, grind the pine nuts in a small food processor or spice grinder.
4. When the squash is cooked and cool enough to handle, with a fork to scrape the flesh toward the center to create long strips. Place the strands into a large bowl.
5. Warm the tomato sauce in a medium saucepan or the microwave. To serve, pour a 1/2 cup of tomato sauce in the center of each plate. Using tongs, twirl one-quarter of the spaghetti squash tightly and mound on top of the sauce. Top each serving with 1 tbsp. of ground pine nuts.

Nutrition: Calories: 205 | Fat: 11 g | Protein: 5 g

528. Roasted Brussels Sprouts with Warm Maple Sauce

(Prep. Time: 5 Min | Cooking: 10 Min | Serving 4)

INGREDIENTS
- 1 lb. (about 30) small Brussels sprouts, trimmed and halved
- 1 tbsp. extra-virgin light olive oil
- 1/4 cup pure maple syrup
- 2 1/2 tbsp. sherry or red wine vinegar
- 3/4 tsp. crushed red pepper flakes
- A pinch of salt + 1/4 tsp. salt
- Pepper to taste

DIRECTIONS:
1. Heat the oven to 450°F. Prep rimmed baking sheet with parchment paper.
2. Throw Brussels sprouts with the oil. If you are oil-free, omit the oil. Season with a pinch of salt and pepper. Spread the Brussels sprouts, cut-side down, on the baking sheet. Roast until tender and browned 20 to 25 minutes
3. Using a saucepan at medium heat, bring the maple syrup to a simmer. Set the heat to low then cook for about 3 minutes Whisk in the vinegar, the remaining 1/4 tsp. salt, and the red pepper flakes and cook, whisking constantly, for another 3 minutes
4. Situate the cooked Brussels sprouts in a large bowl. Add the sauce and toss to coat.

Nutrition: Calories: 132 | Fat: 4 g | Protein: 4 g

529. Baked Oatmeal and Fruit

(Prep. Time: 5 Min | Cooking: 10 Min | Serving 4)

INGREDIENTS
- 3 cups quick-cooking oats

- 3 cups unflavored, unsweetened nondairy milk
- 1/4 cup pure maple syrup
- 1 tbsp. vanilla extract
- 1–2 cups blueberries, raspberries, or both

DIRECTIONS:
1. Preheat the oven to 375°F.
2. In a large mixing bowl, combine all the ingredients. Transfer into a big casserole dish and cover with aluminum foil.
3. Bake for 10 minutes Uncover and bake for another 5 to 10 minutes, or until all the liquid is visibly gone and the edges start to brown.
4. Let cool 5 minutes before serving. Serve with an extra splash of non-dairy milk and a drizzle of maple syrup.

Nutrition: Calories: 365 | Fat: 7 g | Protein: 9 g

530. HEMP AND OAT GRANOLA
(PREP. TIME: 5 MIN | COOKING: 10 MIN | SERVING 4)

INGREDIENTS
- 2 cups old-fashioned rolled oats
- 1 1/2 tsp. cinnamon
- 1/2 cup hemp seeds
- 1/3 cup slivered almonds
- 1/3 cup pure maple syrup

DIRECTIONS:
1. Preheat the oven to 350°F. Prep a big baking sheet with parchment paper.
2. Spread the oats on the lined baking sheet. Sprinkle over the cinnamon and toss. Spread evenly on the baking sheet and toast in the oven for 10 minutes
3. Add the hemp seeds and toss them with the oats. Toast for another 10 minutes Add the almonds, toss, and toast for another 5 minutes
4. Pull out from oven, and drizzle with maple syrup. Toss, spread evenly on the baking sheet, and toast for another 5 minutes
5. Refrigerate covered for up to 5 days.

Nutrition: Calories: 434 | Fat: 20 g | Protein: 17 g

531. WARM FARRO WITH DRIED SWEET CHERRIES AND PISTACHIOS
(PREP. TIME: 5 MIN | COOKING: 9 MIN | SERVING 4)

INGREDIENTS
- 2 cups farro
- 2 1/2 cups water
- 1/4 cups dried sweet cherri
- 1/4 cup shelled unsalted pistachios
- Drizzle of pure maple syrup

DIRECTIONS:
1. Place the farro in a fine-mesh colander and rinse with cool water until the water runs clear.
2. Using a medium saucepan over high heat, boil the water. Stir in the faro and make sure it is completely submerged in the water. Reduce the heat to a gentle simmer. Cover and cook until the farro is chewy and the water is absorbed. Cooking time can vary from 15 to 30 minutes
3. Examine the texture every 5 to 10 minutes
4. Stir in the cherries, and then top with the pistachios.
5. Drizzle with maple syrup. Serve warm.

Nutrition: Calories: 296 | Fat: 3 g | Protein: 10 g

532. PINEAPPLE, CUCUMBER, AND MINT SALAD
(PREP. TIME: 11 MIN | COOKING: 0 MIN | SERVING 4)

INGREDIENTS
- 3 cups chopped fresh pineapple
- 3 cups fresh cucumber, peeled, seeded, and sliced
- 3 scallions, thinly sliced
- 1/4 cup chopped fresh mint
- 1/4 cup fresh lime juice

DIRECTIONS:
1. In a big bowl, incorporate all the ingredients and gently toss.

Nutrition: Calories: 82 | Fat: 0 g | Protein: 2 g

533. BRIGHT, BEAUTIFUL SLAW
(PREP. TIME: 15 MIN | COOKING: 0 MIN | SERVING 4)

INGREDIENTS
- Juice and zest of 2 limes
- 1/4 cup pure maple syrup
- 4–5 cups red cabbage, finely shredded
- 2 mangos or papayas, cut into small chunks
- 2 cups roughly chopped mint leaves
- Salt and pepper to taste

DIRECTIONS:
1. Scourge lime juice and maple syrup. Season with salt and pepper. Set aside.
2. In a medium bowl, add the red cabbage, mango, mint, and lime zest.
3. Add the dressing a little at a time and toss it together. Taste and season again well.

Nutrition: Calories: 177 | Fat: 1 g | Protein: 3 g

534. Baked Apples With Dried Fruit

(Prep. Time: 9 Min | Cooking: 6 Min | Serving 4)

INGREDIENTS
- 4 large apples, cored to make a cavity
- 4 tsp. raisins or cranberries
- 4 tsp. pure maple syrup
- 1/2 tsp. ground cinnamon
- 1/2 cup unsweetened apple juice or water

DIRECTIONS:
1. Preheat the oven to 350°F.
2. Situate apples in a baking dish that will hold them upright. Put the dried fruit into the cavities and drizzle with maple syrup. Sprinkle with cinnamon. Pour the apple juice or water around the apples.
3. Cover loosely with foil and bake for 50 minutes to 1 hour, or until the apples are tender when pierced with a fork.

Nutrition: Calories: 158 | Fat: 1 g | Protein: 1 g

535. Chocolate Protein Bites

(Prep. Time: 5 Min | Cooking: 10 Min | Serving 6)

INGREDIENTS
- 1/2 cup chocolate protein powder
- 1 avocado, medium
- 1 tbsp. chocolate chips
- 1 tbsp. coconut butter
- 1 tbsp. cocoa powder
- 1 tsp. vanilla extract
- A dash of salt

DIRECTIONS:
1. Begin by blending avocado, coconut butter, vanilla extract, and salt in a high-speed blender until you get a smooth mixture.
2. Next, spoon in the protein powder, cocoa powder, and chocolate chips to the blender.
3. Blend again until you get a smooth dough-like consistency mixture.
4. Now, check for seasoning and add more sweetness if needed.
5. Finally, with the help of a scooper, scoop out dough to make small balls.

Nutrition: Calories: 46 | Fat: 2 g | Protein: 2 g | Carbohydrates: 2 g

536. Crunchy Granola

(Prep. Time: 4 Min | Cooking: 10 Min | Serving 1)

INGREDIENTS
- 1/2 cup oats
- A dash of salt
- 2 tbsp. vegetable oil
- 3 tbsp. maple syrup
- 1/3 cup apple cider vinegar
- 1/2 cup almonds
- 1 tsp. cardamom, grounded

DIRECTIONS:
1. Preheat the oven to 375°F.
2. After that, mix oats, almonds, salt, and cardamom in a large bowl.
3. Next, spoon in the vegetable oil, apple cider vinegar, and maple syrup to the mixture.
4. Then, transfer the mixture to a parchment-paper-lined baking sheet.
5. Bake them for 13 minutes or until the mixture is toasted. **Tip:** Check on them now and then. Spread it out well.
6. Return the sheet to the oven for a further ten minutes
7. Remove the sheet from the oven and allow it to cool completely.
8. Serve and enjoy.

Nutrition: Calories: 763 | Fat: 52.4 g | Proteins: 12.9 g | Carbohydrates: 64.8 g

537. Almond Bars

(Prep. Time: 3 Min | Cooking: 11 Min | Serving 6)

INGREDIENTS
- 1 cup almonds
- 1 1/2 cup rolled oats
- 1/3 cup maple syrup
- 1/4 tsp. sea salt
- 5 oz. protein powder
- 1 tsp. cinnamon

DIRECTIONS:
1. For making these delicious vegan bars, you first need to place 3/4 cup of almonds and salt in the food processor.
2. Process them for a minute or until you get them in the form of coconut butter.
3. Now, stir in the rest of the ingredients to the processor and process them again until smooth.
4. Next, transfer the mixture to a greased parchment paper-lined baking sheet and spread it across evenly.
5. Press them slightly down with the back of the spoon.
6. Chop down the remaining 1/4 cup of the almonds and top it across the mixture.
7. Finally, place them in the refrigerator for 20 minutes or until set.

Nutrition: Calories: 166 | Fat: 6 g | Proteins: 12.8 g | Carbohydrates: 17.6 g

538. Spicy Nut and Seed Snack Mix

(Prep. Time: 5 Min | Cooking: 10 Min | Serving 4)

INGREDIENTS
- 1/4 tsp. garlic powder
- 1/4 tsp. nutritional yeast
- 1/2 tsp. smoked paprika
- 1/4 tsp. sea salt
- 1/4 tsp. dried parsley
- 1/2 cup slivered almonds
- 1/2 cup cashew pieces
- 1/2 cup sunflower seeds
- 1/2 cup pepitas

DIRECTIONS:
1. In a small bowl, mix the garlic powder, nutritional yeast, paprika, salt, and parsley. Set aside.
2. In a large skillet, add the almonds, cashews, sunflower seeds, pepitas and heat over low heat until warm and glistening, 3 minutes
3. Turn the heat off and stir in the parsley mixture.
4. Allow complete cooling and enjoy!

Nutrition: Calories: 385 |Fat: 33 g | Proteins: 12 g | Carbohydrates: 16 g

Chapter 9. Smoothie Recipes

539. HEALTHY GREEN SMOOTHIE
(Prep. Time: 10 Min | Cooking: 0 Min | Serving 2)

INGREDIENTS
- 2 cups baby spinach leaves
- 1 stalk celery
- 1 cucumber
- 1 cup water

DIRECTIONS:
1. Place the spinach, celery, and cucumber in a high-speed blender and blend until smooth.
2. Add the water or ice and blend.

Nutrition: Calories: 200 | Fiber: 1.7 g | Protein: 12 g

540. CHOCOLATE MINT SMOOTHIE
(Prep. Time: 14 Min | Cooking: 0 Min | Serving 2)

INGREDIENTS
- 3/4 cup plain greek yogurt
- 1 cup almond milk
- 1/4 cup fresh mint
- 1 cup baby spinach leaves
- 1 tbsp. maple syrup
- 1/4 cup semi-sweet chocolate chips
- 2 cups ice

DIRECTIONS:
1. Place the yogurt, milk, mint, and spinach in a blender and blend on high until frothy.
2. Add the maple syrup and chocolate chips and blend for a few seconds to break up the chocolate chips.
3. Add the ice and blend until thick and smooth.

Nutrition: Calories: 170 | Fiber: 5 g | Protein: 8 g

541. GREEN PUMPKIN SPICE SMOOTHIE
(Prep. Time: 10 Min | Cooking: 0 Min | Serving 2)

INGREDIENTS
- 1 cup frozen spinach
- 1 cup unsweetened almond milk
- 2 scoops vanilla protein powder
- 1 tbsp. smooth nut butter
- 1 tsp. chia seed
- 1 tsp. pumpkin pie spice

DIRECTIONS:
1. Place the spinach in the blender and add the milk and protein powder. Blend to break up the spinach.
2. Add the nut butter, chia seed, and spice and blend until smooth and thick. Add a little more milk if it is too thick.

Nutrition: Calories: 180 | Fiber: 4 g | Protein: 9 g

542. APPLE SPINACH PROTEIN SMOOTHIE
(Prep. Time: 4 Min | Cooking: 10 Min | Serving 0)

INGREDIENTS
- 1/2 cup rolled oats
- 1/2 cup cold water
- 1/2 tsp. cinnamon
- 1/2 tsp. nutmeg
- 1 tbsp. coconut butter
- 1 cup unsweetened almond milk
- 1 scoop vanilla protein powder
- 1 large apple
- 4 cups spinach leaves
- 5 ice cubes

DIRECTIONS:
1. Place the oats and cold water in a blender and pulse a few times. Let it sit for three to four minutes before proceeding.
2. Add the cinnamon, nutmeg, and coconut butter; pulse a few times to mix.
3. Pour in half a cup of almond milk and the protein powder and pulse.
4. Add the apple and blend until somewhat smooth.
5. Add the spinach leaves in two to three batches, blending until smooth each time.
6. Add the rest of the almond milk and the ice; then blend until thick.

Nutrition: Calories: 175 | Fiber: 9 g | Protein: 11 g

543. BANANA BERRY TROPICAL BREEZE
(Prep. Time: 13 Min | Cooking: 0 Min | Serving 2)

INGREDIENTS
- 1 banana
- 1/4 cup frozen pineapple
- 1/3 cup frozen raspberries

- 1 cup frozen strawberries
- 1/2 cup unsweetened almond milk.

DIRECTIONS:
1. Place the banana in the blender along with the pineapple, raspberries, and strawberries. Blend until almost smooth.
2. Add the almond milk and blend until smooth and creamy.

Nutrition: Calories: 190 | Fiber: 4 g | Protein: 7 g

544. Banana Peanut Butter Cranberry Protein Smoothie
(Prep. Time: 12 Min | Cooking: 0 Min | Serving 2)

INGREDIENTS
- 1 tbsp. chia seed
- 1 1/2 tbsp. hemp seed
- 1 cup unsweetened coconut milk
- 2 tbsp. natural peanut butter
- 1 banana
- 1/4 cup dried cranberries
- 3 or 4 ice cubes

DIRECTIONS:
1. Grind the chia and hemp seed in a coffee grinder and add them to the coconut milk in the blender. Pulse to combine the seeds and milk.
2. Add the peanut butter, frozen banana slices, and dried cranberries and blend to combine until smooth.
3. Add the ice cubes one by one and blend in to thicken the smoothie. You may only have to use three of the four. Sprinkle with some shredded coconut if desired.

Nutrition: Calories: 200 | Fiber: 6 g | Protein: 13 g

545. Blueberry Oatmeal Protein Smoothie
(Prep. Time: 13 Min | Cooking: 0 Min | Serving 3)

INGREDIENTS
- 1/2 cup water
- 1/2 cup rolled oats
- 1 cup almond milk
- 1 cup blueberries
- 4 ice cubes
- 1 scoop vanilla protein powder
- 2 tbsp. chia seed
- 1 tbsp. coconut butter

DIRECTIONS:
1. Combine the water, oatmeal, and coconut or almond milk in the blender and pulse a few times. Let sit for three to four minutes
2. Add the blueberries and ice cubes and blend until just combined.
3. Add the protein powder, ground chia seeds, and coconut butter. Blend until everything is smooth and thick. Add more ice if needed to balance the consistency.

Nutrition: Calories: 195 | Fiber: 9 g | Protein: 8 g

546. Carrot Orange Smoothie
(Prep. Time: 11 Min | Cooking: 0 Min | Serving 2)

INGREDIENTS
- 2 tbsp. flax seeds
- 1/2 cup unsweetened coconut milk
- 2 oranges, peeled, pieces separated and frozen
- 1-inch ginger, peeled and grated
- 2 large carrots, peeled then cut into small chunks

DIRECTIONS:
1. Grind the chia seeds with a coffee grinder and place them in the blender.
2. Pour in the coconut milk and frozen orange segments; pulse to mix until chunky.
3. Add the ginger and carrots, blending until smooth and creamy.

Nutrition: Calories: 210 | Fiber: 9 g | Protein: 11 g

547. Chocolate-Strawberry Heaven
(Prep. Time: 14 Min | Cooking: 0 Min | Serving 2)

INGREDIENTS
- 1 tbsp. chia seeds, ground
- 1 cup almond milk
- 1 scoop chocolate protein powder
- 2 tbsp. raw almonds
- 1 cup frozen, sliced strawberries

DIRECTIONS:
1. Grind the chia seeds and place them in a blender with the almond milk.
2. Add the chocolate protein powder and almonds and pulse mix everything together.
3. Add the strawberries and blend until smooth and rich and thick.

Nutrition: Calories: 209 | Fiber: 8 g | Protein: 9 g

548. Cherry Limeade Smoothie
(Prep. Time: 10 Min | Cooking: 0 Min | Serving 2)

INGREDIENTS
- 1 heaping cup of frozen pitted cherries
- 1 ripe peach, peeled and sliced
- 1 tbsp. ground chia seeds
- 1 cup almond milk
- 1–2 limes, juiced
- 1 handful of ice

DIRECTIONS:
1. Add the cherries and peach slices to the blender and pulse.
2. Add the ground chia seeds and pulse.
3. Pour in the almond milk, lime juice, and ice; blend until smooth and thick. Add ice if more thickness is needed.

Nutrition: Calories: 211 | Fiber: 10 g | Protein: 12 g

549. Layered Smoothie

(Prep. Time: 13 Min | Cooking: 0 Min | Serving 2)

INGREDIENTS
- 1 1/4 cups frozen mango pieces
- 1 cup almond milk, divided
- 2 tsp. stevia
- 1 cup frozen strawberries, hulled and cut in half
- 1 cup fresh spinach

DIRECTIONS:
1. Place the mango pieces in the blender, pour in a third of the milk, and add a third of the sweetener. Blend until smooth, then pour into the bottom of a large glass.
2. Place the strawberries in the blender along with another third of the milk and the sweetener; blend this until smooth. Pour gently over the mango layer in the glass.
3. Place the spinach and the remaining milk and sweetener in the blender and blend until smooth. Pour on top of the strawberry layer.

Nutrition: Calories: 208 | Fiber: 5 g | Protein: 9 g

550. Eat Your Kale Smoothie

(Prep. Time: 10 Min | Cooking: 0 Min | Serving 3)

INGREDIENTS
- 1/2 cup frozen mixed berries
- 1 medium ripe banana
- 2 cups fresh kale, stems removed
- 1 heaping tbsp. hemp seed
- 2/3 cup pomegranate juice
- 3/4–1 1/2 cups water

DIRECTIONS:
1. Place the frozen berries and banana in a blender and pulse to break up.
2. Add the kale and blend until somewhat smooth
3. Add the hemp seed, pomegranate juice, and a quarter cup of water, blending until smooth. If your smoothie is too thick at this point, add water a bit at a time until you get the consistency you like.

Nutrition: Calories: 210 | Fiber: 8 g | Protein: 10 g

551. Green Apple Orange Banana Spice

(Prep. Time: 10 Min | Cooking: 0 Min | Serving 2)

INGREDIENTS
- 1 medium Granny Smith apple, cut into slices
- 1 cup orange juice
- 1 banana, peeled, sliced, and frozen
- 1 1/2 cup kale
- 1 tsp. ginger root, peeled and minced
- 1 tbsp. chia or flaxseed, ground
- 1/2 tsp. ground cinnamon

DIRECTIONS:
1. Place the apple in the blender and pulse to break it up.
2. Add the orange juice and frozen banana slices and pulse again to break up and roughly combine.
3. Add the kale and blend.
4. Add the gingerroot, chia, or flax seed and cinnamon; blend until smooth and thick.

Nutrition: Calories: 207 | Fiber: 6 g | Protein: 9 g

552. Maple Fig Smoothie

(Prep. Time: 10 Min | Cooking: 0 Min | Serving 2)

INGREDIENTS
- 3/4 cup rolled oats
- 1 cup preferred milk
- 6–8 figs, stemmed and cut in half
- 1 banana, peeled, cut into slices, and frozen
- 2 tbsp. almond, cashew, or peanut butter
- A pinch ground ginger
- A pinch cinnamon
- A pinch cayenne pepper
- 1/4 cup cocoa powder
- 1/4 cup coconut oil
- 1/4 cup maple syrup

DIRECTIONS:
1. Combine the oats and milk in the blender, pulse, and let sit for about two minutes
2. Add the figs and banana slices and pulse.

3. Add the nut butter, ginger, cinnamon, and cayenne pepper; blend until smooth.
4. In a bowl, combine the cocoa powder, coconut oil, and maple syrup. Whisk until thoroughly mixed, then pour most of it into the blender and blend until smooth and creamy.
5. Divide among individual glasses, drizzling the rest of the syrup on top as an artistic garnish.

Nutrition: Calories: 196 | Fiber: 6 g | Protein: 8 g

553. Mint Protein Smoothie

(Prep. Time: 10 Min | Cooking: 0 Min | Serving 2)

INGREDIENTS
- 1 tbsp. chia seeds, ground
- 1 tbsp. hemp seeds, ground
- 1 tbsp. flax seed, ground
- 1/2 cup mango pieces, frozen
- 1 large orange, peeled and divided
- 1 banana, peeled, chopped in pieces, and frozen
- 1 scoop vanilla protein powder
- 3/4 cup unsweetened coconut milk
- 6 fresh mint leaves

DIRECTIONS:
1. Grind the chia, hemp, and flaxseed and place them in a blender.
2. Add the frozen mango, the orange pieces, and the frozen banana pieces to the blender and pulse a few times.
3. Add the protein powder and coconut milk; pulse again to combine.
4. Add the mint leaves and blend until smooth. If the smoothie is too runny, add a few ice cubes and blend again until thick and smooth.

Nutrition: Calories: 204 | Fiber: 4 g | Protein: 9 g

554. Chocolate Smoothie

(Prep. Time: 6 Min | Cooking: 0 Min | Serving 3)

INGREDIENTS
- 1/4 cup coconut butter
- 1/4 cup unsweetened cocoa powder
- 1/2 cup coconut milk can
- 1 cup almond milk, unsweetened

DIRECTIONS:
1. Freeze almond milk into cubes with an ice cube tray. Prep ahead
2. Process everything until desired thickness.
3. Serve

Nutrition: Calories: 147| Fat: 13 g | Protein: 4 g

555. Mint Smoothie

(Prep. Time: 8 Min | Cooking: 0 Min | Serving 2)

INGREDIENTS
- 2 tbsp. sweetener
- 2 drops mint extract
- 1 tbsp. cocoa powder
- 1/2 avocado, medium
- 1/4 cup coconut milk
- 1 cup almond milk, unsweetened

DIRECTIONS:
1. Blend all ingredients at a high-speed blender.
2. Stir in four ice cubes.

Nutrition: Calories: 401 |Fat: 40 g | Protein: 5 g

556. Cinnamon Roll Smoothie

(Prep. Time: 2 Min | Cooking: 0 Min | Serving 1)

INGREDIENTS
- 1 tsp. cinnamon
- 1 scoop vanilla protein powder
- 1/2 cup of almond milk, unsweetened
- 1/2 cup of coconut milk
- Sweetener of your choice

DIRECTIONS:
1. In a high-speed blender, add all the ingredients and blend.
2. Add two to four ice cubes and blend until smooth.
3. Serve immediately and enjoy!

Nutrition: Calories: 107 | Carbohydrates: 17 g | Protein: 33.3 g

557. Coco Milk Smoothie

(Prep. Time: 4 Min | Cooking: 0 Min | Serving 1)

INGREDIENTS
- 1 tsp. chia seeds
- 1/8 cup almonds
- 1 cup coconut milk
- 1 avocado

DIRECTIONS:
1. Incorporate all the ingredients.
2. Stir in the desired number of ice cubes then blend again.

Nutrition: Calories: 584 | Carbohydrates: 22.5 g | Protein: 8.3 g

558. Almond Smoothie

(Prep. Time: 6 Min | Cooking: 0 Min | Serving 3)

INGREDIENTS
- 1/2 tsp. vanilla extract
- 1 scoop maca powder
- 1 tbsp. coconut butter
- 1 cup almond milk, unsweetened
- 2 avocados

DIRECTIONS:
1. Blend all the ingredients until smooth.

Nutrition: Calories: 758 | Carbohydrates: 28 g | Protein: 9 g

559. Blueberry Smoothie
(Prep. Time: 5 Min | Cooking: 0 Min | Serving 1)

INGREDIENTS
- 1/4 cup pumpkin seeds shelled unsalted
- 3 cup blueberries, frozen
- 2 avocados, peeled and halved
- 1 cup almond milk

DIRECTIONS:
1. In a high-speed blender, add all the ingredients and blend until smooth.
2. Add two to four ice cubes and blend until smooth.
3. Serve immediately and enjoy!

Nutrition: Calories: 401 | Carbohydrates: 6.3 g | Protein: 5 g

560. Nutty Protein Shake
(Prep. Time: 5 Min | Cooking: 0 Min | Serving 1)

INGREDIENTS
- 1/4 avocado
- 2 tbsp. powdered peanut butter
- 1 tbsp. cocoa powder
- 1 tbsp. peanut butter
- 1 scoop protein powder
- 1/2 cup almond milk

DIRECTIONS:
1. In a high-speed blender, add all the ingredients and blend until smooth.
2. Add two to four ice cubes and blend again.
3. Serve immediately and enjoy!

Nutrition: Calories: 694 | Carbohydrates: 30.8 g | Protein: 40.8 g

561. Cinna-Pear Smoothie
(Prep. Time: 2 Min | Cooking: 0 Min | Serving 2)

INGREDIENTS
- 1 tsp. cinnamon
- 1 scoop vanilla protein powder
- 1/2 cup of the following:
  - Almond milk, unsweetened
  - Coconut Milk
- 2 pears, cores removed
- Sweetener of your choice

DIRECTIONS:
1. Blend all the ingredients.
2. Stir in two ice cubes and blend again.

Nutrition: Calories: 653 | Carbohydrates: 72 g | Protein: 28 g

562. The Perfect Milkshake
(Prep. Time: 7 Min | Cooking: 0 Min | Serving 3)

INGREDIENTS
- 2 cup ice cubes
- 2 tsp. vanilla extract
- 6 tbsp. powdered erythritol
- 1 cup cream of dairy-free
- 1/2 cup coconut milk

DIRECTIONS:
1. Using a high-speed blender, mix all ingredients.
2. Situate ice cubes and blend.

Nutrition: Calories: 125 | Carbohydrates: 6 g | Protein: 1.2 g

563. Berry Protein Shake
(Prep. Time: 6 Min | Cooking: 0 Min | Serving 2)

INGREDIENTS
- 1/4 avocado
- 1 cup raspberries, frozen
- 1 scoop protein powder
- 1/2 cup almond milk
- Ice cubes to taste

DIRECTIONS:
1. At high speed, blend all the ingredients until lumps disappear.
2. Put in ice cubes and blend again.

Nutrition: Calories: 756 | Carbohydrates: 80 g | Protein: 27 g

564. Raspberry Nut Smoothie
(Prep. Time: 6 Min | Cooking: 0 Min | Serving 2)

INGREDIENTS
- 10 almonds
- 3 tbsp. coconut butter
- 1 cup almond milk
- 1 cup raspberries

DIRECTIONS:
1. Mix all the ingredients at high speed.
2. Serve immediately and enjoy!

Nutrition: Calories: 448 | Carbohydrates: 26 g | Protein: 14 g

565. Chocolate Strawberry Almond Protein Smoothie
(Prep. Time: 10 Min | Cooking: 0 Min | Serving 1)

INGREDIENTS
- 1 cup of organic strawberries
- 1 1/2 cup homemade almond milk
- 1 scoop chocolate protein powder
- 1 tbsp. organic coconut oil
- 1/4 cup organic raw almonds
- 1 tbsp. organic hemp seeds
- 1 tbsp. organic maca powder

DIRECTIONS:
1. Put all the ingredients inside a blender and beat until they are well combined.
2. **Optional:** Garnish with organic hemp seeds or organic cocoa beans.
3. Enjoy it!

Nutrition: Calories: 720 | Carbohydrates: 39 g | Protein: 44 g

566. Beet Blast Smoothie
(Prep. Time: 5 Min | Cooking: 0 Min | Serving 1)

INGREDIENTS
- 1 1/2 cups unsweetened plant-based milk
- 1 Granny Smith apple, peeled, cored and chopped
- 1 cup chopped frozen beets
- 1 cup frozen blueberries
- 1/2 cup frozen cherries
- 1/4-inch fresh ginger root, peeled

DIRECTIONS:
1. In a blender, mix all the ingredients and blend until smooth. Serve immediately.

Nutrition: Calories: 324 | Carbohydrates: 70 g | Protein: 5 g

567. Green Power Smoothie
(Prep. Time: 5 Min | Cooking: 0 Min | Serving 1)

INGREDIENTS
- 3 cups fresh spinach
- 1 1/2 cups frozen pineapple
- 1 cup unsweetened plant-based milk
- 1 cup fresh kale
- 1 Granny Smith apple, peeled, cored and chopped
- 1/2 small avocado pitted and peeled
- 1/2 tsp. spirulina
- 1 tbsp. hemp seeds

DIRECTIONS:
1. In a blender, incorporate all the ingredients and blend until smooth. Serve.

Nutrition: Calories: 431 | Carbohydrates: 70 g | Protein: 13 g

568. Tropical Bliss Smoothie
(Prep. Time: 5 Min | Cooking: 0 Min | Serving 1)

INGREDIENTS
- 2 cups frozen pineapple
- 1 banana
- 1 1/4 cups unsweetened coconut milk
- 1/4 cup frozen coconut pieces
- 1/2 tsp. ground flaxseed
- 1 tsp. hemp seeds

DIRECTIONS:
1. In a blender, situate all the ingredients and blend until smooth. Serve.

Nutrition: Calories: 396 | Carbohydrates: 71 g | Protein: 6 g

Chapter 10. Juice Recipes

569. SWITCHEL: THE ORIGINAL SPORTS DRINK
(PREP. TIME: 5 MIN | COOKING: 0 MIN | SERVING 2)

INGREDIENTS
- 4 cups (960 ml) water
- 2 tbsp. apple cider vinegar
- 2 tbsp. maple syrup
- 1-inch (2.5 cm) piece ginger, minced
- 1/4 tsp. sea salt, or to taste

DIRECTIONS:
1. Shake all the ingredients together, refrigerate overnight, strain, and drink.

Nutrition: Calories: 110 | Fat: 0 g | Carbohydrates: 28 g| Protein: 0 g

570. LEMON-LIME ELECTROLYTE DRINK
(PREP. TIME: 5 MIN | COOKING: 0 MIN | SERVING 2)

INGREDIENTS
- 4 cups (960 ml) water
- 2 tbsp. maple syrup
- 1 tbsp. apple cider vinegar
- 1 tbsp. fresh lime or lemon juice
- 1/4 tsp. sea salt, or to taste

DIRECTIONS:
1. Shake all the ingredients together, refrigerate overnight, strain, and drink.

Nutrition: Calories: 98 | Fat: 0 g | Carbohydrates: 21 g | Protein: 0 g

571. SWITCHEL SPORTS DRINKS WITH JUICE
(PREP. TIME: 5 MIN | COOKING: 0 MIN | SERVING 3)

INGREDIENTS
- 4 cups (960 ml) water
- 1 cup (240 ml) juice (see suggestions below)
- 2 tbsp. apple cider vinegar
- 2 tbsp. maple syrup
- 1/4 tsp. sea salt, or to taste

DIRECTIONS:
1. Shake all the ingredients together, refrigerate overnight, and drink.

Nutrition: Calories: 97 | Fat: 1 g | Carbohydrates: 28 g | Protein: 2 g

572. CUCUMBER-LIME ELECTROLYTE DRINK
(PREP. TIME: 5 MIN | COOKING: 0 MIN | SERVING 2)

INGREDIENTS
- 4 cups (960 ml) water
- 1/4 cup (50 g) chopped cucumber
- 2 tbsp. maple syrup
- 1 tbsp. apple cider vinegar
- 1 tbsp. fresh lime juice
- 1/4 tsp. sea salt, or to taste

DIRECTIONS:
1. Shake all the ingredients together, refrigerate overnight, strain, and drink.

Nutrition: Calories: 117 | Fat: 4 g | Carbohydrates: 21 g | Protein: 2 g

573. CRANBERRY-CITRUS ELECTROLYTE DRINK
(PREP. TIME: 5 MIN | COOKING: 0 MIN | SERVING 2)

INGREDIENTS
- 4 cups (960 ml) water
- 1 cup cranberry juice blend
- 2 tbsp. maple syrup
- 2 tbsp. orange juice
- 1 tbsp. apple cider vinegar
- 1 tbsp. fresh lime juice
- 1 tsp. fresh lemon juice
- 1/4 tsp. sea salt, or to taste

DIRECTIONS:
1. Shake all the ingredients together, refrigerate overnight, strain, and drink.

Nutrition: Calories: 110 | Fat: 0 g | Carbohydrates: 28 g | Protein: 0 g

574. Miso-Maple Electrolyte "Broth"
(Prep. Time: 5 Min | Cooking: 0 Min | Serving 2)

INGREDIENTS
- 1 tbsp. maple syrup
- 1 tbsp. white miso
- 1–2 tbsp. lime juice, to taste
- 1/2 tsp. minced fresh ginger or garlic, optional
- 2 cups (480 ml) hot but not boiling water

DIRECTIONS:
1. Whisk together the maple syrup and miso. Add the lime juice and ginger, if using. Add the hot water. Pour immediately into your thermos or water bottle.

Nutrition: Calories: 95 | Fat: 1 g | Carbohydrates: 21 g | Protein: 2 g

575. Umeboshi Electrolyte Drink
(Prep. Time: 5 Min | Cooking: 0 Min | Serving 2)

INGREDIENTS
- 2 cups (480 ml) water
- 1 1/2 tbsp. coconut sugar
- 1 tsp. Umeboshi paste

DIRECTIONS:
1. Combine all the ingredients in a water bottle or a jar with a lid. Shake well, then drink.

Nutrition: Calories: 73 | Fat: 0 g | Carbohydrates: 18 g | Protein: 0 g

576. Frozen Matcha Latte
(Prep. Time: 5 Min | Cooking: 0 Min | Serving 1)

INGREDIENTS
- 1 cup (240 ml) vanilla almond milk
- 1 cup (30 g) spinach or (15 g) kale, optional, for added color and nutrition
- 1/2–1 cup (70 to 140 g) ice
- 1 frozen ripe banana, in chunks for ease of blending
- 1 scoop vanilla protein powder, optional
- 2 tsp. Matcha powder
- 1/8 tsp. vanilla bean powder

DIRECTIONS:
1. Combine all the ingredients in a high-speed blender until smooth and drink.

Nutrition: Calories: 320 | Fat: 4 g | Carbohydrates: 57 g | Protein: 18 g

577. Margarita Recovery Drink
(Prep. Time: 3 Min | Cooking: 0 Min | Serving 1)

INGREDIENTS
- 1 cup (140 g) ice
- 1 cup (240 ml) water
- 1/4 cup (60 ml) fresh lime juice (from 2 limes)
- 2 tbsp. orange juice
- 4 dates, pitted
- 1 scoop protein powder, optional
- 1 tsp. coconut oil (OF: coconut milk)

DIRECTIONS:
1. Combine all the ingredients (except the ice if you want to serve this on the rocks) in a blender until smooth. Serve however you like your margaritas!

Nutrition: Calories: 251 | Fat: 5 g | Carbohydrates: 33 g | Protein: 16 g

578. "Bulked-Up" Drink
(Prep. Time: 3 Min | Cooking: 0 Min | Serving 1)

INGREDIENTS
- 3 cups (85 g) mixed baby greens
- 1 cup (240 ml) almond milk
- 1 cup (140 g) ice, optional
- 1/2 cup (100 g) cooked cannellini, adzuki, or black beans
- 1/2 cup (75 g) berries, optional
- 1/4 cup (24 g) GF old-fashioned rolled oats
- 1 banana
- 2 tbsp. coconut butter
- 1 tbsp. unsweetened cocoa powder

DIRECTIONS:
- Combine all the ingredients in a high-speed blender and drink.

Nutrition: Calories: 712 | Fat: 26 g | Carbohydrates: 105 g | Protein: 29 g

579. Banana Weight Loss Juice
(Prep. Time: 10 Min | Cooking: 0 Min | Serving 1)

INGREDIENTS
- 1/3 cup of water
- 1 apple sliced
- 1 orange sliced
- 1 banana sliced
- 1 tsp. lemon juice

DIRECTIONS:
1. Looking to boost your weight loss? The key is taking in fewer calories; this recipe can get you there.

2. Simply place everything into your blender, blend on high for 20 seconds, and then pour into your glass.

Nutrition: Calories: 289 | Carbohydrate: 2 g | Fat: 17 g | Fiber: 2 g | Protein: 7 g

580. Citrus Detox Juice
(Prep. Time: 10 Min | Cooking: 0 Min | Serving 4)

INGREDIENTS
- 3 cup of water
- 1 lemon sliced
- 1 grapefruit sliced
- 1 orange sliced

DIRECTIONS:
1. While starting your new diet, it is going to be vital to stay hydrated. This detox juice is the perfect solution and offers some extra flavor.
2. Begin by peeling and slicing up the fruits. Once this is done, place in a pitcher of water and infuse the water overnight.

Nutrition: Calories: 269 | Carbohydrate: 2 g | Fat: 14 g | Fiber: 2 g | Protein: 7 g

581. Metabolism Water
(Prep. Time: 10 Min | Cooking: 0 Min | Serving 1)

INGREDIENTS
- 3 cup of water
- 1 cucumber sliced
- 1 lemon sliced
- 2 mint leaves
- Ice to taste

DIRECTIONS:
1. At some point, we probably all wish for a quicker metabolism! With the lemon acting as an energizer, cucumber for a refreshing taste, and mint to help your stomach digest, this water is perfect!
2. All you will have to do is get out a pitcher, place all of the ingredients in, and allow the ingredients to soak overnight for maximum benefits!

Nutrition: Calories: 301 | Carbohydrate: 2 g | Fat: 17 g | Fiber: 4 g | Protein: 8 g

582. Stress Relief Detox Drink
(Prep. Time: 5 Min | Cooking: 0 Min | Serving 1)

INGREDIENTS
- 1 cup of water
- 1 tbsp. Mint
- 1 lemon sliced
- 2 pcs. basil leaves
- 1 cup strawberries sliced
- Ice to taste

DIRECTIONS:
1. Life can be a pretty stressful event. Luckily, there is water to help keep you cool, calm, and collected! The lemon works like an energizer, the basil is a natural antidepressant, and mint can help your stomach do its job better. As for the strawberries, those are just for some sweetness!
2. When you are ready, take all of the ingredients and place them into a pitcher of water overnight and enjoy the next day.

Nutrition: Calories: 189 | Carbohydrate: 2 g | Fat: 17 g | Fiber: 0 g | Protein: 7 g

583. Strawberry Pink Drink
(Prep. Time: 10 Min | Cooking: 5 Min | Serving 4)

INGREDIENTS
- 1 cup of boiling water
- 2 tsp. coconut sugar
- 1 acai tea bag
- 1 cup coconut milk
- 1/2 cup frozen strawberries

DIRECTIONS:
1. If you are looking for a little treat, this is going to be the recipe for you! You will begin by boiling your cup of water and seep the tea bag in for at least five minutes
2. When the tea is set, add in the sugar and coconut milk. Be sure to stir well to spread the sweetness throughout the tea.
3. Finally, add in your strawberries, and you can enjoy your freshly made pink drink!

Nutrition: Calories: 321 | Carbohydrate: 2 g | Fat: 17 g | Fiber: 2 g | Protein: 9 g

584. Spiced Buttermilk
(Prep. Time: 5 Min | Cooking: 0 Min | Serving 2)

INGREDIENTS
- 3/4 tsp. ground cumin
- 1/4 tsp. sea salt
- 1/8 tsp. ground black pepper
- 2 mint leaves
- 1/8 tsp. lemon juice

- 1/4 cup cilantro leaves
- 1 cup of chilled water
- 1 cup vegan yogurt, unsweetened
- Ice as needed

DIRECTIONS:
1. Place all the ingredients in the order in a food processor or blender, except for cilantro and 1/4 tsp. cumin, and then pulse for 2 to 3 minutes at high speed until smooth.
2. Pour the milk into glasses, top with cilantro and cumin, and then serve.

Nutrition: Calories: 211 Carbohydrate: 7 g | Fat: 18 g | Fiber: 3 g |Protein: 17 g

585. MEXICAN HOT CHOCOLATE MIX
(PREP. TIME: 5 MIN | COOKING: 0 MIN | SERVING 2)

INGREDIENTS
For the hot chocolate mix:
- 1/3 cup chopped dark chocolate
- 1/8 tsp. cayenne
- 1/8 tsp. salt
- 1/2 tsp. cinnamon
- 1/4 cup coconut sugar
- 1 tsp. cornstarch
- 3 tbsp. cocoa powder
- 1/2 tsp. vanilla extract, unsweetened

For serving:
- 2 cups milk, warmed

DIRECTIONS:
- Place all the ingredients of hot chocolate mix in the order in a food processor or blender and then pulse for 2 to 3 minutes at high speed until ground.
- Stir 2 tbsp. of the chocolate mix into a glass of milk until combined and then serve.

Nutrition: Calories: 160 | Fat: 6 g | Protein: 26 g | Sugar: 7 g

586. HEALTH BOOSTING JUICES
(PREP. TIME: 10 MIN | COOKING: 15 MIN | SERVING 2)

INGREDIENTS
For red juice:
- 4 beetroots, quartered
- 2 cups of strawberries
- 2 cups of blueberries

INGREDIENTS for an orange juice:
- 4 green or red apples, halved
- 10 carrots
- 1/2 lemon, peeled
- 1-inch of ginger

For a yellow juice:
- 2 green or red apples, quartered
- 4 oranges, peeled and halved
- 1/2 lemon, peeled
- 1-inch of ginger

For a lime juice:
- 6 stalks of celery
- 1 cucumber
- 2 green apples, quartered
- 2 pears, quartered

For a green juice:
- 1/2 a pineapple, peeled and sliced
- 8 leaves of kale
- 2 fresh bananas, peeled

DIRECTIONS:
- Place all ingredients in a juicer, chill and serve.

Nutrition: Calories: 316 | Carbohydrates: 13.5 g | Protein: 37.8 g | Fat: 12.2 g

587. THAI ICED TEA
(PREP. TIME: 5 MIN | COOKING: 10 MIN | SERVING 4)

INGREDIENTS
- 4 cups of water
- 1 can of light coconut milk (14 oz.)
- 1/4 cup of maple syrup
- 1/4 cup of muscovado sugar
- 1 tsp. vanilla extract
- 2 tbsp. loose-leaf black tea

DIRECTIONS:
1. In a large saucepan, over medium heat bring the water to a boil.
2. Turn off the heat and add in the tea, cover and let steep for five minutes
3. Strain the tea into a bowl or jug. Add the maple syrup, muscovado sugar, and vanilla extract. Give it a good whisk to blend all the ingredients together.
4. Set in the refrigerator to chill. Upon serving, pour 3/4 of the tea into each glass, top with coconut milk, and stir.

Nutrition: Calories: 844 | Carbohydrates: 2.3 g | Protein: 21.6 g | Fat: 83.1 g

588. COLORFUL INFUSED WATER
(PREP. TIME: 5 MIN | COOKING: 1 MIN | SERVING 8)

INGREDIENTS
- 1 cup of strawberries, fresh or frozen
- 1 cup of blueberries, fresh or frozen
- 1 tbsp. baobab powder
- 1 cup of ice cubes
- 4 cups of sparkling water

DIRECTIONS:
1. In a large water jug, add in the sparkling water, ice cubes, and baobab powder. Give it a good stir.
2. Add in the strawberries and blueberries and cover the infused water, store in the refrigerator for one hour before serving.

Nutrition: Calories: 163 | Carbohydrates: 4.1 g | Protein: 1.7 g | Fat: 15.5 g

589. Hibiscus Tea
(Prep. Time: 1 Min | Cooking: 5 Min | Serving 2)

INGREDIENTS
- 1 tbsp. raisins, diced
- 6 almonds, raw and unsalted
- 1/2 tsp. hibiscus powder
- 2 cups of water

DIRECTIONS:
1. Bring the water to a boil in a small saucepan, add in the hibiscus powder and raisins. Give it a good stir, cover, and let simmer for a further two minutes
2. Strain into a teapot and serve with a side helping of almonds.

Nutrition: Calories: 139 | Carbohydrates: 2.7 g | Protein: 8.7 g | Fat: 10.3 g

590. Lemon and Rosemary Iced Tea
(Prep. Time: 5 Min | Cooking: 10 Min | Serving 4)

INGREDIENTS
- 4 cups of water
- 4 earl grey tea bags
- 1/4 cup of coconut sugar
- 2 lemons
- 1 sprig of rosemary

DIRECTIONS:
1. Peel the two lemons and set the fruit aside.
2. In a medium saucepan, over medium heat combine the water, sugar, and lemon peels. Bring this to a boil.
3. Remove from the heat and place the rosemary and tea into the mixture. Cover the saucepan and steep for five minutes
4. Add the juice of the two peeled lemons to the mixture, strain, chill, and serve.

Nutrition: Calories: 229 | Carbohydrates: 33.2 g | Protein: 31.1 g | Fat: 10.2 g

591. Lavender and Mint Iced Tea
(Prep. Time: 5 Min | Cooking: 10 Min | Serving 8)

INGREDIENTS
- 8 cups of water
- 1/3 cup of dried lavender buds
- 1/4 cup of mint

DIRECTIONS:
1. Add the mint and lavender to a pot and set this aside.
2. Add eight cups of boiling water to the pot. Sweeten to taste, cover and let steep for ten minutes Strain, chill, and serve.

Nutrition: Calories: 266 | Carbohydrates: 9.3 g | Protein: 20.9 g | Fat: 16.1 g

592. Pear Lemonade
(Prep. Time: 5 Min | Cooking: 10 Min | Serving 2)

INGREDIENTS
- 1/2 cup of pear, peeled and diced
- 1 cup of freshly squeezed lemon juice
- 1/2 cup of chilled water

DIRECTIONS:
1. Add all the ingredients into a blender and pulse until it has all been combined. The pear does make the lemonade frothy, but this will settle.
2. Place in the refrigerator to cool and then serve.

Nutrition: Calories: 160 | Carbohydrates: 6.3 g | Protein: 2.9 g | Fat: 13.6 g

593. Energizing Ginger Detox Tonic
(Prep. Time: 5 Min | Cooking: 10 Min | Serving 4)

INGREDIENTS
- 1/2 tsp. of grated ginger, fresh
- 1 small lemon slice
- 1/8 tsp. cayenne pepper
- 1/8 tsp. ground turmeric
- 1/8 tsp. ground cinnamon
- 1 tsp. maple syrup
- 1 tsp. apple cider vinegar
- 2 cups of boiling water

DIRECTIONS:
1. Pour the boiling water into a small saucepan, add and stir the ginger, then let it rest for 8 to 10 minutes, before covering the pan.
2. Pass the mixture through a strainer and into the liquid, add the cayenne pepper, turmeric, cinnamon and stir properly.
3. Add the maple syrup, vinegar, and lemon slice.

4. Add and stir an infused lemon and serve immediately.

Nutrition: Calories: 443 | Carbohydrates: 9.7 g | Protein: 62.8 g | Fat: 16.9 g

594. Warm Spiced Lemon Drink
(Prep. Time: 2 Min | Cooking: 12 Min | Serving 12)

INGREDIENTS
- 1 cinnamon stick, about 3 inches long
- 1/2 tsp. whole cloves
- 2 cups of coconut sugar
- 4 fluid of ounce pineapple juice
- 1/2 cup and 2 tbsp. lemon juice
- 12 fluid oz. orange juice
- 2 1/2 quarts of water

DIRECTIONS:
1. Pour water into a 6-quarts slow cooker and stir the sugar and lemon juice properly.
2. Wrap the cinnamon, the whole cloves in cheesecloth and tie its corners with string.
3. Immerse this cheesecloth bag in the liquid present in the slow cooker and cover it with the lid.
4. Then plug in the slow cooker and let it cook on a high heat setting for 2 hours or until it is heated thoroughly.
5. When done, discard the cheesecloth bag and serve the drink hot or cold

Nutrition: Calories: 523 | Carbohydrates: 4.6 g | Protein: 47.9 g | Fat: 34.8 g

595. Soothing Ginger Tea Drink
(Prep. Time: 5 Min | Cooking: 10 Min | Serving 8)

INGREDIENTS
- 1 tbsp. minced gingerroot
- 2 tbsp. honey
- 15 green tea bags
- 32 fluid oz. white grape juice
- 2–4-quart of boiling water

DIRECTIONS:
1. Pour water into a 4-quarts slow cooker, immerse tea bags, cover the cooker and let stand for 10 minutes
2. After 10 minutes, remove and discard tea bags and stir in the remaining ingredients.
3. Return cover to slow cooker, then plugin and let cook at high heat setting for 2 hours or until heated through.
4. When done, strain the liquid and serve hot or cold.

Nutrition: Calories: 232 | Carbohydrates: 7.9 g | Protein: 15.9 g | Fat: 15.1 g

596. Nice Spiced Cherry Cider
(Prep. Time: 5 Min | Cooking: 8 Min | Serving 16)

INGREDIENTS
- 2 cinnamon sticks, each about 3 inches long
- 6 oz. cherry gelatin
- 4-quart of apple cider

DIRECTIONS:
1. Using a 6-quarts slow cooker, pour the apple cider and add the cinnamon stick.
2. Stir, then cover the slow cooker with its lid. Plugin the cooker and let it cook for 3 hours at the high heat setting or until it is heated thoroughly.
3. Then add and stir the gelatin properly, then continue cooking for another hour.
4. When done, remove the cinnamon sticks and serve the drink hot or cold.

Nutrition: Calories: 78 | Carbohydrates: 13.2 g | Protein: 2.8 g | Fat: 1.5 g

597. Classic Switchel
(Prep. Time: 5 Min | Cooking: 0 Min | Serving 4)

INGREDIENTS
- 1-inch piece ginger, minced
- 2 tbsp. apple cider vinegar
- 2 tbsp. maple syrup
- 4 cups water
- 1/4 tsp. sea salt, optional

DIRECTIONS:
1. Combine all the ingredients in a glass. Stir to mix well.
2. Serve immediately or chill in the refrigerator for an hour before serving.

Nutrition: Calories: 110 | Fat: 0 g | Carbohydrates: 28.0 g | Protein: 0 g

598. Lime and Cucumber Electrolyte Drink
(Prep. Time: 5 Min | Cooking: 0 Min | Serving 4)

INGREDIENTS
- 1/4 cup chopped cucumber
- 1 tbsp. fresh lime juice
- 1 tbsp. apple cider vinegar
- 2 tbsp. maple syrup

- 1/4 tsp. sea salt, optional
- 4 cups water

DIRECTIONS:
1. Combine all the ingredients in a glass. Stir to mix well.
2. Refrigerate overnight before serving.

Nutrition: Calories: 114 | Fat: 0.1 g | Carbohydrates: 28.9 g | Protein: 0.3 g

599. Trope-Kale Breeze

(Prep. Time: 5 Min | Cooking: 0 Min | Serving 4)

INGREDIENTS
- 1 cup chopped pineapple (frozen or fresh)
- 1 cup chopped mango (frozen or fresh)
- ½ to 1 cup chopped kale
- ½ avocado
- ½ cup coconut milk
- 1 cup water, or coconut water
- 1 teaspoon matcha green tea powder (optional)

DIRECTIONS:
1. Purée everything in a blender until smooth, adding more water (or coconut milk) if needed.

Nutrition: Calories: 566 | Fat: 36g | Carbs: 66g | Fiber: 12g | Protein: 8g

600. Mango Madness

(Prep. Time: 5 Min | Cooking: 0 Min | Serving 4)

INGREDIENTS
- 1 banana
- 1 cup chopped mango (frozen or fresh)
- 1 cup chopped peach (frozen or fresh)
- 1 cup strawberries
- 1 carrot, peeled and chopped (optional)
- 1 cup water

DIRECTIONS:
- Purée everything in a blender until smooth, adding more water if needed.

Nutrition: Calories: 376 | Fat: 2g | Carbs: 95g | Fiber: 14g | Protein: 5g

Conclusion

A plant-based diet is any diet that emphasizes foods derived from plant sources.

It is also a term that refers to a way of eating that focuses on consuming whole, plant-based foods. These foods are usually unprocessed (meaning they haven't been altered from their natural state) and ideally organic.

Since plant-based dishes are naturally low in simple sugars and calories, they allow you to eat more without the guilt associated with other diets.

The plant-based diet is generally a healthier way of eating, but you'll also be able to lose weight when you incorporate it into your life.

In a nutshell, this cookbook offers you a world full of options to diversify your plant-based menu. People on this diet are usually seen struggling to choose between healthy food and flavor but, soon, they run out of options. Give each recipe a good read and try them out in the kitchen. You will experience tempting aromas and binding flavors every day.

The book is conceptualized with the idea of offering you a comprehensive view of a plant-based diet and how it can benefit the body. You may find the shift sudden, especially if you are a die-hard fan of non-vegetarian items. But you need not give up anything that you love. Eat everything in moderation.

The next step is to start experimenting with the different recipes in this book and see which ones are your favorites. Everyone has their favorite food, and you will surely find several of yours in this book. Begin with breakfast then work your way through. You will be pleasantly surprised at how tasty a vegan meal really can be.

You will love reading this book, as it helps you understand how revolutionary a plant-based diet can be. It will help you to make informed decisions as you move toward more remarkable change for the greater good. What are you waiting for? Have you begun your journey on the path of the plant-based diet yet? If you haven't, do it now!

Now you have the whole thing you need to get ongoing making budget-friendly, healthy plant-based recipes. Just follow your essential shopping list and follow your meal plan to get started! It's easy to shift over to a plant-based diet if you have your meals prearranged out and temptation locked away. Don't forget to clean out your kitchen before starting, and you're sure to meet all your diet and health goals.

You need to plan if you are thinking about dieting. First, you can start slowly by just eating one meal a day, which is vegetarian, and gradually increasing your number of vegetarian meals. Whenever you are struggling, ask your friend or family member to support you and keep you

motivated. One important thing is also to be regularly accountable for not following the diet.

Suppose dieting seems very important to you, and you need to do it right. In that case, it is recommended that you visit a professional such as a nutritionist or dietitian to deliberate your dieting plan and optimizing it for the better.

No matter how much you want to lose weight, you cannot decrease your calorie intake to an unhealthy level. Losing weight does not mean that you stop eating. It is done by carefully planning meals.

A plant-based diet is straightforward once you get into it. At first, you will start to face many difficulties, but if you start slowly, you can face all the barriers and achieve your goal.

Swap out one unhealthy food item each week that you know is not helping you and put in its place one of the plant-based **INGREDIENTS** that you like. Then have some fun creating the many different recipes in this book. Find out what recipes you want the most so you can make them often, and most of all, have some fun exploring all your recipe options. I wish you good luck with the plant-based diet!

Printed in Great Britain
by Amazon